Economic Behavior and Distributional Choice

Selected Writings of Harold M. Hochman

Harold M. Hochman

William E. Simon Professor of Political Economy, Department of Economics and Business, Lafayette College, USA

Edward Elgar

Cheltenham, UK • Northampton, MA, USA

Published by
Edward Elgar Publishing Limited
Glensanda House
Montpellier Parade
Cheltenham
Glos GL50 1UA
UK

Edward Elgar Publishing, Inc.
136 West Street
Suite 202
Northampton
Massachusetts 01060
USA

A catalogue record for this book
is available from the British Library

Library of Congress Cataloguing in Publication Data

Hochman, Harold M.
    Economic behavior and distributional choice : selected writings of Harold M. Hochman
    / Harold M. Hochman.
        p. cm.
    Includes bibliographical references and index.
    1. Economics—Moral and ethical aspects. 2. Distributive justice. I. Title: Selected writings of Harold M. Hochman. II. Title.

HB72 .H653 2002
174—dc21

2002024367

ISBN 1 84064 398 6
Printed and bound in Great Britain by MPG Books Ltd, Bodmin, Cornwall

Contents

PART II   PUBLIC POLICY

A   Tax Policy

B   Urban Economics and Urban Policy

C   Addictive Behavior

Acknowledgements

The author and publisher wish to thank the following who have kindly given permission for the use of copyright material.

Academic Press, Inc. for article: 'Contractarian Theories of Redistribution', in E. Helpman, A. Razin and E. Sadka (eds), *Social Policy Evaluation: An Economic Perspective*, 1983, 211–34.

American Economic Association for articles: 'Pareto Optimal Redistribution', with James D. Rodgers, *American Economic Review*, **59**, September 1969, 542–57; Richard A. Musgrave, 'Pareto Optimal Redistribution: Comment', *American Economic Review*, **60**, December 1970, 991–3; 'Pareto Optimal Redistribution: Reply', with James D. Rodgers, *American Economic Review*, **60**, December 1970, 997–1002; 'Individual Preferences and Distributional Adjustments', *American Economic Review*, **62**, May 1972, 353–60; 'Social Problems and the Urban Crisis: Can Public Policy Make a Difference?', with Worth Bateman, *American Economic Review*, **61**, May 1971, 346–53.

Elsevier Science Publishers BV for article: 'Concepts of Extended Preference', with Shmuel Nitzan, *Journal of Economic Behavior and Organization*, **6**, 1985, 161–76.

Kluwer Academic Publishers for article: 'Public Choice Interpretations of Distributional Preference', *Constitutional Political Economy*, **7**, Winter 1996, 3–20.

The Manhattan Institute for article: 'Clearing the Regulatory Clutter', in Peter Salins (ed.), *New York Unbound: The City and the Politics of the Future*, New York: Basil Blackwell, 1988, 93–108.

MIT Press Journals for article: 'On the Income Distribution as a Public Good', with James D. Rodgers and Gordon Tullock, *Quarterly Journal of Economics*, **87**, May 1973, 311–15.

The National Bureau of Economic Research, Inc. for article: 'The Simple Politics of Distributional Preference', with James D. Rodgers, in F. Thomas Juster (ed.), *The Distribution of Economic Well-Being*, National Bureau of Economic Research, 1977, 71–107.

The National Tax Association for article: 'The Optimal Tax Treatment of Charitable Contributions', with James D. Rodgers, *National Tax Journal*, **30**(1), March 1977, 1–18.

Oxford University Press for article: 'Addiction as Extreme-Seeking', with Thomas Barthold, *Economic Inquiry*, **26**, January 1988, 89–106.

The Urban Institute Press for article: 'Rule Change and Transitional Equity', in Harold M. Hochman and George E. Peterson (eds), *Redistribution Though Public Choice*, Columbia University Press, 1974, 320–41.

Urban Studies for article: 'New York and Pittsburgh: Contrasts in Community', *Urban Studies*, **29**(2), April 1992, 237–50 (Special Issue: *Problems of Urban Agglomeration, 1961–91, Essays in Honor of Benjamin Chinitz*).

Preface (Dedication)

Drafting this in the backwash of terrorist acts in New York and Washington, lingering sadness and visceral anger dominate the emotions. Yet, as we know, it will not always be so. The scholar hopes that, thanks in part to the knowledge he creates, future generations will live in a better world. This book reflects that belief. The articles it contains are, in large part, about distributive justice and pluralism, and the place, in social science, of human behavior that nurtures a just society in which our will is the guarantor of both freedom and survival.

A collection like this is assembled, primarily, for one's profession, but also for one's children and grandchildren. So I dedicate this book, and the hopes it encompasses, to Betsy Ann Hochman and Sandra Ellen Lesikar, and, of course, to Brook Ellen Lesikar, age two months, and thus fortunate enough not to comprehend what transpired, little over a month ago, in places her grandparents have called home.

Someday, hopefully, they will inspect its contents, at least briefly.

Durham, Pennsylvania and Sunapee, New Hamphire
October, 2001

Introduction

This collection best illuminates, I think, my intellectual odyssey as an economist. In addition, it brings a few of my articles, including some personal favorites originally published in obscure places, to a new audience.

I try, in this introductory essay, to supply context for the articles that follow. The essay, while substantive, inevitably contains some elements of autobiography. Forgive me! For me, this makes the papers, at least their tone, easier to comprehend and satisfies some primal urge. I see this introduction, most of all, as a singular opportunity for introspection: to gain a glimmer of insight into my life's voyage from there to here; to judge whether, or when, it has amounted to more than simple self-indulgence, like so much of academic enterprise, and life; and, not least, to reminisce.

Some are bound to disagree, but I do not think of economics as pure science; too much is going on that muddies the waters. Like history, academic writings in economics are decidedly path-dependent, the product of accumulated knowledge, personal and communal, and of life experience.

The contents of this book reveal that more than half the articles (my *better* ones?) were co-authored. Of these, most were written with James Rodgers, who began as my student in 1966, then seemed, for a decade, to be my alter ego. Thus, for much of my professional life, but (decidedly) not always, the voyage has not been lonely. Properly, the contributions of authors are inseparable in joint writings; this is true, for the most part, in the articles reprinted here. So, to each of my co-authors, especially Jim Rodgers, my debts transcend, by far, the printed product.

More than most of my contemporaries, I am the antithesis of the solitary scholar, perhaps to a fault. I find intensive interaction with colleagues and students essential to the expression of ideas; it wards off distraction, to which I am inordinately sensitive, and converts work to diversion. At sixty-five I no longer care to speculate about the reasons, or to pay a practitioner of a different discipline to discern them. Moreover, trained in the 1950s, my technical skills have always been quite limited[1] (as I am occasionally reminded, unnecessarily) and I have almost no patience for drudgery; so I do not prosper as well on my own. (This last is one reason, though pragmatic, not philosophical, why the seemingly compulsive positivism of much present-day economics is not for me.)

All but a handful of the selections relate to or derive from Chapter 1, my first article with Rodgers, titled 'Pareto Optimal Redistribution', which spells out the relationship between utility interdependence and the logic of redistributive income transfers, effected through fiscal means. (Judged by citations, it is also the most widely read of my papers.) Yet all of the papers share a theme; they tinker, in some simple and, I hope, meaningful way with the behavioral margins of neoclassical economics. Whatever an article's immediate focus, I like to think that it addressed an intellectual puzzle, even if time has turned this puzzle into a commonplace. However, none of the articles claim revolution; typically, they proceed incrementally, often by modifying some customary assumption, as utility interdependence does, and trace implications. To the well-schooled, antecedents are transparent, and influence never concealed.

Like my teaching, my writings evince a growing concern with the capability of my discipline, as structured reasoning, to distinguish right from wrong, with (borrowing Michael McPherson's phrase) the relationship of morals to markets. Particularly in distributional matters, history and life experience (not abstraction) validate the centrality of moral concerns. Ultimately, it is impossible to separate efficiency from justice, commutative or procedural, or from human well-being, private or communal, at any operational level. Even if we prefer that the argument remains analytic and, save for productivity concerns, value-free, justice intrudes when anything important is at stake. So, by implication, there is no neat separation between efficiency and equity (the term economists typically use when speaking of fairness) in discussing human welfare. This is the focal problem with which the distributional choice articles grapple.[2]

Could it be otherwise? I suspect not, at least for me. Perhaps it is enough that I am, like the twentieth-century British philosopher Isaiah Berlin, 'a Jew of the Holocaust generation,' touched intimately, distance notwithstanding, by the unholy events of my childhood – though these were incomprehensible to me at the time and, in many ways, still are. Again, for reasons like Berlin's, I have never sought bright-line, but simplistic binary answers to the normative quandaries of my mind. So, there is a real sense in which my writings have never resolved anything; they have, instead, helped to delimit debate, whether they dealt with a democratic regime with predefined property rights (the earlier articles) or constitutional expression (the later ones). It sufficed, for me, to point out that distributional indeterminacy, as it relates to the question of a social optimum, is probably much narrower than the nihilism of mid-1960s welfare economics led most economists to believe.

Broadly, my approach to economics, like my teaching, reflects a pro-market bias, but in the large, not the small. I consider *the market* an instrumental process, not a quasi-religious icon, like some modern-day apostles of minimum government. Mental benefit–cost calculations lead me to prefer that market and not administrative processes do most of the allocating, economic and other. However, because externalities and informational imperfections do not figure in the base model, though they are clearly material in both the narrow economic and the broad constitutional sense, the sufficiency of market allocation is ever in dispute. In this sense, I counsel – as Irving Kristol (1978) once did – but 'Two Cheers for Capitalism'. I suspect this is a lot closer to the views of many free-market advocates than they like to admit, especially when confronted with poverty or, for that matter, the various evils of which human beings are capable. After all, economics may not be pure science, but it is not a cult.

A consequence of this perspective is that Rodgers and I have found enemies on both the left and the right. In the first case, this is because we treated path-dependent preferences, revealed through choice, as legitimate, and accepted, for the argument's purposes, initial property rights.[3] In the latter, it is because we argued that transfers from rich to poor might actually be Pareto Optimal, so that, subject to the boundaries of community, they benefit everyone and are necessary for allocative efficiency, interpreted as a minimal condition of welfare maximization. If, with the same sentences, we managed to offend both ideological extremes, my convictions are strengthened.

Early on, the demonstration that income transfers can be Pareto Optimal, the theme (or assumption) that unifies all but the last of the Hochman–Rodgers papers, led a few (unnamed) friends to claim, largely in conversation, that Rodgers and I had demonstrated the identity of efficiency and justice, so long as the distributional problem is properly defined. Yet this was never *our* position. It sufficed, for us, that neither Benthamite cardinal utility nor a *strong* social welfare function, the weakest links in the intricate logic of welfare economics, were required to justify redistributive transfers.[4]

Biographical prologue

Formative years

I offer, as lighter fare, a few tidbits of biographical detail, covering the period before the articles in this book were written. Though distorted by memory's lens, I hope they will provide some insight into who I am, personally and professionally.

I was born in New Haven, Connecticut in 1936 and brought up in a nearby industrial town called Shelton, a half hour away. My parents, both of whom had immigrated as children (from 'Russia', or Lithuania, loosely defined) had relocated from Brooklyn, where my maternal grandparents and most of their families resided. In Shelton, they operated a shirt factory, started in the depths of the Depression when labor was plentiful.

Though hardly wealthy, we were comfortable, much more so than most of my school friends. For my parents, my education was uppermost, though more for practical than philosophical reasons.[5] Over its thirty years of existence, the factory, according to my father, 'lost money'; yet, somehow, it paid taxes annually. Additionally, it contributed, in two ways, to my education. Foremost, it cultivated a distaste for real work, though my role (from teens on) had a vaguely managerial cast; I did not mind the bossing, but disliked the manual labor and *detested* the grind. Small wonder I was drawn to academia. Second, from the ninth grade on, when the education finally took, it financed my tuition at the Hopkins Grammar School in New Haven (since renamed to accommodate coeducation) and then, through both undergraduate and graduate years, at Yale.

Symbolically, acceptance by Yale seemed more important to relatives than to me.[6] Family concerns dominated the college choice. My mother, never really well, had taken ill and died during the spring of my senior year at Hopkins, the first major trauma of my rather sheltered life as an only child; so, for my father, needing both company and occasional help with the factory, it was better for me to be in New Haven. It did not hurt, of course, that this came with regular pick-up and delivery of laundry, including shirts professionally pressed in the factory. For the economist, benefits and costs are everything.

As an undergraduate at Yale, I majored in economics because I took to it; besides, it raised fewer red flags than the viable alternatives. After all, the expectation of the extended family, my aversion notwithstanding, had been that I would advance dutifully to a respectable career in medicine, or possibly law, and if neither, the family business.

Edward Budd, who force-fed economic theory to the honors students (nine in all) and C.E. Lindblom, who made us range outside conventional bounds and actually think, were my most influential undergraduate teachers. To attest to the strength of the program, at least two of my honors classmates, Donald Hester and Harald Malmgren, have enjoyed highly successful careers as economists.

I met my wife, Kappie, then a Wellesley freshman, as a blind date for a football weekend, arranged by an ex-girlfriend who wished, the story goes, to rid herself of me for good, and succeeded. My recollection is that I did not attend the football game, being otherwise occupied with the Graduate Records Exam; Kappie somehow managed to overlook this and the romance prospered. It is not in my interest to inquire whether she has regrets. Upon graduation, despite a fellowship offer from MIT, which would have put me closer to Wellesley, I decided to remain at Yale, persuaded by the sales pitch of John Perry Miller.

The Yale program was then entering its heyday, thanks to the acquisition of the Cowles Foundation a year or two earlier. I studied theory with James Tobin and Arthur Okun and read welfare economics with Richard Ruggles. After a few iterations, I wrote my dissertation with William Fellner (with whom, more than anyone else, I came to identify), as well as Okun and, until he left Yale for greener pastures, Michael Lovell. The thesis dealt with macroeconomic policy and evaluated the investment implications of depreciation acceleration. Though the topic was not unusual, given the times at Yale, my colleagues today find my connection to it astonishing. The writing process was sheer torture, the stuff of recurrent nightmares, but I considered the product to be decent; nonetheless, I did not consider the article that derived from the thesis for inclusion in this book. My classmates, who taught me as much as my professors, included William Brainard, Mordecai Kurz, and T.N. Srinivasan, friends to this day.[7]

In 1962 I accepted a position at the US Treasury in Washington, two years of teaching at Yale and a half-finished thesis (an optimistic evaluation) in hand. Including undergraduate years, I had been at Yale for nine years, seemingly forever; and, because I thought of New Haven as home, leaving seemed strange, even with a wife and expectations of an early return to academia. At the Treasury I quickly learned that bureaucracy was as much fun as the shirt factory, and after only six months I moved to the Institute for Defense Analyses (IDA), recruited by Malmgren, who had preceded me there, and Steven Enke, and lured by a promise of release time to complete the dissertation.

I was at IDA for almost three years, and recall two major accomplishments. First, after two years I finally wrapped up the dissertation, with more angst than joy. Then, with the support and encouragement of Bill Niskanen, to whom I reported, I successfully completed a major study (regrettably classified) of *Military Assistance Planning and Programming*. The highlight, for Kappie and for me, was a round-the-world fact-finding trip, our first foreign adventure (during which I enjoyed, at age twenty-nine, a full colonel's perks). Addiction to foreign travel followed with minimal lag. I subsequently learned that non-academic publications, regardless of significance, counted for little in the academic arena; at least I was free to discuss the trip.

Later in the same year, 1965, I moved to a full-time academic position at the University of Virginia, as the junior and least distinguished of a three-person team of public economists, with James Buchanan and Gordon Tullock as my colleagues.[8] Most of all, I enjoyed teaching the graduate students and listening to the stories of Bill Breit – student of Abba Lerner and the Jackie Mason (or was it Harry Golden?) of economists – with whom I edited the erstwhile 'best-seller', *Readings in Microeconomics*. However, it took a while to learn (too late, as it happened) that publication, along with a certain reticence, was what really counted in academe.

It was in Charlottesville that Kappie and I met Carmen and Francesco Forte, who gave us (with Betsy, then one year old) the chance to live in Italy during the late summer and fall of 1968.[9] We spent the first six weeks in Santa Margherita on the Ligurian coast, then moved to Turin for the remainder of our stay, during which I co-authored an article (not reprinted) with Forte. Coincidentally, we studied Piemontese cuisine and wine, quite intensively, and made lifelong friends among the economists at (as it was then known) the Laboratorio di Economia Politica, of whom I single out Giorgio Brosio and Piervincenzo Bondonio, masters of a dialect (in addition to Piemontese) I can best characterize as scatological.[10]

The last thirty years

In September, 1969, shortly before 'Pareto Optimal Redistribution' (Chapter 1) appeared in print, I moved from Virginia to the Urban Institute in Washington. I had been a lesser victim of the internecine skirmishes that led Buchanan and Tullock to depart not long before, and others, like Breit, John Moore (my first doctoral student and later a colleague), and Leland Yeager, not long thereafter. Truth to tell, while we had enjoyed many friendships, academic and non-academic, in Charlottesville, I had never been entirely comfortable, partly for reasons of ideology and partly because my personal style is ill-suited, in obvious ways, to the Upper South.

At the Urban Institute, then in its infancy and troubled by an identity crisis – whether its role was to be advocacy or research on urban process or the *official* social problems of the times – my responsibilities expanded rapidly, as my relationships with Bill Gorham (its President) and Worth Bateman (Research Vice-President) developed. My (theoretical) research on distributional choice was secondary, at most. Instead, I was preoccupied with administration (largely learning-by-doing) as Director of the Research Program in Urban Public Finance, coordinating a staff and designing a diverse program in a substantive corner of public economics that was (surprising as this now seems) still relatively undeveloped. Overall, this was a heady period: productive and, judged by the volume and innovative content of the group's writings, successful. I had the luxury of working directly with many first-rate economists, including (to name but a few) Harvey Galper, Claudia Scott, George Peterson, Richard Wagner, Dennis Young, and (each summer) Mitch Polinsky.

Still, with funding from the National Science Foundation and the encouragement of James Blackman, Director of its Economics Program, my work on distributional choice continued throughout my six years at the Institute (less a year at Berkeley and a three-month sabbatical in London). The high point was the conference on *Redistribution Through Public Choice* that George Peterson and I organized in March, 1973; the papers presented, including 'Rule Change and Transitional Equity' (Chapter 10), were published by Columbia University Press in 1974.

For better or worse, it was my intention, throughout this period, to return eventually to academia, partly because I missed the student contact (more than the teaching itself) and partly for three additional, and compelling reasons, *June, July* and *August*. Thus, in 1972, when Charlottesville friends decided to sell their New Hampshire cottage on Lake Sunapee, we purchased it, almost sight unseen, and have spent nearly 30 summers (and occasional winter months) there ever since, while residing in Washington, DC (until 1975), Scarsdale, New York (while at the City University of

New York (CUNY) from 1975 through 1992), and Durham, Pennsylvania (since moving to Lafayette College in 1992).

Several factors prompted my decision to move to CUNY, where I divided my time, for more than 15 years, between Baruch College and the City University Graduate Center, which houses the Economics PhD Program. These included the interest in the urban economy I had developed at the Urban Institute; the opportunity to teach in a program with Abba Lerner and Donald Gordon (*the 'economist's economist'*), both of whom I had long admired;[11] and a wish to escape perpetual payment of private school tuition for our two daughters, Betsy and Sandy, who were then seven and five years of age.

All in all, the New York experience was bittersweet. New York's and CUNY's financial straits, in combination with the disparate qualities of the university and a demand-driven focus on the study of financial economics, made it all but impossible to create a quality research, or teaching, environment conducive to my substantive interests; one rarely saw more than a small handful of able students in any year; and, finally, in Scarsdale it was difficult to keep up on a professor's salary. Yet both CUNY and New York have much more to offer, academically, culturally, and culinarily, so there were great many high points and, almost by reflex, I now think of New York as home.[12]

While at CUNY I was able to arrange a number of leaves at other colleges and universities. Overseas, we spent almost a year at the Hebrew University of Jerusalem in 1980–81, as Lady Davis Visiting Professor, and in 1988 we visited the University of Turin (naturally). In the mid-1980s, as my research career began to wind down, I decided to do something different and sampled teaching at an undergraduate liberal arts college, selective in its choice of students, by visiting Wesleyan and Williams. This led me, shortly thereafter, to Lafayette, when the William E. Simon Chair in Political Economy became open. Since moving to Lafayette in the fall of 1992, we have continued our travelings, visiting Turin (again) in 1996; teaching for a term and shepherding a lively group of Lafayette students during their Study Abroad Program at Vesalius College in Brussels in 1997; then, in 1999, spending a little over a month at Deakin University in Australia, the only country in which I have ever been where, even among economists, I did not witness even a shred of paranoia.

Pareto optimal redistribution

Origins and responses
In some ways, the continuing professional interest in 'Pareto Optimal Redistribution' (Chapter 1) and the literature it has engendered have surprised us, but in others not at all.[13] The central idea, that a progressive income tax (in more general terms, redistributive fiscal incidence) can readily be justified, within a neoclassical frame of reference, by utility interdependence, was worked out while I was teaching public finance to a graduate class in which Jim Rodgers was a second-year student.[14]

Readers who are old enough or rely (even now) on the wrong textbooks are familiar with the standard utilitarian justifications of progressive taxation, cast in terms of the *sacrifice* of utility that is both cardinally measurable and interpersonally comparable – simple enough provided one can swallow the assumptions. Of course, these sacrifice arguments are a chimera. Nobody has yet figured out how to calculate cardinal utility of this sort, or whether it is valid to assume, like the theory, that all agents have the same marginal utility of money function. So, thus constructed, the case for progressive taxation as a means of evening out a society's distribution of income is logically weak (or, as Blum and Kalven (1953) argued in a persuasive essay, *uneasy*) and rests, in truth, on simple faith or egalitarian ideology, not analysis. Nonetheless, a significant part of the curriculum in virtually every public finance course was devoted to discussion of redistribution.

At the time, political philosophy, then in its mid-century doldrums, offered little help, even as general guidance, in discussing these issues; John Rawls's work was in its formative stages,[15] and most economists, especially novices like me, were trained to think in terms of a self-contained paradigm, or were too unsophisticated to do otherwise.

Since, at Virginia, Buchanan and Tullock both preferred students with enough background to discuss their cutting-edge research constructively, it fell to me to teach the initial graduate course in public finance (to guide the recruits through, as it were, basic training).[16] When, the second time I did this, I came to the segment on redistributive taxation, it struck me that I had been teaching nonsense. This led me, in preparing notes, to jot down a few calculations, indicating the tax patterns that would be chosen, assuming neutrality in the Lindahl sense,[17] if the well-being of lower-income individuals enters systematically into the utility functions of others with higher initial (essentially market-determined) incomes. As it turned out, simple and, on the surface, reasonable interdependence patterns, coupled with realistic assumptions about the shape of the distribution itself (shades of an earlier research apprenticeship with Ed Budd) implied that tax progressivity would be Pareto Optimal. In other words, fiscal incidence that reflects a redistribution of real income from rich to poor could improve the welfare status of all parties. Hence, the article's title, which almost everyone, me included, had hitherto considered a contradiction in terms.

At the next morning's class, I presented the rudiments of the argument. Jim Rodgers picked up on it immediately and, within the hour, we agreed to work together to turn it into an article. From the start, it seemed clear that we were onto something and, because it built on basic facts about human relationships, that it might augur a sea change in the way economists, at least in normative analysis, viewed redistributive transfers.[18]

First, we worked out the implications of simple interdependence for the two-person case, then, accounting for free-rider behavior, for its *n*-person analogue, which converts the transfer into a public good. To do this, we traced patterns of redistribution implied by two stylized assumptions about interdependence and two different (initial) income distributions, one rectangular and the other a rough approximation of the actual distribution in the US.[19] We then spent a few weeks writing and rewriting, encouraged by the comments of colleagues, especially Buchanan, and shipped off the article to the *American Economic Review*, believing we were wasting the department's postage and anticipating an early rejection.

Happily, when Gary Becker visited Charlottesville a month or so later, he let it slip to one of my colleagues (Buchanan, I believe) that he had recently read an article by two young economists from the University of Virginia, suggesting that he was the referee. Because our article's thrust was normative, reputationally counter, of course, to Becker's predilections, Buchanan was pessimistic. Fortunately, he was wrong. Not too long thereafter, an odd-sized envelope from the National Bureau of Economic Research appeared in my mailbox, which I took to be advertising and left unopened for a few days; it was, in fact, a letter from Becker, accompanied by a draft paper of his that covered much, but not all, of the same ground as ours (not the welfare economics, I seem to recollect). It was followed a week or so later by a letter from John Gurley, then editor of the *American Economic Review*, indicating tentative acceptance, provided we made some revisions, all relatively inconsequential (based on my own recent experience as editor of the *Eastern Economic Journal* from 1992 through 1998). Rodgers and I were, truth to tell, stunned; in 1968, after all, a major publication in the *AER* was a big deal for a young economist, all the more for one like Rodgers, who had yet to take qualifying exams.[20]

I then, so to speak, took the show on the road, starting with the fall term in Italy.[21] During that year I presented the article countless times: in Turin, where I developed it into a series of lectures;[22] at Brown, Dartmouth, and other schools in the US; and at Sheffield and York in England, invitations attributable to Alan Peacock's apparent belief that Rodgers and I had, for public economics, accomplished something of real worth. Rodgers started his dissertation (Rodgers, 1970), which used the utility interdependence argument, among other things, to challenge the free-market tenet that cash transfers are always preferable to transfers-in-kind, because they afford the recipient more options and thus higher utility. I consider the point of his argument to be quite important: the conventional thinking, near and dear to egalitarians and libertarians alike, fails to recognize that donor preferences, grounded in property rights, impel the transfer process in the first place, and the form of the transfers influences the *total* amount that donors, acting politically in an *n*-person setting, transfer 'willingly.'[23]

On publication of 'Pareto Optimal Redistribution', my anticipations were (at least for me) uncharacteristically optimistic, but the reception, especially the amount of commentary the work engendered, still surprised us. Within a month or two, George Borts (Gurley's successor as Editor) had sent us at least a half dozen written comments for review; three were published a year later (Goldfarb, 1970; Meyer and Shipley, 1970; Musgrave, 1970). One was Musgrave's, which I reprint here (Chapter 2) with our response (Chapter 3) because I consider it central to the professional acceptance of our argument, which he heartily endorsed, by dividing his Distribution Branch, henceforth, into two compartments and designating Pareto optimal transfers as *secondary redistribution*.[24] Of the others, the comment by Paul A. Meyer and J.J. Shipley pointed out some (possible but, in the larger scheme, substantively inconsequential) technical difficulties with our presentation, interpreting this aspect of the argument more strictly than we intended, while Robert Goldfarb's paper dealt with translation of the two-person into the *n*-person example, and the question of whether (and when) it is best to conduct redistributive activities collectively rather than privately.

Other exchanges, all lively, followed for two or three years, with distinguished economists like Geoffrey Brennan and Cliff Walsh (Brennan, 1973; Brennan and Walsh, 1973), E.J. Mishan (1972), and John Head (1970) (see also Hochman, 1970).

In addition, George von Furstenberg and Dennis Mueller (1971), and Mark Pauly (1973) published full-length articles, criticizing or elaborating upon the original argument. I list these,with others, in the Bibliography, but have chosen not to summarize or respond to them here. Much of what was said is incorporated in our later writings. Moreover, since it is more than a quarter century since the discussion was first joined, I think it unseemly to debate technicalities or worry about intellectual property rights, for the ideas in question have become, through time, common property. It makes far more sense to treat the various commentators, instead, as collaborators, taking their contributions as a compliment.

I wrote 'Individual Preferences and Distributional Adjustments', the last article in this initial section of the book (Chapter 4), for an invited session of the American Economic Association meetings in January, 1972, while visiting the London School of Economics and the Centre for Environmental Studies in London for three months.[25] For me, the invitation signified that our interpretation of the rationale for redistributive transfers had attained respectability.

This essay, after an initial restatement, added a few new twists, which I wish I had done more to develop, somewhere. One was a rudimentary attempt to rationalize the taxation of intergeneration transfers at death in terms of utility interdependence. This hinges on the diminishing ability of living individuals to identify heirs, as specific persons, as they project into the future, an argument that connects with the models of Abba Lerner and John Harsanyi. The other is an initial attempt to connect the distributional argument to the Tiebout model and to constitutional choice. These were to become recurring themes, in my subsequent articles and the general literature.

Developing the theme

The seven remaining articles in Part I of this book, which divide into three sections, develop these themes. The first group consists of two conceptual papers on utility interdependence and its implications: a comment (with Rodgers and Gordon Tullock) on a thought-provoking contribution by Lester Thurow and a taxonomic paper on extended preference written (with Shmuel Nitzan) during my sabbatical year at the Hebrew University. The second section tackles, in a rudimentary way, the issue of empirical validity (in two articles with Rodgers). The final section contains three essays, written (without co-authors) over a period of 20 years, which expand formal discussion and think through the relationship of my work on distributional choice to the broader question of *economic justice*.[26]

Conceptual articles

The first of the conceptual articles (Chapter 5) was written in the fall of 1969, shortly after I moved from Charlottesville to the Urban Institute. Prompted by Musgrave, then Editor of the *Quarterly Journal of Economics*, Rodgers and I joined up with Gordon Tullock, who had submitted a related piece, to craft a public choice response to an interesting and, technically, provocative essay by Lester Thurow (1971). It was Thurow's contention that the income distribution, within any bounded society, can itself be construed as a public good, providing a rationalization of redistributive transfers additional to and arguably independent of utility interdependence. Our comment suggested that Thurow's distinction was, in effect, redundant, because it is utility interdependence, either in general or in specific-commodity form, that is responsible, motivationally, for the public good characteristics of the redistributive actions. We held, in other words, that the taste for distributional equality derives from such externalities. In retrospect, as my perspective has adapted to contractarian and communitarian theory, our arguments seem closer to Thurow's than they did at the time, and I see his contribution (like Goldfarb's comment) as another (entirely independent) attempt to contend with the preferential basis of redistribution, well before this became integral to standard discourse.

In the fall of 1980, not long after I arrived in Jerusalem on my sabbatical, Shmuel Nitzan attended a talk I gave at Bar-Ilan University in Tel-Aviv. Two articles resulted from the conversations that ensued, largely late at night, after my co-author had returned home from the moonlighting that was *de rigeur* for Israeli academics.

The first of these collaborations, 'Concepts of Extended Preference' (Chapter 6), expanded upon the (by then familiar) utility interdependence assumptions of the earlier redistribution articles, which had only considered simple benevolence. The early going describes a taxonomy for the full range of utility interactions, both sympathetic and (adding a bit of cynicism and realism) antipathetic, or negative (a topic that had been touched upon in the literature, with little rigor, under rubrics like *malice* or *envy*). Central to the article is a simple expository device: division of a fixed endowment of a single good, income, between a reference individual, whose property rights are well-established, and a second person. Though simple, this two-person model clears up a great deal of semantic confusion, by defining, non-trivially and (one hopes) unambiguously, such concepts (some local and some global) as generosity, altruism, self-orientation, acquisitiveness, willingness to begrudge, and destructiveness. It relates these concepts to initial conditions and to the exchange rate or terms of trade at which donors (willing or, with antipathy, unwilling) can carry out the transfers (the technology). One thing made clear – though common usage suggests that it remains ill understood – is the distinction between the broad concept of utility interdependence (sympathy) and the narrower concept of altruism, terms which are far from synonymous. The article utilizes its definitions in a number of illustrations, which include charitable giving and taking (or crime).[27]

Empirical articles

Geoffrey Brennan tells me that I am a theorist at heart, though, of course, in no way that any graduate of a present-day doctoral program might recognize. Actually, I suspect Brennan was being kind and trying to say, with more tact than I deserve, that I lack the patience for painstaking empirical work, especially when the necessary data are not laid out before me. Unfortunately, I suspect he is right; I have always been happier, when writing, to stress the conceptual. Rodgers and I were aware from the start, however, that the impact of our income redistribution story on public economics and welfare economics would be greater if we could demonstrate, not just intuitively but empirically, that the interdependence we had in mind is more than wishful thinking and actually does motivate individuals, privately and as taxpayers. Yet because there was (and is) no direct way to garner systematic (non-anecdotal) evidence of utility interdependence, and it did not cry out unambiguously from any of the major databases that economists used (or use, even now) in behavioral research, this proved to be a tall order.

Even so, it seemed better to tackle the problem with imperfect (in their fit to theory) hypotheses and funky data than to do nothing at all, to put welfare economics on an empirical basis (paraphrasing Harvey Leibenstein). Rodgers and I started on this even before 'Pareto Optimal Redistribution' appeared in print. Our first instinct was to look at charitable giving as (proximate) evidence of benevolent interdependence, though manifested in private rather than political behavior, to examine its variation with socioeconomic characteristics and to probe, indirectly, the extent to which it might justify observed fiscal incidence.

The resulting article, 'Utility Interdependence and Income Transfers Through Charity' (Chapter 7) was presented, in December 1969, at a meeting of the Society for the Study of Grants Economics and published, ultimately, in a collection edited by Kenneth E. Boulding and Martin Pfaff. It examined, with very limited success, the variation of reported contributions with the mean and dispersion of community income and community size (to indicate the potential for free-rider behavior and measure the relationship between interdependence and social pressure) in a small sample of US metropolitan areas. The regressions, though elementary, found significant associations between charitable contributions and some of the independent variables, but not community size. Of course, the data were hardly a perfect fit to the hypotheses; utility interdependence is but one explanation of private charity and, as ever the case with this topic, motivation is impossible to untangle. In the end, though hardly satisfied, we considered it a start.[28]

A while later, after I had settled into the Urban Institute, we were asked to give a paper at a National Bureau of Economic Research (NBER) Income and Wealth Conference in Ann Arbor. When we finally got around to writing it in 1974, I was visiting the Graduate School of Public Policy at the University of California at Berkeley and interacting regularly with Aaron Wildavsky, Bill Niskanen, Arnold Meltsner, and Nelson Polsby, midway through my most enjoyable year as an academic. As one might expect, since the paper was written for a National Bureau function, 'The Simple Politics of Distributional Preference' (Chapter 8) took another crack at empirical verification (loosely defined) of the utility interdependence rationale. This time, instead of charitable giving, we examined survey evidence of political support for redistributive transfers on the part of California voters.[29] While the data were more accessible and we had first-rate students to help with its processing, the *chutzpah* required for the conceptual exercise – association of poll responses to qualitative survey questions with our assumptions about utility interdependence, interpreted through simple median voter models of direct and representative democracy – easily exceeded a lifetime's allotment. Still, despite the tentative nature of its conclusions, the article was remarkably well received, all the more given its audience of empiricists.

The major finding is that benevolence need not be widespread, much less universal, to have a significant impact on the distributional outcome. Democracy requires only that benevolence be *sufficient*, at the margin, for a coalition (minority or majority, depending on political assumptions) of recipients, who support redistribution out of self-interest, and donors to control the outcome. In representative democracy, the efficacy of this coalition depends on its dispersion across jurisdictions. So far as distributional preference is concerned, the data suggest that non-recipient supporters of welfare programs, save those close to the top of the income distribution, appear to support redistributive transfers because they dislike the manifestations of poverty rather than out of *pure* benevolence.[30]

Economic justice

Of the three essays reprinted in this section, the first and third are reviews, while the second was written, early in 1973, for the Urban Institute conference I organized with George Peterson.

'Contractarian Theories of Redistribution' (Chapter 9) dates to the late 1970s, roughly a decade after I began working with Rodgers. It pulls together my thinking on distributional choice and income equality, as of, more or less, the mid-point of my career.

Initially, this essay restates, in non-technical terms, the constitutional and post-constitutional rationalizations of redistribution; it then turns to a discussion of the preference-based limits to redistributive action. I limit myself here to a few observations.

The first is the seemingly innocent, yet consequential, finding that '... freedom is certainly likely to require *some* redistribution. But it is unlikely to be consistent with either *negligible* or *pervasive* redistribution' (p. 215). One might, skeptically, ask why this is consequential. The reason is that it seems independent of specific assumptions and implies a rejection of extremes, in ideology and policy, on the fiscal adjustment of market-based distribution.

The second point relates to my increasing interest, during the 1970s, in writings of contemporary political philosophers on economic justice,[31] especially John Rawls (1974), and their relationship to the earlier, more traditional utilitarian models of writers like Abba Lerner (1944) and John Harsanyi (1955). My article argues that the Hochman–Rodgers argument can produce utilitarian conclusions, without their baggage, with an extreme assumption about benevolence.

Finally, following up on Robert Nozick's (1974) contention, it argues that attempts to eliminate inequalities in the *time-slice distribution* (Nozick's term) would bring about other inequalities that might, ethically, prove even less acceptable, assuming normal behavioral responses.

Of all the articles reprinted here, 'Rule Change and Transitional Equity' (Chapter 10)[32] may best reflect the hard lessons taught me by Buchanan and Tullock. The central argument is straightforward. If incompletely anticipated, all changes in existing rules, regardless of efficiency implications, have distributional effects, because they alter pre-existing claims and expectations, producing windfall gains and losses. Whether this warrants social concern depends not only on the nature of these gains or losses, but also on the legitimacy of the rules that are changed and the process, legal and economic, that governs the change.[33] If, in some constitutional sense, pre-existing rules are legitimate, justice requires that prospective social gains – measured, as they usually are, in comparative static terms – be weighed, invoking a criterion of fairness, against their transitional costs of implementation.[34]

Constitutional law makes this explicit through the Fifth Amendment's *takings* clause, which requires the payment of *just compensation*, when private property is condemned for public use. Nowadays, the courts also recognize, as an issue of fairness, *regulatory takings*, which occur when effects of regulation approximate those of condemnation.[35] However, while there is no mistaking the conceptual analogy, no such requirement applies to administrative or legislative acts, like changes in tax law, that are not takings in the Fifth Amendment sense.

The policy dilemma is at once normative and pragmatic. Ideally, democratic decisions reflect constituent preferences, expressed through voting. Even if a rule change appears to be efficient in benefit–cost terms, it may not be enacted if enough voters, acting on narrow and extended self-interest, prove unwilling to bear the transitional losses it entails. Thus, feasibility requires a rule change to pass a dual test, as Frank Michelman (1967) (incidentally, my college classmate) showed, by introducing the concept of *demoralization costs*, in a classic article on 'just' compensation.

It is patent nonsense to treat rules, by virtue of simple existence, as if they were etched in stone and rule out all reform, however desirable, because some people will suffer transitional losses. However, it is not only simple common sense, but ethical obligation, to devise measures (grandfathering and deferred implementation are examples) that can temper these effects, just as safeguards against transitional inequity are built into democratic process itself through restrictive voting rules, logrolling, and extensive public discussion of proposed change.[36] The overall effect is to make reform both more feasible and, in terms of equity, more desirable.

The most recent of the essays is 'Public Choice Interpretations of Distributional Preference' (Chapter 11), an amalgam of two public lectures, one to the European Public Choice Society in 1992 and the other my Inaugural Lecture at Lafayette. It is a personal statement, unsparing of editorial comment, that summarizes my current thinking about distributional choice and economic justice, as informed by economics and ethics. I confess, in the end, to views that are 'admittedly subjective … neither morally antiseptic nor ahistorical'; after all, even the base economic model entails (though some economists are congenitally loathe to admit it) considerable subjectivity.

Initially, I discuss old ground, market process and the role of government in the economy, then proceed to the constitutional and post-constitutional explanations of redistributive activities, emphasizing the centrality of ethical or impersonal choice and its relationship to utility interdependence. This is followed by a brief summary of some very suggestive experimental findings, which support my contention that individuals, in registering distributional preference, prefer a more egalitarian outcome than markets are likely to generate, but stop well short of equality. Finally, turning to the thesis of *Spheres of Justice* (Walzer, 1983), the essay questions the *normative* meaning of *equality* itself and, appealing to Michael Walzer's distinctions, tries to think through the connections of simple equality, complex equality, and dominance to pluralism and economic freedom. In concluding, I contend that a restatement of the argument in terms of *complex equality* – defined as an absence of *dominance*, in which inequalities are not transferable across normative spheres – tends to strengthen the case for market allocation.

Public policy

The five articles in Part II differ, topically, from the rest of the volume, but close reading reveals similar methodological themes. Unlike distributional preference, my interest in these topics has waxed and waned with other obligations, and with research grants. The first article, which deals with tax policy, derives from the exploration of charitable contributions as evidence of utility interdependence. The three that follow, which are in urban economics, stem from my activities at the Urban Institute in the early 1970s and at CUNY a decade later. The final article, written with Thomas Barthold, develops a model of addictive behavior, one of my current research interests.

Taxation policy

In preparing for the Ann Arbor conference, Rodgers and I revisited the subject of charitable contributions, but in a different light, that of optimal tax policy (Chapter 12). Of our ten co-authored papers, this was not only the most difficult to execute, but the last.

To oversimplify, tax discussion typically portrays deviations from the nominal rate structure of the individual income tax as *tax-expenditures*, with pejorative connotations for fiscal equity. Statements about *optimality* generally require an autonomous value judgment (a social welfare function) that defines preferred (but by whom?) tradeoffs between equity and efficiency.[37] Unfortunately, this can mislead, at least in thinking about tax preferences like deductions and exclusions, with incidence that deviates, by intent, from standard equity norms (redistributive goals). Without further probing, it is all too easy to interpret such deviations from the nominal rate structure as unwarranted grants from government – thus assumed, by implication, to hold property rights in the foregone tax – to privileged taxpayers.

For us, this interpretation ignores the logic of taxation, as enunciated by Wicksell and Lindahl. Taxation is the way citizens finance their demands for public goods, supported by property rights and expressed through voting.[38] Thus, we turn the optimal tax reasoning around, interpreting the contributions deduction, ideally, as a Lindahl-efficient device for apportioning the cost of philanthropic activities between high-demanders (those making private donations) and taxpayers-at-large. Such cost sharing does two things. It diminishes underprovision, which is a characteristic of publicness, and it reduces tendencies toward government monopoly in the provision of impure public goods.

Looking at the problem this way, we concluded that fiscal efficiency would be improved by replacing the existing deduction with a tax credit, available (in the US) to both non-itemizing *and* itemizing taxpayers (the latter tend to have higher incomes). The key to this argument is the extensive discussion (see Part III of the article) of the proper relationship between the private price and income elasticities of charitable giving and the rates at which the fisc (under the Lindahl logic) should subsidize contributions.

Frankly, I found this argument more convincing, in the end, than Rodgers did. Still, I was surprised by the extent to which it caught on, as evidenced by its inclusion in Susan Rose-Ackerman's book, *The Economics of Nonprofit Institutions* (1986), and its frequent citation, especially in law journals.[39]

Urban economics and urban policy

While my writings on urban affairs broke less ground, conceptually, they attracted some attention, and represented a major commitment of my resources. Accordingly, I include, as Chapters 13 through 15, three articles on the urban economy and urban society. These try, in different ways, to cast old, seemingly intractable issues in a new interpretive light.

I wrote the first paper, 'Social Problems and the Urban Crisis: Can Public Policy Make a Difference?', with my colleague Worth Bateman, at a time when we were immersed in the research program of the Urban Institute and all too aware of the racial tensions in American society and, concomitantly, the academy. Not long before, Edward Banfield, the conservative political scientist, had published *The Unheavenly City* (1970), a provocative book that could properly be characterized as the antithesis of *political correctness*. We had but limited sympathies for Banfield's thesis, which attributed the *urban crisis*, in the large, to an intractable *culture of poverty*, rooted in *present-orientedness*, among the lower classes and recommended, too fatalistically, a policy of *benign neglect*; nonetheless, like many Americans, we shared his frustrations. An invitation from John Kain to present a paper at the American Economic Association meetings in Detroit, then a prime example of urban decay, afforded us a welcome opportunity to revisit some of the issues Banfield had raised.

Relative to Banfield's, our take on the urban crisis was abstract. True, an apparent culture of poverty, reinforced by population concentration, discrimination, and *de facto* segregation, virtually guaranteed that short-run programs could not cure troubled cities. Moreover, by heightening aspirations, modest improvements in the status of the disadvantaged would heighten perceptions of inequity. Any quest for a panacea was bound to fail; success required a renewal of belief in democratic process and the legitimacy of government.

We argued that urban programs, to have a chance of success, would have to be systemic and capable of countering deep-seated perceptions of distributive injustice, so that everyone, including Banfield's lower classes, could approach the future with some optimism. Moreover, to sustain constitutional credibility and the rule of law, it was essential that the processes through which change is engineered be perceived as fair.[40] This directed government, in acting to ameliorate urban pathology, to look to changes in the *rules of the game* and the *effective constitution* (property rights issues) rather than short-term palliatives, which the electorate is less likely to perceive as Pareto Optimal. In other words, prescription must foster a moral consensus to succeed – a tall order, and one unlikely to be widely understood, especially among the poor, at the time. Yet, looking back, I like to think that this is what has transpired, albeit incompletely, during the intervening thirty years.

'Clearing the Regulatory Clutter' (Chapter 14) examines a different dimension of urban life, the over-regulation of consumer and business activities for which New York City has long been notorious. However, at base, it is also about the allocative and distributional implications of the institutional setting and the legitimacy of rules. The article derives from a group project, funded by a grant from the US Department of Housing and Urban Development (HUD), that I directed a year or so after moving to CUNY, in the midst of the notorious budget crisis of the 1970s.[41]

While regulations, ostensibly adopted to protect the community from predatory behavior, were not the root cause of the extensive deterioration of New York's economic fortunes, they certainly made things worse. Taken one at a time, *good* reason could be adduced for virtually all of New York's regulations – licensing, development (land and building), and price controls – but the totality betrayed a failure to measure benefits adequately against real costs. However admirable the intentions, the regulatory network, as a whole, betrayed a deep-seated distrust of market process; added to the struggles of an economy in transition from manufacturing to services; and impeded economic recovery. Fortunately, favorable institutional changes have, in recent years, improved the business climate, contributing (at least up to the time of the World Trade Center travesty in September 2001) to New York's remarkable reversal of fortunes.

The third selection in this section, 'New York and Pittsburgh: Contrasts in Community' was written in the early 1990s for a session honoring Benjamin Chinitz at the meetings of the Regional Planning Association. Stylistically, it is a retrospective, largely a new and different take on his 1961 article, 'Contrasts in Agglomeration', supplemented by comment on the rise and decline, between 1970 and 1990, in the academic popularity of urban economics.[42]

Agglomerative externalities operate through spatial concentration and urban scale, impelled by personal interaction and historical interplay. Their power resides in factorial or exponential effects on the urban environment. Chinitz's essay focused on positive economies of agglomeration, which encourage and facilitate entrepreneurship, risk-taking, and other salutary behavior. In contrast, my essay emphasizes the dark side of agglomeration, negative externalities that stimulate the transference of destructive values and, by subverting a city's life-support system, deepen urban pathology. With increased density and scale, I hypothesize, the negative face of agglomeration ultimately overtakes the positive. This helps to explain why (at least until the mid-1990s) Pittsburgh, in emerging from a long urban decline, seemed to enjoy more success than New York.[43]

Addictive behavior
Since the early 1980s, I have redirected my thinking, by chance more than design, to addictive behavior (treated as a deviation from textbook assumptions) and the problems, clinical and social, associated with extreme behavior.[44] To date, these inquiries have produced three papers, two on addiction and one on political extremism. Only the first of these, a theoretical paper with Thomas Barthold entitled 'Addiction as Extreme-Seeking' appears here (Chapter 16).[45]

The Barthold–Hochman article, through its representation of individual choice, tries to identify suitable directions for the treatment of individual patients and for public policy. The model distinguishes between the apparent extreme-seeking behavior (unconventional, perhaps pathological) of some individuals with strong addictions (psychological *or* physiological) and continuous adjustment, which is typical of what economics ordinarily considers to be rational behavior. Its assumption is that extreme-seeking can be captured by concave segments of indifference curves.

Additionally, borrowing from Stigler and Becker (1977), the model assumes that addictive behavior is driven, intertemporally, by a capital effect, which captures personal consumption history. In the short-run, this magnifies addictive tendencies, and in the long-run it deepens them by making indifference curves more concave; yet it can also produce behavior reversals. Over time, addictive behavior is limited by thresholds, related to consumption of the addictive good and the limits it places on the consumption of necessities.

This analysis has a number of implications. One is the observation that the best – read *most effective* – way to modify an existing addiction, tastes given, may be to transfer it, through substitution, to something less harmful. Examples include the replacement of hard drugs with methadone, alcohol with religious commitment, and compulsive eating with dieting. Of course, as in the article by Becker and Murphy (1988), it is even better if, somehow, tastes changes can be induced.

When, fifteen or so years ago, I started to think this line of reasoning through, I was, frankly, more sanguine about the model than I am now. To be sure, most people have irrational moments, which may correspond to our indifference curve concavities; and with deep addiction these can stretch into weeks or months. Yet, for most addicts most of the time, the *rational addiction model* (Becker–Murphy) seems to ring true. As with any model designed with econometric verification in mind, however, it seems to me that the rational addiction approach does less well with extremes, with the deviant or pathological behavior that shows up in the outliers. It is these cases, I suspect, the ones that are most likely to entail intensive clinical intervention, that our model, I believe, accommodates more readily.

A common hypothesis about behavioral differences between addicts and non-addicts focuses on the discounting of future prospects. Some writers, including George Ainslie (1975), and Richard Herrnstein and Drazen Prelec (1992), have argued that addicts discount hyperbolically (leading, for the most susceptible, to extreme-seeking behavior?) rather than exponentially (the standard in economics) and, as a consequence, over-weight near-term payoffs. For the economist, of course, this argument has major intuitive appeal, because it pegs behavior to tradeoffs that are both observable and standard; however, it does nothing to resolve the even more basic question of why.

One virtue of the discounting argument is that it can be investigated through controlled experiments; research is not dependent on autonomous data. Recently, Louis Levy-Garboua and a number of his associates (at the University of Paris) conducted a set of such experiments, which examine whether addicts under treatment display different responses than a control group to uncertain choices and intertemporal tradeoffs. Their initial iteration, which involved a series of experimental games, was suggestive, but found no conclusive evidence of behavioral differences. Working with two Lafayette colleagues, Rose Marie Bukics and Edward Gamber, and two students, Matthew Rutherford and Mark Commanducci, I have been trying to replicate these experiments at Lafayette College, using samples drawn from the local population, with results, thus far, that look similar to those of the French researchers.[46]

Conclusion

To conclude my story, it remains only to sum up; yet, in the main, the previous commentary has already done this for me. Tempting as it is to try to say something, in summation, that might seem profound, it is better not to try; such wisdom is usually contrived.

I have long thought of economics, like mathematics (almost), as a young person's game, and this self-executed retrospective of my career has not altered this view.

There is a profound temporal mismatch, throughout our professional life cycle, between technical skills and intuition, and insight into the unorthodox conceptual issues, especially if normative, that entail the crossing of disciplinary boundaries. In this respect, academic incentives are prone to sabotage progress. By the time most economists can constructively redirect their energies away from academic fashion, their technical skills are passé.

I consider myself fortunate to have focused, from early in my career, on a number of troubling conceptual issues, of a type, more or less, that young economists usually avoid. So, in this sense, my technical deficits, strictly defined, may have been a hidden strength. Yet it is not one I ever wished to have, for the price has been high. I could never push the analysis as far as I might have liked, and it is never in one's career interests to be deviant.

The articles in this book have been, for me, a continuing source of satisfaction. As a scholar little can match the exhilaration of discovering, in the course of class preparation, that something as ordinary as sympathetic feelings can make redistributive transfers much easier to justify, analytically, than most economists had thought. Even more satisfying is the sense that I have contributed, even a bit, to extending the concept of *economic man* to accommodate caring and decency, repelling an avenue of attack on our paradigm and opening new avenues of multidisciplinary investigation.

While none of this can it be traced to some global life plan, worked out in a flash of post-adolescent insight, neither did it evolve autonomously. It derives, at base, from the way I learned, and the teachers and friends I was fortunate enough to have, many of them of the postwar generation, with firm roots in the Old World. This, in itself, produced an intimate knowledge of the consequences of injustice, commutative or distributional, and a full understanding of the limitations of economic reasoning. Whether generations trained, in the main, by master technicians will benefit in the same way from the vision of their elders remains for the future to reveal. Yet technicians, too, become wiser as they mature and, from what I have seen in the past few years, there is more reason for hope than despair.

I am not nearly objective enough to judge or predict the long-run impact of my writings on the topics I have, by choice or circumstance, examined. Let it suffice that I am without regret, save for the wish to have done more.

Notes

1. Mine was the last cohort of economists for whom econometrics was not a mandatory element of professional training, undergraduate or graduate, something virtually incomprehensible to my younger colleagues. I see this as a weakness, but not a fatal one. And because it forces me to have greater respect for the metaphysical, it is sometimes a strength.
2. Of course, we can sometimes use the economist's magic trick, *other things equal*, to set distributional concerns aside, as in discussing excess burden. If theoretical boundaries are finely drawn, we can act as if institutions are chosen for efficiency alone and rectify the resulting inequities *ex post facto* with lump-sum fiscal adjustments. But this is pure artifice, not least because politics intervenes.
3. Archibald and Donaldson (1976), for example, referred to the Hochman–Rodgers model of 'Pareto Optimal Redistribution' as a *master-dog* model, because it is driven by the preferences of the *donors* in redistributive relationships, who are typically wealthier than recipients. Yet they miss the point. With utility interdependence donor preferences are enough to turn visceral opposition to redistributive transfers on its head as long as the marginal utility of money of recipients is positive. Thus, such critics should be happy, not perturbed. Although 'Pareto Optimal Redistribution' (Chapter 1) inquires into the optimality of fiscal incidence, it does not deal with whether economic justice requires additional transfers.

4. Candidly, it sufficed, as it would have for most young academics, that a major journal accepted our article.

5. I doubt, for example, they would have had much interest in the contents of this book; nonetheless, they would have been proud. I am reminded, here, of the time when my father's elder sister, who came to the English language rather late in life, introduced me as 'my nephew, the e-communist.' Dangerous for the times. Now, of course, this would be taken to mean that I am some sort of *avant garde* entrepreneur.

6. For my maternal grandfather, a tailor by trade and a man both courtly and kind, with a benign taste for *schnapps*, I suspect my attendance at Yale, one of the few universities of which he had heard, was a high point of life. (As I reread this description of my grandfather, it is small wonder I was drawn, ultimately, to Fellner.)

7. With these friends to consult, it is no surprise that I did not feel a crying need to develop a command of mathematics.

8. So far as I am aware, I am the only economist to have been tutored by both Tobin and Okun (formally) and by Buchanan and Tullock (by immersion). Thus, serendipity doubtless played a role in the genesis of this article.

9. It was natural that, when professional travel became a part of my life, we would gravitate to Italy. When I was growing up, both Shelton and New Haven were home to large numbers of Italian-Americans, including many of my friends (and my parents' employees). My early life did not lack for warmth, but its steady diet of Eastern European (Jewish, specifically, *Litvak*) 'cuisine' could not compare with the pungent aromas we associate with Italian food (all the more because Italian meat dishes, being non-kosher, were technically beyond my reach).

   However, the impression that my parents were observant, or even religious, would be mistaken. Prior to marriage, my mother pursued a business career in New York and developed, though not to my father's knowledge, a marked fondness for red roast pork and other Chinese fare. Since I share these proclivities, and haunts, are tastes genetically determined? My father, though adamant about the evils of ham, regularly consumed bacon, a taste acquired while serving in the US army at the tail end of World War I, peeling potatoes. Yet, especially for him, I was not to become a fallen angel; at least, it was important for me not to descend too far. So, for the sake of *my* soul, uppermost in our household, the regular fare included fresh-killed but thrice-boiled chicken; gefilte fish ('filthy fish' to our Tennessee-bred housekeeper); and other light fare – invariably accompanied by complaints about my inability to maintain a reasonable body weight.

10. That we have had a long romance with Italy, particularly Piemonte, would be understatement. We now count three extended stays in Torino, and around 25 visits; at least for Americans, we fancy ourselves experts on esoterica like agnolotti, salciccia crudo (raw pork sausage) and such oenological rarities as pelaverga, as well as the relative merits of Italian economists.

11. Unfortunately, both Gordon and Lerner soon left CUNY. Gordon, however, returned to Baruch for seven years in 1979.

12. Specifically, I have fond recollections of my associations with two of the more colorful administrators at CUNY, diametric opposites politically, Julius C.C. Edelstein, Vice-Chancellor for Urban Affairs, and Joel Segall, President of Baruch College. For a time, I coordinated, with two of my colleagues, lectures and seminars in Philosophy, Politics, and Economics that nurtured my (academic) interest in distributive justice, and I enjoyed some success as the initial Research Director of the (independent) International Center for Economic Policy Studies (now the Manhattan Institute) and as Gordon's successor as Director of the Center for the Study of Business and Government at Baruch.

13. In addition to many excellent contributions, the published literature contains a few that betray a failure to understand what we were trying to say. I find it a bit distressing that *quality* correlates less well with journal reputation than one might expect.

14. While the germ of this idea had long been around, the argument had not been developed, in public finance or welfare economics. Buchanan (1960) mentioned it in a book review published in the *Southern Economic Journal*, but I was not aware of this until our paper was in draft.

    I trace my concern with welfare economics, in particular, with its distributional indeterminacy, to endless re-reading of Jan de V. Graaff's (1957) *Theoretical Welfare Economics* in James Tobin's first-year graduate theory course at Yale – shortly before Challis Hall, teaching public finance, required us to read up on the traditional utilitarian justifications of progressive taxation, then the rather unsatisfactory state of thinking on this subject.

15. The first that most people (but few economists) even heard of Rawls was through his 1958 essay, 'Justice as Fairness', in *Philosophical Review*.

16. This field, thanks to the presence, physical and spiritual, of Buchanan and Tullock accounted for about half the graduate curriculum in economics at the University of Virginia.

17. By 'in the Lindahl sense' I mean that individualized payments for public goods would be

distributionally neutral. In other words, they would reflect willingness-to-pay, to wit, what individualized prices would be if it were not for the free-rider problem.

18. It is often said that ideas have their time, and so with this one. Between writing and publication we learned that several others, including Edgar Olsen (1969), Richard Zeckhauser (1971) and, foremost, Serge-Christophe Kolm (1969), had been covering some of this ground.

19. I sometimes wonder whether the message did as much to make the argument catch on as the title, with its touch of irony, and our use of Mutt and Jeff (two long-forgotten cartoon characters) as the names of the donor and recipient in the two-person case. (The latter was, on my recollection, all Rodgers.)

20. Becker never published this paper. I have always interpreted this as an act of uncommon generosity. A few years later he incorporated its core argument in 'A Theory of Social Interaction' (1974).

21. To date myself yet again, we sailed, with Betsy, then a baby, an Old English Sheepdog, and baggage enough for a regiment, on the ocean liner *Michelangelo*, a period experience we could not repeat now, even if we wished to do so.

22. I am reminded here of a mildly amusing story, pertaining to the discomfiture of the Italian graduate assistants who (doubtless to please Forte) attended these lectures, especially my friend Bondonio. He complained that my lectures were difficult to understand, not because I had consumed a bottle of dolcetto (a Piemontese red wine) at lunch but because, as an American, *I* spoke poor (American and not *English*) English.

23. This portion of Rodgers' dissertation was subsequently published in *Public Finance Quarterly* (1973), and incorporated in an essay, 'Explaining Income Redistribution', in *Redistribution Through Public Choice* (1974).

24. Even 30 years after its appearance the article continues to be cited with some frequency. What accounts for this? In addition to implications for public finance and welfare economics, it helps that the argument crosses, at least implicitly, the boundaries of other social sciences, presenting a real challenge to the assumption of simple self-interest and raising questions about the nature of preferences and preference formation, the logic of philanthropy, and the meaning of distributive justice.

25. The London visit stands out for many reasons, not least my conversations about justice with Amartya Sen and my discussions with famous scholars as disparate as Harry Johnson (sometimes accompanied by *doubles* of scotch whiskey, because 'singles are no goddamn good') and Richard Titmuss. But the biggest treat was a performance of Eugene O'Neill's *A Long Day's Journey into Night* that starred Sir Laurence Olivier. I also recall a lunch at which Lord Robbins waved off my contention that economists might, after all, have something meaningful to add to discussions of distributional choice.

26. *Economic justice* has long been a subject of discussion among political philosophers, from Aquinas to Rawls and Nozick, though logical positivists have tended to downplay it; economists, save those who rejected the neoclassical paradigm, often treated the term as an oxymoron. Since Rawls, however, and such others as Amartya Sen, this has turned around.

27. I decided, after some vacillation, not to reprint 'Tiebout and Sympathy' (Hochman and Nitzan, 1983), my other article with Nitzan, essentially because both of us like the title (as a play on words) more than the article. It is a rather technical piece, out of character for me. The article, which is related to a seminal argument of Pauly's, applies our taxonomy (Chapter 6) to the Tiebout process.

28. Even if the data requirements could have been untangled, conceptually, it is unlikely that suitable data would have been available. In the US most of what we know about charitable contributions comes from individual income tax returns. As contributions are defined for tax purposes, it is difficult to attribute a high proportion to utility interdependence or, for that matter, to escape all manner of heroic assumptions.

29. Our inquiry followed in the tradition of an on-going line of research in political science, using, so far as we could, the interpretive methods of public choice. The classic in this literature was the much-cited discussion of *other-regardingness* (the political scientist's term for utility interdependence) by Harvard's James Q. Wilson and Edward Banfield (1964). Political scientists, it appears, had been less prone to equating rationality and *narrow* self-interest, or committing the cardinal sin of imbuing self-interest with normative significance.

30. Of course, the assumption here is that the utility interdependence is activated by income differentials. This need not be the case if contributions are motivated by other factors, as they were in the aftermath of the World Trade Center disaster.

31. In retrospect, this was a reluctant, but fortunate response to the prodding, none too subtle, of a philosopher–colleague at the Urban Institute, Peter Brown.

32. This article was prepared, immediately after I returned from London, for the Urban Institute–National Science Foundation conference that George Peterson and I organized in 1973.

33. Whether the prior claims are monetary is of no consequence, so long as they are valued by the claimants.

34.   The subject of this article seemed, in temporal context, decidedly impolitic, but I considered it important to address, especially then, with some force. In pointing out that the *status quo*, if legitimate, must be respected, it may appear that I am condoning and counseling conservatism. Not so; I am simply saying that policy must, like law, respect precedent, by considering not only its goals but also the route it takes to attain them. So if this essay is politically incorrect, likewise our constitution.
35.   Another contextual comment is warranted here. In the 1950s and 1960s collective action (government) was often seen, uncritically, as a universal agent of *desirable* change. This was, I suspect, a residual conceit of our Keynesian heritage, which reflected an incomplete understanding of the connection between political rights and property rights. In the abstract, this denied 'voice' to transitional losers.
36.   Examples range from the relatively mundane (tax law) to the emotionally charged (desegregation). A worst case example, cited in the article, would reverse traffic conventions, so that red meant go and green stop.
37.   Often, sometimes implicitly, 'equity' is simplified to 'equal,' as if equal distribution were unambiguously definable. Allocative efficiency is interpreted as minimization of excess burden.
38.   To be more precise, I refer here to the *public characteristics* of goods.
39.   I attribute this to the article's introduction of a different way of thinking through tax issues to a set of scholars, academic lawyers, who had historically worked within a Pigovian framework, without bringing property rights or public goods into the conversation.
40.   This was the genesis of the 'transitional equity' argument of Chapter 11.
41.   The project on local regulation was funded, thanks to John Weicher, by the US Department of Housing and Urban Development. The primary researchers were Richard Coffman, Raymond Domanico, and James Suarez.
42.   However, most of all it was an expression of thanks for Chinitz's advice, his help, and his kindness, which he dispensed freely, to me and to others, indeed to anyone, occasionally on request.
43.   A credible (but obviously incomplete) explanation of the dynamism of New York's economic rebirth in the 1990s is that Mayor Giuliani's administration put reduction of some of the most obvious diseconomies of agglomeration at the top of its priority list.
44.   Until the 1980s addictive behavior received little attention from economists, at least conceptually. Now, however, a major literature exists, with Gary Becker and Kevin Murphy (1988), Michael Grossman, Thomas Schelling, and Gordon Winston (1980) among the primary contributors.
45.   The other article on addictive behavior, written with my Lafayette colleague Susan Averett (Averett and Hochman, 1994), tried, in a preliminary way, to determine whether available data enable us to identify a class of extreme-seeking individuals, with very limited success. The third article, 'Is Democracy an Antidote for Political Extremism?' (Hochman, 2002), which applies median voter analysis to a discussion of the long-term viability of political extremes, was not published until this manuscript had been completed.
46.   It is always a mistake to dismiss negative results, if only because they suggest that the research might better proceed in (slightly?) different directions, which dig deeper than the obvious hypotheses. We plan to modify the original experiments (and samples) in the hope of obtaining more definitive evidence. It is of special interest to us, of course, whether the experiments can discern differences between hard-core or pathological addicts (extreme-seekers?) and others.

Bibliography

Ainslie, George (1975), 'Specious Reward: A Behavioral Theory of Impulsiveness and Impulse Control', *Psychological Bulletin*, **82**, July, 463–96.

Archibald, G.C. and David Donaldson (1976), 'Non-paternalism and the Basic Theorems of Welfare Economics', *Canadian Journal of Economics/Revue Canadienne d'Economique*, **9**, August, 492–507.

Averett, Susan L. and Harold M. Hochman (1994), 'Addictive Behavior and Public Policy', Supplement to *Public Finance/Finances Publique*, **49**, 244–58 (Proceedings of the 49th Congress of the International Institute of Public Finance, Berlin, 1993).

Banfield, Edward C. (1970), *The Unheavenly City: The Nature and Future of Our Urban Crisis*, Boston: Little, Brown.

Becker, Gary S. (1968), 'Interdependent Preferences: Charity, Externalities and Income Taxation', National Bureau of Economic Research, March, unpublished manuscript.

Becker, Gary S. (1974), 'A Theory of Social Interactions', *Journal of Political Economy*, **82**, Nov–Dec, 1063–93.

Becker, Gary S. and Kevin Murphy (1988), 'A Theory of Rational Addiction', *Journal of Political Economy*, **96**, August, 675–700.

Blum, Walter J. and Harry Kalven, Jr. (1953), *The Uneasy Case for Progressive Taxation*, Chicago: University of Chicago Press.

Boulding, Kenneth E. (1962),'Notes on a Theory of Philanthropy', in Frank G. Dickinson (ed.), *Philanthropy and Public Policy*, New York: National Bureau of Economic Research.

Breit, William and Harold M. Hochman (eds) (1968), *Readings in Microeconomics*, New York: Holt, Rinehart and Winston. Second Edition, 1971; Third Edition, St. Louis: Times Mirror/Mosby College Publishing, 1986; Italian translation, Milano: ETAS KOMPASS, 1972 (3 Vols); Spanish translation, Mexico: Interamericana, 1973.

Brennan, Geoffrey (1973), 'Pareto Desirable Redistribution: The Case of Malice and Envy', *Journal of Public Economics*, **2**, April, 173–83.

Brennan, Geoffrey and Cliff Walsh (1973), 'Pareto-Optimal Redistribution Reconsidered', *Public Finance Quarterly*, **1**, April, 147–68.

Buchanan, James M. (1960), 'The Theory of Public Finance', *Southern Economic Journal*, **26**, January, 234–38.

Chinitz, B. (1961), 'Contrasts in Agglomeration: New York and Pittsburgh', *American Economic Review: Papers and Proceedings*, May, 279–89.

Forte, Francesco and Harold M. Hochman (1969), 'Monetary and Fiscal Policy: Ambiguities and Definitions', in Heinz Haller and Horst Claus Recktenwald (eds), *Finanz-und Geldpolitik im Umbruch*, Mainz: v. Hase & Kochler Verlag, 357–87.

Goldfarb, Robert S. (1970), 'Pareto Optimal Redistribution: Comment', *American Economic Review*, **60**, December, 994–96.

Graaff, Jan de V. (1957), *Theoretical Welfare Economics*, London: Cambridge University Press.

Harsanyi, John C. (1955), 'Cardinal Welfare, Individualist Ethics, and Interpersonal Comparisons of Utility', *Journal of Political Economy*, **63**, August, 309–21.

Head, John G. (1970), 'Equity and Efficiency in Public Goods Supply', *Public Finance/Finances Publique*, **25**(1), 24–41.

Herrnstein, Richard J. and Drazen Prelec (1992), 'A Theory of Addiction', in George Loewenstein and Jon Elster (eds), *Choice Over Time*, New York: Russell Sage Foundation, 331–60.

Hochman, Harold M. (1970), 'Professor Head on Equity and Efficiency: Comment and Addendum', *Public Finance/Finances Publique*, **25**(3), 536–45.

Hochman, Harold M. (2002) , 'Is Democracy an Antidote to Extremism?', in Albert Breton, Gianluigi Galeotti, Pierre Salmon, and Ronald Wintrobe (eds), *Political Extremism and Rationality*, New York: Cambridge University Press, 139–51.

Hochman, Harold M. and Shmuel Nitzan (1983), 'Tiebout and Sympathy', *Mathematical Social Sciences*, **6**, November, 195–214.

Hochman, Harold M. and James D. Rodgers (1971), 'Is Efficiency a Criterion for Judging Redistribution?', *Institut International de Finances Publiques*, Congress de Leningrad, September 1970, 238–47.

Hochman, Harold M. and James D. Rodgers (1973), 'Brennan and Walsh Reconsidered (Mutt and Jeff Ride Again)', *Public Finance Quarterly*, **1**, October, 359–71.

Kolm, Serge-Christophe (1969), 'On the Optimal Production of Social Justice', in J. Margolis and H. Guitton, (eds), *Public Economics*, New York: St Martin's Press, 145–200.

Kristol, Irving (1978), *Two Cheers for Capitalism*, New York: Basic Books.

Lerner, Abba P. (1944), *The Economics of Control*, New York: Macmillan.

Meyer, Paul A. and J.J. Shipley (1970), 'Pareto Optimal Redistribution: Comment', *American Economic Review*, **60**, December, 988–90.

Michelman, Frank (1967), 'Property, Utility, and Fairness: Comments on the Ethical Foundations of "Just Compensation"', *Harvard Law Review*, **80**, April, 1165–1258.

Mishan, Edward J. (1972), 'The Futility of Pareto-Efficient Distribution', *American Economic Review*, **62**, December, 971–76.

Musgrave, Richard A. (1959), *The Theory of Pubic Finance*, New York: McGraw-Hill.

Nozick, Robert (1974), *Anarchy, State and Utopia*, New York: Basic Books.

Olsen, Edgar O. (1969), 'A Normative Theory of Transfers', *Public Choice*, **6**, Spring, 39–58.

Pauly, Mark V. (1973), 'Income Redistribution as a Local Public Good', *Journal of Public Economics*, **2**, February, 35–58.

Rawls, John (1958), 'Justice as Fairness', *Philosophical Review*, **67**, April, 164–94.

Rawls, John (1974), *A Theory of Justice*, Cambridge: Belknap/Harvard University Press.

Rodgers, James D. (1970), 'Utility Interdependence and Income Redistribution', unpublished doctoral dissertation: University of Virginia.

Rodgers, James D. (1973), 'Distributional Externalities and the Optimal Form of Income Transfers', *Public Finance Quarterly*, **1**, July, 266–99.

Rodgers, James D. (1974), 'Explaining Income Redistribution', in H.M. Hochman and G.E. Peterson, *Redistribution Through Public Choice*, New York: Columbia University Press, 165–205.

Rose-Ackerman, Susan (ed.) (1986), *The Economics of Nonprofit Institutions: Studies in Structure and Policy*, New York: Oxford University Press.

Stigler, George J. and Gary S. Becker (1977), 'De Gustibus Non Est Disputandum', *American Economic Review*, **67**, March, 76–90.

Thurow, Lester C. (1971), 'The Income Distribution as a Pure Public Good', *Quarterly Journal of Economics*, **85**, May, 327–36.

Vickrey, William (1962), 'One Economist's View of Philanthropy', in Frank G. Dickinson (ed.), *Philanthropy and Public Policy*, New York: National Bureau of Economic Research.

Von Furstenberg, George and Dennis Mueller (1971), 'The Pareto Optimal Approach to Income Redistribution: A Fiscal Application', *American Economic Review*, **61**, September, 628–37.

Walzer, Michael (1983), *Spheres of Justice: A Defense of Pluralism and Equality*, New York: Basic Books.

Wilson, James Q. and Edward C. Banfield (1964), 'Public Regardingness as a Value Premise in Voting Behavior', *American Political Science Review*, **58**, December, 876–87.

Winston, Gordon C. (1980), 'Addiction as Backsliding: A Theory of Compulsive Consumption', *Journal of Economic Behavior and Organization*, **1**, December, 295–324.

Zeckhauser, Richard (1971), 'Optimal Mechanisms for Income Transfers', *American Economic Review*, **61**, June, 324–34.

PART I

PARETO OPTIMAL
REDISTRIBUTION

A

The Central Argument

Pareto Optimal Redistribution

By HAROLD M. HOCHMAN AND JAMES D. RODGERS*

The neoclassical approach to public finance identified with Richard Musgrave [10, Ch. 1] divides the process of budget determination and the functions of government into three parts or branches.[1] The allocation branch, justified by the failure of the market to satisfy the demand for public goods, engages in explicit reallocative measures required to rectify this failure and achieve allocative efficiency. The distribution branch is charged with the purely normative responsibility of bringing about the desired size distribution of income, or optimal Lorenz curve, through taxation and transfer payments. The stabilization branch performs the conventional macroeconomic fiscal functions of attaining full employment, price stability, and a satisfactory rate of economic growth.

Though the interdependence of these three branches is generally recognized, their conceptual separation serves both a methodological and heuristic purpose. The distinction between actions designed to promote efficient use of resources and actions designed to make the distribution of income more equitable avoids the " . . . confusion of the underlying issues at the planning stage" that would result if the budget were viewed " . . . in consolidated terms from the outset" [10, p. 38] and helps the analyst to sort out the diverse issues with which public finance deals.[1] However, the neoclassical approach adopts

the tripartite separation not only because it offers the analyst a useful intellectual framework, but because it also serves as a foundation on which a normative theory of the budget based on the value postulate of consumer sovereignty can be constructed. This, as argued elsewhere [4], raises logical difficulties. This normative theory permits only allocation activities, and even here only the provision of public goods that are not merit wants, to be judged in terms of the Pareto criterion. Its implication is that redistribution and stabilization cannot (or should not?) be consistent with consumer sovereignty.

We believe that this line of reasoning is misleading. It implies that redistribution yields no benefits to the parties who finance it, so that from this viewpoint it imposes a simple deadweight loss. The implication is rather unappealing, to say the least. If accepted, redistribution carried out by government institutions can only be explained as legalized Robin Hood activity, and redistribution through private institutions would seem to imply individual irrationality. While it is plausible to assume that some portion of governmental redistribution simply reflects the political power of the recipients, it is also plausible that part of this redistribution is beneficial to the taxpayers as well as to the recipients. The benefit to the former group would appear to stem from two sources, which need not be mutually exclusive. One

* The authors are, respectively, a member of the research Staff at the Urban Institute, on leave from the University of Virginia, and assistant professor of economics at Pennsylvania State University. The paper was prepared while the latter was a graduate student at the University of Virginia. Among the many to whom we are indebted, we wish without implicating to give special acknowledgment to Gary S. Becker, James M. Buchanan, Alberto di Pierro, John R. Haring, and Edgar O. Olsen.

[1] It is, of course, an oversimplification to associate the sharp separation of allocation and distribution problems with Musgrave alone. This treatment is characteristic in neoclassical economics generally, and in particular in the "new welfare economics." See, for example, [1] and [9]. We cite Musgrave because his treatise is a core part of virtually every graduate course in public finance.

542

is the preference for security against drastic future income fluctuations, and the second is interdependence among individual utility functions. In the analysis which follows, a model is developed to explain redistribution in terms of this latter source of benefit—interdependent preferences.

Given interdependence among individual utility functions, it is possible that some redistribution will make everyone better off.[2] Efficiency criteria can be applied, therefore, to redistribution of income through the fiscal process.[3] If, for example, the utility of individuals with higher incomes depends upon and is positively related to the incomes of persons lower in the distributive scale, tax–transfer schemes which raise the disposable incomes of those in the poorer group may improve everyone's utility level. Where this is true, as we shall assume, Pareto optimality, contrary to the orthodox approach to public finance, is not only consistent with but requires redistribution. Both allocation and redistribution can be dealt with in terms of the same methodology and the same criterion —efficiency. Then it can be argued that the distributive goal of vertical equity is contained within the Paretian concept of efficiency.

A simple example, involving two persons, will clarify this approach to redistribution. Suppose that Mutt, the taller, has an annual income of $10,000 and Jeff, the shorter, an annual income of $3,000. Suppose, further, that Mutt's utility level varies directly with Jeff's income (i.e., $\partial U_M/\partial Y_J > 0$ where U_M is Mutt's utility and Y_J is Jeff's income). In determining the appropriate extent of redistribution between Mutt and Jeff, the neoclassical approach, as we interpret it, would not focus on this externality. Instead, it would refer to a social welfare function with a capacity for making interpersonal comparisons. This function would be either a social ordering of the Bergson type or a Benthamite cardinal utility calculus that permits judgments about the equity of distributional adjustments to be couched in terms of objective measures of sacrifice. Indeed, this is inherent in its strictly normative interpretation of redistribution. Our approach, in contrast, implies that redistributive activities can be justified without a social welfare function that makes interpersonal comparisons, provided that utility interdependence is recognized and taken into account in formulating social policy. If, because increases in Jeff's income affect Mutt's utility favorably, gains from trade through redistribution are possible, and if there is no appropriate private vehicle through which Mutt will donate a portion of his income to Jeff,[4] the establishment of collective institutions through which such an income transfer can be processed may increase the welfare of both parties. Redistribution through the fiscal process is just as necessary for the attainment of Pareto optimality in these circumstances, as the collective provision of conventional public goods.[5]

---

[2] Provided this interdependence takes the form of an external economy.

[3] Similar logic can be applied to the stabilization function. Aggregate targets, too, are public goods, and government action can be justified in terms of the "paradox of isolation." We shall, however, say nothing more about stabilization in this paper.

[4] Voluntary transfers, as within families, would likely occur in the two-person case. In the N-person case, however, individuals, unless coerced, may choose to be "free-riders" and it is the incentive to behave in this way that may be viewed as the raison d'etre of government. Since we are interested, ultimately, in the N-person case, we rule out voluntary transfers in the present two-person example. And when we turn to the N-person case, we assume that the possibility of voluntary redistribution through private charity has been exhausted, thus focusing attention on the incremental redistributive activities carried out under public auspices. For a thorough discussion and analysis of the conditions under which private charity can or will internalize Pareto-relevant interdependence, see David B. Johnson [8].

[5] An alternative way of viewing the problem posed in this paper is in terms of the utility possibility function, a construction frequently employed in welfare

So much for our rationale.[6] Section I examines the possible patterns of utility interdependence in the two-person case and, for one of these, devises a simple model of Pareto optimal redistribution. Section II generalizes this model to the N-person case and discusses it in the context of two alternative representations of the size distribution of income. Section III examines the actual pattern of fiscal incidence in the United States, speculates about the conditions under which this pattern might be Pareto optimal, and offers some conjectures as to why actual incidence departs from the hypothetical patterns derived in Section II. Section IV contains some concluding remarks.

I. *Patterns of Utility Interdependence and Pareto Optimal Adjustments in the Two-Person Case*

It is a fairly simple matter to identify the possible patterns of utility interdependence between two persons with unequal incomes and to select, for further analysis, those which are consistent with realistic distributional adjustments. Consider the utility functions of the two individuals, Mutt and Jeff, who are the only members of our hypothetical community:

(1) $$U_M^0 = f_M(Y_M^0, Y_J^0)$$

(2) $$U_J^0 = f_J(Y_M^0, Y_J^0),$$

where U_M^0 and Y_M^0 are the initial values of

TABLE 1—POSSIBLE PATTERNS OF UTILITY INTERDEPENDENCE

		$\partial U_J/\partial Y_M$ (Evaluated at Y_M^0, Y_J^0)		
	Mutt \ Jeff	>0	=0	<0
$\partial U_M/\partial Y_J$ (Evaluated at Y_M^0, Y_J^0)	>0	I	II	III
	=0	IV	V	VI
	<0	VII	VIII	IX

Mutt's utility index and income, respectively, prior to any redistribution, and U_J^0 and Y_J^0 are the corresponding values for Jeff. As before, we assume that Mutt has the higher income, i.e., $Y_M^0 > Y_J^0$. Interdependence is present because U_M depends on Y_J and because U_J depends on Y_M.[7]

Nine possible pairs of marginal interrelationships between the two utility functions can be identified,[8] and these are given by the cells in Table 1.

Most of these cases can be ruled out, so

---

economics. The existence of external economies can result in this function having upward sloping portions, positions which cannot be efficient in the Pareto sense. The problem we analyze is one of moving, by means of redistributive transfers, from such an inefficient point to a point where the function no longer slopes upward. See [7, p. 59 ff.] or [13, p. 73 ff.].

[8] Since the initial writing of this paper, other research by Becker [2] and Olsen [12] which makes much the same point has come to our attention. Becker's paper, in particular, develops a theoretical apparatus in which the model we use is, in effect, a special case. It deals briefly, in a similar vein, with the fiscal issues on which we focus.

[7] Of course, variables other than income, e.g., wealth' consumption level, or consumption of particular commodities, could be the source of the interdependence. Income is employed here because it simplifies the analysis.

[8] Situations in which externalities are inframarginal are excluded from our consideration. An inframarginal externality exists when

$$\frac{\partial U^i}{\partial Y_j} = 0 \quad \text{and} \quad \int_0^{Y_j} [\partial U^i/\partial Y_j] dY_j \gtrless 0.$$

In such cases no transfer is appropriate, though one would be if, given the ith person's income and the assumption that the externality is an external economy, the jth person's income were sufficiently smaller than Y_i. In our two-person example, utility interdependence might not be marginally relevant because Mutt's income is too low for his demand for Jeff's income to have become effective or because the initial difference between Mutt's and Jeff's incomes ($Y_M^0 - Y_J^0$), on which we focus, is less than some critical minimum. In this paper, however, we shall apply no restrictions on either far as rationalizing distributive adjustments is concerned, by making a relatively weak assumption and by imposing certain reasonable restrictions. We assume (a) that both Mutt and Jeff, given prevailing prices of goods and services and the prevailing interest rate, have marginal utilities of income for own-consumption greater than zero (i.e., $\partial U_M/\partial Y_M$, $\partial U_J/\partial Y_J > 0$). We require, in addition, that (b) all transfers be Pareto optimal (i.e., harm neither Mutt nor Jeff) and that (c) all transfers flow from the person with the higher income to the person with the lower income. Therefore, since Y_M exceeds Y_J, only one-way transfers from Mutt to Jeff are permitted. Furthermore, transfers large enough to reverse the initial distributional ordering are not allowed. For the two-person case, therefore, the transfer can be no greater than $(Y_M^0 - Y_J^0)/2$.

Using assumption (a) and restrictions (b) and (c), all interdependence patterns except those in the top row of Table 1 can immediately be eliminated. Cases IV and VII would require a transfer from Jeff to Mutt, violating restriction (c). Case V represents the situation of utility independence, the orthodox neoclassical assumption; a transfer in either direction, given (c), would harm one of the parties, violating (b). This same conclusion holds also for Cases VI, VIII, and IX. There is no possible transfer, in either direction, that would harm neither Mutt nor Jeff.

Hence only Cases I, II and III remain. The externality patterns of Cases II and III are, for purposes of indicating the Pareto optimal pattern of redistribution, one-way patterns, which imply that only Mutt's preferences need be consulted. So

Y_M^0 or $Y_M^0 - Y_J^0$, save the requirement that $Y_M^0 - Y_J^0$ exceed zero, in ascertaining whether interdependence is marginally relevant and, therefore, calls for a redistributive transfer. For rigorous definitions of the various types of externalities and their conceptual significance, see J. M. Buchanan and .W C. Stubblebine [5].

long as Jeff's utility is either independent of Mutt's income (Case II) or varies inversely with it (Case III), his utility function can be ignored; in either case, a transfer to Jeff, given (b), is certain to improve his welfare. In Case I, on the other hand, it is not certain that a transfer from Mutt to Jeff will increase Jeff's utility because the reduction in Mutt's disposable income that it implies makes Jeff feel worse. However, for Jeff to be harmed by a transfer from Mutt, his marginal utility of own-consumption $(\partial U_J/\partial Y_J)$ must be more than offset by the external diseconomy generated by the reduction of Mutt's income $(\partial U_J/\partial Y_M)$. Obviously, this is most unlikely, and in the analysis that follows, we assume that $(\partial U_J/\partial Y_J > \partial U_J/\partial Y_M)$, so that any transfer that Jeff receives, benefits him. It makes no difference, therefore, which of the three interdependence patterns in the top row of Table 1 is assumed. In all of them, transfers, given consumer sovereignty, are entirely a matter of Mutt's volition, and the process of determining a Pareto optimal redistributive transfer can concentrate on his preferences alone.

Hypothetical Patterns of Pareto Optimal Transfers

Suppose, now, that an increase in Y_J (as in Case II) augments Mutt's utility. How large a transfer will Mutt desire to make to Jeff? To answer this question, consider Figure 1, which is concerned with Mutt's choice of how much of his income to retain for himself and how much to transfer to Jeff. This choice will obviously depend both on Y_M^0 and Y_J^0. We assume, largely because it facilitates our examination of redistribution in the N-person case, that the size of the transfer depends upon the differential $Y_M^0 - Y_J^0$, rather than, among other specifications, either the absolute levels of Y_M^0 and Y_J^0 or the initial ratio, Y_M^0/Y_J^0. Thus the ordinate of Figure 1

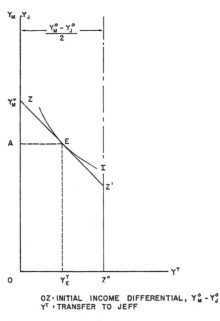

OZ : INITIAL INCOME DIFFERENTIAL, $Y_M^0 - Y_J^0$
Y^T : TRANSFER TO JEFF

FIGURE 1

measures the excess of Y_M^0 over Y_J^0, and the abscissa measures transfers from Mutt to Jeff, Y^T. The situation in which $Y_M^0 = Y_J^0$ is represented by the origin of Figure 1. (It is labeled "0" because this is where the differential is zero and where the transfer size is zero, not because Jeff's initial income Y_J^0 is 0.) The terms on which Mutt is able to exchange own-consumption for increments in Jeff's income is given by the slope of $ZZ'Z''$, Mutt's opportunity locus or "budget line." The budget line becomes vertical at Z' because of the restriction that Y^T must not be so large as to reverse the distributional ordering. The slope of the ZZ' segment is -1, since a given size transfer to Jeff reduces the amount of income that Mutt retains for his own use by the same amount. I is one of Mutt's (convex) indifference curves containing points which indicate the terms at which Mutt is will-

ing to exchange own-consumption for increments in Y_J.[9] The positive dependence of U_M on Y_J is reflected by the negative slope; if U_M did not depend on Y_J, Mutt's indifference map would simply consist of a set of horizontal lines. If the initial incomes are given by Y_M^0 and Y_J^0, so that the initial differential is equal to $0Z$, transfers to Jeff of any amount up to Y_E^T raise Mutt's utility level and a transfer of Y_E^T allows Mutt to attain equilibrium at E, where the marginal utility of a dollar of own-consumption equals the marginal utility of a one dollar increment in Jeff's income. Thus, point E, by definition, is a Pareto optimum.[10,11]

Having provided an analysis to determine the size of the transfer that Mutt desires to make to Jeff for a given income differential, the next step is to determine how this amount varies with the differential, so that the structure of a Pareto optimal, explicitly redistributive tax-transfer system can be ascertained.

[9] Because both axes in Figure 1 are measured in terms of units of the numeraire, the only feasible points for Mutt lie on the budget line itself. With no transactions or administration cost and no charitable deductions to reduce Mutt's tax obligations, a dollar increase in Y^T implies a dollar decrease in Mutt's income for own-use.

[10] There are transfers greater than Y_E^T that would reduce Mutt's utility relative to the level implied by I but would leave him better off than he would have been in the absence of any transfer at all, i.e., on the indifference curve (not represented in Figure 1) that cuts the ordinate at Z.

[11] Note, however, that although the presence of an external economy is a necessary condition for Pareto optimal transfers, it is not a sufficient condition. If the slope of Mutt's indifference curves were everywhere less than unity in absolute value, he would regard the price of any income transfer, in terms of own-consumption foregone, as excessive. In this situation, there is no transfer to Jeff, either voluntary or coerced, that would be Pareto optimal.

Similarly, concave indifference curves (not represented in Figure 1) would also imply a corner solution at Z or an equilibrium at Z', the kink in the budget line. Whether the equilibrium, in this case, would be at Z (implying that no transfer is Pareto optimal) or at Z' (implying that income equality is required for Pareto optimality) would depend on the precise shapes of the concave indifference loci.

How should the tax on Mutt vary with the income differential? (1) Should it be a constant amount or fixed sum, or should it vary as the initial income differential $Y_M^0 - Y_J^0$ ($=0Z$) varies? If the latter, should it increase (2) in proportion to $0Z$ or (3) less than proportionately? Or should it vary (4) inversely with the differential? The answer, in the two-person model, depends on the elasticity, with respect to $Y_M - Y_J$, of Mutt's demand for increments in Jeff's income, which we shall refer to as Mutt's transfer-elasticity and denote as E_M.[12] Figures 2 through 5 illustrate these four cases. Changes in the size of the initial differential, $0Z$, produce parallel shifts of the budget line, which generate a locus of equilibrium positions. E_M, in these diagrams, is the elasticity of this locus, the income-differential consump-

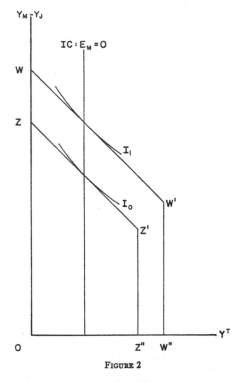

FIGURE 2

---

[12] Transfer-elasticity differs only slightly from the more familiar income-elasticity of demand. Income-elasticity would measure the responsiveness of Mutt's demand for transfers to Jeff to changes in Y_M itself. Transfer-elasticity, on the other hand, measures its responsiveness to changes in $0Z = Y_M^0 - Y_J^0$, the initial differential, regardless of whether these are due to a change in Y_M^0 with Y_J^0 constant, a change in Y_J^0 with Y_M^0 constant, or changes in both Y_M^0 and Y_J^0.

The transfer-elasticity concept, indeed our use of $Y_M^0 - Y_J^0$ as the key variable, is clearly a simplification of reality. Our choice of the specific form that this formulation implies to attach to the utility functions specified earlier in general terms is based on intuition and convenience. To look at Figure 1 as a subset of Y_M, Y_J space with the axes shifted by the amount of Y_J^0 would yield a more general analysis, but one which would be much less manageable than ours, which is general enough to enable us to make the points in which we are interested. Our argument is illustrative rather than definitive, and adoption of the differential as the crucial variable simplifies the illustrations in the N-person case of Section II, by allowing us to abstract from abolute levels of income in our calculations.

However, the implications of this simplification should be pointed out. Under our assumption, equal absolute increases in Mutt's and Jeff's incomes would leave the optimal transfer to Jeff unchanged. Nor does the response to a change in the differential depend on the starting income levels. If, instead, the optimal transfer were an increasing function of, say, the ratio of Y_M to Y_J, rather than the difference between them, it would decrease if Y_M and Y_J increased by the same absolute amount.

tion (IC) line.[13] The IC lines in Figures 2 through 5 require the particular tax-transfer patterns indicated in the four questions posed above, assuming that the equilibria are always to the left of Z'. If, for example, $E_M = 0$, a fixed sum transfer is Pareto optimal; if $E_M = 1$, the optimal transfer increases in proportion to $0Z$.

II. *Pareto Optimal Adjustments in the N-Person Case*

The N-Person Model

Must a Pareto optimal structure of redistributive taxes be progressive, propor-

---

[13] The IC line is analogous to the income-consumption line. The difference is that $Y_M^0 - Y_J^0$ is variable here, whereas Y_M varies in the case of the income-consumption line. Because of the choice of axes on which to measure the transfer and initial differential, E_M varies inversely with the absolute slope of IC.

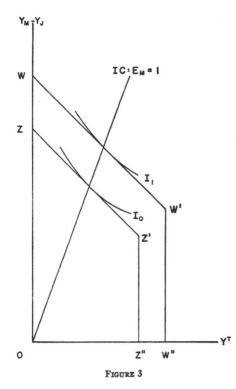

FIGURE 3

tional, or regressive? What pattern of fiscal residuals does such a tax structure imply? Answers to such questions require that our analysis be extended to the N-Person case.

We assume an institutional setting in which free-riding, i.e., strategic behavior, is precluded so that the political mechanism through which interdependence is internalized accurately reflects the distributional preferences of individuals in this regard. To secure the gains from trade that are possible because of interdependence, individuals choose to compel themselves to make redistributive transfers, just as they compel themselves to pay taxes to finance the provision of other collective goods. As in the two-person case, it is assumed that the tax transfer process does not change the initial distributional

ordering, so that relative positions in the income scale are unaffected. It is assumed, further, that individuals have identical tastes[14] (so that all would exhibit the same consumption patterns at any given income level), and that income taxation produces no incentive effects or excess burden (i.e., the supply of labor or demand for leisure are perfectly inelastic).

Only two of the IC configurations are considered, the cases in which $E_M = 0$ (implying that Pareto optimality requires fixed-sum transfers) and $E_M = 1$ (implying that transfers proportional to $(Y_M^0 - Y_J^0)$ are optimal). It is assumed that each individual (1) makes a transfer to (permits himself to be taxed on behalf of) every person with a lower income (in a lower income bracket) and (2) receives a transfer from each individual with a higher income. Except for those in the lowest and highest income brackets, then, all individuals pay some redistributive taxes (are in Mutt's status relative to some persons) and receive some redistributive transfers (are in Jeff's status relative to others). Each individual's net outcome is the algebraic sum of the outcomes in the pairwise equilibrium relationships that emerge with all persons who have initial incomes different from his. Thus, in the N-Person model, Pareto optimal tax payments and transfers received depend on both E_M's

---

[14] Obviously, this assumption is unrealistic. Any real-world blanket redistributive tax would, of course, deviate from Pareto optimality not only because of differing transfer elasticities on the part of different individuals (Mutts) whose preferences exhibit row 1, Table 1 interdependence, but also because the preferences of some Mutts are characterized by row 2 or row 3. It does not follow from this, however, that interpersonal utility comparisons, in terms of a crude cardinal utility calculus or a more refined social welfare function, are needed to justify all redistribution. But it does raise the question of what governmental unit should intermediate redistributive transfers, and more broadly, of the optimal redistributive areas in a fiscal federalism, a question analogous in some respects to that of determining optimum currency areas in the theory of international trade.

(one's own and others') *and* the shape of
the size distribution of income. E_M and
$(Y_M^0 - Y_J^0)$ determine the Pareto optimal
transfer between each pair of individuals.
One's position in the income scale determines the number of persons to whom he
will make transfers and the number from
whom he will receive them. Each individual's aggregate tax payments (summed
over all Jeffs), transfer receipts (summed
over all Mutts), and fiscal residual (receipts minus payments) depend, therefore,
on both considerations.[15,16]

Pareto Optimal Patterns of Redistribution

Pareto optimal distributional adjustments are derived for two distributional
settings, a rectangular distribution (D_r)
and a summary representation of the actual
income distribution in the U.S. in 1960
(D_a). This is done twice for each distribution; once on the assumption that the
E_M's of all N individuals are zero and once
assuming that the E_M's are unity. Results

[15] Our efforts to identify the incidence of Pareto
optimal redistributive adjustments under different
assumptions about E_M should not be confused with the
problem of determining the appropriate incidence of
the overall tax structure. We assume that the costs of
allocative activities are distributed on a benefit basis,
before redistribution is contemplated at all, and, there
fore, deal only with the marginal incidence of distributional adjustments, ignoring the feedbacks of redistribution that might confound this prior application
of the benefit principle. An overall Pareto optimum is,
obviously, a matter of transfer-elasticity (or some
analogous measure of distributional preferences) and
these income-elasticities. Hence, we are implicitly
assuming away any changes in evaluations of conventional public goods that the Pareto optimal transfers might bring about. Another way of putting the
matter is to say that we are assuming that individuals,
in choosing their consumption mixes, fully anticipate
the transfers they are to receive.

[16] N, the absolute size of the community, is of no
significance in our calculations. We can either assume
that N is constant or that the fiscal residuals of individuals are unaltered, if it changes. This assumption
requires that (1) changes in N are spread proportionately among all income classes, preserving the relative
distribution; (2) the levies on individual Mutts are
varied in inverse proportion to the number of Jeffs
concerned; and (3) administration of the tax-transfer
process is subject to constant returns to scale.

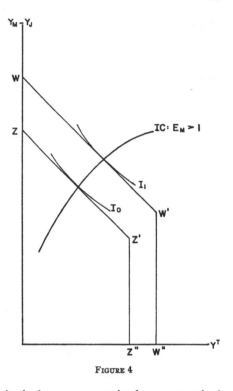

FIGURE 4

in the four cases examined are summarized
in the tables indicated in Table 2.

D_r, which is a useful benchmark case, is
described numerically in the first two columns of Tables 3 and 4. It is a simple

TABLE 2—PARETO OPTIMAL REDISTRIBUTIONS
CLASSIFIED BY TRANSFER ELASTICITY AND
INCOME DISTRIBUTION

	Income Distributions		
	E_M ⟍ D	D_r	D_a
Transfer-Elasticity	$E_M = 0$	Table 3	Table 5
	$E_M = 1$	Table 4	Table 6

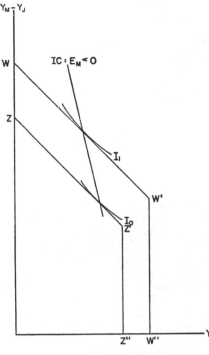

FIGURE 5

rectangular distribution for a community of five persons and contains five income classes of identical width. Each class contains one individual having an income equal to the mean of the class limits.

D_a, the second distribution, is described in the first two columns of Tables 5 and 6. It is the summary distribution, for the U.S. in 1960, which Gillespie [6] used in reporting his estimates of fiscal incidence in the U.S. (discussed in Section III). In using D_a, we assume, for convenience, that the community contains one hundred individuals or families, an assumption that permits us to use relative frequencies instead of the absolute distribution in our analysis. D_a contains seven income classes of varying width, with an open-ended class ($10,000 and over) at the top. Within income classes, families are treated as if they were identical in size. All incomes in the five intermediate classes are assumed to be equal to the mean of the class limits, referred to in the tables as the "representative class income."[17] To specify representative class incomes for the "under $2,000" and "$10,000 and over" classes, a linkage procedure was used, producing estimates of $800 for the first bracket (under $2,000) and $15,000 for the top bracket ($10,000 and over).[18]

[17] This simplifies our calculations and assures that modest redistributive adjustments cannot reverse the distributional ordering.

[18] We calculated the total income received by each unit of one percent of all families in the two bottom and two top income brackets in D_a from Gillespie's distribution of aggregate income by size class [6, p. 174, Table 13, line 1]. We then computed the ratios of these figures for the two bottom brackets (.32) and the two

TABLE 3—PARETO OPTIMAL REDISTRIBUTIONS

Rectangular Income Distribution (D_r): Transfer-Elasticity (E_M) = 0

Income	Number of Individuals	Fixed-Sum Transfers of $100			Tax Structure	
		Tax Paid ($)	Transfer Received ($)	Pareto Optimal Fiscal Incidence ($)	Marginal Rate	Average Rate
1,000	1	—	400	+400	—	—
2,000	1	100	300	+200	.10	.050
3,000	1	200	200	0	.10	.067
4,000	1	300	100	−200	.10	.075
5,000	1	400	—	−400	.10	.080

HOCHMAN AND RODGERS: OPTIMAL REDISTRIBUTION   551

TABLE 4—PARETO OPTIMAL REDISTRIBUTIONS

Rectangular Income Distribution (D_t): Transfer-Elasticity $(E_M) = 1$

| | Transfer 5 Percent of Income Differential | | | | Tax Structure | |
Income	Number of Individuals	Tax Paid ($)	Differential Transfer Received ($)	Pareto Optimal Fiscal Incidence ($)	Marginal Rate	Average Rate
1,000	1	—	500	+500	—	—
2,000	1	50	300	+250	.05	.025
3,000	1	150	150	0	.10	.050
4,000	1	300	50	−250	.15	.075
5,000	1	500	—	−500	.20	.100

Let us consider D_r. If E_M is zero for all individuals making transfers, the Pareto optimal tax structure is degressive, as Table 3 indicates. In our example, each of the five persons in the community, one at each income level, transfers $100 to each individual in a lower bracket.. Thus, the individual with an income of $1,000 is exempt, while those with higher incomes are taxed at a constant marginal rate of 10 percent. The average rate increases, monotonically, from zero to 8 per cent, and the Pareto optimal fiscal residuals (distributional transfers received less taxes paid, after accounting for conventional public goods on a benefit basis) are symmetrical, by virtue of D_r's symmetry.

This outcome suggests that Pareto optimality requires more progressivity if, with a rectangular distribution, $E_M > 0$. This conclusion, with its implication that progressive taxation can be justified without interpersonal utility comparisons, is illustrated by Table 4, which summarizes the outcomes for the case in which all E_M's are unity. In this case the implied

top brackets (1.77). Our estimate of average income in the bottom bracket ($800) was derived by multiplying the representative class income of $2,500 in the second ($2,000 to $2,999) bracket by .32 and rounding the product to the nearest $100. Our estimate of average income in the top bracket ($15,000) was obtained by multiplying the representative class income of $8,750 in the $7,500 to $9,999 bracket by 1.77 and rounding.

marginal rates of tax rise from zero to 20 percent. In our example, the factor of proportionality, k, is assumed to be .05, making the implied transfer between any pair of individuals in different income brackets .05 $(Y_M^0 - Y_j^0)$.

The results can be recast in terms of the IC lines of Figures 2 and 3. In Figure 2, $E_M = 0$ and Pareto optimality requires a degressive tax (degressivity). In Figure 3, $E_M = 1$, and the IC line has a zero intercept and a slope equal to the reciprocal of k. In this case, the Pareto optimal tax structure is clearly more progressive than it is with a vertical IC line; and, in general, implied progressivity is greater, the smaller the slope of the IC line.

The outcomes with D_r tell us something about the incidence of Pareto optimal redistributive adjustments in the context of any distribution in which frequencies vary monotonically with income. With declining frequencies, the ratio of Jeffs (to whom transfers must be made) to Mutts (from whom transfers are received) increases more rapidly with income than it does with a rectangular distribution. Thus, if E_M is the same for all individuals, the Pareto optimal tax structure is necessarily more progressive than it is with D_r. In the unlikely case in which frequencies increase with income, the converse would hold true.

We turn now to D_a. (See Tables 5 and

TABLE 5—PARETO OPTIMAL REDISTRIBUTIONS

Actual Income Distribution (D_a): Transfer-Elasticity $(E_M)=0$

Represen- tative Class Income[a]	Percent of Families[b]	Fixed-Sum Transfer of $5			Tax Structure	
		Tax Paid ($)	Transfer Received ($)	Pareto Optimal Fiscal Incidence ($)	Marginal Rate	Average Rate
800	14	—	430	+430	—	—
2,500	9	70	385	+315	.042	.028
3,500	9	115	340	+225	.045	.033
4,500	11	160	285	+125	.045	.036
6,250	28	215	145	− 70	.032	.034
8,750	15	355	70	−285	.056	.040
15,500	14	430	—	−430	.011	.028

[a] Class mid-points for all but bottom and top brackets. Procedure for obtaining "representative class incomes" for bottom and top brackets is discussed in fn. 18.
[b] Implies a community consisting of 100 families or individuals.

6.)[19] Unlike D_r, which is symmetrical, D_a is skewed to the right.[20] Where $E_M=0$, the implication of this asymmetry is that the

[19] The size of the fixed-sum transfer (for Table 5) and the value of k (for the computations underlying Table 6) make no difference in the shape of the pattern of residuals and are thus analytically irrelevant. The values used in our computations were chosen for their convenience, to facilitate subsequent comparisons of our hypothetical residuals and the actual residuals reported by Gillespie.

[20] Columns (1) and (2) of Tables 5 and 6 show 71 percent of all families with incomes under $7,499, which is less than half the assumed mid-point of the top bracket, $15,500.

structure of Pareto optimal taxes is not uniformly progressive throughout the distribution. With "fixed-sum" transfers of $5 (Table 5) this tax structure is progressive up to, but not including, the model income bracket ($5,000–$7,499); in this bracket the marginal tax rate decreases from 4.5 to 3.2 percent. This decline in the marginal rate occurs because the percentage change in "representative class income" between the fourth and fifth income brackets exceeds the percentage change in the number of individuals entitled to

TABLE 6—PARETO OPTIMAL REDISTRIBUTIONS

Actual Income Distribution (D_a): Transfer-Elasticity $(E_M)=1$

Represen- tative Class Income	Percent of Families	Transfer 0.1 Percent of Income Differential $(k=.001)$			Tax Structure	
		Tax Paid ($)	Transfer Received ($)	Pareto Optimal Fiscal Incidence ($)	Marginal Rate	Average Rate
800	14	—	553	+558	—	—
2,500	9	24	412	+388	.014	.010
3,500	9	47	335	+288	.023	.013
4,500	11	79	267	+188	.032	.018
6,250	28	154	167	+ 13	.043	.025
8,750	15	333	94	−239	.072	.038
15,500	14	914	—	−913	.086	.059

receive transfers. After this decline, the marginal rate increases to 5.6 percent in the sixth bracket ($7,500–$9,999) and then declines again to 1.1 percent in the "$10,000 and over" class.

When optimal incidence patterns are derived for D_a under the assumption that $E_M=1$ (see Table 6) this complex rate structure is not obtained. The Pareto optimal tax structure is, rather, uniformly progressive. With k, the factor of proportionality, equal to .001, marginal rates of tax rise from 1.4 percent in the first bracket ($2,000–$2,999) to 8.6 percent for families with incomes of "$10,000 and over."

These examples have demonstrated a means of determining Pareto optimal redistributive adjustments, albeit under highly restrictive assumptions and only for certain special cases.[21] The structure of the Pareto optimal redistributive taxes, whether progressive, proportional, regressive, or lacking uniformity, depends on the values of the transfer-elasticities and the shape of the initially existing distribution of income, as determined by initial endowments and the operation of the market economy.

III. *Actual Incidence and Pareto Optimal Redistribution*

Granting all of the other assumptions we have made, under what assumptions about utility interdependence would the actual fiscal structure be Pareto optimal? To answer this question, among others, Table 7 compares the Pareto optimal fiscal residuals computed in Section II, for D_a, with one of the sets of residuals estimated by Gillespie [6, p. 162, Table 11]. Columns (1) and (2) of Table 7 describe D_a. Column (3), which reports the actual residuals, is derived from Gillespie's estimates of the consolidated fiscal incidence of federal,

[21] We have considered only two values of the transfer-elasticities and two income distributions, and have assumed identical utility maps. While the analysis could be generalized by a mathematical formulation, there seemed to us to be virtue in simplicity.

state, and local taxes and expenditures in the U.S. for 1960.[22] To obtain the figures in Column (3), we multiplied Gillespie's estimates of fiscal incidence in each income bracket, which he reported in proportional terms, by the "representative class income." Thus Column (3) indicates, in absolute terms, the fiscal residuals (benefits of expenditures and transfers received, less taxes paid) which accrued to average individuals in each bracket. For comparison we report, in Columns (4) and (5), the Pareto optimal fiscal residuals with D_a in the "fixed-sum" ($E_M=0$) and "proportional transfer" ($E_M=1$) cases of Tables 5 and 6, respectively.[23]

[22] Needless to say, Gillespie faced many difficult problems, requiring essentially arbitrary choices, in compiling these estimates. One such problem was that of choosing an income base. The base for which the estimates in Column (3) of Table 5 are derived is adjusted broad income, money income adjusted for transfers, government expenditures, and taxes. Other problems included (1) distribution of the burdens of specific taxes, (2) imputation of the benefits of specific expenditures to beneficiary groups, and (3) distribution of these beneficiary groups among income classes. For taxes, Gillespie could use published material, e.g., Musgrave's study [11]. For expenditures, he had less to go on in the way of prior research. Since demand prices for public goods are not revealed, the only practicable alternative was to allocate benefits on the basis of some measure of cost undertaken on behalf of individuals. Perhaps the most intractable problem was the distribution of general (nonallocable) expenditures, e.g., national defense, among individuals and income groups. In Table 11 [6, p. 126], which we used as our source of Column (3), such expenditures are distributed on an income (rather than, say, on a per capita) basis.

[23] The appropriate interpretation of Column (3) differs slightly from that of Columns (4) and (5). The latter indicate the net gain or loss, in strictly monetary (i.e., not welfare) terms, that would accrue to each individual from a Pareto optimal redistributive process. In addition to redistributive adjustments, the figures in Column (3) include imputations of the aggregate benefits accruing to individuals from public goods, minus the taxes paid to obtain these benefits. From our viewpoint, however, this difference in interpretation is of little importance. This may be seen by assuming (as we have) that the political mechanism, in providing public goods, accurately reflects individual preferences, and that both redistribution in kind and in money terms are consistent with such preferences, in the same sense in which monetary transfers alone internalize the general externalities taken into account in our simpler model.

Both of the hypothetical patterns of residuals, Columns (4) and (5), vary inversely with income. The real-world residuals in Column (3), however, do not fully conform with this pattern. The most obvious differences between the actual and hypothetical residuals occur in the first, second, and sixth income brackets. Instead of decreasing between the first and second brackets, the fiscal residual actually increases, almost in proportion to income, i.e., from \$441 to \$1,110. Furthermore, in the "\$7,500–\$9,999" bracket, the fiscal residual is positive, not negative. In terms of the absolute deviation from either of the hypothetical residuals (for $E_M=0$ or 1), the first of these abberations is more significant,[24] especially when compared to the level of income in the bracket in which it occurs. We choose, consequently, to ignore the abberation in the sixth bracket and discuss only the one in the second.

The fact that the fiscal process seems to subsidize the 14 percent of all families in the "under \$2,000" bracket less heavily than the 9 percent in the \$2,000–\$2,999 bracket does not coincide with our hypothetical computations in which the Pareto optimal residuals decrease monotonically as income increases. It is worthwhile to explore alternative explanations of this outcome.

One possibility is that the first bracket may well consist, to a greater extent than those just above it, of rural poor. In rural areas, communities are smaller and social pressure to interact is consequently greater. Payment of income in kind is likely to be more common, and simple bilateral or multilateral transfers through private charity are more likely to be feasible, reducing

[24] For example, in the second bracket the deviation of the actual residual from the computed residual in Column (5) is \$1,110–\$388; relating this deviation to income in the second bracket, we obtain (\$1,110–\$388)/\$2,500=.31. This proportional deviation is much greater than that in the sixth bracket: (\$148+\$239)/\$8,750=0.04.

dependence on the fiscal process as a redistributive mechanism. In urban areas social conditions may not fit this model as well. Urban poverty, moreover, is readily apparent to more individuals with relatively high incomes, and general interdependence among individuals in different income groups is by virtue of proximity even more pronounced. Fiscal machinery is more likely to enjoy a clear advantage as the mechanism of redistribution, because the social group is large and private arrangements that can overcome "free rider" behavior to the degree required are more difficult to devise.

A second, less benign, explanation is that those who are really poor, i.e., families with incomes under \$2,000, may be almost devoid of political power. Their welfare counts for less than that of individuals with higher incomes in the calculations of politicians, just as their preferences count for less in the market sector. This argument, implying that political power and effective demand go hand in hand, may be extended to a hypothesis that the actual fiscal structure reflects a coalition among middle income groups, that is, among families whose incomes lie between the bottom and top brackets. It should be noted, however, that this hypothesis is diametrically opposed to the notion that the actual fiscal structure comes at all close to being Pareto optimal; for, if it were Pareto optimal, families in the top bracket would, by definition, prefer the disproportionate tax burden they now bear, according to Gillespie's estimates, at least to a situation without redistribution, so no such coalition would be necessary.

A third, less provocative, though possibly more realistic explanation might attribute the apparent plight of the "under \$2,000" group to quirks in the statistical procedures underlying Gillespie's estimates and our own calculations. Many difficulties are encountered in imputing the

TABLE 7—COMPARISON OF FISCAL INCIDENCE UNDER ALTERNATIVE TAX-
TRANSFER ASSUMPTIONS

(1)	(2)	(3)	(4) $E_M=0$	(5) $E_M=1$ Transfer 0.1
Representative Class Income ($)	Percent of Families	U.S. Fiscal Structure, 1960ᵃ	Fixed-Sum Transfers of $5ᵇ	Percent of Income Differential ($)ᶜ
800	14	+ 441	+430	+558
2,500	9	+1,110	+315	+388
3,500	9	+ 648	+225	+288
4,500	11	− 58	+125	+188
6,250	28	− 131	− 70	− 13
8,750	15	+ 148	−285	−239
15,500	14	−2,046	−430	−913

ᵃ U. S. Fiscal Structure, 1960: Gillespie [6, p. 162, Table 11, line 11]. Reported figures are the product of "representative class incomes" and effective rate (expenditure benefits and transfers received minus taxes paid) of fiscal incidence.
ᵇ Table 5.
ᶜ Table 6.

burdens of taxation and the benefits of expenditures. Thus, the increase in residuals between the first and second brackets might, at least to some degree, be attributed to such factors as the imputation of the benefits of general expenditures, e.g., national defense, on an income-related rather than per capita basis.

Despite aberrations and ambiguity, it is interesting to ask, "If the actual residuals in Table 7 are Pareto optimal, what are the implied patterns of utility interdependence?" If we suppose that the actual residuals reflect the exact amount of redistribution required to internalize such interdependence, so that the actual fiscal structure is by implication, Pareto optimal, we can infer something about the values of transfer-elasticities at various income levels and the shapes of individuals' *IC* lines. In general, the residuals with $E_M=1$, the "proportional transfer case," seem to be better correlated with the actual pattern of incidence than the residuals in the "fixed-sum" case ($E_M=0$). This is particularly clear in the top income bracket, which seems, according to Column (3), to finance the lion's share of any

redistribution that actually occurs.[25] Residuals in the second through the seventh brackets, taken as a group, suggest that individuals in high brackets have larger transfer-elasticities than those in lower brackets; thus, instead of remaining constant, as Column (5) assumes, E_M appears to increase with income.[26] Furthermore, since the middle income groups (brackets four through six) seem, more or less, to break even in the fiscal process, it would appear that utility interdependence increases in significance as income increases and becomes really significant only when income reaches a level of $10,000 or more.[27]

[25] Thus, so far as vertical equity is concerned, our observations suggest that typical discussions of the U.S. fiscal structure might overstate the normative significance of erosion of the tax base.
[26] Except for the minor lapse in the $7,500–$9,999 class.
[27] If, however, the actual residuals are not Pareto optimal, an alternative explanation of the disproportionate fiscal burden on the $10,000 and over group is required. The obvious alternative, that this burden reflects political weakness, controverts the generally held belief in the correlation of political and economic power. Our analysis, unfortunately, provides neither an answer to this riddle nor a criterion for choosing between such polar explanations of observed fiscal incidence.

In terms of the diagrams, this suggests that the *IC* line coincides with the ordinate (and has a slope equal to or only slightly different from infinity) until the income differential begins to exceed, say, $6,000–$8,000. At this point its slope becomes finite (E_M begins to exceed zero). Thereafter, as $0Z = (Y_M^0 - Y_J^0)$ increases, E_M increases and the *IC* line, as in Figure 4, bends downward to the right. Thus, to return to our general example, where individuals are in Mutt's status, the income or consumption levels of those with Jeff's status appear to be normal goods. Stated a bit differently, the general implication is that the ratio of the marginal utility of own-consumption to the marginal utility of others' consumption declines over the income range considered.

IV. *Conclusion*

In trying to reconcile income redistribution (e.g., through a negative income tax) with consumer sovereignty and an individualistic interpretation of the fiscal and political processes, we have experimented with alternative hypotheses about utility interdependence. In the presence of such interdependence, Pareto optimality may not only be consistent with redistribution, but may require it. If so, the necessary fiscal adjustments depend on the implicit transfer-elasticities and the shape of the size distribution of income.

Pursuing this line of thought, we have calculated, for several situations, the patterns of tax burdens, transfers, and fiscal incidence that would be Pareto optimal. We have also tried to determine the type of utility interdependence that is implied by the actual fiscal residuals prevailing in the U.S. in 1960, on the assumption that those residuals were Pareto optimal.

An important implication of our analysis is the finding that the case for progressive taxation, aimed at redistributing income,

may be far less "uneasy"[28] than most of us have come to believe. Quite to the contrary, progressive taxation, for explicit redistributive purposes, may be fully consistent with the Pareto criterion under quite reasonable conceptual assumptions. Progressivity, given such assumptions, may be interpreted as a matter of revealed preference, which does not require interpersonal utility comparisons for its justification. Whether these assumptions are empirically valid is, of course, another question, but one that should yield to empirical investigation.

All this does not pretend to claim that fiscal reality does not deviate from the requirements of Pareto optimality. It does. But the fact that it does may be a technical matter and not a conceptual necessity. Departures of the actual fiscal structure from the Pareto ideal may simply reflect an operational inability to correctly juxtapose individual preferences and fiscal incidence. We are suggesting, therefore, that if more could be learned about utility interdependence through empirical investigation of private and public choice patterns and processes, it might turn out to be possible to utilize this information to achieve a fiscal structure more in accord with the individualist ethic that underlies the economist's model of resource allocation.

Of course, one might personally feel that the amount of redistribution dictated by the Pareto criterion will not be "enough." We are not saying that society should necessarily follow only the Pareto rule. It is possible, however, to develop a theory of redistribution based on such a rule, and considerable redistribution might be indicated if it were operationally possible to

[28] Blum and Kalven [3] is the classic discussion of progression. Their treatment, which examines progression as traditionally justified in terms of sacrifice and interpersonal comparisons, reinforced the pre-existing skepticism of the profession.

devise a fiscal structure consistent with this criterion.

REFERENCES

1. F. M. BATOR, "The Simple Analytics of Welfare Maximization," *Amer. Econ. Rev.*, Mar. 1957. *47*, 22–59.
2. G. S. BECKER, "Independent Preferences: Charity, Externalities and Income Taxation." Unpublished manuscript, Mar. 1968.
3. W. J. BLUM AND H. KALVEN, JR., *The Uneasy Case for Progressive Taxation.* Chicago 1953.
4. J. M. BUCHANAN, "The Theory of Public Finance," *Southern Econ. J.* Jan. 1960, *26*, 234–38.
5. ———, AND W. C. STUBBLEBINE, "Externality," *Economica*, Nov. 1962, *29*, 371–84.
6. W. I. GILLESPIE, "Effect of Public Expenditures on the Distribution of Income," in R. A. Musgrave, ed., *Essays in Fiscal Federalism*, Washington 1965, pp. 122–86.
7. J. DE V. GRAAFF, *Theoretical Welfare Economics*, New York 1957.
8. D. B. JOHNSON, "The Fundamental Economics of the Charity Market." Unpublished doctoral dissertation, Univ. Virginia, 1968.
9. E. J. MISHAN, "A Survey of Welfare Economics, 1939–59," *Econ. J.*, June 1960, *70*, 197–256.
10. R. A. MUSGRAVE, *The Theory of Public Finance.* New York 1959.
11. ——— et al, "Distribution of Tax Payments by Income Groups: A Case Study for 1948," *Nat. Tax J.*, Mar. 1951, *4*, 1–53.
12. E. O. OLSEN, "A Normative Theory of Transfers," *Public Choice*, spring 1969, *6*, 39–58.
13. J. ROTHENBERG, *The Measurement of Social Welfare.* Englewood Cliffs, 1961.

[2]

Pareto Optimal Redistribution: Comment

By Richard A. Musgrave*

The analysis by Harold Hochman and James D. Rodgers of redistribution qua exercise in Pareto optimality offers a helpful and down-to-earth addition to other recent efforts in this direction.[1] Now that the case has been made, it is indeed difficult to see why this aspect had so long been neglected. However, the following comments seem in order.

I

The degree of "redistribution" which occurs in the context of the Hochman-Rodgers scheme is a function of a) people's rate of substitution between the satisfaction derived from retaining income and that derived from giving it, and b) the "initial" distribution of earnings which exists before giving occurs. Whatever the values of a), the outcome will differ depending on b). Such, at least, will be the case unless everybody's rate of substitution is such that complete equality results. Pareto optimal redistribution thus constitutes a *secondary redistribution* which depends on the initial distribution of earnings. This distribution is determined by such factors as inheritance, earning capacities, education, and market structure. It may itself be changed through the political process. Such changes, referred to here as *primary redistribution*, are not a matter of voluntary giving, but of taking.

How is this primary redistribution decided upon? To the extent that it operates within the legal framework, it is performed through the voting mechanism. At a normative level, this explanation is not very helpful, however, since it merely raises the next issue, i.e., how the distribution of votes and the voting rules are to be decided on. Eventually, the problem becomes one of social-contract determination. At a positive level, primary redistribution depends on the social structure and balance of power between income groups. As these change, corresponding changes occur in the voting decisions and/or voting rules.

II

Turning to an application of these concepts, how can the primary or non-consent component be distinguished from the secondary or Pareto component? Private redistribution or charity in the United States now accounts for about $12 billion.[2] Assuming (somewhat unrealistically) that this giving is truly voluntary, it must be interpreted as being of the secondary type. But how should one interpret the much larger block of budgetary redistribution, which may well exceed $30 billion?[3]

---

[2] Charitable contributions claimed for itemized deductions in 1969 amounted to about $11.5 billion and the resulting tax revenue loss to over $3 billion, leaving about $8 billion of privately financed contributions. To this let us add, say, $3.5 billion to account for contributions made by returns using the standard deduction, giving a total of about $12 billion of private contributions. This figure does not cover interfamily giving. Using the family as a unit, this is not considered a part of redistribution.

The figure of $3.5 billion for nonitemized deductions is based on the following conjecture. Applying the ratio of contribution to *AGI* for returns with itemized deductions to returns with standard deductions, we obtain an upper limit of $6.5 billion. This, however, is surely an overestimate since nonitemizers may be expected to have a lower contribution ratio. The figure of $3.5 billion sets this ratio at roughly 50 percent of that for itemizers.

[3] This amount is the estimated total gain in net benefits (gain from public expenditures minus loss from taxation) on the part of those whose net benefits are positive. Obviously such estimates are difficult to obtain since they imply the entire scope of both tax and expenditure incidence, including the imputation of benefits from public services. For a discussion of the problems involved in estimating expenditure benefits, see I. Gillespie. The figure of $30 billion corresponds to Gillespie's estimate of $17.5 billion for a 1960 budget total of $133.6 billion, raised to allow for a budget total of $300 billion. The underlying figure of $17.5 billion

* Professor of economics, Harvard University.
[1] See the Hochman and Rodgers *Review* article and the references there given. To these should be added S. C. Kolm's paper on the optimal production of justice.

991

Hochman and Rodgers assign this entire amount as well to the secondary category. This follows from their assumption of ". . . an institutional setting in which free-riding, i.e., strategic behavior, is precluded so that the political mechanism through which interdependence is internalized accurately reflects the distributional preferences of individuals in this regard" (p. 548). This permits them to treat the large number case as if it involved small numbers, but the assumption is not permissible.

Rather, the situation is similar to that of provision for social goods. Let us specify that Mutt's satisfaction from giving to Jeff derives from the fact that Jeff's consumption is increased. Mutt, therefore, derives the same satisfaction if the transfer originates with Sam. With small numbers, Mutt and Sam get together and negotiate their giving to Jeff.[4] But the situation differs if Mutt is confronted with 60 million Jeffs and Sams (households) instead of one. He will readily conclude that his giving will not contribute significantly to the welfare of the Jeffs, so that uncooperative behavior on his part will not meet with retribution by the Sams. Some way must be found by which preferences are revealed and concerted action is agreed upon. Hence secondary (Pareto optimal) redistribution must be implemented through the political process, just as such a process is needed for the provision of social goods. This is why secondary redistribution extends into the budgetary process.

But if so, how can it be distinguished from primary redistribution which also operates through the budget? The distinction is subtle but nonetheless important. In its

secondary redistribution component, the budgetary process reflects an attempt to approximate what in the small number case would be accomplished voluntarily by individual bargains, and without compulsion. Since numbers are large, compulsion (the mandatory application of the voting decision) is needed to secure revelation of preferences, but it is a necessary evil only, not an objective in itself. Budgetary redistribution in its primary component, on the contrary, involves compulsion by its very nature: the Jeffs succeed in taking from the Mutts and Sams against their will.

The existing pattern of budgetary redistribution, therefore, includes both a secondary and a primary component. While I suspect that a substantial part is of the primary type, there is no simple test by which the two components may be distinguished in practice. Indeed, it would not be realistic to think of particular redistribution dollars as being assignable entirely to one or the other group. Both aspects are present and intertwined in determining the redistributional pattern.

III

Finally, a word about the bearing of secondary redistribution on my distinction between allocation and distribution policy, a distinction which was formulated with primary redistribution in mind.[5] Allowing for the possibility of secondary redistribution moves part of the distribution issue into the framework of Pareto optimality, and in this sense aligns it with the "allocation branch." But this does not mean that policies to secure an efficient *product* mix must involve distributional considerations, and vice versa.

The Hochman-Rodgers approach looks at Pareto optimal redistribution and I think correctly so, in terms of money income. Thus, two Pareto games are being played in two adjoining boxes: One involves the distribution of money income, while the other involves the determination of the product mix with any given distribution. Mutt derives welfare from Jeff's increase in income, but accepts Jeff's preference pattern and

---

assumes allocation of benefits from general expenditures (expenditures which do not permit specific allocation) in line with income. If such benefits are allocated on a per capita basis, the level of redistribution is nearly doubled.

[4] The situation is similar if Mutt derives value from Jeff's giving because this maintains his net (after-giving) income position relative to Jeff's. While Sam's position is improved, this does not carry adverse implications because he is too far down the line. If, on the other hand, Mutt's satisfaction derives from the fact that the gift originates with *himself*, he will be indifferent to gifts by others. In this case secondary giving will not call for budgetary action and be wholly private.

[5] See my *The Theory of Public Finance*.

decision on how to divide this income between oranges and apples.[6] As long as the interpersonal utility argument in Mutt's utility function is individualistic, my essential point of separation between allocation and distribution policies is retained. Redistribution should be handled in terms of income transfers, and not by pricing policy. I shall be pleased henceforth to divide my Distribution Branch into two compartments, D' being Pareto optimal and D'' primary, but this is all that is needed.

The situation differs if Mutt values Jeff's consumption of oranges and apples in accordance with his own (Mutt's) rates of substitution. In this case, allocation and distribution are inseparable. The provision for merit goods may be interpreted in these terms, and is frequently linked with redistribution.[7] Equivalent in nature to a cash grant earmarked by the donor for specified

---

[6] Dr. Mutt, at his most sophisticated, realizes that his welfare gain from giving depends on Jeff's welfare from receiving, and that the latter depends not only on changes in money income but also in relative prices. In this sense the allocation effects of giving are linked to the distribution effects. Dr. Mutt will take into account prevailing price and market structures. In this connection, the problem is the same as that discussed in my defense of separation between allocation and primary redistribution issues. See my 1966 article.

[7] I have suggested this approach as an explanation to the prevalence of merit goods in my 1966 article.

uses, redistribution in kind may be of the secondary or primary type, but there is some presumption that it is secondary, since the claimant would hardly wish to restrict his choice in the primary case.

Redistribution, it appears, involves a complex set of transfers, primary or secondary, in cash or in kind, and operating both inside and outside of the budget. While the exploration of cash-giving in terms of Pareto optimality is instructive, it covers but a part of the problem and cannot claim to explain the entire phenomenon at hand.

REFERENCES

I. Gillespie, "Effect of Public Expenditures on the Distribution of Income," in R. A. Musgrave, ed., *Essays in Fiscal Federalism*, Washington 1965.

H. M. Hochman and J. D. Rodgers, "Pareto Optimal Redistribution," *Amer. Econ. Rev.*, Sept. 1969, *59*, 542–57.

S. C. Kolm, "The Optimal Production of Justice," in J. Margolis and H. Guitton, eds., *Conference on The Analysis of the Public Sector, Barritz, 1966*, New York 1969.

R. A. Musgrave, *The Theory of Public Finance*, New York 1958.

——, "Provision for Social Goods," in J. Margolis and H. Guitton, eds., *Conference on The Analysis of the Public Sector, Biarritz, 1966*, New York 1969.

[3]

Pareto Optimal Redistribution: Reply

By HAROLD M. HOCHMAN AND JAMES D. RODGERS*

The comments raise two objections to our discussion of "Pareto Optimal Redistribution." The first objection, discussed by Paul A. Meyer and J. J. Shipley, relates to our two-person model, while the second, introduced by Richard A. Musgrave, deals with the extent to which redistribution can be explained in terms of utility interdependence and the analytic device through which we extend our analysis from the two-person to the N-person case. Robert Goldfarb's comment contains a partial reformulation of our N-person model, which establishes the link between Stephen Marglin's analysis and ours, thus indicating how some of the difficulties that Musgrave cites can be resolved.

I. *Meyer and Shipley*

The Meyer and Shipley comment, though helpful in that it points the way to a needed clarification of our model, is overstated. Their first point, which alleges that the slope of the budget line in our Figure 1 should be -2 rather than -1, betrays a failure to understand what the vertical axis of our diagram measures. This axis measures the *initial* income differential $((Y_M - Y_J)^0$, the intercept of the budget line), and *the portion of the initial income differential which Mutt retains for own use.* This, of course, is $(Y_M - Y_J)^0 - Y^T$, where Y^T is Mutt's transfer to Jeff. *The vertical axis does not measure the post-transfer income differential.* The increase in Jeff's income (above its initial level) which the transfer brings about is measured on the horizontal axis. Hence, the "slope of the ZZ' segment of the budget line is -1, since

a given size transfer to Jeff reduces the amount of income that Mutt retains for his own use by the same amount" (Hochman and Rodgers, p. 546). This should be clear from our discussion of what is measured in Figure 1, as well as from our definition of Mutt's equilibrium at E, "where the marginal utility of a dollar of own-consumption equals the marginal utility (to Mutt) of a one dollar increment in Jeff's income." (p. 546).[1] Unfortunately, however, our labeling of the vertical axis (as indicating "$Y_M - Y_J$") was ambiguous and an understandable source of confusion.

The second point in the Meyer and Shipley comment is that our Figures 2–5, illustrating the alternative configurations of Mutt's preferences, are technically incorrect, because our "IC lines which are the loci of equilibrium differential-transfer points . . . , are not consistent with (our) assumptions." Our assumptions, they argue, imply that "Mutt has an infinitely elastic demand for increments to Jeff's income."

The first half of this criticism is technically correct, though it imputes more importance to the formal characteristics of our model than we intended and is easily repaired without altering the sense of the argument. The inconsistency that Meyer and Shipley identify derives from our *ceteris paribus* assumption that the size of the transfer which Mutt wishes to make to Jeff depends only on the initial differential between their money incomes. Specified in general terms, Mutt's utility function, in our model is $U_M = f_M(Y_M, Y_J)$. Our analysis, however, focuses

* Director of studies in urban public finance, The Urban Institute, and department of economics, Pennsylvania State University, respectively. The authors wish to acknowledge the support of the National Science Foundation, under Research Grant GS-2805 to the Urban Institute. They are indebted, for useful insights, to James M. Buchanan, Francesco Forte, William Hamburger, William McEachern, and A. Mitchell Polinsky.

[1] We note, in passing, one way of improving our representation. In place of our restriction precluding transfers which reverse the distributional ordering, we might make the reasonable assumption that the slopes of Mutt's indifference curves are zero or less where they intersect a 45° ray from the origin. By doing this, we eliminate the need for the $Z'Z''$ segment of our budget line and the strict prohibition of some Pareto optimal transfers that our original formulation implies.

997

on the subset of (Y_J, Y_M) space with origin $Y_M = Y_J$ and coordinates which measure the portion of the initial differential which Mutt retains for own use and Y_E^T, Mutt's equilibrium transfer to Jeff. In the two-person case, the assumption that Mutt's transfer depends only on the differential restricts Mutt's utility function to a particular form, which implies, as Meyer and Shipley point out, that Mutt's IC line must have a constant positive slope with an intercept on the positive portion of the vertical axis. This holds true for a diagram representing all of (Y_J, Y_M) space, such as Figure 2 in the Meyer and Shipley comment, and for the diagrams which our paper employs in illustrating the two-person model.[2] It must be recognized, however, that the two-person case, in our view, is just a building block on which the N-person extension can be based. Provided that our diagrams are viewed in an N-person context and that it is recognized that Mutt's desired transfer to any given Jeff at a particular point in time is not independent of the incomes which other Jeffs in the community receive, the Meyer-Shipley criticism does not invalidate the diagrams depicted in our Figures 2–5.[3]

While our paper did not explicitly recognize how severe a restriction our formulation of the two-person case imposes on Mutt's preferences, relaxation of this restriction leaves our essential argument intact. Moreover, as we noted, our formulation of the two-person case can be repaired in either of two ways. First, we might simply admit that the utility function differs in form for each of the diagrams and for each of the alterna-

[2] Note that the representation in Figure 3 of the Meyer and Shipley comment is incorrect. Their budget line should have a slope of -1 and the IC line should have a positive slope.

[3] Suppose, for example, that Mutt has an income of \$5,000 and that two Jeffs (J_1 and J_2) have incomes of \$2,000 and zero, respectively. Let the size of Mutt's preferred transfer to J_1 be $Y_{J_1}^T$ and the size of his preferred transfer to J_2 be $Y_{J_2}^T$. Now suppose J_2's income rises to \$2,000 while J_1's remains at \$2,000. As a result the Pareto optimal transfers become $Y_{J_1}^{T*}$ and $Y_{J_2}^{T*}$. It is not generally true that $Y_{J_1}^{T*}$ need equal $Y_{J_1}^T$ nor that $Y_{J_1}^{T*}$ need equal $Y_{J_2}^T$. Hence, in an N-person model our figures are not inconsistent with our assumption that transfers depend on the initial income differential.

tive numerical examples; conceptually, however, this is not very satisfying. As an alternative, we can redefine the conceptual experiment through which the amount of the Pareto optimal transfer is derived, so that the restrictive IC outcome that Meyer and Shipley describe does not result, thus eliminating the problem. Originally, in setting up our model, we did not distinguish between changes in $Y_M - Y_J$ (changes in the intercept of the budget line on the ordinate) that result from (1) changes in Y_M and (2) changes in Y_J, implying thereby that our analysis was capable of registering the effects of diagonal movements in Y_J, Y_M space.[4] This is the source of the restrictive outcome. By redefining our conceptual experiment, so that the changes in $(Y_M - Y_J)^0$ which we consider derive only from changes in Y_M, with Y_J held constant (or the reverse,) diagonal movements in (Y_J, Y_M) space are ruled out as objects of our analysis and our two-person case becomes fully consistent with all of the IC lines that our paper goes on to discuss.

So much for our discussion of this problem. We might comment briefly, however, on the Meyer and Shipley claim that our assumptions imply that Mutt has an "infinitely elastic demand for increments to Jeff's income" (p. 990). Presuming that their reference, in saying this, is to income elasticity (since the price of a transfer, i.e., the slope of ZZ', is always -1 in the two-person case), this statement cannot be correct, as a matter of simple arithmetic. There is no way in which the response of Y^T to a change in Mutt's income (or, for that matter, to a change in $(Y_M - Y_J)^0$) can be infinitely large.

II. *Musgrave*

The essential argument of our paper was that Paretian welfare economics, contrary to the conventional view, can help to resolve dissatisfaction with the size distribution of income. Once the interdependence of utility functions is admitted, the range of distribu-

[4] We had claimed, in fn. 12 on p. 549, that it makes no difference whether a change in the initial income differential derives from a change in Y_M or a change in Y_J.

COMMUNICATIONS

tional conflict is narrower than economists have supposed, to the extent that inter-dependence implies that the initial or market-determined income distribution is not co-incident with the distribution of welfare. The relevant implication of interdependence is that some portion or portions of the utility-possibility locus, in the two-person case, may slope upward, so that some of its points (each of which corresponds to an initial distribu-tion of money income) are dominated.

Musgrave argues that this line of reason-ing, while correct, resolves only a part of the social issue of distributional justice. He re-classifies redistribution under two headings: "primary" redistribution, involving a choice among points on the efficient segment of the utility-possibility frontier; and Pareto opti-mal redistribution (which Musgrave calls "secondary") involving a movement from an inefficient (positively-sloped) to an effi-cient portion of this locus.

Primary redistribution, at the normative level, is a matter of "social contract," which evolves from the process of constitutional choice through which a society establishes its structure of common and individual rights to human, physical, and natural resources. Any society, in doing this, must settle not only on an optimal distribution of current income, but, more generally, on rules for distributing rights and opportunities to earn and expend money income and consume leisure. The "distributional" outcome, in a total sense, is achieved through a bargaining process, in which "free" individuals, seeking agreement, revise their preferences and/or opt in or out of the political community. The society which is produced by the contracting process, emerging from a consensus of free indi-viduals, has institutional (including "distri-butional") characteristics that are, by defini-tion, Pareto optimal (in the sense that those persons who cannot subscribe to its constitu-tion choose exclusion from the community). Interpreted as an element in this process, "primary redistribution" cannot be a matter of "taking" rather than "voluntary giving," as Musgrave claims (p. 991). Taking, per se, is in fact inimical to the notion of the social contract that characterizes the constitutional

choice process (which is in turn the basis of modern theories of democracy).

The issues that primary redistribution involves are therefore broader than the tradi-tional public finance literature admits, or than Musgrave's dichotomy implies. Still, if the only distributional issue addressed is the apportionment of current income, as in the conventional framework, Musgrave's dis-tinction between primary redistribution, which makes some individuals worse off, and secondary redistribution, which makes no one worse off, is well taken. But the terms primary and secondary, which Musgrave has chosen to designate such distributional ad-justments, are misleading, for the logical ordering of the two components of the re-distributive process that they imply is in-correct. Specifically, one cannot determine in welfare terms, whether the initial or market-determined distribution of income is satisfactory *until* Pareto optimal transfers have occurred.

However, when we turn to the very different question of real world redistribu-tion, we can certainly agree with Musgrave that its primary and secondary components are "intertwined in determining the redis-tributional pattern" (Musgrave, p. 992). To argue that all redistribution is in the Pareto optimal category would be unrealistic, just as it would be unrealistic to argue that all re-distribution is primary or that all charitable contributions are voluntary. Surely, we did not intend such an impression, and Mus-grave, in criticizing our assignment of all government redistribution to the Pareto optimal category, has misinterpreted us. The first and second sections of our paper dealt with a hypothetical situation in which only *Pareto optimal* transfers were considered. Then, for argument's sake, its third section asked what pattern of utility interdepen-dence might be implied if (again hypo-thetically) the actual pattern of fiscal residuals were Pareto optimal. But it did all this in an explicitly heuristic spirit, without false pretense to realism.

In criticizing our discussion of the *N*-person case, Musgrave contends that treat-ing " . . . the large number case as if it involved small numbers . . . is not permissible" (Musgrave, p. 992). However, whether such a simplification is admissible or not depends on one's assumptions about the precise character of the motivation that underlies the income transfers. One possible case, as Musgrave suggests, is that in which Mutt's satisfaction derives "from the fact that the gift originates with himself." But, Mutt's benefit, alternatively, might derive from the improvement in the recipient's welfare which the transfer produces. In this latter case Mutt's motivation might be genuine concern for the recipient's plight *or* the belief that the gift will reduce the likelihood that the recipient will participate in antisocial behavior (e.g., in riots which affect the value of Mutt's private property). If each benefactor's benefits derive only from transfers that he makes himself and not from transfers which other persons make, simple aggregation of pairwise transfers is the proper method of analysis in the N-person case and our straightforward extension of the two-person model to the case of a community-at-large is appropriate. Since the market would not "fail" in this case, as Musgrave notes, a Pareto optimal outcome is attained through private redistribution, and the intermediation of the fiscal structure is not required. In the second case, however, a Mutt's transfer to any particular Jeff yields spillover benefits to other Mutts, and, unless highly qualified, the simple aggregation of pairwise transfers is not a correct procedure, except as an explicit matter of heuristic convenience. Transfers are a collective good which benefit all individuals in Mutt's income status vis-à-vis the recipient, implying an argument for coerced redistribution that is strictly analogous to the argument that "national defense" must be financed through the fiscal process. When there is a large number of potential benefactors, the attainment of a Pareto optimum through voluntary action is difficult, inasmuch as each participant has a private incentive to remain a "free rider" and stands to gain from a collective agreement which coerces him into participating in the transfer process. In these circumstances, attainment of a Pareto optimum requires

that all marginally affected Mutts must share in the transfer to a particular Jeff, with the cost of increasing a given Jeff's income by one dollar being apportioned among the Mutts (assuming application of the benefit principle) on the basis of their marginal evaluations.[5]

Regarding the implications of our paper for Musgrave's division of the public sector into allocation and distribution branches, several comments are in order.

Where the interrelationships among utility functions are such that a large number of non-participants benefit from the process of redistribution, interpersonal transfers pose exactly the same kind of "market failure" problem as "national defense." Such transfers are, therefore, a collective good, albeit one that is not resource-using. Thus, in Musgrave's schema, they should logically be provided for by the allocation branch, since, concisely stated, its function is to carry out the public activities needed to assure a Pareto optimal allocation of resources.

At least for classification purposes, we see no difference between the case in which Mutt's benefit derives from an increase in Jeff's income or welfare and the case in which Mutt's benefit derives from an increase or decrease in Jeff's consumption of a particular commodity. Contrary to Musgrave's claim, the issue of whether a money or in-kind transfer is appropriate does not, in itself, indicate whether allocation and distribution are separable or inseparable. If each of the interested Mutts permits himself to be coerced into financing an in-kind transfer to Jeff (in the form of a consumption subsidy) that induces him to alter his consumption pattern and Jeff accepts the transfer on their terms, we have evidence that all of the individuals involved, including Jeff, have moved

[5] We reemphasize, however, that the issue of the appropriate formulation of the N-person case is separate and distinct from the main point that we wished to demonstrate with our simplifying assumptions, that is, the normative distributional implications of utility interdependence. At the same time it should certainly be clear that a realistic treatment of the N-person case, as suggested by Musgrave, and developed in part by Goldfarb, is a natural extension of our analysis and adds to its relevance.

to preferred situations. Jeff's acceptance, of course, unquestionably implies that he is better off than he would have been with *no transfer at all*. It is this *ex ante* state of affairs, rather than what the welfare outcome would have been if the transfer had been in general purchasing power, that is the appropriate basis of comparison. Transfers of general purchasing power, in Musgrave's terminology, can be *either primary* (in which case they are purely a distributional phenomenon) or *secondary* (in which case their allocative and distributive aspects are inseparable). However, one could argue that *all* earmarked or in-kind transfers are of the secondary type since recipients, if they had the power to institute redistribution in their favor, would prefer cash. An estimated 43 percent of all federal aid to the poor in 1968 took the in-kind form (see M. S. March).[6]

III. *Goldfarb*

While Goldfarb's useful insight into the nature of the *N*-person case requires no rejoinder,[7] some aspects of his comment, on which we shall dwell briefly, trouble us.

Goldfarb remarks that "In short, if the utility functions of the rich have the particular form we postulated, a 'large' government poverty program may be justified on Pareto optimization grounds, even though private charity programs, for the poor do not receive any contributions," (p. 995). This suggests a failure to understand why some collective wants are satisfied voluntarily, through charity or other private means of provision, while others must be provided for through the fiscal process. The size of a

[6] All this suggests that the notion of merit wants is redundant. The phenomena to which this generally refers are simply cases of particular-commodity utility interdependence. In such situations "gains from trade" are possible, and their realization may require collective action, just as national defense requires it. Musgrave himself recognizes that merit wants might best be explained in terms of interdependent utility in his Biarritz paper (see p. 143). Also see Buchanan (1960). The ideas discussed in this paragraph are discussed in more detail in Rodgers (1969).

[7] One of the authors deals with the *N*-person case in a similar way but in more detail than Goldfarb's comment. See Rodgers (1970).

redistribution program in itself indicates nothing at all about whether it is justifiable in terms of the Pareto criterion, regardless of whether the *mechanism* through which it is put into effect is private or public. What matters is whether the collective marginal evaluations warrant the program. Whether private or public means of provision are appropriate depends on the costs of obtaining voluntary agreement. The real thrust of Goldfarb's observation, then, is that the free-rider problem will make the level of voluntary transfers suboptimal.

Moreover, Goldfarb's assertion to the effect that a society with the same number of poor but more rich people is more likely to have a Pareto optimal redistribution *available*, other things equal, hinges on an implicit assumption that *all potential recipients* must share in any transfers actually made. But whatever a community's size, a "rich" man, by earmarking his contributions, can bring about the same redistribution to any particular "poor" man that a community can accomplish vis-à-vis all poor men. This, of course, is what happens in families in which income recipients make continuing transfers to the other members.

IV. *Conclusion*

Our paper, as we have pointed out, questioned the neoclassical approach to distributional issues,[8] but it " . . . does not pretend to claim that fiscal reality does not deviate from the requirements of Pareto optimality" (Hochman and Rodgers, p. 556). We can, however, go beyond our original findings and suggest a number of other conclusions to which we have come in the course of our further thought on the subject. First, the logic of utility interdependence, as we have noted, implies that in-kind redistribution is in the Pareto optimal category. Second, so long as there are no legal or economic impediments to mobility among political jurisdictions, Pareto optimal transfers are the only kind of redistributive transfers possible at the state and local jurisdictional levels. Third, the fact that individuals do accede to the social con-

[8] Another recent paper, which deals with the same question, is by S. C. Kolm.

tract and participate in the redistribution, despite their preference to free ride, suggests that redistributive transfers are a social good.

The question of how to decompose redistribution into its primary and secondary components and the development of theories capable of explaining each of these classes of transfers is worth further study, both at the theoretical and the empirical levels. For the theory our paper discussed to have practical relevance, research in this area must, among other things, determine whether utility functions are in fact interdependent and whether, where observed, such utility interdependence is benevolent, as our discussion has assumed. It appears, at this point, that the most fruitful way of beginning to do this is to examine the available data on private contributions to charity.[9]

[9] We have made a start in this direction. See our forthcoming article "Utility Interdependence and Income Transfers Through Charity."

REFERENCES

J. M. Buchanan, "The Theory of Public Finance," *South. Econ. J.*, Jan. 1960, *26*, 234–38.

—— and G. Tullock, *The Calculus of Consent*, Ann Arbor 1962.

H. M. Hochman and J. D. Rodgers, "Pareto-Optimal Redistribution," *Amer. Econ. Rev.*, Sept. 1969, *59*, 542–57.

—— and ——, "Utility Interdependence and Income Transfers through Charity," in K. E. Boulding and M. Pfaff, eds., *Transfers in an Urbanized Economy: Theories and Effects of the Grants Economy* (forthcoming).

S. C. Kolm, "On the Optimal Production of Social Justice," in J. Margolis and H. Guitton, eds., *Public Economics*, New York 1969, 145–200.

M. S. March, "Public Programs for the Poor: Coverage, Gaps, and Future Directions," in S. J. Bowers, ed., *Proceedings of the National Tax Association*, New York 1967, 606–19.

S. A. Marglin, "The Social Rate of Discount and the Optimal Rate of Investment," *Quart. J. Econ.*, Feb. 1963, *77*, 95–112.

R. A. Musgrave, "Provision for Social Goods," in J. Margolis and H. Guitton, eds., *Conference On the Analysis of the Public Sector, Biarritz, 1966*, New York 1969, 124–44.

J. D. Rodgers, "On the Optimal Form of Income Transfers," Urban Institute Working Paper #1200–04, Washington 1969.

——, "Utility Interdependence and Income Redistribution," unpublished doctoral dissertation, Univ. Virginia 1970.

Individual Preferences
and Distributional Adjustments

By Harold M. Hochman*

Common, by training, to economists is a belief that distributional adjustments must rest on an extra-economic social welfare function, capable of the interpersonal utility comparisons which ordinal utility precludes. Without such an ordering of social states—which need not be true to the preferences of citizen-consumers—welfare economics, as a basis for advocacy, is limited to Pareto-efficient measures, which are thought to preclude distributional counsel. It is, therefore, open to criticism that it institutionalizes the status quo.

This assessment, if correct, is crippling. It suggests that for economists ethics and justice are intractable, even though ethics is largely a matter of men's preferences on rules of behavior in dealing with others, and preferences are the cornerstone of the neoclassical theory of value. It is troubling because economic policy can only avoid distributional side effects under the most restrictive of assumptions, thus calling into question all normative judgments, couched in language of Pareto efficiency, which claim independence of equity considerations. As our radical colleagues have chided us, conventional economics, in downgrading the distributional component of social policies, all too often produces semi-answers to semi-problems, with dubious relevance.

This essay explores whether the limits of economics, as the Pareto criterion reflects them, are as restrictive as they seem, or whether neoclassical logic, duly modified, permits meaningful answers to distributional questions. Starting with individual preferences, it spells out what economists can conclude about the desirability of distributional adjustments, though it nowhere implies that the Pareto criterion is a proper limit on social policy or that the Paretian ethic identifies a uniquely preferred income distribution.

I. Distributional Adjustment in a Neoclassical Setting

Recent developments suggest, conceptually, that the Pareto criterion need not rule out normative discussion of distribution. As a discipline, political economy, through a new understanding of external effects, has again come into its own, facilitating the explanation of collective action in terms of constituent preferences

* Director of Studies in Urban Public Finance, The Urban Institute, Washington, D.C. James Buchanan, Peter Brown, Harvey Galper, John Johnston, George Peterson, A. Mitchell Polinsky, Walter Williams, and, as another among my debts to him, James Rodgers criticized an earlier draft. I should also like to thank the Centre for Environmental Studies in London and Christopher Foster, Morris Perlman, Alan Prest, and Amartya Sen of the London School of Economics, where I was in residence while this paper was written, and the National Science Foundation, which supported its preparation under Grant #GS-2805 to The Urban Institute.

353

and, in so doing, freeing economics from artificial substantive boundaries. The dimensions of the community, thus costs of agreement, determine whether publicness is internalized privately through voluntary exchange or publicly through political decisions. In parallel, attempts to explain certain types of "irrational" behavior have enriched the concept of "economic man." Individual utility functions have been recast in lifetime terms and modified to take account of such unconventional or unmarketed goods as time and interpersonal welfare interdependencies. These developments, which bring many of the behavioral factors that radicals claim conventional economists have ignored into the neoclassical domain[1], have a strong bearing on the meaningfulness of the separation of efficiency and equity, a distinction basic to public finance and central to the question of distributional choice.

Assume (until section IV) that the structure of property rights is given, and consider the implications of differing distributions of income in a political community of two individuals. If preferences and production functions are all well-behaved and there are no Pareto-relevant external effects, the utility-possibility locus, everywhere concave from below, is the welfare frontier, along which there remains no scope for mutually advantageous joint actions. One or more Pareto-preferable points on the frontier correspond to each point within it. Without interpersonal comparisons, however, there is no basis for choosing among these outcomes, each of which implies a different distribution of income and welfare.

Distributional considerations intrude for two reasons. First, some external effects are inherently distributional, imply-

ing that individual welfare is not entirely a function of own-income and own-use. Second, the real-world fiscal measures through which communities internalize publicness are not lump-sum; thus, even if fiscal authorities, seeking the distributional neutrality of a Lindahl solution, try to link the pricing of collectively provided goods to marginal evaluations, there will be redistributive effects. In this paper I focus on the first of these arguments and its implications for our ability, *qua* economists, to offer distributional counsel.

(1) If, as in families, individual utility functions are interdependent, the competitive relationship among individual welfare levels is incomplete. Some portion(s) of the utility-possibility locus will be upward-sloping and the distributions implied by points on such segment(s) of the locus are Pareto-inferior to other points. In such cases, the distinction between Pareto efficiency and vertical equity (as welfare criteria) is blurred, and both parties to an income transfer, as donor and recipient, can benefit from it. In larger communities, such income transfers, which are essential to the attainment of a Pareto optimum, become a public good. Even though a "best" distribution (from those that are mutually preferred) cannot be identified, it is possible to indicate the amount *and* the form of the minimum transfer the attainment of a Pareto optimum requires, given an inefficient initial distribution.

(2) Individuals, to mesh opportunities with preferences, reallocate their income streams intertemporally. Such intrapersonal income transfers may be channeled, during a given time period, either through private interpersonal gifts or through a public social security program.

(3) Income transfers may be Pareto-preferable because of external effects in production. Such transfers, through explicit manpower retraining programs or

---

[1] But the radicals, ironically, write in apparent innocence of these developments in the mainstream literature (see, for example, Herbert Gintis and Michael Zweig).

macro economic income and employment policies, may increase the expenditure options that face both donors and recipients.

Though these arguments suggest that the Paretian logic may be able to explain significant aspects of distributional choice, they do not define or produce "social justice." After all Pareto-optimal transfers, the community must still choose, somehow, among a residual set of Pareto-optimal distributions, each of which corresponds to a different system of rules and rights to property and human capital. No one of these distributions is uniquely optimal, and each, potentially, is Pareto-efficient. Still, once the argument is brought this far, consideration should be given to the usefulness of extending the Paretian line of reasoning to the constitutional level of abstraction at which rights and rules are themselves determined.

II. Utility Interdependence and Income Distribution

It seems fair to argue that the notion of social justice is neither meaningful nor operational unless at least one individual's welfare, in his own thinking, depends on what happens to others. But while even casual observation of private behavior discredits the assumption that utility functions are independent, this assumption has persisted, obscuring much of what the Pareto criterion can tell us about distributional adjustments.

To indicate the distributional implications of utility interdependence, consider again a two-person political community, where A's utility is related positively *and* marginally not only to own-consumption but to B's income, consumption, or income-producing activities. Assume, further, that A's initial income is higher than B's and that A's marginal interest in B's welfare dominates B's concern for his well-being. Thus, over some range of initial distributions, A's own-welfare varies in-

versely with disposable income and A's equilibrium consumption bundle includes a voluntary transfer to B. This transfer benefits both parties, though its amount depends only on A's preferences.

Moving from this small group case, in which voluntary transfers are likely, to N-person political communities, the number of such paired comparisons of status between potential donors and potential recipients is multiplied. The political provision of Pareto-optimal transfers encounters the same types of measurement problems and transactions costs as the provision of ordinary public goods. In the two-person community, justification of a Pareto-optimal cash transfer requires that the donor value the recipient's utility increment at unity, inasmuch as the medium of the transfer, cash, is the numeraire. In the N-person case, however, the *sums of the marginal evaluations of all potential donors* vis-a-vis each recipient are relevant. The increase in community size reduces each potential donor's effective demand for a given increment in a particular recipient's disposable income and, by affording donors with opportunities to be free riders, opens up the prospect of strategic behavior. Thus, collectivization of the transfer process through the fiscal structure, through progressive taxation or nonzero fiscal residuals, is required to effect Pareto-optimal redistribution.

Only if distributional externalities are "general" is the traditional theorem, that transfers in cash are preferable to transfers in kind, unambiguously valid. With general interdependencies, only the recipient's welfare or utility index is an argument in the donor's utility function. Cash transfers afford the recipient more options, enabling him to attain a higher utility level than restricted transfers of the same monetary value. If the paired linkages among donors and recipients are specified in relative income terms, the implied transfers tend to equalize the income distribution. And, under what seem to be reasonable assumptions about donors' elasticities of demand for increments in recipients' disposable incomes, it is appropriate to finance such transfers through progressive taxation.

The Pareto-optimal form of an income maintenance program differs with the specific assumptions made about citizen-consumer preferences. If, for example, donors' marginal rates of substitution between own-consumption and income transfers depend only on income differences and all pairwise income comparisons are made simultaneously, such an income maintenance program levels up incomes from the bottom. No individual is a transfer recipient as long as others have disposable incomes lower than his, and the initial distribution is, as it were, truncated. On the other hand, if empathy intrudes and donor choices, made on a one-by-one basis, reflect marginal rates of substitution that vary with initial incomes of potential recipients as well as initial income differences, the implied incidence pattern is different. All individuals, except those at the extremes of the distribution, are both donors and recipients of Pareto-optimal income transfers, resulting in an across-the-board condensation of the initial distribution.

If, at the donor's margin of choice, utility interdependence is of the "particular commodity" rather than "general" class, the unambiguous case for cash transfers collapses (see, among others, James Rodgers) and attainment of a Pareto-efficient distribution requires in-kind transfers through commodity grants or price subsidies.[2] The donor's concern, here, may either be with the recipient's consumption of specific commodities *or* with his allocation of potential income between labor and leisure. If, specifically, the donor is concerned with the level of the recipient's consumption but is averse to the work disincentives which a higher money income might produce, an optimal income maintenance program would combine a cash guarantee or in-kind transfer with a wage subsidy (see G. E. Peterson). This outcome contrasts with the positive marginal tax on wages implicit in most income maintenance proposals.

To justify *or* explain real-world income transfer programs in terms of utility interdependence requires not only evidence of distributional externalities[3] but the consistent variation of individual tastes with objective criteria. Using this argument to explain such programs also requires that the political process be a perfect fit to the democratic model and that there be sufficient evidence to refute alternative hypotheses, in particular, political power hypotheses which view transfers as a matter of taking rather than giving.

Still, it seems worthwhile to consider efficiency aspects of equity before turning to a "strong" social welfare function. Even the present argument suggests that the case for progressive taxation *need not be* "uneasy," given but marginal change in the neoclassical paradigm, and that consumer sovereignty *need not imply* a universal preference for cash transfers if "no man is an island," because someone's freedom (donor's or recipient's) may be infringed whether transfers are in cash *or* in kind. If it is correct, liberal economists, in opposing in-kind transfers, can no longer base their argument on consumer sovereignty *per se*, but are reduced to arguing that in-kind transfers are more costly to

---

[2] Note that in-kind transfers, to be effective, cannot be inframarginal to the recipient's consumption bundle and that retrading must be uneconomic or illegal. Viewed in these terms, transfers which reflect putative "merit wants" need not have paternalistic connotations unless they actually reduce the recipient's utility *and* his disposal costs are nonzero.

[3] Patterns of interdependence might be inferred (cautiously, to avoid circularity) from data on charitable contributions, referendum results in voting on redistributive programs, or measured fiscal residuals.

administer than cash transfers or, that in requiring a more elaborate bureaucracy, they pose a greater potential threat to personal freedom. But this argument is difficult to square with modern theories of political economy—just as liberal in origin —which relate legitimate actions of democratic governments to citizen-consumer preferences for goods that are provided more efficiently if provided collectively.

III. Intertemporal and Intergeneration Income Transfers

Even if their expectations are certain, individuals, expecting intertemporal income variation, engage in saving and dissaving to bring about optimal patterns of lifetime consumption. Though such intertemporal transfers may imply no redistribution if incomes are examined in lifetime terms, they may, in cross-section measures, suggest a substantial amount of interpersonal redistribution (see A. Mitchell Polinsky 1971). While such intertemporal but intrapersonal transfers can be carried out without fiscal intervention, nonzero transactions and information costs (making terms of borrowing and lending asymmetrical) and administrative economies of scale may give rise to the partial collectivization of the intertemporal transfer process.

Uncertainty in income expectations is, however, a more likely rationalization of the fiscal collectivization of saving. Quite aside from administrative efficiency, public provision, under uncertainty, may provide a better hedge against inflation. Indeed, risk-averse individuals, if uncertain of their expected income streams, might vote unanimously, *ex ante*, for transfers which produce cross-section redistribution. Such transfers can be interpreted as a means of self-insurance against the prospect of financial adversity. The more imperfect are income and status expectations, the more favorable individuals are likely to be toward equality and the broader will

be the community through which they collectivize their demands for social insurance. Since risk pooling is the output under demand, collectivization is essential, though public provision is not.

In the limiting case, risk-aversion implies that an equal division of incomes is appropriate. The argument, which is similar to Lerner's, can be interpreted in terms of Harsanyi's (1953) model, in which:

> [the] value judgment(s) [of risk-averse individuals] on the distribution of income show impersonality to the highest degree . . . [and an individual's choice of] a particular income distribution [is made in] complete ignorance of what his own relative position (and the position of those near to his heart) would be within the system chosen. This would be the case if he had exactly the same chance of obtaining the first position (corresponding to the highest income) or the second or the third, etc., up to the last position (corresponding to the lowest income) available within that scheme.

Thus distributional choice, in a "state of nature" in which own prospects cannot be discerned, is impersonal and individuals, facing such a situation, opt for equality.

Taken together, the utility interdependence and income insurance explanations of income transfers suggest a number of important methodological insights. They point out, for one thing, which types of changes in individual tastes the Paretian logic can accommodate. This is important not only because tastes, taken as given in static welfare economics, are endogenous in intertemporal choice, but because in-kind transfers may fail to fulfill their objectives *unless* they alter the preferences of their recipients. For another, they provide us with a way of examining and understanding intergeneration transfers and linking the taxation of estates or bequests to citizen-consumer preferences.

To deal, though briefly, with these issues, think of an individual as an evolving decision-making unit, with age and experience changing both preferences, as revealed in market and political choices, and perceived opportunities. Describe his preferences in terms of a series of one-period utility functions (as of different individuals, living in series) which are linked intertemporally by *benevolent* and *marginally relevant* interdependencies. Assume, aside from time preference and diminishing one-period marginal rates of substitution between general purchasing power and particular commodities, that the individual is intertemporally indifferent between consumption in one period and consumption in another, that there is, in other words, no "rivalry" among his period-specific utility functions.

With this definition of the individual, the Paretian terms of reference can accommodate taste changes of two types, even though both are irreversible. "Corrective" changes, reflecting improvement in the individual's knowledge of his "true" preferences and alternatives, are the first type. The implication is that actual choices are stochastically related to "true" preferences and that decision-making errors decrease with age and experience. Transfers in kind may be an effective means of transmitting such information, or, in such forms as education, may fulfill an enabling function. The effect is to make later period-specific utility functions more definitive than earlier ones. Taste changes which reflect a widening of options, attributable to technical change or increases in income that awaken latent demands, are the second type. In neither case is there any implication that the individual, in the past, would have acted differently than he did, given the information and the options then available. Thus, these types of taste change do not run afoul of the Pareto criterion.

Similarly, intended intergeneration transfers, through gifts or bequests, may reflect nonrivalry between the utility func-

tions of donors and beneficiaries. Relative to the relationship between a given individual's period-specific utility functions, nonrivalry is reduced, but not eliminated, when he considers the preferences and opportunities of his heirs.[4] But, practically speaking, when wealth-owners project forward more than a generation or two, they cannot identify their heirs, so that the utility interdependence and impersonal choice foundations of intergeneration transfers merge and estate taxation becomes more acceptable as an alternative to specific bequests.

IV. Paretian Interpretations of Constitutional Choice

The discussion, to this point, only implies that some income distributions are not Pareto-efficient, given the values that underlie the Pareto criterion and the structure of rights to property and human capital on which the allocation of resources is based. While it has demonstrated that individuals may unanimously prefer some distributions to others, it has enabled us to designate neither an optimal distribution of income nor an optimal structure of property rights, except in the state of nature in which choice is entirely impersonal.

Here, I turn to the process of constitutional choice through which political communities settle on such rights and rules and determine, through this "social contract," which distribution will materialize. This structure of rights, rules, and opportunities —the total distributional context—is a higher level public good, which remains to be dealt with after Pareto-optimal transfers have taken place. The extent to which it is meaningful to interpret this higher level "choice of game" as a Pareto-optimal process is the question at hand.

There are at least two ways in which

---

[4] It might be possible to use data on the characteristics of bequests and life insurance policies to quantify such interdependencies.

individual choices, taken collectively, move communities toward agreement on rules of the game and narrow the residual set of Pareto-efficient distributions. Even if a change in rules injures some members of the political community, its aggregation with other issues in political decision-making *and* the extension of the time horizon in terms of which it is evaluated may make it acceptable to all. Opportunities for such grouping of issues, including distributional issues, through logrolling or vote-trading are contingent on the assumption that individuals hold single-issue positions with differing intensities. However, while issue-grouping makes limited consensus more likely, including consensus on the rules that underlie the income distribution, it does nothing to resolve conflict once such potential gains are exhausted.[5] Consensus at the constitutional level requires that the grouping exclude at least some alternatives. Thus, while logrolling can reduce the scope of distributional conflict, it cannot eliminate it. Similarly, lengthening of the time horizon, to judge policies in terms of long-run effects (see Polinsky 1972), can resolve some distributional conflict. Some rule changes, however, produce negative long-run effects for at least some members of the community, and single-period returns which imply bankruptcy are irretrievable.[6]

These arguments, which broaden the frame of reference in which the income distribution issue is considered, can be used in the evaluation of social decision rules, whether set up to decide single issues or to establish rules of the game that apply in repeated trials. Thus, while majority rule might be unacceptable if outcomes are evaluated in single-issue terms, it is compatible with democracy if they are construed as episodes in a convergence process, itself having the essential properties of logrolling. Even under the Paretian ethic, majority rule *may* be satisfactory, given appropriate preference patterns, because the overall outcome is preferred to the inaction that would result from issue-by-issue judgments constrained by the Pareto criterion.[7]

The Tiebout model of residential location can also be interpreted as a constitutional choice mechanism that can resolve some distributional conflict. In this model, individuals, in locating in a political jurisdiction, decide on the local or national community that offers the most favorable fiscal structure (fiscal residuals) and environmental characteristics. Mobility, by changing the locus of political participation, fosters long-run change in fiscal and legal rules, with entry and exit bringing about marginal adjustments.

Interpreted as a model of "club" formation, the Tiebout mechanism can assure that the rules under which individuals live *and* the rules that govern constitutional change are acceptable to all, provided one begins *de novo* or assumes a world in which incomes are equal and only tastes differ. But in the real world, with its pre-existing environment, this is not very useful, for it is tautological, an argument that reality is uniquely optimal because it would not have materialized were it not. While individuals, by relocating, can mitigate their dissatisfaction, their clustering cannot

---

[5] One difficulty with logrolling as a means of gaining consensus through compromise is that the compensation of individuals who oppose changes in distributional rules may, under unfavorable terms of trade, undo the desired redistribution, leaving the initial conflict intact.

[6] Nevertheless, the increasing uncertainties which appear when changes in distributional rules are considered in a multiperiod context move the logic of the argument toward the impersonal choice construction, as it applies in the "state of nature," and, in so doing, make it more forceful.

[7] Thus, issue-grouping is much like uncertainty in its effect, in making choice more impersonal. The difference is in the "averaging" mechanism, in one case an expansion in the number of issues considered and in the other an equi-probability assumption about the outcomes of single trials.

undo the dependence of their claims on initial endowments of physical and human capital. The existence of such endowments is enough to assure the normative insufficiency of the Tiebout mechanism.

V. Conclusion

Unhappily, but not unexpectedly, this discussion has returned to its point of departure, that economics, as a science of choice, cannot define or establish a "just" or "proper" distribution. Its odyssey, however, has taken us well beyond the standard disavowal of distributional competence and has indicated that the Pareto criterion, despite its ultimate insufficiency, has much to tell us about distributional choice. It has, for example, discussed equity in terms of Pareto efficiency and suggested that individual behavior, through private or public income transfers, can move communities from dominated to preferred distributions. In a limited sense, such adjustments assure minimal justice and incorporate ethical propositions, founded on testable hypotheses about individual preferences and social choice, within the logic of economics.

That economists can have much to say about distributional matters is not nearly so surprising as its history of neglect. The failure of the neoclassical paradigm to fully define distributive justice does not excuse the discussion of allocative issues in a distributional vacuum. Nor does it mean that the economist's logic cannot be used in examining distributional issues and in identifying the logical origins of redistributive programs.

For me, a belief that economics, adapting both form and substance, must probe more deeply into interpersonal relationships and ethical issues is the primary lesson of radical criticism. Economists, if they are to contribute to the solution of social problems, cannot be so cavalier as their wont has been in dealing with issues in the traditional domains of sociology and political philosophy. But persistent adaptation of neoclassical thought, as in the emerging theories of public choice and human interaction, lead me, in assessing such criticism, to Knightian skepticism rather than a quest for a new paradigm, less true to methodological individualism and resting on even shakier normative foundations.

REFERENCES

H. Gintis, "Neo-Classical Welfare Economics and Individual Development," *URPE Occasional Paper*, No. 3, July 1970.

J. Harsanyi, "Cardinal Utility in Welfare Economics and the Theory of Risk Taking," *J. Pol. Econ.*, Oct. 1953, *61*, 434–35.

J. Johnston, "Utility Interdependence and the Determinants of Redistributional Public Expenditures," unpublished dissertation, 1971.

G. E. Peterson, "Welfare, Work Fare and Pareto Optimality," Working Paper No. 1200–12, The Urban Institute, 1970.

A. M. Polinsky, "A Note on the Measurement of Incidence," Working Paper No. 1200–15, The Urban Institute, 1971.

——, "Quasi-Paretian Justice," *Quart. Jour. Econ.*, May 1972.

J. D. Rodgers, "Distributional Externalities and the Optimal Form of Income Transfers," Working Paper No. 1200–04, The Urban Institute, 1971.

M. Zweig, "A New Left Critique of Economics," in D. Mermelstein, ed., *Economics: Mainstream Readings and Radical Critiques*, New York 1970.

B

Conceptual Articles

[5]

ON THE INCOME DISTRIBUTION AS A PUBLIC GOOD *

Harold M. Hochman, James D. Rodgers, and Gordon Tullock

I

Lester Thurow's provocative paper,[1] which considers the circumstances in which attainment of a Pareto optimum requires income redistribution, unfortunately does as much to obscure and confuse as to clarify the logic of distributional adjustments.

As Thurow sees it, there are three reasons why redistribution may be necessary to achieve a Pareto optimum: (1) one man's income may be an argument in the utility function of another;[2] (2) utility may derive from the act of giving per se, rather than its effect on the recipient; and (3) the distribution of income — i.e., a measure of inequality — may itself be an argument in the utility function. This third situation, Thurow argues, can arise because of externalities (different crime rates, degrees of political stability, etc.) associated with alternative income distributions, *or* (even if there are no externalities) because of individual tastes for equality or inequality.

Though Thurow recognizes that (1) and (3) "shade into one another," and that all three cases "can lead to substantial income transfers," he concentrates on (3), since it implies that "income transfers take on a different characteristic than when they are generated by either of the other two motives." In this case, he argues, *"The income distribution is a pure public good"* (his emphasis,[3] whereas it is not if transfers are a matter of "deriving utility from the incomes of others and from giving gifts."[4]

But the implication that a market failure problem exists only if the income distribution itself enters individual functions is erroneous. This very same type of public good problem arises if utility derives from the incomes of others. If A's income level Y_A affects

* The authors are indebted to the National Science Foundation for its support, given under Research Grant GS-2805 to the Urban Institute and Research Grant GS-2974 to Pennsylvania State University. Thanks for comments on earlier drafts are due, without implication, to David Harrison, Harvey Galper, John Johnston, George Peterson, A. Mitchell Polinsky, and Walter Williams.

1. Lester C. Thurow, "The Income Distribution as a Pure Public Good," this *Journal*, LXXXV (May 1971), 327–36.
2. See Harold M. Hochman and James D. Rodgers, "Pareto Optimal Redistribution," *American Economic Review*, LIX (Sept. 1969), 542–57.
3. Thurow, *op. cit.*, p. 328.
4. *Ibid.*, p. 329, note 4.

other persons — or, for that matter, just one other person — Y_A is a pure public good, meeting the conditions of nonexcludability and nonrivalry and producing market failure in a group of sufficient size. However, if *all* individuals derive utility *only* from the *act of giving* per se and derive no utility from the *effects of their gifts*, there are no externalities, and there is no market failure. A giver's welfare depends only on his own gift, not on the recipient's income or behavior as affected by this giver's transfer or the transfers of others. The correct distinction is not, as Thurow suggests, situation (3) as opposed to situations (1) and (2), but situation (2) as opposed to situations (1) and (3).

Moreover, it is doubtful whether anything is gained by including a distributional index in individual utility functions rather than maintaining the more general externality formulation. If the nonpoor find such manifestations of poverty as crime, political instability, or dilapidated housing to be offensive, it may not be the distribution of income at all but, instead, particular consumption or production activities of the poor that enter (with negative partial derivatives) the utility functions of the nonpoor.[5] It would seem, therefore, that a generalized version of (1) is more useful than Thurow's construction, both in the positive sense of predicting the types of welfare programs the nonpoor prefer and in the normative sense of specifying the *form* of the transfers that are needed to attain Pareto optimality.[6] Moreover, a necessary condition for distributional preferences to be summarized in the manner Thurow suggests, is that interdependence must involve only the incomes of the poor and not their specific activities. It would seem, therefore, in view of the impossibility of uniquely summarizing the degree of inequality by a single number, that formulation (1) is preferable to (3). And certainly one would not want to use both (1) and (3) simultaneously; to include both interdependence arguments *and* a distributional index in the utility functions of the nonpoor is redundant, much as it would be to include both food *and* the nourishment it provides.

Thurow's suggestion that a distributional index might itself enter utility functions, *where there are no externalities*, poses another

5. This point has been stressed by James M. Buchanan, "What Kind of Redistribution Do We Want?" *Economica*, XXXV (May 1968), 185–90. To assert that redistribution is the Pareto-efficient response to such negative externalities implies that the nonpoor consider income transfers to be the least costly method (as opposed, e.g., to more stringent criminal penalties or higher police expenditures) of reducing such offensive activities by given amounts.
6. See James D. Rodgers, "Distributional Externalities and the Optimal Form of Income Transfers," *Public Finance Quarterly*, forthcoming.

THE INCOME DISTRIBUTION: COMMENT

problem. To argue as he does that individuals engaging in redistribution are merely exercising an "aesthetic taste for equality or inequality," and that their utility rises and falls with variations in this abstract measure X, is to ignore the motivational basis of such transfers. Preference for a particular distribution, it would seem, must derive from a preference for an environment with attributes that the individual thinks this particular distribution is best able to produce. One may, for example, prefer a more equal distribution because he considers it a precondition of effective equality of opportunity. But he can hardly hold such views if he is not concerned with the welfare (or the consumption or the production activities) of others. Thus, Thurow's distinction between distributional concerns deriving from externalities and from "an aesthetic taste for equality or inequality" is wholly artificial. A taste for equality is in itself evidence of externalities.[7] Moreover, it is immaterial to this point whether the externalities are generated by identifiable individuals, though this *is* relevant to the form of the desired transfers and the size and scope of the political community that effects them.

II

Additional difficulties plague Thurow's technical discussion of the attainment of a Pareto optimal distribution through income transfers. The principal difficulty is his numerical example, which implicitly grants credence to a counter-intuitive assumption.

Assume as does Thurow that attaining a Pareto optimal distribution requires equalizing transfers. Normally, one would expect a poor man to favor such transfers.[8] However, Thurow's Figure I,[9] which depicts his model in a community of three persons (B_1, B_2, B_3), implies the opposite — to induce the poor individual to accept a transfer he must be compensated. To go from the initial distribution X_0 to an optimum at X_1 (where the distribution is more equal)[1]

7. There is a case in which income distribution might enter a person's utility function even if there are no interpersonal externalities. The risk-averse individual may, for example, expect that he will some day be poor and to hedge may opt for a more equal distribution. But the problems of uncertainty, intertemporal distribution, and social rule making, which arise here, are not issues that Thurow addresses.

8. Indeed, even in the odd circumstance in which a poor person was averse to equalization, one would expect that the transfer received would more than offset the welfare loss he would suffer because of his taste for inequality. If he favors more equality, equalizing transfers would benefit him in both ways.

9. Thurow, *op. cit.*, p. 330.

1. The most natural inference from Thurow's numerical example is that $Y_1 > Y_2 > Y_3$ in the initial distribution. For other orderings, it is not at all ob-

both equalizing transfers *and* compensatory payments are needed. In Thurow's numerical example B_1 pays a tax of $500, B_2 pays a tax of $250 and receives a transfer of $400, and B_3 (by assumption, "a man with a relatively low income") receives a transfer of $200 and a compensatory payment of $150 (since his postulated taste is for inequality). Thus, on balance, B_1 gives up $500, with $150 of this amount going to B_2 and $350 going to B_3.

Other things equal, the idea that B_3 must be compensated to induce him to accept a transfer quite plainly implies that he has an aversion to income transfers and prefers his initial income. But, while B_3 and his peers might have a taste for inequality, it seems doubtful that this taste is so strong that they prefer to comprise the lower tail of the distribution themselves in order to satisfy it.[2]

The counter-intuitive nature of Thurow's example notwithstanding, assume for the moment that wealthier individuals favor more equality, while the poor prefer less. Thus, to satisfy the wealthy, there must be a net transfer to the poor. But, to convince B_3 to accept a transfer of $200, he must be given compensation (a bribe) of $150. Thus, once all is said and done, B_3 receives $350, not $200. If, however, he is averse to equalizing transfers more compensation is required for him to accept $350 than $200. Problems of realism aside, one wonders then about another issue, namely the determinacy of equilibrium in Thurow's example. If, to switch assumptions, B_3 feels that a redistribution of income in which he gains $350 at the expense of B_1 is desirable, it is very difficult to see what meaning, if any, there is in Thurow's assumption that B_3 objects to the new distribution and must be compensated to accept it.

III

A final comment is in order on Thurow's policy inference that "society must control the distribution of taxes and expenditures at

---

vious that the pattern of redistribution Thurow postulates in his numerical example would produce a movement *toward equality*. For example, one would expect his "perfect measure" X to move toward less equality if at X_0, $Y_3 > Y_2 > Y_1$, while the direction of movement would be uncertain (without knowing how X is to be computed) if at X_0, $Y_2 > Y_1 > Y_3$.

2. If it is assumed that the nonpoor wish more equality and it is maintained at the same time that the poor must be compensated for any movement toward equality, one can imagine a situation in which the poor, though recipients of transfers, would be unwilling to accept them for lack of sufficient compensation! In the real world, as opposed to Thurow's construction, this would require (in an N-person example in which all who are poor receive transfers) that peer envy be stronger than the private desire for income and wealth, for at least some recipients. There is no indication that this is what Thurow had in mind.

the local level," [3] since everyone must live in a society with one income distribution. Only in this concluding remark does Thurow indicate that his *implicit* frame of reference is national government, and thus the nation-wide distribution of income is the empirical analogue of his "distribution as a public good." However, as he recognizes in his earlier reference to the "neighborhood" distribution,[4] individuals in consuming public goods may live in many "neighborhoods" at once, and distributional externalities that enter individual utility functions may be "local" rather than national. Thus, despite Thurow's reservations about decentralization,[5] distributional considerations are a matter of local as well as national interest; and centralization, though it focuses discussion on "one distribution," is no more the touchstone of efficiency than polycentrism. Clearly, the problems of distributional efficiency in a federal system, as raised by Thurow in his concluding remarks, are far too complex — and far too important — for dispatch in a casual paragraph.

THE URBAN INSTITUTE
PENNSYLVANIA STATE UNIVERSITY
VIRGINIA POLYTECHNIC INSTITUTE AND STATE UNIVERSITY

3. Thurow, *op. cit.*, p. 335.
4. *Ibid.*, p. 328.
5. *Ibid.*, p. 335.

[6]

Journal of Economic Behavior and Organization 6 (1985) 161–176. North-Holland

CONCEPTS OF EXTENDED PREFERENCE

Harold M. HOCHMAN*

Baruch College of The City University of New York, New York, NY 10010, USA

Shmuel NITZAN*

Bar-Ilan University, Ramat-Gan, Israel

Received September 1983, final version received November 1984

This paper remedies ambiguity in the discussion of interdependent preferences by developing a consistent set of distinctions, which span the full range of sympathetic and antipathetic interaction, for the two-person case without reactive behavior. It defines concepts such as benevolence, generosity, altruism, destructiveness, and willingness to begrudge transfers to others and indicates how their use can clarify the discussion of economic behavior. The definitions take account of preferences (indicated by rates of substitution) and prices (indicated by rates of exchange) at critical income allocations.

> 'If charity cost no money and benevolence caused no heartache, the world would be full of philanthropists.'
>
> *Yiddish proverb*

1. Introduction

If people did not act as if they care about others, our everyday language could accomodate neither love nor hate, nor simpler concepts of extended preference. Nonetheless, economics contains no systematic characterization of utility interactions, linking non-selfish behavior to ordinary language, or to simple representations of opportunity and choice.

This paper, which examines the full range of extended preference — sympathetic (when interdependence is positive) and antipathetic (when negative) — attempts to bring order to economic discussion of this subject. To keep to basics, it focuses on the simplest distributional problem, allocation of a fixed endowment of a single good, income, between a representative individual and one other person. But even this primitive

*We thank the Lady Davis Fellowship Trust of the Hebrew University for financial support, the Maurice Falk Institute for Economic Research in Israel for hospitality, Ephraim Kleiman and Edward Saueracker for a number of insights, and Susanne Freund for editorial assistance.

framework can span the range of human character, from Albert Schweitzer to Nero Caesar.[1]

To be sure, economics has not ignored this class of external effects. 'Hume, Smith Edgeworth and Marshall' [see Collard (1978, p. 3)] and, more recently, such major theorists as Boulding (1962) and Vickrey (1962) have treated utility interdependence as a serious concern. Until the late 1960's, however, the main body of economics, sustaining a narrow interpretation of 'rational' behavior, left this discussion, after fragments of insight, to the tender, if often ineffectual, ministrations of other disciplines.

A glance at recent journals will convince anyone that this is no longer so. Economists now concern themselves with the full range of social interaction, from empathy to alienation and generosity to niggardliness [see Becker (1974, and Scott (1972)]. Utility interdependence is integral to models of income transfers, through private philanthropy and public redistribution [see, among others, Hochman and Rodgers (1969 and 1977b)]. It is central, as well, to economic discussion of the donation of human blood [Culyer (1977)] and assistance to victims of natural disaster [De Alessi (1975)].

While such contributions add realism to our interpretation of human behavior,[2] their treatment of utility interactions is neither complete nor consistent, even for a two-person world without reactive behavior. Some of the resulting difficulties are semantic. However, semantic and substantive confusion go hand in hand, all the more when the subject violates disciplinary boundaries. Especially in fields like ethics and welfare economics, the meaning of concepts is fundamental; ambiguous language not only makes communication more difficult but results in muddled analysis.

Ostensible antonyms need not be opposites. 'Benevolence', which dictionaries define as 'disposition to do good', hardly seems the opposite of 'malevolence', which connotes 'intense, often vicious ill-will, spite or hatred'. Conversely, terms as complex as altruism and envy should not be used, without qualification, to describe positive and negative utility interactions. It is also improper to treat altruism as a synonym for 'generosity' (or 'giving') or to refer to giving as altruistic without considering its price and the relative endowments of donor and recipient [see, e.g., Becker (1974)]. On the other hand, altruism is not an 'empty economic box,' simply because self-interest

---

[1]We do not even try to come to grips with the relationship between utility interdependence and ethics, or the subsidiary subject of 'paternalistic' or 'meddlesome' preferences [see Archibald and Donaldson (1976)]. Discussion of paternalism requires at least two distinct goods. We also eschew discussion of interactive behavior (which could be examined with game-theoretic tools) and the existence of equilibrium, a problem when many persons act out interdependent preferences in a political environment [see Arrow (1979)].

[2]If preferences are sympathetic, for example, a concern with fairness need not require ignorance of personal identity [as in Rawls (1975)] and optimal patterns of redistribution need not be derived from dubious Benthamite propositions which require utilities be interpersonally comparable.

narrowly construed, cannot accommodate unilateral transfers [as argued in Hochman and Rodgers (1977a)].

Antipathetic interaction is less frequently discussed in the economic literature, perhaps because it cannot [except in an aberrant multi-person example, like Brennan's (1973)] produce Pareto optimal income transfers and perhaps because economists, in subconscious escapism, prefer not to enshrine the seamier side of human behavior in their models. Usually antipathy is loosely specified. No real distinction is made between petty spitefulness or resentment, as between siblings, and destructive behavior; and words like 'malice' and 'envy',[3] as well as malevolence, are used as if they were interchangeable. [See Brennan (1973).]

A firm grasp on everyday language can clear up much of this semantic confusion. In what follows, we suggest consistent distinctions, relating sympathy and antipathy, natural antonyms free of psychological nuance, to opportunities and constraints.

2. Basic structure

The economy distributes but one good, income x, between two individuals, a decision-maker or *reference individual* (designated by subscript 1) and a second individual (designated 2). $U_i(x_1, x_2)$, a continuously differentiable function, represents the preferences of the reference individual. Its first order partial derivatives are $U_i(x_1, x_2) = \partial U(x_1, x_2)/\partial x_i$, where $i = 1, 2$. It is assumed throughout that individual utility is monotonic increasing in own-income $[U_1(x_1, x_2) > 0]$ and quasi-concave.

The initial allocation is denoted by $(\bar{x}_1, \bar{x}_2)$ and the final allocation, which the reference individual retains for own-consumption, by (x_1, x_2). Each individual can spend his endowment on own-consumption; dispose of it at no cost; or exchange x_1 for x_2 at a rate $r(x_1, x_2)$, r for short. In a *neutral* environment r is unity; the individual can trade x_1 for x_2 one-for-one, though whether he does so is a matter of preference. If transactions costs impede transfers or a central authority imposes a tax to discourage transfers, $r < 1$. If the government encourages transfers, as it does in the United States through the tax-deductibility of charitable contributions, $r > 1$, and varies with the marginal tax rate.

We now turn to classification of individuals with interdependent utilities. Obviously, for *homo economicus*, guided by narrow self-interest, $U_2(x_1, x_2) = 0$ at any allocation (x_1, x_2). Such an individual can properly be called *selfish*. The terminology to be suggested for interdependent utilities presupposes, for the relevant allocations, $U_2(x_1, x_2) \neq 0$.

---

[3]Note that 'envy', as defined [as in Varian (1976)] as a condition in which one agent prefers the allocation of another, need not imply utility interdependence. If, however, envy is interpreted as resentful awareness of an advantage enjoyed by another, it can (but need not) be interpreted as one type of antipathy.

3. Sympathy

Individual 1 is defined as sympathetic at (x_1, x_2) if $U_2(x_1, x_2) > 0$, to wit, if he considers the income of individual 2 a good. Thus, if sympathetic, his in-difference curves between x_1 and x_2 have the usual form and are not vertical (see fig. 1).[4] He is *benevolent* at (x_1, x_2) if $0 < [U_1(x_1, x_2)]/[U_2(x_1, x_2] = \mathrm{MRS}$ $(x_1, x_2) < 1$, i.e., if his marginal rate of substitution (MRS) between own-income and individual 2's income at (x_1, x_2) is less than unity. If he finds himself at (x_1, x_2) under neutral terms of trade — if it costs him a dollar to transfer a dollar — he allocates the marginal dollar to a transfer (to individual 2) and not to own-consumption. Since benevolence is defined at a particular allocation (x_1, x_2), it is a local characteristic of preference.

In exploring the effects of interdependent preferences on behavior, a natural starting point is the initial income allocation $(\bar{x}_1, \bar{x}_2)$. If benevolent at

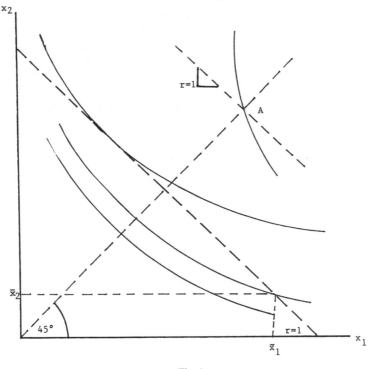

Fig. 1

[4]Whether a sympathetic (as opposed to selfish) person, acting on extended self-interest, can be called an egoist depends on how we choose to define egoism. What matters is whether *egoism* is equated with *egotism*, or self-interest (narrow or extended) is distinguished from abstract or ethical preference, in which probabilistic identity eliminates the distinction between self and other.

$(\bar{x}_1, \bar{x}_2)$, the individual can be called *generous*. Generosity, therefore, implies active or 'effective' benevolence. With $r = 1$, a generous individual, with no special inducement, gives away part of his income, but whether he will actually transfer income depends on r.[5]

This leads us to a definition of charitability. An individual can be considered *charitable* if $0 < \text{MRS}\ (\bar{x}_1, \bar{x}_2) < r$. If, at the initial allocation $(\bar{x}_1, \bar{x}_2)$, the MRS is less than the actual exchange rate, the reference individual will transfer some income to individual 2. Whether $\bar{x}_1 \gtrless \bar{x}_2$ is immaterial to this definition, though charity is more likely, obviously, if $\bar{x}_1 > \bar{x}_2$. Since r depends on the environment (including the tax code and transactions costs) the scope of charitable activity is shaped by the social fabric and political institutions.

Although economists often interpret altruism as a synonym for sympathy, it is a more obscure concept. To us, it seems appropriate to reserve the designation altruistic for a limited class of behavior, in which preferences display a bias toward others and transfers among equals occur in the face of an unfavorable exchange rate.[6] To illustrate, the benevolence and the charitability of a multi-millionaire who gives a (tax-deductible) dime to an orphan is beyond doubt. But is it really proper to describe such a donor as an altruist?[7] Now reverse the status of donor and recipient, and the point is clear.

Our distinction between altruists and non-altruists is based on local benevolence when the initial income is equally divided. An individual is an *altruist* if he is benevolent at $[1/2(\bar{x}_1 + \bar{x}_2), 1/2(\bar{x}_1 + \bar{x}_2)]$ on the 45° ray. If the two individuals start with identical incomes and $r = 1$, individual 1, if altruistic, will transfer some income. Because it does not make every donor an altruist, this interpretation of altruism does not trivialize the phenomenon it tries to explain.

To illustrate these concepts refer to fig. 1. The indifference curves indicate that the richer of the two individuals (the reference individual) is altruistic, as well as generous and charitable. While such other-oriented preferences are not the rule, examples of self-sacrifice come readily to mind — between parents and children, friends and lovers, battlefield comrades, and in such special circumstances as danger or natural disaster, complete strangers.[8]

Thus far our characterization of interdependent preferences has been keyed

[5]Culyer (1977) covers some of the ground of this section in an excellent paper, though one well-concealed from the profession-at-large. We acknowledge his recognition of the significance, for behavior based on utility interactions, of price as well as preference.

[6]Thus, whether altruism and self-interest are consistent is a red herring.

[7]Virginia Held, a philosopher, argues (1977) that an altruistic person is one who puts the net interests of others ahead of his own.

[8]Of course, application of our definition requires an 'appropriate' definition of 'income'. In sociobiology, for example, it may be appropriate to define income in terms of survival probabilities, or some measure that is a function of such probabilities and the stakes of the game, e.g., life and death [see Trivers (1971)].

to local benevolence at the initial income allocation and to r, which describes the environment. The next step is to extend these local concepts to larger subsets of the income space.

If an individual is benevolent at every (x_1, x_2) for which $x_1 = x_2$, he can be called a *global altruist*. Whenever incomes are equal, such an individual is other-oriented. An altruist with homothetic preferences is by implication a global altruist. (The right-hand indifference curve in fig. 1, which intersects the 45° line at A, indicates that the individual depicted is not a global altruist.) If an individual is benevolent at *every* (x_1, x_2), so that his MRS is always less than unity, he can be considered an *extreme altruist*. By implication, an extreme altruist in a neutral environment $(r=1)$ prefers a corner outcome; he transfers his entire income to individual 2. Only if $r < 1$ might we find an extreme altruist retaining some income for own-consumption (an interior solution). The limiting case of extreme altruism occurs when $MRS(x_1, x_2) = 0$ for any (x_1, x_2). The individual is infinitely altruistic, and his indifference map consists of a set of horizontal lines. Extreme and infinite altruism are obviously unlikely and represent a rare commitment, to be found, if at all, only among zealots, committed to an ideological or religious ideal that merges self-interest and ethical preference.[9]

Each of these concepts has a negative complement. A sympathetic individual can, of course, be non-benevolent at an allocation (x_1, x_2). This occurs when $MRS(x_1, x_2 \geq 1$. He can be non-generous if $MRS(\bar{x}_1, \bar{x}_2) \geq 1$ or non-charitable if $MRS(\bar{x}_1, \bar{x}_2) \geq r$. If $MRS[\bar{x}_1 + \bar{x}_2/2, \bar{x}_1 + \bar{x}_2/2] \geq 1$, the individual is *self-oriented*. If this condition holds at all income allocations along the 45° ray, he is globally self-oriented and quasi-concavity implies that he is not benevolent at any bundle (x_1, x_2) at which $x_1 < x_2$. Thus, for sympathetic individuals, self-orientation is the mirror image of altruism. If there is no bundle at which the individual is benevolent, he can be called *acquisitive*. If acquisitive in the limit, he is simply selfish, with $MRS(x_1, x_2) = \infty$ at all income allocations and vertical indifference curves.

Except in the limit cases, giving is a function of price. While an infinite altruist will always be charitable and a selfish person will never make a voluntary transfer, none of the other concepts has clearcut implications. Local and global sympathy, generosity, altruism, and even global or extreme altruism need not lead to charity. On the other hand, ungenerous, self-oriented, and even acquisitive individuals may be charitable if the price is right. Knowledge of initial conditions, $\bar{x}_1 \gtrless \bar{x}_2$, renders the outcome more determinate. In a neutral environment (if $r=1$) a relatively rich altruist $(\bar{x}_1 > \bar{x}_2)$ will always be generous and charitable; if $r < 1$, however, this need not be true. A relatively poor altruist, although charitable if r is sufficiently

---

[9]It is tempting to characterize the infinite altruist as an ascetic, who views self-denial as a good in and of itself. Ephraim Kleiman, however, has pointed out that a true ascetic believes that others would also be better off with less material wealth.

more than unity, need not be generous; but in a neutral environment a relatively poor $(\bar{x}_1 < \bar{x}_2)$ self-oriented individual will always be ungenerous and will never be charitable.

Charitable giving with identical preferences

Thus defined, sympathy is basic to public choice explanations of income transfers. While such transfers are likely to be private and voluntary in the small-number case, they are generally public with large numbers. If the demand for transfers cannot command a political majority, it becomes the domain of organized charity. [See Hochman and Rodgers (1977a and 1977b).] Such discussion of Pareto optimal income transfers presents a suitable vehicle for illustration.

Suppose, in a two-person community, identical preferences: $U^1(x_1, x_2) = U^2(x_2, x_1)$ for every income allocation (x_1, x_2). If positions were reversed, the two individuals would simply switch consumption bundles. Assume $r = 1$. Thus we have as neutral an environment as can be devised.

While the two individuals may have identical preferences, they may wish to transfer different amounts. If both are self-oriented and $\bar{x}_1 = \bar{x}_2$, neither will make a transfer. Should their initial allocations differ, however, individual 1, who is relatively rich, may make a voluntary transfer; but the other individual, who is relatively poor, will never do so.

Fig. 2 spells this out. Since neither individual can force the other to give up income, only the shaded area of the budget set is feasible. Individual 1's situation is depicted in fig. 2(a). The initial income allocation is $(\bar{x}_1, \bar{x}_2)$. Since his optimal allocation is (x_1^1, x_2^1), he is willing to make a transfer of $(\bar{x}_1 - x_1^1)$. In fig. 2(b), individual 2's situation, the axes are interchanged, but all else remains the same. Since the optimal allocation is $(\bar{x}_2, \bar{x}_1)$, individual 2 retains his initial endowment. Could he have forced a transfer from individual 1, however, he would have preferred (x_2^2, x_1^2). Thus, because incomes differ, individuals with the same benevolence patterns transfer different amounts, despite identical terms of trade.

The situation is essentially unaltered if we permit the rate of exchange between x_1 and x_2 to differ, as it does if charity is tax-deductible $(r > 1)$ or transactions costs differ between rich and poor $(r < 1)$. Here, though preferences are identical, the range of possible transfer patterns expands. If both agents are self-oriented, it is not only possible for the rich one to make a transfer while the poor one does not, but for the poor one to make the larger transfer. The simple observation that an individual contributes to charity tells us less about his character than we think.

4. Antipathy

While it may be a less appealing subject, there is a comfortable symmetry

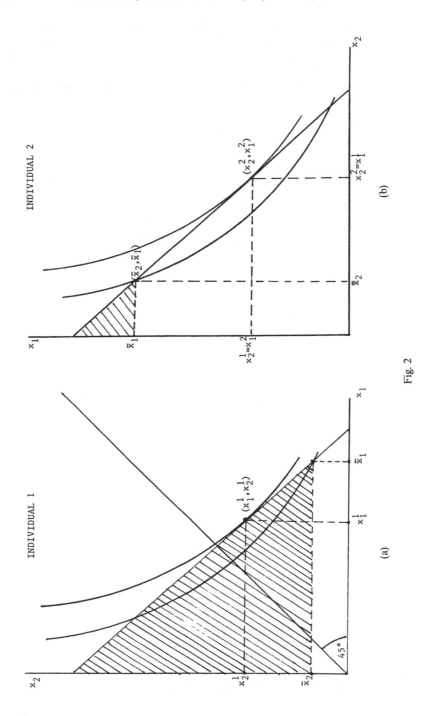

Fig. 2

about the concept of antipathy. An individual is antipathetic at (x_1, x_2) if $U_2(x_1, x_2) < 0$ — if, given (x_1, x_2), he considers the income of the other individual a 'bad'. Antipathy is therefore the natural counterpart of sympathy. A person who is *neither* sympathetic *nor* antipathetic is selfish. Local antipathy implies indifference curves with positive slopes. Again, if preferences are quasi-concave and the antipathy is universal, these indifference curves exhibit diminishing slope (the local measure of antipathy increases) as x_1 increases (see fig. 3).

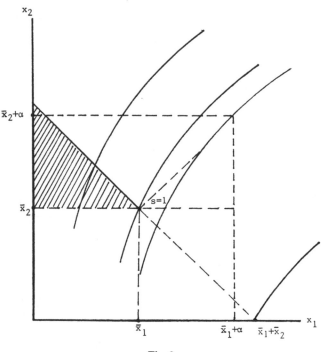

Fig. 3

A universally antipathetic individual is never benevolent and, in the two-person case, never transfers income voluntarily. With a sympathetic person transfers supply their own compensation; but an unwilling donor requires positive compensation for any improvement in the position of his fellow man. All preferred allocations are corner solutions on the x_1 axis. The reference individual in fig. 3 would be best off at $(\bar{x}_1 + \bar{x}_2, 0)$, if however, he cannot force negative transfers (reduce individual 2's income), his feasible set is the shaded triangle, and the prefers $(\bar{x}_1, \bar{x}_2)$.

Whether the slope of an indifference curve exceeds or falls short of unity is crucial to the characterization of antipathetic preference. An antipathetic individual is *not destructive* at (x_1, x_2) if $MRS(x_1, x_2) \leq -1$ and *destructive* if $-1 < MRS(x_1, x_2) < 0$. If destructive he prefers negative simultaneous transfers, reducing x_1 and x_2 by equal amounts, to the status quo.

Destructiveness is a local concept (the analog of benevolence) that refers to a specific allocation (x_1, x_2). The concept that demarcates destructiveness from nondestructiveness at $(\bar{x}_1, \bar{x}_2)$ is *willingness to begrudge equal transfers* (the negative counterpart of generosity). An individual who is not destructive will tolerate equal transfers and prefers simultaneous transfers, which increase x_1 and x_2 by the same amount, to the initial allocation.

Put differently, individual 1, if antipathetic, must be compensated to maintain his original level of utility if the other individual is given a dollar.[10] So long as he is not destructive, such compensation is between zero and $1. A person who is destructive at $(\bar{x}_1, \bar{x}_2)$ requires compensation in excess of $1.[11] The individual described in fig. 3 is willing to begrudge equal transfers. He prefers, e.g., the allocation $(\bar{x}_1 + \alpha, \bar{x}_2 + \alpha)$ to $(\bar{x}_1, \bar{x}_2)$.

The actual response of an antipathetic individual to simultaneous positive transfers hinges on the relationship between $MRS(x_1, x_2)$ and the transfer rate, s^{12} — the ratio of third-party transfers to individuals 1 and 2. The reference individual is *willing to begrudge* increments in both x_1 and x_2 whenever $MRS(\bar{x}_1, \bar{x}_2) \geq s > 0$. Thus, willingness to begrudge transfers is the counterpart of charitability. In fig. 3 the antipathetic individual happens to face a positive transfer rate of unity $(s = 1)$ and is clearly willing to begrudge the indicated transfer. While he will not give up $1 to forestall it, he will pay something — indicated by the slope of his indifference curve at $(\bar{x}_1, \bar{x}_2)$.

Extending the test of local destructiveness to all income allocations, an individual is *extremely destructive* if there is *no* (x_1, x_2) at which he tolerates equal transfers. Since he prefers the origin (at which he receives nothing) to the initial allocation, a relatively poor individual who is extremely destructive is self-destructive. In the limit case, *all-consuming destructiveness*, no amount of compensation can induce an antipathetic person to begrudge a transfer, however small. $MRS(x_1, x_2) = 0$ for every (x_1, x_2); the indifference map consists of a set of parallel horizontal lines with the critical allocations along the x_2 axis. The individual will fiddle, like Nero, while Rome burns. In the

---

[10]Of course, the source of this transfer must be a third party (the state) since individual 1, if antipathetic, will not make the transfer voluntarily.

[11]This situation describes the two donors in Brennan's (1973) model of Pareto-desirable redistribution with malice and envy. Brennan transforms the income reductions into positive transfers to a third party, to whom the donors are indifferent. Our only quarrel with Brennan is terminological, because he contrasts altruism with malice and envy as if they were operationally identical antonyms of altruism.

[12]Consider two antagonistic social groups. Whether one will tolerate community programs that benefit the other hinges on its willingness to begrudge transfers. Thus, the concept applies to such diverse topics as revolution and vote-trading on issues with distributional side-effects.

other limit case, in which $MRS(x_1, x_2) = \infty$ for a non-destructive individual, we return to the selfish stereotype.[13]

Compensation plays the same role with antipathy as price with sympathy. With sufficient compensation, agents may cooperate, despite antagonism. Political alliances (e.g., between the western allies and the Soviet Union during World War II and among rival politicians of the same political party) are clear examples. These are to be contrasted with the self-sacrificing actions of hunger strikers and kamikaze pilots, or for that matter, political assassins, whose acts often lead to their own destruction.

4.1. Harmony and conflict in marriage

Concepts of antipathy are ideally suited to the discussion of coalitions among conflicting parties. Conflict is inevitable with antipathy because compensation is impossible in zero-sum games — in which a 'cake' of fixed size in distributed. With a variable cake, however, cooperation can be consistent with antipathy; so long as total income is increasing, simultaneous transfers to all parties are feasible. But antipathetic individuals can also benefit when the cake becomes smaller — if they are destructive.

It is less obvious that global sympathy can also accommodate a wide range of conflict. When all parties are acquisitive (i.e., never benevolent) conflict is likely. If the exchange rate is biased against transfers, however, altruists may also conflict, provided the terms of trade dominate their preferences.

Marriage, the most venerable of social institutions, illustrates this line of reasoning. A happy marriage not only requires sympathy, but benevolence and generosity, and is improved by altruism.[14] But a failed marriage need not imply antipathy. Though our wives may swear that the example is apocryphal, there are 'amicable' divorces. Even if antipathetic, some divorced couples remain cordial, out of concern for their children or a mutual desire to limit the costs of litigation — provided they are not destructive. If, however, bitterness dominates and husband and wife are unwilling to begrudge each other the spoils of marital war, the preference direction may be negative. If at least one of the antagonists is destructive, only the lawyers are likely to benefit.

4.2. 'Taking' in a model with extended preference

In giving to charity the individual allocates own-income. But he can also

---

[13]Nothing is gained by distinguishing between destructiveness along the 45° ray and destructiveness at other income allocations, as in formulating the concept of altruism.

[14]The O. Henry story, 'The Gift of the Magi', presents a poignant illustration of reciprocal altruism. The husband sacrifices his watch and the wife her hair — their most precious possessions — to buy Christmas gifts for each other — combs for her hair and a golden chain for his watch.

allocate effort or income to 'taking', to increase own-consumption, by legal or illegal means, at the expense of others. While antipathy may enter the picture, it need not.[15]

The economic model of crime and punishment [Becker (1968)] interprets illegal activities as consumer decisions about occupational choice, motivated by expected utility maximization, within a portfolio model of time allocation. All benefits and costs are monetary, including the 'wealth equivalents' of psychic gains and losses. Typically, sympathy and antipathy are ignored. We simplify this by assuming risk-neutrality and incorporating but two arguments, x_1 and x_2, in the utility function of the reference individual. Initial income; the return to illegal activity, if successful; the probability that it will be unsuccessful; and the monetary penalty if it is unsuccessful determine the opportunity set — the technology of crime.

A selfish individual will engage in taking if it 'pays': if its expected (monetary) return exceeds its expected (monetary) cost. While this may describe those who engage in crime for profit, it ignores the fact that antipathetic individuals may turn to taking even if they do not expect it to pay. In general, antipathetic persons are more likely to commit crimes, at given levels of risk aversion, than selfish ones, whose preferences are neutral.[16]

We turn now to a series of illustrations. Fig. 4 describes the opportunity set. The reference individual, by giving, can move from A to any point in the triangle ARM. Taking permits him to move toward the horizontal axis as well. If taking is costless, the transformation curve has a constant slope of -1; he can move from $(\bar{x}_1, \bar{x}_2)$ to a point like I; if, however, victims retaliate or the community protects itself, AL is not feasible. The outcome may lie within $RALO$; a positive price must be paid for controlling part of the other individual's income.

If, starting at A, the reference individual, investing BA, enters an illegal activity, three outcomes are possible. First, because the expected benefit of BC is less than the expected cost of BA, taking may not pay. In the final reckoning BC is subtracted from individual 2's income and added to individual 1's ($BC = CD$), leaving him at D, which had not been in his feasible set at the outset. Second, an investment of BA may be equal to the expected benefit, $BE = BA = EF$, enabling him to move from A to F. Third, the net return may be positive, reducing individual 2's income by $BG > BA$ and transferring $BG = GH$ to individual 1 (bringing him to a point like H in triangle AKL). If taking always pays, the set of feasible income allocations

---

[15]Consider, in this light, the redistributive activities of Robin Hood, which did not reflect antipathy, even to the victims.

[16]Preferences of individuals engaging in illegal activities may be fundamental to determining strategies of deterrence. Extreme forms of antipathy call for a different social response from the theft of food by the mother of ten starving children.

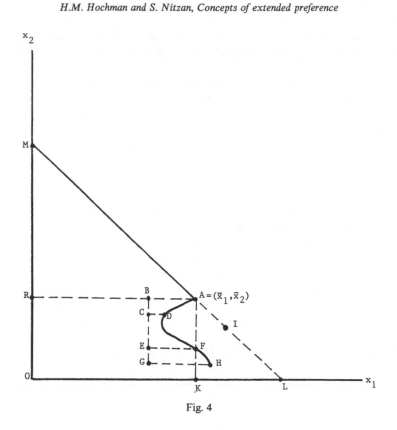

Fig. 4

consists of the line segment MA and a curve that lies within AKL; but if illegal activities are unsuccessful, MA and a curve contained within the rectangle $ORAK$ define the set of feasible and efficient allocations.

This characterization of taking can now be employed, in the panels of fig. 5, to illustrate our distinctions among concepts of extended preference:

Fig. 5(a): Only if ungenerous will a sympathetic individual be involved in taking. If generous at $(\bar{x}_1, \bar{x}_2)$ he prefers, by definition, to make a transfer; but if he is ungenerous [prefers (x_1^1, x_2^1)] and, therefore, engaged in taking, a sufficient transfer from a third party, shifting the budget line to the right, can alter his behavior. If the transfer is large enough, taking may cease, and the individual may become generous.

Fig. 5(b): If crime pays a sympathetic individual can be indifferent between giving and taking [between (x_1^1, x_2^1) and (x_1'', x_2'')]. It may be easier to deter taking by making it cheaper to transfer income (shifting out the upper segment of the opportunity locus) than by altering the price of illegal activity (shifting in the lower segment, by making punishments more severe or spending more on law and order). The government, through a marginal

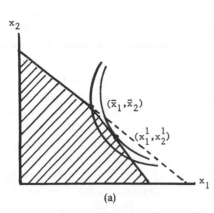

(a)

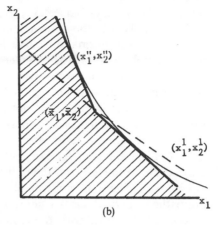

(b)

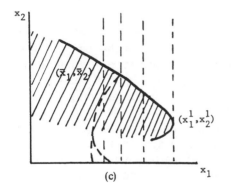

(c)

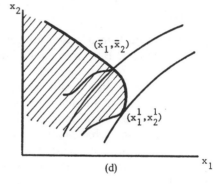

(d)

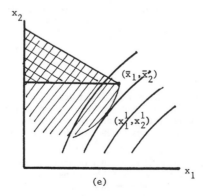

(e)

Fig. 5

increase in the incentive to make transfers, may be able to move the reference individual from (x_1^1, x_2^1) to (x_1'', x_2'').

Fig. 5(c): This is the standard case in the economic theory of crime. So long as the transformation curve is negatively sloped, a selfish individual, with vertical lines for his indifference map, engages in taking. The one exception occurs when x_2 is exhausted before taking becomes profitable (the transformation curve intersects the horizontal axis to the left of $\bar{x}_1$).

Fig. 5(d): Even if crime does not pay, an antipathetic person may engage in taking; however, deterrence is possible. Here, preferences are given, but law enforcement varies. The unconstrained equilibrium is (x_1^1, x_2^1), with taking of $(x_1^1 - \bar{x}_1)$. But enforcement can shift the right-hand portion of the transformation curve to the left, and the optimum to $(\bar{x}_1, \bar{x}_2)$, the initial endowment.

Fig. 5(e): There is no iron-clad guarantee against illegal activities by antipathetic individuals — short of absolute deterrence, under which the feasible set coincides with the cross-hatched triangle. But even this may not be enough to neutralize all-consuming destructiveness.

5. Summary

The classification of extended preferences suggested in this paper is by no means complete. But for economic behavior, in which maximization of own-utility is the central behavioral assumption and the subject of analysis is the representation of desire, not motivation,[17] it covers the full range of utility interactions, from infinite altruism to all-consuming destructiveness. By providing precise definitions, consistent with ordinary English usage, to terms like benevolence, charitability, willingness to begrudge transfers, and destructiveness, this classification seems a proper starting point in resolving our muddled attempt to build utility interdependence into models of human interaction.

> 'The question is,' said Alice, 'whether you can make words mean so many different things.' 'When I use the words,' Humpty Dumpty said in rather a scornful tone, 'it means just what I choose it to mean — neither more nor less.'
>
> Lewis Carroll, *Through the Looking Glass*

References

Archibald, G.C. and David Donaldson, 1976, Non-paternalism and the basic theorems of welfare economics, Canadian Journal of Economics/Revue Canadienne d'Economique 9, 492–507.
Arrow, Kenneth J., 1979, Optimal and voluntary income distribution, Technical report no. 288 (Institute for Mathematical Studies in the Social Sciences, Stanford University, Stanford, CA).

[17]This view of consumer theory is as old as modern economic analysis. Irving Fisher argued in his '*Mathematical Investigations,*' that 'the plane of contact between psychology and economics is *desire* ... whether the necessary antecedent of desire is 'pleasure' or whether independently of pleasure it may sometimes be 'duty' or 'fear' concerns a phenomenon in the second remove from the economic act of choice and is completely within the realm of psychology.'

Becker, Gary S., 1968, Crime and punishment: An economic approach, Journal of Political Economy 76, 169–217.

Becker, Gary S., 1974, A theory of social interactions, Journal of Political Economy 82, 1063–1093.

Boulding, Kenneth E., 1962, Notes on a theory of philanthropy, in: Frank G. Dickinson, ed., Philanthropy and public policy (National Bureau of Economic Research, New York).

Brennan, Geoffrey, 1973, Pareto desirable redistribution: The case of malice and envy, Journal of Public Economics 2, 173–183.

Collard, David, 1978, Altruism and economy: A study in non-selfish economics (Martin Robertson, Oxford).

Culyer, Anthony J., 1977, Quids without quos — a praxeological approach (Institute for Economic Affairs, London).

De Alessi, Louis, 1975, Towards an analysis of postdisaster cooperation, American Economic Review 65, 127–138.

Fisher, Irving, 1925, Mathematical investigations in the theory of value and prices (Yale University Press, New Haven, CT).

Held, Virginia, 1977, Rationality and reasonable cooperation, Social Research 44, 708–744.

Hochman, Harold M. and James D. Rodgers, 1969, Pareto optimal redistribution, American Economic Review 59, 542–557.

Hochman, Harold M. and James D. Rodgers, 1977a, The simple politics of distributional preference, in: F. Thomas Juster, ed., The distribution of economic well-being, National Bureau of Economic Research: Studies in Income and Wealth no. 41 (Ballinger, Cambridge, MA) 770107.

Hochman, Harold M. and James D. Rodgers, 1977b, The optimal tax treatment of charitable contributions, National Tax Journal 30, 1–18.

Rawls, John, 1975, A theory of justice (The Belknap Press of Harvard University Press, Cambridge, MA).

Scott, Robert Haney, 1972, Avarice, altruism and second party preferences, Quarterly Journal Of Economics 86, 1–24.

Trivers, R.L., 1971, The evolution of reciprocal altruism, Quarterly Review of Biology 46, 35–57.

Varian, Hal R., 1976, Two problems in the theory of fairness, Journal of Public Economics 5, 249–260.

Vickrey, William, 1962, One economist's view of philanthropy, in: Frank G. Dickinson, ed., Philanthropy and public policy (National Bureau of Economic Research, New York).

C

Empirical Articles

Harold M. Hochman and
James D. Rodgers:
**Utility Interdependence and
Income Transfers through Charity**

Introduction

Recent years have witnessed a heightened concern with the problem of poverty, as evidenced by a growing literature in the social sciences,[1] culminating in the proposed Family Assistance Program and the work of the President's Commission on Income Maintenance, particularly its negative income tax proposal.[2] This literature has focused on specific proposals for adjusting the size distribution of income. Accordingly, the lion's share of the attention has been devoted to measuring the incidence of poverty, analyzing the incentive effects of various transfer schemes, and estimating the number of families that would be raised above the "poverty line" by changes in existing income maintenance programs.

Still, some of the most important issues, positive *and* normative, associated with income transfers have received little attention. At the conceptual level little has been done to rationalize the increased interest in income transfers and welfare programs save, conventionally, by reference to overt value judgments that equate reductions in income inequality with "social justice." Distribution has been interpreted as a matter of equity and has been divorced from the Paretian criterion of economic efficiency, in terms of which economists judge the allocation of resources.[3] Although this is due to

1. A sample of useful recent works dealing with poverty and income maintenance includes O. Eckstein, ed., *The Economics of Income Maintenance Programs* (Washington, D.C.: The Brookings Institution, 1967); C. Green, *Negative Taxes and the Poverty Problem* (Washington, D.C.: The Brookings Institution, 1967); and C. Wilcox, *Toward Social Welfare* (Homewood, Ill.: Richard D. Irwin, 1969).

2. The President's Commission on Income Maintenance Programs, *Poverty Amid Plenty: The American Paradox* (Washington, D.C.: U.S. Government Printing Office, 1969).

3. A typical example of the prevailing view is that "judgment on questions of income redistribution lies beyond the purview of economic analysis. By wide acceptance, economic theory plays a subordinate role in matters of this kind: one is confined to questions of ways and means and to pointing out unintended effects of a proposed measure." (D. Berry, "Modern Welfare Analysis and the Form of Income Redistribution," in *Income Redistribution and Social Policy*, ed. A. T. Peacock [Oxford: Alden Press, 1954], p. 41.)

economists' agnosticism with respect to questions of distribution, it can be shown that this, in part at least, derives from an inadequate model of individual choice and an incomplete conception of what constitutes rational behavior.

The fact is that our profession lacks a theory that can cope with distributional issues, at either the normative or the positive level. It has neither a normative theory that can be used in guiding policy, indicating *how much redistribution ought to be brought about* through income transfer programs, nor a positive theory explaining *why the observed amount of redistribution does in fact occur.* Further, we have only recently begun to develop effective methods of determining empirically how much redistribution actually does occur through fiscal activities,[4] and no good estimates of the redistributive effects of private interpersonal transfers are even available.

This paper, by relaxing a common assumption, will fill part of this lacuna. Instead of viewing distributional questions in the traditional formulation of rational behavior, in which individuals relate to each other *only* through market transactions, we assume "benevolent and Pareto-relevant interdependence"[5] among their utility functions, so that economic efficiency requires income transfers.[6]

As an initial attempt to verify this model, which we developed in our earlier paper, we try to ascertain whether private gifts and contributions are correlated with the dispersion of the community's income distribution and other socioeconomic variables, as they should if they are motivated by utility interdependence. At the positive level this approach can improve our understanding of the logic of income transfers. At the normative level, it is, to use Harvey Leibenstein's phrasing, a step toward "the establishment of

---

4. See W. I. Gillespie, "Effect of Public Expenditure on the Distribution of Income," *Essays in Fiscal Federalism* (Washington, D.C.: The Brookings Institution, 1965), pp. 122–86; and *Tax Burdens and Benefits of Government Expenditures by Income Class, 1961 and 1965* (New York: Tax Foundation, 1967). For a criticism of these studies see H. Aaron and M. C. McGuire, "Benefits and Burdens of Government Expenditures," *Econometrica* (in press).

5. "Benevolent interdependence" simply refers to the situation in which one person receives satisfaction from increments in the welfare or income of other persons. Whether this results from altruism, from a distaste for the manifestations of poverty, or from fear of antisocial behavior of the poor makes no difference in our analysis of transfers. See our earlier paper, "Pareto-Optimal Redistribution," *American Economic Review 59* (September 1969): 542–47. Another, more rigorous treatment of this subject is G. Becker, "A Theory of Social Interactions" (Chicago, September 1969).

6. Milton Friedman, who put forward the basis elements of this argument in *Capitalism and Freedom* (Chicago: University of Chicago Press, 1962), argued that transfers occur because of altruistic interdependence among individual utility functions. However, Friedman did not develop this point, and neither its welfare implications nor the possibility of explaining actual transfers in terms of interdependence had been explored before the recent efforts we have mentioned.

welfare economics on an empirical basis."[7] Appropriately extended, our analysis of utility interdependence may well suggest some norms or guidelines for policy in the distributional area.[8]

Interdependent Preferences and Consumer Choice

The thrust of our argument is that charity, as a vehicle for income transfers, indicates utility interdependence, which gives rise to individual dissatisfaction with the initial size distribution of income. The notion that every individual may find *some* income distributions, including the initial or pretransfer distribution to be unacceptable is intriguing, for it opens the way to use of the Pareto criterion in discussing distributional questions, and it therefore challenges the neoclassic doctrine.[9]

In our paper "Pareto-Optimal Redistribution"[10] we examined the normative implications of benevolent utility interdependence, first in a two-person model and then for the N-person case. Its analysis assumed that an individual's desire to make an income transfer (in the two-person case) is a matter of his preferences and the initial difference between his market-determined income and the other person's. It also assumed that preferred or Pareto-optimal transfers reduce income inequality – that is, that no individual wishes to make a transfer to someone with a higher initial income. Construing the N-person case as a simple aggregation of pairwise outcomes, an individual's "propensity to transfer" or "rate of benevolence" (with respect to own-income) in this model turns out to be a matter of his income or transfer elasticity[11] and his position in the distribution of income (which determines how many individuals he will make transfers to and how many

---

7. H. Leibenstein, "Long-Run Welfare Criteria," in *The Public Economy of Urban Communities*, ed. Julius Margolis (Washington, D.C.: Resources for the Future, 1965), p. 41.

8. However, a word of caution is in order. Although our model may suggest that utility interdependence makes some distributions inefficient, there remains a residual set of income distributions, all of which are Pareto optimal among which a society cannot choose without stronger ethical judgments than those implicit in the Pareto criterion.

9. For a clear statement of the traditional view, which sharply separates allocation (efficiency) and distribution (equity) questions, see R. A. Musgrave, *The Theory of Public Finance* (New York: McGraw-Hill Book Co., 1959), chap. 1.

10. Hochman and Rodgers, "Pareto-Optimal Redistribution." The simplifying assumptions of our model of Pareto-optimal redistribution are spelled out in this paper and clarified further in Hochman and Rodgers, "Pareto-Optimal Redistribution: A Reply," *American Economic Review* 60 (December 1970): 997–1002.

11. "Transfer elasticity" is analogous to *income elasticity* but differs because our model of Pareto-optimal redistribution treats the initial income differential as the critical independent variable in the two-person case. See Hochman and Rodgers, "Pareto-Optimal Redistribution," p. 547.

he will receive transfers from in the N-person situation). This in turn implies, for reasons to be expanded later, that the total volume of Pareto-optimal transfers in any community should vary with its mean income and the dispersion of its income distribution.

In "Pareto-Optimal Redistribution," we assumed that the fiscal structure should be the mechanism of redistribution, which we measured as net fiscal incidence, defined in terms of fiscal residuals.[12] The existence of nonzero fiscal residuals can be interpreted as necessary (though not sufficient) evidence of utility interdependence. However, this procedure has one major defect. It assumes that fiscal outcomes, which are generated through coercive means, accurately reflect individual preferences – in this instance, individual tastes for the consumption of others, at the cost of own-consumption and own-accumulation. Although one would predict some rough correspondence between tastes and government activities, redistribution effected by government is the outcome of a complex set of influences, originating in the past as well as in the present. This paper, which tries to test the empirical validity of our utility interdependence model, focuses on individual charity, which, though by no means completely free of coercion (in terms of social pressure to contribute) more closely approximates voluntary behavior.[13] The virtue of considering income transfers through charity, for present purposes, is that they are *not* channeled through the fiscal process and are therefore relatively more suitable for testing the implications of our utility interdependence model.[14]

Let us now consider momentarily the relevance and the deficiencies of a "charitable contributions" variable in indicating and measuring the extent to which private behavior reveals Pareto-relevant utility interdependence. Although all income transfers by definition produce income redistribution, not all the redistributive effects reduce income inequality. Similarly, not all charitable contributions result in income transfers. Some expenditures, nominally contributions, are simply private purchases of collective services. This may be true, for example, of many, perhaps most, religious contributions; "indulgences," to cite an extreme example, involved the purchase of

---

12. The fiscal residual for any income level is the difference between benefits and tax burdens imputed to the average individual with that income.

13. Note that the household itself is a logical place to look in studying utility interdependence, because in its internal behavior it is to a considerable extent a transfer economy. Although we do not develop this point, it does suggest the economist's need for useful sociological data.

14. There is another reason why it is preferable to focus on voluntary transfers. If one's ultimate concern is with devising norms for distribution policy based on individual preferences, it may be methodologically invalid to use observed fiscal incidence to infer norms for establishing the desired pattern of fiscal incidence. This point ought not to be stretched too far, however. Methodologically it may be quite acceptable to use preferences revealed in the fiscal structures of one jurisdictional level or unit of government in deciding on the distribution policy or incidence pattern that is appropriate for another unit or level of government.

a private good, "salvation." However, all charitable contributions, whether or not income transfers are the intended effect and whether or not they are equalizing, result in an improvement in the contributor's welfare. If this were not so, such contributions would not occur, because in a legal sense they are voluntary.

In the model we discussed the income transfers required by utility interdependence are equalizing. Moreover, they can be brought about, in principle if not in fact, through either private or public action. If the model is at all accurate in its representation of individual preferences, the amount of distribution-equalizing income transfers in any political community varies directly with the generosity of its members in contributing to charity – even though charity is surely an imperfect measure of such transfers. Thus, for the initial test of the utility interdependence formulation, to be described here, we shall simply postulate that charitable contributions, a variable for which measurements are available, are a satisfactory proxy for private equalizing income transfers.

This is not to imply that a charity variable is free from ambiguity. Voluntarism, except in such special cases as the purchase of CARE packages, is not absolute. Although failure to contribute does not invoke legal sanctions, "social pressure" is present and it can result in other, equally real sanctions: noncontributors can be ostracized.[15] Moreover, given the deductibility of charitable contributions for purposes of income tax computations, charity is not independent of the existing fiscal structure; the community at large shares as a partner in all itemized contributions, which have both price and income effects on consumer choice.[16]

The division of income transfers between public and private modes hinges in the first instance on the size of the group of individuals experiencing distributional externalities and on whether this group coincides with the dominant coalition of voters in the political community. Given existing political boundaries, transfers tend to be carried out by government. The problem is left for private charity when this condition is not met, either because the externalities are narrower than any existing political unit or because they cut across such units within which they cannot command effective majorities.[17]

---

15. For an analysis of the effect of social pressure on incentives to contribute to charity, see D. B. Johnson, "The Fundamental Economics of the Charity Market" (Ph.D. diss., University of Virginia, 1968), chap. 7.

16. The implications of deductibility are discussed in M. K. Taussig, "Economic Aspects of the Personal Income Tax Treatment of Charitable Contributions,"*National Tax Journal 20* (March 1967): 1–19.

17. The division is, of course, not so clear cut as these statements might imply, because tradition is also a significant factor, and adjustments to new political boundaries and social values take time. Still, it seems the best conceptual basis for distinguishing between situations in which private and public transfer mechanisms are operative.

An Empirical Test of the Utility Interdependence Explanation of Charitable Giving

This section reports on our initial effort to estimate a "propensity-to-transfer" function by determining whether intercity variation in charitable giving can be explained by the independent variables suggested by our model. In constructing our empirical test, let us explain first why the utility interdependence model suggests that contributions vary directly with income (the community mean income) and its dispersion. The basic reason (returning to the two-person model) is that the benefactor's desired transfer varies directly with his income if such transfers are a normal good. Increases in the higher-income individual's income may increase his desired transfer or lead individuals who had not been making transfers before to make them, because evaluated at lower own-incomes, marginal utility of own-consumption had exceeded the marginal utility of increments in the donee's income. When the benefactor's income increases, such latent utility interdependence becomes marginally relevant.

Similarly, there is ample reason to expect the level of transfers to vary with the dispersion or degree of inequality in the community's income distribution. So long as individuals' marginal propensities to transfer (vis-à-vis initial income differentials) are positive, the levels of their preferred transfers increase when pairwise income differentials become larger, which is what happens, *ceteris paribus*, when dispersion increases.[18] In the present analysis the implications of the initial income differential for the Pareto-optimal level of transfers enters through the dispersion variable – the more divergence there is among relative levels of well-being, as indicated by income, the higher we can expect the level of contributions to be.[19]

A third variable that might be relevant (on *a priori* grounds) is the number of persons in the political community. The theory of public goods distinguishes between cases in which a large number of persons benefit from provision of a collective good and cases in which the number of beneficiaries is small. Large groups are characterized by anonymity, and the benefits an individual receives from the transfer process depend almost

---

18. Although there are also other reasons why desired transfers might vary with income, they are not relevant here inasmuch as the income variable we consider is a community average. If, as in the first instance, the initial demand is marginally relevant, an increase in income alters the desired transfer because it improves the benefactor's rank in the income distribution, thus confronting him with more potential beneficiaries. If the desired transfers vary more than proportionally with the initial income differential, the Pareto-optimal transfer increases even more because the increase in the benefactor's income widens the initial differentials between his income and the incomes of potential recipients.

19. A similar prior argument for a positive association between income inequality and charitable transfers is made in R. A. Schwartz, "Private Philanthropic Contributions – An Economic Analysis" (Ph.D. diss., Columbia University, 1966), p. 31.

entirely on what others contribute and only slightly on his own contribution. Hence, "free-rider" behavior is likely to prevail. Conversely, individuals in a small group cannot vary their contributions without affecting the behavior of other contributors, so social pressure and the recognition that one's own contribution may be relatively important can be expected to reduce "free riding."

Because noncontributors can still benefit, assuming the benefits of charity are a public good, there is reason to expect the level of private charity to be suboptimal. The amount by which giving falls short of its optimum might well be less, however, in a small community. Charity, reflecting private provision of collective wants, should be more prevalent in smaller communities, implying higher levels of per capita contributions, and *ceteris paribus*, lower per capita government budgets.

Such reasoning is the heart of Friedman's contention that urbanization, by increasing the size of the group over which interdependence extends, reduces social pressure and necessitates the collectivization of charity.[20] Friedman's argument implicitly assumes that charity is motivated by expected improvements in the welfare of its beneficiaries. The argument holds equally well for the case in which contributors desire to eliminate the more noxious manifestations of poverty – for example, shabbiness of dress and high incidence of violence in slum areas. Either of these motivations implies that an individual can benefit from charity whether or not he contributes himself, so long as the income or other characteristics of the recipients (which charity alters) enter his utility function. However, if the simple joy of giving or the publicity contributions attract is what motivates donors, the free-rider problem disappears; charity becomes a private good, or, at least, donors think of it as such, and the attainment of its benefits requires a personal contribution. Thus, paradoxically, altruism is more likely than egoism to result in a suboptimal level of charitable giving.

As an initial, though very rough, test of the hypothesis that free-rider behavior is less prevalent in small groups than in large, we include population in one set of our estimates of a propensity-to-transfer function. However, it is an imperfect measure of community size, in the sense required. It may be more appropriate to use other locational breakdowns, and ethnic background or racial characteristics may be more important than geographic boundaries in demarcating the community within which utility interdependence is found.[21] Still, it is plausible to assume that the community of individuals who have marginally relevant interdependent preferences is larger, the larger the population of the political community in which they reside. Hence, assuming that the benefits of contributions are in fact collective,

---

20. See M. Friedman, *Capitalism and Freedom*, p. 191.

21. With reference to this point, see the discussion of public and private regardingness in J. Q. Wilson and E. Banfield, "Public-Regardingness as a Value Premise in Voting Behavior," *American Political Science Review 58* (December 1964): 876–87.

free-rider behavior should increase with population, and per capita contributions may be expected to vary inversely with city size.

If the population variable were statistically significant, the results would confirm the importance of social pressure in small groups as a stimulus to charity and would support the view that most people regard its benefits as a public good. Failure of this hypothesis, however, must be interpreted more cautiously, because it might either be attributed to a failure of social pressure to diminish as a group size increases or to the fact that the benefits of charity are not a public good. Because social pressure is irrelevant if charity *is not* a public good, either of these mutually exclusive explanations could in itself account for a poor showing of the population variable.

The Data and the Regression Equations

Translated into operational form, suitable for explaining intercommunity differences in charitable giving, our model, which attributes transfers through charity to utility interdependence, reduces to the propensity-to-transfer function:

$$T_k = g(\overline{Y}_k, D_k, N_k). \tag{1}$$

In (1) T_k is the average transfer through charity (level of charitable contributions) made by individuals in a community; this is a function of $\overline{Y}_k$, which is per capita income in the *kth* community; D_k, which is a measure of the dispersion of its distribution of income; and N_k, which is its population. Our test of the utility interdependence formulation is then a cross-section analysis of intercity differences in contributions. While there is no assurance that the relationship specified, if significant, is inconsistent with other models as well, significance can at least tell us whether the data are consistent with our model.

Appropriate empirical counterparts of the variables in (1) are reported for a sample of thirty-two United States metropolitan areas in the *Survey of Consumer Expenditures* (SCE), taken during the period 1959–61 by the Bureau of Labor Statistics.[22] The SCE examines household income allocations, and the figures it reports, which are sample averages for various expenditure categories, include the variables we require for preliminary tests of our propensity-to-transfer function. The SCE expenditure breakdown includes an item entitled "gifts and cash contributions," defined as "cash contributions to persons outside the family and to welfare-religious, educational, and other organizations; and the cost of goods and services purchased in the survey year and given to persons outside the family."[23]

---

22. U.S. Department of Labor, Bureau of Labor Statistics, *The Survey of Consumer Expenditures* (Washington, D.C.: U.S. Government Printing Office).

23. *Ibid.* See report for any of the cities covered; for example, for San Francisco, see BLS Report No. 237–52, April 1964 (Second Advance Report).

The SCE also reports average after-tax income and the distribution of after-tax income in each city's sample. The reported figure for average gifts and cash contributions is taken as the empirical counterpart of R_k, and average after-tax income is the empirical counterpart of $\overline{Y}_k$.[24]

The income variable, per capita after-tax income, is the appropriate measure of per capita income – what the average individual would have had if he had not given to charity, plus the tax saving. Our distribution variable – measuring income dispersion or inequality – was calculated from the distribution of after-tax income among families sampled in each city. It was defined arbitrarily as the sum of the percentage of sample families with incomes less than 50 percent of the recorded mean and the percentage with incomes more than 50 percent above this level.[25] Conceptually, D_k thus calculated is independent of the value of $\overline{Y}_k$ itself.

N_k, which is supposed to measure community size, cannot be determined empirically, as we have pointed out. Thus population is used as a rough and perhaps inadequate proxy. The population figures used were obtained from the 1960 census.[26]

In addition to these measurable variables we also experimented with dummy variables for four geographic regions of the country (broadly defined, the West, the South, the Midwest, and the Northeast). These dummy variables were supposed to provide a rough test of whether the propensity to transfer through contributions differs among regions. In theory, interregional differences could result, because perceptions of utility interdependence vary in strength among the subcultures in the society at large, or alternatively, because the fiscal structure is a more adequate mechanism for internalizing such externalities in some sections of the country than in others.

Conventional multiple-regression procedures were used to estimate the propensity-to-transfer function. Both linear and logarithmic (or elasticity) specifications of (1) were estimated. In the logarithmic form the independent variables have a multiplicative effect on contributions. Within this frame of reference we experimented (see table 1) with formulations, including and omitting the regional dummy variables and specifications, which forced the

---

24. $\overline{Y}_k$, as used here, reflects only the increasing "marginal relevance" of utility interdependence, the first of the factors cited in our earlier discussion. However, if our estimation procedure had used cross-section observations for individual spending units or for different income classes in a single community rather than averages, $\overline{Y}_k$ would also reflect distributional changes (see footnote 19). This suggests that it might be worthwhile to look at pooled observations broken down by communities *and* income classes. (This will be done in a later paper.)

25. This measure of dispersion is easy to compute and is probably as useful for our purposes as the Gini coefficient, given the crudity of the data and the small samples involved.

26. Population figures are taken from U.S. Bureau of the Census, *U.S. Census of Population: 1960, Vol. I, Characteristics of the Population*, Part I, "United States Summary" (Washington, D.C.: U.S. Government Printing Office, 1964). Population in the thirty-two sample cities ranged from 13,311 for Fairbanks, Alaska, to 3,550,404 for Chicago, Illinois. Note that even 13,311 may be above the size range in which social pressure and free-rider behavior, which the population variable is intended to reflect, vary significantly.

equation through the origin. All of the equations (1a–1f) were estimated twice, once with the population included, as in the estimates summarized in table 2(a) and once with the population variable excluded, as in table 2(b).

The Regression Results

The regression results, as reported in tables 2(a) and 2(b) are generally consistent with the hypothesis that utility interdependence is a reasonable explanation of charitable giving:

1.   All equations show a significant association between contributions and the independent variables. The *F* values for all of the regressions indicate significance at the 1 percent level.

2.   The coefficients of after-tax income ($\overline{Y}_k$) and the dispersion in the distribution of after-tax income (D_k) are positive, as predicted, and in each regression are significant at the 1 percent level.

3.   The population coefficient, our improvised measure of "community size," *never* differs significantly from zero. Although its sign is negative in most cases, conforming to the *a priori* expectation, its absolute effect is miniscule. In view of our reservations this is not surprising, and further, more formal investigation of the socioeconomic and demographic factors associated with utility interdependence is warranted.[27] It should also be

Table 1. Regression Equations

(1a)	$C_k = B_1\overline{Y}_k + B_2 D_k + B_3 N_k + B_4 X_{1k} + B_5 X_{2k} + B_6 X_{3k} + B_7 X_{4k} + e_k$
(1b)	$C_k = B_0 + B_1\overline{Y}_k + B_2 D_k + B_3 N_k + B_4 X_{1k} + B_5 X_{3k} + B_6 X_{4k} + e_k$
(1c)	$C_k = B_1\overline{Y}_k + B_2 D_k + B_3 N_k + e_k$
(1d)	$C_k = B_0 + B_1\overline{Y}_k + B_2 D_k + B_3 N_k + e_k$
(1e)	$\text{Log } C_k = B_0 + B_1 \text{ Log } \overline{Y}_k + B_2 \text{ Log } D_k + B_3 \text{ Log } N_k + B_4 X_{1k} + B_5 X_{3k} + B_6 X_{4k} + e_k$
(1f)	$\text{Log } C_k = B_0 + B_k \text{ Log } \overline{Y}_k + B_2 \text{ Log } D_k + B_3 \text{ Log } N_k + \text{Log } e_k$

Variables:

C_k = Average reported charitable giving in the *i*th city.

$\overline{Y}_k$ = Average after-tax income in the *i*th city.

D_k = Dispersion of after-tax income in the *i*th city.

N_k = Population of the *i*th city.

X_{1k} = Dummy variable for the western cities.
$\quad$ $X_1 = 1$ if *i* is a western city.
$\quad$ $X_1 = 0$ if *i* is not a western city.

X_{2k} = Dummy variable for southern cities.

X_{3k} = Dummy variable for midwestern cities.

X_{4k} = Dummy variable for northeastern cities.

e_k = Error term.

27.   What is needed, of course, is experimentation with other proxies for group size and social identification – for example, measures of ethnic and racial homogeneity. See, for example, Wilson and Banfield, "Public-Regardingness."

noted that because of the insignificance of the population variable, the question of whether the charitable expenditures employed as data here are a collective good remains undecided.

4. In the linear regressions the coefficients of the geographic dummy variables either did not differ significantly from zero at any level of confidence or were significant only at the relatively low levels of 10 or 15 percent. In the logarithmic form the coefficient of X_3, the dummy for midwestern cities, is significant at the 5 percent level. This coefficient was consistently *negative* and was larger than any of the other dummy coefficients.

These results are open to opposing interpretations. The dummy coefficients might be interpreted as indicating that the public sector is more adequate in satisfying redistributive collective wants in the Midwest than elsewhere, in particular in the South. On the other hand, it might be inferred that midwesterners are slightly less generous than city dwellers in other geographical areas and that southerners are the most generous geographical group, once the influence of income and its distribution on giving has been removed.

5. The logarithmic or elasticity form [(2e) and (2f)] gives a slightly better fit than the linear regressions, as indicated by its higher R^2. This improvement in "goodness of fit" indicates that the relationship between contributions and the independent variables Y and D may be multiplicative rather than linear. However, because the improvement is small, we cannot place a great deal of confidence in this conclusion.

The Measurement of "Benevolence": Pitfalls and Prospects

Our income transfer model, which reflects a set of explicit assumptions about utility interdependence, seems capable of explaining a substantial amount of the variation in private giving. With this in mind, let us turn to the question of how useful the model is, not just in measuring utility interdependence or benevolence but in devising norms for distributional policy that are grounded in individual preferences.

In our earlier paper, "Pareto-Optimal Redistribution," we demonstrated that "altruistic" or "benevolent" utility interdependence may require a society to engage in redistribution if it is to attain Pareto optimality.[28] Individuals, in addition to engaging in voluntary redistribution through

---

28. See Hochman and Rodgers, "Pareto-Optimal Redistribution." With interdependence, the utility-possibility locus is no longer uniformly downward sloping. (For external economies this is true for as few as two persons; for external diseconomies upward-sloping portions require three or more persons.) Its upward-sloping portions, for obvious reasons, are inefficient, provided that malevolence is ruled out; in the minds of all nonmalevolent members of the society, any point on them is dominated by some point or points along the downward-sloping portion.

Table 2. Estimates of a Propensity-to-Transfer Function:
(a) Population Included as an Independent Variable

Equation	Intercept	Y	D	N	X_1	X_2	X_3	X_4	$\bar{R}^2$	F	SEE	N	K
1a	*	0.517[a] (0.093)	203.5[a] (81.1)	-0.004 (0.010)	-83.4[d] (76.8)	-75.0[d] (68.2)	-91.7[c] (70.1)	-70.1[d] (71.7)	0.644	7.5[a]	41.2	32	7
1b	-75.0	0.516[a] (0.093)	203.5[a] (81.1)	-0.004 (0.010)	-8.3 (26.6)	—	-16.7 (21.7)	4.1 (30.8)	0.644	7.5[a]	41.2	32	7
1c	*	0.425[a] (0.029)	136.6[a] (51.6)	-0.007 (0.009)	—	—	—	—	0.611	22.7[a]	40.0	32	3
1d	-76.2	0.508[a] (0.074)	202.5[a] (74.2)	-0.007 (0.009)	—	—	—	—	0.631	15.9[a]	39.6	32	4
1e	-1.48	1.161[a] (0.191)	0.184[a] (0.074)	0.000 (0.017)	-0.061 (0.082)	—	-0.093[b] (0.067)	-0.024 (0.094)	0.676	8.7	0.127	32	7
1f	-1.1	1.093[a] (0.154)	0.191[a] (0.071)	-0.006 (0.016)	—	—	—	—	0.646	17.2	0.125	32	4

Estimates of a Propensity-to-Transfer Function:
(b) Population Excluded

Equation	Intercept	Y	D	P	X_1	X_2	X_3	X_4	R^2	F	SEE	N	K
1a'	*	0.515[a] (0.092)	202.5[a] (79.8)	—	-83.8[d] (75.6)	-93.7[d] (67.1)	-71.0[c] (68.8)	-71.0[d] (70.1)	0.641	9.3[a]	40.6	32	6
1b'	-74.9	0.515[a] (0.092)	202.5[a] (79.8)	—	-8.9 (26.2)	—	-18.8 (20.7)	3.9 (30.3)	0.641	9.3[a]	40.6	32	6
1c'	*	0.427[a] (0.031)	139.1[a] (52.6)	—	—	—	—	—	0.601	45.1	39.4	32	2
1d'	-77.8	0.506[a] (0.073)	200.8[a] (73.6)	—	—	—	—	—	0.624	24.0	39.3	32	3
1e'	-1.487	1.161[a] (0.187)	0.183[a] (0.069)	—	-0.061 (0.081)	—	-0.093 (0.064)	-0.024 (0.092)	0.676	10.8[a]	0.125	32	6
1f'	-1.138	1.098 (0.151)	0.182 (0.066)	—	—	—	—	—	0.646	26.5	0.124	32	3

*=Intercept is suppressed.
SEE=Standard Error of Estimate.
N=Number of observations.
K=Number of independent variables

[a] Significant at the 1 percent level.
[b] Significant at the 5 percent level.
[c] Significant at the 10 percent level.
[d] Significant at the 15 percent level.

charity, may coerce themselves through the fiscal process into implementing additional distributional adjustments. The reason for this, of course, is market failure. Private transfers, if not augmented by fiscal activities, may produce "too little" income redistribution. Potential Pareto-optimal transfers that can make everyone better off remain.

Thus distribution policy must face up to the same problem encountered in deciding how much of a conventional public good to provide. This preference-revelation problem, itself inherent in market failure, makes the information required to determine and to achieve an optimum level of provision difficult to obtain. To obtain this information one must, in Paul Samuelson's words, know "the shapes of the marginal-utility curve of the public good to each man." Hence there is no question that the problem of determining "rates of benevolence" is difficult.[29]

We accept this readily enough, but the issue that concerns us here is not whether the problem is difficult but whether it is tractable. The implication of this paper is that it may well be. Our contention is that it may be possible to use what we know about redistribution through charity – albeit in an inefficient amount – in resolving the social question of how much redistribution ought to be brought about under public auspices to achieve a Pareto optimum.[30]

Two problems that inevitably confront any attempt to implement this line of reasoning must be mentioned again. First, in the short run charity is itself affected by the fiscal structure by virtue of the price and income effects of its deductibility. Nonetheless, it seems reasonable to think of the fiscal structure in this context as parametric, so that patterns of charitable giving remain valid evidence of the incremental distributional adjustments that individuals wish to implement.[31] Second, some charitable contributions may

---

29. P. A. Samuelson, "Pitfalls in the Analysis of Public Goods," *Journal of Law and Economics* 10 (October 1967): 199–204.

30. A similar argument, suggesting that "discussion of a theory of charity might be appropriate in the study of local government fiscal behavior," can be found in a paper by C. M. Tiebout and D. B. Houston, "Metropolitan Finance Reconsidered: Budget Functions and Multi-Level Governments," *Review of Economics and Statistics* 44 (November 1962): 412–17 (quotation from p. 416).

31. We are, as the analytic portion of this paper has suggested, in argument with Boulding's statement:

> The almost complete neglect by economists of the concepts of malevolence and benevolence cannot be explained by their inability to handle these concepts with their usual tools. There are no mathematical or conceptual difficulties in interrelating utility functions provided that we note that it is the perceptions that matter. The familiar tools of our trade, the indifference map, the Edgeworth box, and so on, can easily be expanded to include benevolence or malevolence, and indeed, without this expansion many phenomena, such as one-way transfers cannot be explained.

The appendix to Boulding's paper in the NBER volume on philanthropy, "Altruism and Utility," demonstrates how "benevolent" utility interdependence can be taken into account within the Edgeworth box construction. See K. E. Boulding, "Economics as a Moral Science"; and K. E. Boulding, "Altruism and Utility," in *Philanthropy and Public Policy*, ed. F. G. Dickinson (New York: Columbia University Press, 1962).

not be motivated by interdependence at all; some contributors may benefit only from the act of giving per se, not from the gifts of others. In such cases the market does not fail, and charity does not tell us anything about the distributional adjustments required by the Pareto criterion. The fact does remain, however, that the major share of all private transfers *are likely to be* of the collective good type, affecting the welfare of individuals other than their immediate donors and recipients. Thus on the basis of the evidence discussed, we remain hopeful that further development of the line of reasoning on which this paper is based will be of some help in deriving norms for distributional judgments that are consistent with the Pareto criterion of efficiency and in delimiting the extent to which this "weak" welfare norm can be used in evaluating distributional questions. Conceptual hazards notwithstanding, additional research on utility interdependence, both theoretical and empirical, seems to be warranted – for its own sake, to enrich our understanding of individual preferences, and for the sake of its implications for distributional policy. This opens up several intermediate lines of inquiry.

First, to ascertain both the motivating factors underlying charity and the effects of charity, private transfers must be disaggregated. It is important for these purposes to identify contributors to various types of charity in terms of income and other demographic and ethnic characteristics. This suggests the need to *uncover and utilize* knowledge that is usually thought to be more sociological than economic.

Examination of incidence outcomes in areas of mixed private and public activity, like the production of medical care and research and the provision of education, is also an essential part of research on utility interdependence. Cost and benefit imputations for these areas can be interpreted in light of *a priori* hypotheses about the externalities that justify public action to determine whether the methods of financing now in use are consistent with the Pareto criterion. Fiscal outcomes should also be examined to ascertain whether the utility interdependence explanation of income transfers is superior to alternative explanations of redistribution through the public sector. The interdependence explanation must be viewed within models of the collective decision-making process, and the manner in which this process channels individual preferences into government programs and political actions must be studied.

Just how useful this exercise will be is difficult to assess. However, if it is determined that observed patterns of redistribution, either through charity or public finance, can be explained in terms of utility interdependence, it may be possible to use such knowledge, particularly at lower levels of government, in designing fiscal structures that accord – more closely than fiscal structures now do – with the Pareto norm.

HAROLD M. HOCHMAN
City University of New York

and

JAMES D. RODGERS
Pennsylvania State University

The Simple Politics of Distributional Preference

Income redistribution, in its many facets, poses extraordinarily difficult and complex problems for both normative and positive economics. For normative economics, it has, until recently,[1] meant irreconcilable conflict. With regard to how much redistribution should occur, scholars, notwithstanding long debate, remain agnostic, as they have been since Lord Robbins shattered the scientific illusion of classical utilitarianism.[2]

For positive economics, the realm of this paper, efforts to interpret redistribution have exposed the limited extent of our progress in over-

NOTE: When this paper was written, Hochman was visiting lecturer in the Graduate School of Public Policy, University of California at Berkeley. Denis Aitken, William Bicker, Mickey Levy, Edward Neuschler, and Ted Radosevich deserve credit for assistance with the data. Research support from the National Science Foundation is gratefully acknowledged: Hochman's grant was GS-33244X; Rodgers' was GS-33224X. Data for this study, originally collected by the Field Research Corporation, were provided by the State Data Program of the Institute of Governmental Studies, with the assistance of the Survey Research Center, University of California at Berkeley. These organizations are not responsible for the analysis and interpretation of data appearing here.

71

coming the conundrums of empirical measurement and modeling. The measurement problem itself poses two broad problems. One relates to the adequacy and availability of data and the other to the conceptual difficulties encountered in determining the incidence of public expenditures. While there exist studies of the redistributive impact of individual programs,[3] general-equilibrium problems have befuddled efforts to develop convincing estimates of the overall amount of redistribution.[4]

The development and empirical testing of positive theoretical models intended to explain the extent to which individuals and communities choose to engage in income redistribution has also produced but limited progress. Existing positive research can be divided into two parts, one dealing with transfers carried out in the private sector (through charity, donations of time, and intergeneration gifts)[5] and the other, on which this paper focuses, with income redistribution through government programs.

In a society with a democratic government,[6] there are at least two different, though complementary, ways in which the analysis of public redistribution may be approached. The first inquires into how much redistribution will occur and what its pattern may be expected to be.[7] The second starts with the overall pattern of redistribution produced by an existing government, or by the existence of a particular redistributive program, and attempts to construct a theory to account for it. In one sense these two approaches are similar. Both call for a theory that contains not only a model of individual behavior subject to constraints, but also a model of the political process through which preferences for goods and services with "public" characteristics are transmitted. The difference is that the first approach asks a question that is open-ended, while the second starts with a particular pattern of redistribution.

This paper adopts the second approach. Its concern is with explaining, in terms of individual preferences, public redistribution to low-income persons—to be specific, those distributional adjustments, taken as a group, that are commonly referred to as "welfare" programs.

A number of recent papers have argued that income redistribution, through tax-financed, poverty-alleviating income transfers, may represent a collective response to the existence of nonmarket interactions between the poor and the nonpoor, the nonpoor being concerned, for a variety of reasons, with the well-being, or the consumption-leisure choices, of the poor.[8] One ground on which this explanation of income transfers has been criticized is that transfer recipients, as well as taxpayers, have the franchise, so that observed transfers may well be attributable to the political power of the former rather than to the preferences of the nonpoor.[9] Thus, provided that transfer recipients exercise their right to vote, the conventional assumption of universal independent preferences, combined with direct or representative decision making by majority rule, may in itself be sufficient to account for transfers to the poor.

While we have no intention of denying that transfer recipients, through voting, will support programs that provide them with benefits, either monetary or in kind, the thrust of our argument will be that the support of recipients, given the voting rules in force, cannot itself account for the existence of such programs. This does not mean that self-interest considerations play no part in generating support for redistribution to the poor. But it does mean that something must be present, in addition to simple recipient self-interest, to account fully for the redistribution that is observed.

The remainder of this paper presents the analytical basis for these remarks and some evidence of individual preferences which seems to support them. In Part I, we discuss the basis of nonrecipient support for redistribution. Part II contains a model of redistribution in direct democracy. In Part III, this model is extended to a setting of indirect or representative democracy, and we explore how much nonrecipient support the enactment of redistribution requires. In Part IV, an effort is made to derive real-world measures of distributional preference from the responses of a panel of California citizens to queries about welfare spending and other redistributive expenditures. In Part V, the implications of these responses are examined in terms of the political models developed in Parts II and III. Part VI, set at a more general level, offers a few concluding remarks about the line of reasoning pursued in this paper.

I. THE BASIS FOR NONRECIPIENT SUPPORT FOR REDISTRIBUTION

A major theme of this paper is that the political base on which support for redistribution rests extends well beyond its direct recipients. We imply by this that many nonrecipients do not behave like simplistic "economic men," concerned with their own disposable incomes and the goods and services these incomes can buy for own-use, and nothing else.

Some nonrecipients, of course, may support redistribution to the poor for reasons that seem almost as straightforward as those of recipients. A nonrecipient may support welfare programs because (a) he expects, with high probability, to himself be a direct recipient at some future time; (b) he may derive income from some activity that is favorably affected by such redistributive programs (e.g., farmers presumably have higher incomes because of food stamps, and social workers receive higher salaries because of Aid to Families with Dependent Children); or (c) he may view transfer programs as substitutes for transfers he would otherwise feel obliged to make privately, entirely on his own (e.g., persons with parents drawing Old Age Assistance).

But the basis of nonrecipient support for redistributive programs may extend beyond simple self-interest. Transfers to the poor may be viewed, as mentioned earlier, as a collective response to nonmarket interactions between the status or activities of the poor and nonpoor members of the community. Such nonmarket interactions may take several forms. Non-recipients may be concerned, for a variety of reasons, with the well-being of the poor, or at least interested in seeing that all individuals have access to minimum amounts of certain commodities and services, such as food, housing, and medical care. Thus, the individual's utility function may include, as an argument, the welfare (or some proxy for welfare like income) of other persons, as in

(1) $U^A = U^A(Y^A, Y^C)$

As specified in (1), A's utility function includes not only his own income, Y^A, but C's income, Y^C. With this specification, A will desire to make a transfer to C whenever the rate at which he is willing to trade increments in own-consumption for increments in C's consumption (his marginal rate of substitution between own-consumption and C's) exceeds the rate at which such trades can be made. In the N-person case, where such demands are satisfied (for familiar reasons) through the political process, A may well feel that welfare spending, as financed by taxation, satisfies this condition. Alternatively, if A cares about C's consumption pattern, e.g., with the food or housing that C consumes, the specification of A's utility function will be

(2) $U^A = U^A(X_1^A, \ldots, X_n^A, X_1^C)$

where $X_1^A, \ldots, X_n^A$ are the rates of consumption of each of the n goods consumed by A and X_1^C is the amount of X_1 which C consumes. In this case, A will favor transfer activities aimed at increasing C's consumption of the particular commodities with which he, A, is concerned. He will tend to favor, say, price subsidies for consumption of these goods to programs providing C with cash payments.[10]

Nonmarket utility interactions may also arise, however, because A sees the existence of poverty as a source of negative externalities. Although A may not "care" about C for C's own sake, he may be affected adversely by particular aspects of C's behavior. In such cases, transfers for him are a kind of input used to "produce" a reduction in such social maladies as crime and public health inadequacies.

In the discussion that follows, actions directed to the reduction of such negative externalities, as well as to the maximization of own-consumption (as opposed to utility) or to the minimization of private costs (payments for goods and services, directly or through taxes) are considered to be based on self-interest. Thus, if all individuals act only on self-interest, to be more precise, "narrow" self-interest, nonrecipient support for redistributive transfers must derive from nonmarket utility interactions that are negative or from the motives described as (a) and (b) in our first set of examples.

On the other hand, we define behavior which results from *positive* nonmarket interactions among utility functions as *benevolence*. Nonrecipient support for redistributive transfers that derives from utility inter-dependencies, as described in the two-person example of equation 1, and from the motive described as (c) are included in this category.

Our discussion of the implications of nonrecipient support for redistribution concerns itself only with the existence, not the pattern, of benevolence. At issue is whether individuals, through the mechanisms of public choice, support transfer programs that enable others to augment their consumption, not whether the beneficiaries are relatives or friends or anonymous persons, identified only by, say, inferior income status.

Note also that benevolence, in our definition, is fully consistent with the maximization of own-utility. Individuals support transfers that are based on benevolence because they reflect preferred income allocations. Such transfers are, then, a matter of "rational" calculus, consistent with the private utility functions of the actors. It is for this reason that such choices can be accommodated within the corpus of economic theory.

Nothing that we say implies that benevolence is based on altruism. Altruism, which Webster's dictionary defines as "unselfish concern for the welfare of others," relates to motivation, not preference, and implies something more; namely, selflessness. Strictly speaking, therefore, in an analysis grounded in the postulate that choice is "rational," in the sense of being consistent with an objective function that is internal to the individual, altruism is an empty box.

II. REDISTRIBUTION IN DIRECT DEMOCRACY

This section begins our attempt to determine the circumstances under which a political democracy may be expected to produce redistribution to the poor. It deals, as a first step, with the simple but revealing case of direct democracy, in which the political community votes directly in referenda on public programs rather than for representatives who vote on such programs in legislatures. Part III then turns to the more complex and realistic case of representative democracy.

One important determinant of the amount of redistribution is the voting rule through which the community reaches its decisions. If unanimity is required, preference independence and income certainty, taken together, suffice to rule out all redistribution. Only if the unanimity requirement is relaxed can redistribution occur in a model that abstracts from both interdependent preferences and uncertainty. More plausible, however, is the assumption that simple majority rule prevails, implying that a motion will be adopted if favored by $(N+1)/2$ of the voters. What we wish to determine is whether, with this voting rule, redistribution favoring the poor is likely to be enacted.

Assume that (a) each person has one vote and (b) the distribution of income among persons is unequal. One might predict, then, following Anthony Downs (1957), that the 51 percent of the voters with the lower incomes would enact a tax on the 49 percent with the higher incomes and transfer the proceeds to themselves, each member of the "coalition" receiving an equal share of the redistributive pie.

A three-person model provides the simplest example that can illustrate this kind of redistributive outcome of direct democracy. Suppose three voters, A, B, and C, have initial incomes of Y_A^0, Y_B^0, and Y_C^0, where $Y_A^0 > Y_B^0 > Y_C^0$. By assuming away incentive effects so that each party maintains his market income at Y^0, regardless of which redistributive policies are adopted, the situation can be characterized as a constant-sum game. If income redistribution among the three members of the community is the only issue with which public choice deals, and if revenue is obtained from the members of the group through the taxation of income at a single tax rate, t, the characteristic function of this game can be identified in terms of the payoffs to the various coalitions that may form.

(3)   *i.* $V(A) = V(B) = V(C) = 0$

       ii. $V(A, B) = tY_c$; $V(A, C) = tY_b$; $V(B, C) = tY_a$

No payoff is available to one-member coalitions such as $V(A)$. Two-member coalitions receive an amount tY_i, where the income that is taxed is that of the excluded party. Since $Y_A^0 > Y_B^0 > Y_C^0$, the payoffs in the three possible two-member coalitions are ranked as $V(B, C) > V(A, C) > V(A, B)$. The highest payoff is earned by the coalition (B, C) which excludes A, the highest-income voter, and this result is the basis for the Downsian conclusion that the 51 percent coalition will consist of the voters with the lowest incomes in an N-voter model.

The second part of this Downsian solution, which specifies that B and C will share equally in the gains, is not necessarily compelling. To obtain this result, one seems forced to make some very special assumptions about expectations. *B* and *C*, for example, may anticipate that unequal sharing would significantly enlarge the chance of their coalition proving unstable. The prospect that the (*B*, *C*) coalition will disintegrate and permit the formation of another coalition from which one of them is excluded must be assumed so unfavorable that neither will risk demanding a disproportionate share of the coalition gains. There is no compelling reason, however, why either *B* or *C* must be so risk averse.[11]

We may now inquire how likely it is that the redistribution that democratic societies effect on behalf of the poor will reflect the kind of coalition that emerges in our example, viz., a (*B*, *C*) coalition with equal sharing. Clearly, one of the main problems with this is that the maximum income at which a voter can remain eligible for transfers in the real world is far below the median. A substantial number of those at the top of the bottom 51 percent receive zero cash transfers and, absent all interdependencies positive or negative, would vote for transfers only if they view the existence of such programs as a means of generating private income (i.e., as suppliers) or as a kind of insurance against the hazard of becoming impoverished.[12] That these motives apply for all those in the bottom 51 percent of voters with incomes too high to be eligible for redistributive transfers is open to considerable doubt. Those nonrecipients who see private gain in transfer programs, after accounting for their shares of the tax costs, are unlikely to be more than a very small minority of the voting population. Nor is the receipt of welfare payments now treated as a right to which persons are "entitled." The barriers erected to exclude the "undeserving" poor from recipient status and to prevent cheating serve also to reduce the insurance value of the programs to those who are not poor. There is, moreover, no reason for the nonpoor to content themselves with programs that provide only insurance benefits, as they would surely be better off with actual transfers. For various reasons then, existing welfare programs, in which means tests exclude a large number of voters with incomes below the median from benefits, are not easily accounted for by the simple Downsian coalition hypothesis.

Within the context of a direct democracy model, what alternative hypothesis can we invoke to account for transfers to the poor? One alternative is to assume that voters with above-median incomes have utility functions that reflect interdependence. This being the case, they may support and willingly consent to finance transfers to that one-fifth to one-quarter of the population that they classify as poor.

As far as the theory of redistribution in direct democracy is concerned, what does such nonrecipient support imply? In terms of our three-person model, the fact that high-income *A* may derive benefits from transfers can be examined on the assumption that such benefits are greater if the recipient is low-income *C*, rather than *B*. This would be true, presumably, if the source of *A*'s benefits is positive utility interdependence, as in equations 1 and 2. It would also be true if *A* perceives a link between low income and crime.

On these assumptions, it is clear that a coalition of *A* and *C* is much more likely, relative to one of *B* and *C*, than it was in the previous analysis. *B*'s support need no longer be obtained to enact a transfer program, and *A* has an incentive to break up a (*B, C*) coalition if it should form, not just to reduce his tax bill, but to assure that the transfers will be used in what he thinks to be a more appropriate way (going just to *C* instead of to *B* as well as *C*).

These conclusions may now be applied to an *N*-voter model. If some individuals with above-average incomes benefit from income transfers to the poor, a phenomenon that simple self-interest models, with no recognition of externalities, are hard put to explain, ceases to be a mystery. Given a transfer program which restricts net payments to, say, the low 20 percent of the income distribution, it is very difficult to assure the support of a majority in a model which ignores utility interdependence. But recognition of nonrecipient support surmounts this difficulty.

III. REDISTRIBUTION IN REPRESENTATIVE DEMOCRACY

Political models in which public decisions are made by popular vote describe but a limited number of real-world situations. The lion's share of collective decisions are made in representative bodies. Thus, it is to an analysis of the redistributive policies that may be expected to emerge from such representative assemblies or legislatures that we now turn.

Consider a hypothetical community of 25 persons, divided geographically into five equal parts, among which there is no short-run mobility.[13] These parts can be considered districts, provinces, counties, or states. In each district one person is elected by simple majority vote to serve as member of the community's legislature. It is assumed that this person clearly perceives the preferences of the majority responsible for his election and honors these preferences when voting in the legislature. Decisions in the legislature are also made by simple majority rule and, for purposes of the present argument, on an issue-by-issue basis with no vote trading. Finally, the legislature concerns itself only with policies explicitly designed to redistribute income—its jurisdiction is a kind of special district with a distributional mandate.

Assume initially that voters, as in the Downs model, have independent preferences and that no person fails to exercise the franchise.[14] Thus, each voter unfailingly votes for the candidate who supports programs that yield him the largest positive fiscal residual (the transfers he receives less the taxes he pays). A description of the decision-making process implicit in these assumptions is provided in Figure 1. Each column represents one

FIGURE 1

D_1	D_2	D_3	D_4	D_5
X	X	X	O	O
X	X	X	O	O
X	X	X	X	X
O	O	O	O	O
O	O	O	O	O

of the five districts, D_1 to D_5, and the five cells in each column represent the five voters in this district. A representative is elected by majority vote from each district, and the assembly therefore contains five representatives. In Figure 1, an X is displayed in a cell if the voter approves and votes for a proposal; an O is displayed if the voter opposes it. As is apparent from Figure 1, with simple majority rule, both in voting for representatives and in voting on legislation, a motion *may* be enacted if favored by a *minimum* of nine voters. This is because three representatives must vote for enactment, and each, to be elected, must be favored by at least three constituents.[15]

To illustrate the implications of such a model, we may examine several situations. These differ in their assumptions about (a) the number of people eligible for transfers and (b) their dispersion among the districts. Throughout, the redistributive program is assumed to be explicit, with upper-income groups being taxed at a uniform rate *t* and the receipts being distributed uniformly to those with incomes below some specified level. We are not concerned with what this level is or how it is decided, but take it as given. In the illustrations that follow, each person in each district is either eligible for transfers and thus designated "poor" and identified by an X, *or* pays taxes to finance transfers, in which case he is called "rich" and is identified by an O.

A distribution of poor voters among districts like that represented in Figure 1 illustrates the situation in which the number of "poor" people (assuming simple self-interest—no utility interdependence—on the part of the rich) required to enact redistribution is at its minimum of nine. If one of the poor were to shift from D_1 to, say, D_4, the redistributive proposal would fail. Hence, it is clear that the spatial distribution of supporters is crucial. Another way of demonstrating this is to consider the situation represented by Figure 2. Here, even though the "poor" number sixteen, they are unable to vote themselves income transfers from the wealthy.

FIGURE 2

D_1	D_2	D_3	D_4	D_5
X	X	X	X	X
X	X	X	X	X
O	O	O	X	X
O	O	O	X	X
O	O	O	X	X

The general implication of these illustrations is that redistribution is bound to be enacted, no matter what the distribution of the poor among districts, if their number exceeds sixteen—with a population of twenty-five and majority rule in force—and that redistribution will never occur if the poor are less than nine. However, if the poor number between nine and sixteen, inclusive, their distribution among districts determines whether redistribution will occur. In the general case of K districts, each with N persons, at least 25 percent of the population must be poor if redistribution on their behalf is to occur, and it is enacted in this case only if the poor are evenly distributed over $(K + 1)/2$ districts and absent entirely from the remaining $(K - 1)/2$.[16]

Now consider the implications of utility interdependence on the part of the nonrecipient rich. Assume, for the sake of argument, that there is no negative externality basis for redistribution, so this interdependence is entirely a matter of benevolence. If there are more than sixteen poor, the effect of introducing such interdependence into the twenty-five person model is nil, inasmuch as redistribution would be enacted in any case. However, with sixteen poor or less, interdependence can bring about redistribution which would not occur without it. This effect can be illustrated for two extreme cases:

    a. If there are sixteen poor, distributed as in Figure 2, only one of the nonrecipients in D_1, D_2, or D_3 must be benevolent, to a degree sufficient to be made better off by redistribution, to reverse the outcome.

b.   With, say, but one poor person in each district, a much higher proportion of nonrecipients must be benevolent, as Figure 3 illustrates.

FIGURE 3

D₁	D₂	D₃	D₄	D₅
X	X	X	X	X
O	O	O	O	O
O	O	O	O	O
O	O	O	O	O
O	O	O	O	O

Here, six is the minimum number of benevolent nonrecipients (the minimum of nine supporters minus the three poor blokes in any three of the other five districts). The maximum number of rich who can be benevolent without assuring legislative enactment of redistribution is eleven, the maximum of sixteen less the five poor, distributed one to a district.[17]

For the relevant cases (situations in which the number of poor is less than seventeen), the implications of nonrecipient benevolence can conveniently be summarized in a table of "minimum requirements," such as Table 1. While the transfer recipients must number at least nine (must exceed 32 percent of the population) with no benevolence, its introduction can reduce the minimum number of recipients to one. The implicit arithmetic is simple. In political effect, the rich, if benevolent, are perfect substitutes for poor recipients. Depending on the overall spatial distribution of supporters, a benevolent minority among the nonpoor can assure the passage of legislation that transfers income to the poor, and this minority need be nowhere near so large as it must be with the same decision rule in direct democracy.[18]

Several issues of practical policy and constitutional politics can be discussed in terms of this model. The first is the impact of reapportionment as a means of long-run recourse open to a defeated opposition on the redistributive outcome. At one level of analysis, the answer to this question must remain indeterminate. To know the effects of reapportion-

TABLE 1   Number of Benevolent Rich Required for Enactment of Redistributive Legislation

Number of Poor (Actual Transfer Recipients)	Poor as a Percentage of Community	Number of Benevolent Rich to Ensure Enactment		Percentage of Rich Who Are Benevolent		Percentage of Benevolent Rich in the Community Population	
		Minimum	Maximum	Minimum	Maximum	Minimum	Maximum
17 (or over)	68	0	0	0	0	0	0
16	64	0	1	0	11	0	4
15	60	0	2	0	20	0	8
14	56	0	3	0	27	0	12
13	52	0	4	0	33	0	16
12	48	0	5	0	38	0	20
11	44	0	6	0	43	0	24
10	40	0	7	0	47	0	28
9	36	0	8	0	50	0	32
8	32	1	9	6	53	4	36
7	28	2	10	11	56	8	40
6	24	3	11	16	58	12	44
5	20	4	12	20	60	16	48
4	16	5	13	24	62	20	52
3	12	6	14	27	64	24	56
2	8	7	15	30	65	28	60
1	4	8	16	33	67	32	64

ment, one must specify the initial situation, the specific inter-district reallocation of voters that it contemplates, and the constitutional constraints under which it operates. But a specific example can illustrate some of the possibilities.

Suppose that the legislature has passed a redistributive proposal and that Figure 4 illustrates the distribution of its supporters, consisting of both the poor and the benevolent rich (denoted by B). In this setting, reapportionment that shifts any individual from district D_4 to D_5 (or vice versa) can have no effect, for both of these districts are opposed to redistribution in any case. But the outcome may be quite different if reapportionment affects one of the districts in which a majority supports redistribution. If, for example, reapportionment shifts a benevolent person from D_3 to D_4, it changes to one in which three out of five representatives (those from D_3, D_4, and D_5) oppose redistribution, resulting in its termination.

FIGURE 4

D_1	D_2	D_3	D_4	D_5
X	X	X	B	B
X	X	X	O	O
B	B	B	O	O
B	O	O	O	O
O	O	O	O	O

At another level of analysis, the possibility of reapportionment, at least in a long-run sense, may make redistribution more difficult to effect. This is true, for example, if significantly less than 50 percent of the community supports redistribution, while a decision to reapportion requires but a simple majority among the electorate. To see this, one need only observe that if, say, only nine persons out of twenty-five secure the enactment of a redistributive program, a substantial majority opposes it. If reapportionment can be carried out in any manner whatsoever, no matter how arbitrary, it is an easy matter for this majority to bring about the redistricting needed to terminate the program. In the real world, of course, reapportionment is constrained by rules governing the geographical basis of representation, rules which require, for example, spatial continuity within jurisdictions. This constraint limits the efficacy of reapportionment as a means of recourse to a defeated majority. Still, on the average, the prospect of reapportionment does increase the minimum level of overall support under which redistribution is likely to be enacted.[19]

Metaphorical swords, however, usually have two edges. Just as the possibility of reapportionment can limit the ability of a minority as small as 9/25 to secure enactment of a redistributive program, so it can also prevent a minority of 9/25 from blocking the passage of such a program. Reapportionment can, for example, easily convert the situation in Figure 2, in which redistribution is favored by 16/25 of the population but fails, into a situation in which redistribution will occur.

It should be noted, finally, that reapportionment can make the outcome of collective decision making in representative democracy more like the outcome under direct democracy only if apportionment decisions are themselves decided by a simple majority rule. In contrast, if, say, three-fourths of the population must approve reapportionment, its potential impact is nullified.

A related issue, similarly elucidated by our model, concerns the effect of the spatial distribution of potential recipients, the poor, on the likelihood that a transfer program will be enacted. Put a bit more pragmatically, it is relevant to ask whether the poor are likely to enjoy more political success (obtain larger per capita transfers) if they are dispersed across districts or concentrated. Our model suggests that this question is relatively easy to resolve. In the absence of nonrecipient support, neither concentration nor an even distribution among districts benefits potential recipients. Where there are ten such persons, the implications of an even distribution of two per district and the concentration of all ten in but two districts are the same—redistributive proposals will fail. To make the most of their numbers, potential recipients must be "semidispersed."[20]

Clearly, the model of representative democracy that this section has presented is innocent of many of the realities of collective decision making. A number of complications are, therefore, apparent. Two of these, hitherto ignored, are discussed here, together with some modifications that they might require.

The first complication is that collective decisions are often outcomes of a logrolling process in which representatives trade votes on different issues. To gain support on issues on which they hold strong views, representatives may either vote for legislation to which they (and, on our assumptions, their constituents) are mildly opposed or vote against legislation which they mildly favor. Such behavior immediately takes us beyond the confines of our simple single-issue model and poses the question of when an extension of the model to accommodate logrolling is essential to the analysis of redistribution through the public sector. What we can point out here is that to the extent that all constituents have intense feelings (either positive or negative) about redistribution relative to other issues, logrolling is not likely to be an important factor.

A second complication, also with some real-world importance, is that rates of voter participation, obviously much less than 100 percent, tend to vary directly with income. The analytic equivalent of such variation in voter participation, in terms of our model, is a disproportionate reduction in population, which eliminates more potential voters with low incomes than with high incomes. Other things equal, inverse voter participation reduces the ability of the poor to gain income transfers through use of the political process. By raising the minimum proportion of nonpoor who must favor a redistributive proposal to obtain its legislative enactment, it increases the importance of nonrecipient support in accounting for observed transfers to the poor.

IV. EVIDENCE OF DISTRIBUTIONAL PREFERENCE

Other things being equal, direct recipients of income transfers, together with those who think themselves likely to become recipients, can be expected to look favorably upon redistributive programs. To assure this, one needs only the comfortable assumption that the marginal utility of net increments in disposable income (the difference between transfers and perceived taxes) is sufficient to offset any implied costs in terms of lost privacy associated with the transfer process itself.[21]

But preferences of nonrecipients, which are transmitted through a political process that sets out to define new programs or to propose changes in the level or content of existing programs, are less transparent. In representing nonrecipient demands, one may, to start, presume that the capacity and taste for redistributing income vary with conventional socioeconomic and demographic indexes. Thus, even if all nonrecipients have identical tastes for redistribution, their willingness to transfer income—the "effectiveness" (marginal relevance) of their demands—will vary with these indexes (in other words, income and other claims, implied by family size, age, and so on, on nonrecipient resources).

Unfortunately, data that indicate the incidence of utility interdependence, benevolent or other—much less the critical levels the enactment of redistributive motions require—are not only difficult to delineate, but are difficult to obtain. Indeed, even if such data were identifiable, the fact that political institutions do not generate data in the required form precludes definitive investigation. Since what one has to work with is fragmentary and imperfect, little choice remains but to arm oneself with such tenuous assumptions about patterns of preference interdependence as seem to fit the evidence and institutions and to proceed.

To examine redistribution in direct democracy, one can turn to, as Wilson and Banfield (1964) have done, voting patterns in public expenditure referenda with redistributive overtones, involving school tax decisions or the capital financing of such facilities as a general hospital with a low-income clientele.[22] Or, in examining referendum voting on such measures as Proposition I (the California tax initiative rejected in November 1973, which proposed the constitutional restriction of public expenditures), one may introduce into the relationship variables used to explain the voting outcomes in precincts or census tracts that putatively reflect utility interdependence, as Levy (1974) has done. Where inference about the prevalence and strength, much less the political significance, of interdependencies is at issue, however, these procedures have a number of drawbacks. Citizen perceptions of the implicit distributional implications of the proposals under study are bound to be imperfect, not just because voters differ in fiscal sophistication, but because such effects are inherently unclear. This may not only affect how people vote but whether they vote. Moreover, the data examined, which represent averages for voting precincts or census tracts, can only provide evidence of central tendency, indicating median voting behavior (in terms of income, education, or other indicators of preference) within such political units. Our political models, on the other hand, indicate that it is the distributional preferences of critical minorities that determine whether proposed redistributive measures are successful. While it is possible to infer something about the size and composition of such minorities from cross-section voting data, provided detailed information on voter characteristics within political units exists, this is at best a tricky business.

Thus, to study actual and (for political acceptance) necessary levels of nonrecipient support for redistribution, it seems worthwhile to seek data in which the individual voter is the unit of observation. Periodic polls of a sample of California voters by the Field Research Corporation appear to be a workable mine of such data. Several of the Field polls conducted during 1970 (in May, August, and November) posed a variety of questions, designed to ascertain attitudes toward government expenditures in general and toward welfare spending in particular, to just over half of their samples of more than 1,100 voters. The focus on welfare spending, the most obvious means of redistribution to the poor, was attributable to the fact that Governor Reagan had made welfare reform a major issue in his reelection campaign. A defect of these data is that they measure intention, without enforcement of performance, rather than revealed preference. In one sense, however, this is a virtue, for it eliminates the distortions of actual distributional preferences that occur in candidate voting, where there is issue packaging, and in logrolling, which figures significantly in legislative decision making.[23]

Distributional preferences, as implied by responses to the welfare spending questions of the 1970 California polls, are summarized in Table 2. Income is the primary classification variable, in recognition of its importance in determining whether utility interdependencies are marginally relevant, and whether respondents are likely to be welfare recipients.[24] The sample responses have been recalculated (producing but minor changes of a percentage point or two) to reflect California population weights, which are, aside from vagaries of voter participation, measures of voting strength. Though the May, August, and November samples from which the data were compiled included different respondents, the responses are assumed to be comparable.

Within each income group (summarized in rows 1 through 3 of Table 2), the responses may be interpreted as the data of a simple cumulative function, though one for which the variable which interests us, attitude toward spending, is qualitative and discontinuous. The family of such functions (one for each income-bracket column in Table 2) describes variation, with income, in respondent satisfaction with particular welfare spending levels, relative to the existing level and to a regime in which there would be no welfare program at all. Rows 1 through 3 of the table each indicate a different respondent attitude. Row 1 measures the percentage of respondents who believe that some level of welfare spending (a level which is greater than zero but by an unspecified amount) must be considered a "moral imperative." Such persons responded with "agree strongly" or "agree somewhat" to the statement: "In spite of some waste in the welfare program, it would be morally wrong to do away with it." Row 2 indicates the proportion who consider the present level of welfare spending either "adequate" (that is, not too frugal) or "insufficient" (that is, desiring that it be increased). Taken together, we interpret these respondents as viewing the present level as "not unduly generous." This is obviously a weaker and more inclusive indication of support than that registered in row 3 by respondents who think that the present level of welfare spending is insufficient and desire more.

On inspection, a number of implications seem clear. First, only a small percentage of persons in any income bracket oppose any and all welfare spending. Only 11 percent do not feel that it is a "moral imperative" to maintain *some* positive level of welfare spending.

Second, in each of the three rows there is in general a systematic break in the relationship between the response percentages and income at roughly $7,000, and this income is interpreted as the breakpoint between the actual and potential welfare recipient population and the nonrecip-

TABLE 2   Derivation of Distributional Preferences from Reactions to Statements on Welfare Spending (Sample percentage responses weighted to reflect California population)

	Income ($1,000) and Income Distribution (in parentheses)							
	Less than 3	3–5	5–7	7–10	10–15	15–20	More than 20	All
	(10%)	(10%)	(11%)	(21%)	(27%)	(14%)	(6%)	(100%)
1. Moral imperative	92	96	96	88	87	93	82	89
1a. Not moral imperative	8	4	4	12	13	17	18	11
2. Present level not unduly generous (adequate or insufficient)	82	64	79	63	60	65	61	66
2a. Present level adequate	44	26	39	44	36	39	47	39
3. Desire more spending	38	38	40	19	25	25	14	27
4. Helps prevent crime	75	68	58	49	48	47	26	65
5. (1) – (4)	18	28	37	39	39	46	56	24
6. Provide housing to those who can't afford it	71	63	49	50	39	42	32	46
7. (1) – (6)	21	33	47	38	48	51	50	43
8. (5) – (6)*	(53)	(35)	(12)	(11)	nil	4	24	(22)
9. Able-bodied men should not collect welfare	72	86	76	78	82	74	79	79
10. (1) – (9)	20	9	19	10	5	19	3	10

Continued overleaf

NOTE: All questions except those in rows 6 and 11 are from the August 1970 poll. Lines 6 and 11 are from the November 1970 poll. Defects in comparability, in addition to those attributable to sample composition, arise because the November (but not the August) poll permitted "undecided" responses (which we treat as "disagreement"). The following explanation relates to the various rows.

1.   Welfare is a moral imperative. Reactions of "agree strongly" and "agree somewhat" to the statement: "In spite of some waste in the welfare program, it would be morally wrong to do away with it." Response that welfare is a moral imperative is taken to imply the marginal relevance of some utility interdependence.
1a. The complement of 1.

2.   Response that "more" spending is desired or current level of spending is "adequate" to the question: "Where should welfare, relief, and poverty programs fit in government spending?" implies that respondent does not believe the current level of the program to be unduly generous.
2a. Response that current level of spending is "adequate."

3.   Response that "more money" should be spent.

4.   Reaction of "agree strongly" or "agree somewhat" to statement that "if it weren't for welfare, there would be a lot more stealing, burglaries, and other crime." Interpreted as the upper limit on support for welfare spending that is based on narrow self-interest rather than benevolence.

5.   The difference between percentage responses under 1 and 4. Interpreted as lower limit of support for welfare that is benevolence-based.

6.   Reactions of "agree strongly" and "agree somewhat" to "it's only fair for government to provide good housing for people who can't afford it."

7.   The difference between the percentage responses under 6 and 1.

8.   The difference between the percentage responses under 5 and 6. Asterisk indicates that the percentages contain negative percentages.

9.   Reactions of "agree strongly" and "agree somewhat" to "no able-bodied man who is healthy enough to work should be allowed to collect welfare."

10. The difference between the percentage responses under 1 and 9.

ient population.[25] The decline in what appear, on the whole, to be favorable attitudes toward welfare spending may be interpreted as reflecting a rise, with income, in its net "price," more than sufficient to offset any increases in "tastes" for redistribution. Several factors contribute to this: (a) direct variation of the tax cost of income transfers with marginal tax rates and (b) inverse variation with income of the monetary benefit of transfers, because the probability of ever being poor declines and welfare programs consequently become a much worse form of insurance.

Third, only in the $3,000 to $5,000 group (where the figure is 25 percent) do less than 36 to 47 percent believe that the existing level of welfare spending is "adequate," a characterization that implies an absence of any demand for increases in such programs. The difference between the 25 percent response rate in this group ($3,000 to $5,000) and the 44 percent response in the lowest group (less than $3,000) seems to be primarily a matter of differences in age composition and in experience with the inadequacies of existing levels of welfare payments.[26]

In examining Table 2, one might inquire why prowelfare sentiment is less than unanimous in those income groups in which direct recipients are likely to be concentrated. Higher levels of redistributive transfers are, after all, in their apparent private interest. Doubtless, a part of the answer is that the Field polls inquired about attitudes toward welfare spending and not, more inclusively, about redistributive transfers or, in even more general terms, about income transfers, including those like social security, which are at least partially (even if more in perception than fact) annuities financed by prior social insurance payments. Some of those in the lowest income groups are, moreover, transients who had incomes that were below long-run expectations in the year concerned. Others, such as the "working poor," may well have taken the survey questions literally, interpreting them as referring to a particular package of welfare programs, monitored through complex rules and regulations that they consider unpalatable. These rules may have made them ineligible or made their participation so uncomfortable that they registered negative responses even though they could be quite favorably disposed toward such familiar systems of "no strings" income transfers as the Family Assistance Plan or a demogrant system of the type proposed by Senator McGovern in 1972. Without probing deeper through further questions (an alternative not available to us) there is no way of telling which of these motivating factors were operative, or to what degree.

The responses themselves offer little in the way of precise basis for inferring the motives of nonrecipient support. In this regard, agreement that "it would be morally wrong to do away with" welfare spending is of some help, inasmuch as it does indicate benevolence, as we have defined it, but it does so, strictly speaking, only for marginal departures from program levels of zero. As Part I has indicated, however, benevolence, deriving from a sense of fairness or caring about the well-being of others, is but one basis of nonrecipient support.[27]

The role of negative externalities, grounded in a distaste for behavior patterns associated with absolute or relative deprivation, must also be considered. It should be stressed that these need not be founded on a dislike of the poor. They may derive, for example, from presumed implications of poverty for the stability of the social and political fabric, or the quality of community life.

A crude, though suggestive, attempt to distinguish positive or benevolent interactions from negative utility interactions as the basis for nonrecipient support of welfare spending is made in rows 4 and 5 of Table 2. For hints into the real-world operation of the models of democracy that Parts II and III have presented, these rows contain some of our most interesting data. Reactions to the statement: "If it weren't for welfare, there would be a lot more stealing, burglaries, and other crime," are recorded in row 4. Among nonrecipients, agreement with this statement (responses of "agree strongly" and "agree somewhat") is here interpreted as an indication of support for redistribution (a belief that welfare spending is desirable) on grounds of negative utility interactions and not on grounds of benevolence. The strong inverse relationship between income and agreement that "welfare prevents crime" is worth noting. It suggests that those most experienced with crime (which in prevalence varies inversely with neighborhood quality and, thus, income) seem most convinced that the statement is correct.

As far as negative interactions deriving from crime itself are concerned, these figures are, of course, at most an upper limit—more likely an overstatement—to which nonrecipient support does not derive from benevolence. Here, however, for the sake of argument, we treat the responses in row 4 as a proxy for all negative sources of nonrecipient support.

Differences between the responses to "welfare is a moral imperative" (row 1) and "welfare prevents crime" (row 4) are reported in row 5. These derived figures are then our measures (in a sense, minimum measures) of the frequencies with which benevolence itself is a factor in distributional preferences, in the sense that nonrecipients prefer *some positive* level of welfare spending.[28] That "net" benevolence, thus measured, varies directly with income is what one would expect if "concern for the well-being of others" is a normal good.

The frequencies in row 5 rise from 18 percent among respondents with incomes under $3,000 to 56 percent among those with $20,000 or more. Among all those who are presumed to be nonrecipients (those over

$7,000) its range is 39 to 56 percent, and its average incidence is 47 percent.[29] However, since some respondents who agree that "welfare prevents crime" did not consider it a moral imperative, the deductions row 4 provides are too large. The 47 percent figure should, therefore, be adjusted upward by 3 percent, producing a corrected estimate of 50 percent. In the context of our political models, in which low frequencies of nonrecipient benevolence can be crucial, this minimum estimate of the incidence of benevolence in nonrecipient preferences must be considered quite significant.

The substantive focus changes in row 6 to the form in which non-recipients prefer their redistributive transfers to the poor to be made. At issue here (and in the remaining rows of Table 2) is whether the levels of self-perceived well-being of recipients—or alternatively, their consumption patterns or work-leisure choices—are the basis of donor concern.

In models of democracy without benevolence, all transfers will be in cash. Transfers in cash provide a wider range of consumption options and will be preferred by recipients who enact redistribution on their own behalf. On the other hand, in models with benevolence (or negative utility interactions), nonrecipient preferences are also relevant, both in determining whether redistribution will occur and in establishing its form and amount. If nonrecipient support does not derive from concern with the self-perceived well-being of transfer recipients, but extends to the sources or uses of their incomes, cash transfers may no longer be preferred. Specifically, if the utility interdependence of the marginal donor in the coalition required to enact a redistributive motion is of the particular-commodity type, the preferred transfers will be in kind and not cash. Row 6, taking up this issue, indicates nonrecipient reactions of "agree strongly" or "agree somewhat" to the statement posed in the November 1970 poll that "it's only fair for government to provide good housing for people who can't afford it." Because a different sample was used in November, comparisons with the August responses for inference about patterns of benevolence and the preferred form of income transfers must be taken with a large grain of salt. Still, provided one has a bit of a speculative bent, such comparisons are enlightening.

The responses in row 6 can be interpreted loosely as evidence of donor concern with the consumption patterns rather than the general well-being of recipients. In the housing case, this might have any of a number of sources: concern with how well recipients are housed, an objection to the aesthetics of ill housing or, to stretch a point, an aversion to the implications of housing inadequacies for social behavior. For the moment, there is no need to discriminate among these explanations; it can simply be assumed that the response frequencies in row 6 are an upper limit on the incidence of particular-commodity interdependence, as opposed to general and nonspecific utility interdependence with which we are concerned here.[30]

Our specific interest in this connection is with the interpretation that might be given of the responses of individuals with incomes above the breakpoint, which is, in this case, $5,000 rather than $7,000. Among such respondents, 38 to 51 percent of those agreeing that welfare is a moral imperative did *not* express the opinion that government is obligated to provide good housing for those who cannot afford it (see row 7). The theory suggests two possible reasons for this. Either these respondents were concerned with the overall welfare and not the consumption patterns of the poor, *or* they were not concerned with the poor at all, but supported welfare spending because of a belief that it prevents crime or ameliorates other undesirable side effects of poverty. To "net out" the effects of such negative interactions, we then deducted the "provide housing" responses from the calculated "net" benevolence levels (in row 8) rather than deducting them only from the "moral imperative" frequencies (as in row 7). Of course, "helps prevent crime" and "good housing" are not mutually exclusive as this procedure taken by itself implies. Many observers would argue that the housing component of welfare spending plays a major role in its effect on crime. Row 8's "net" estimates of benevolence, attributable to general and nonspecific, rather than particular-commodity utility interdependence, are minima in two ways: first, because the "prevents crime" frequencies place an upper limit on nonrecipient support that is not attributable to benevolence; and second, because of overlap among responses to the "prevents crime" and "provide housing" queries.

Taken at face value, the *negative* net frequencies in row 8 of Table 2 suggest that nonrecipient support for redistribution is (strictly) a matter of particular-commodity interdependence for respondents with incomes between $5,000 and $10,000. From $10,000 to $15,000, the net figure is effectively zero and warrants a similar interpretation. Over $15,000, however, it rises from 4 percent to a maximum of more than 24 percent among respondents with incomes over $20,000.[31] This is a large enough frequency to suggest with some force that donor concern with the self-perceived well-being of welfare recipients is a normal good which holds little interest at or near the breakpoint between recipients and nonrecipients but which is in significant demand among voters in the top decile of the income distribution. This inference, based on the indications of distributional preference summarized in Table 2, lends strength to the argument (developed elsewhere)[32] that support of redistribution by the rich, in the coalitions required to enact welfare programs, varies directly with income and is disproportionately derived from those donors with the highest incomes.

Another key issue in the investigation of distributional preference is whether nonrecipient donors are concerned with levels of self-perceived welfare among the recipient population or with the potential levels of their money incomes.[33] Donor aversion to work disincentives is evident in public discussion of redistributive proposals (in connection, for example, with the family assistance legislation and, in particular, with income-maintenance experimentation) and is corroborated by the almost uniformly positive poll responses to the statement that "no able-bodied man who is healthy enough to work should be allowed to collect welfare" (summarized in rows 9 and 10 of Table 2).[34]

Within the present frame of reference, the differences between non-recipient responses on the "moral imperative" and "able-bodied man" issues may be taken as evidence of a minimum level of interdependence in which the recipient's welfare, pure and simple, rather than his earned income is what counts. The average of these differences, which vary but little across income classes, approximates 10 percent. This contrasts with the 50 percent estimate of the incidence of "net" benevolence implied by the differences between the responses to the "moral imperative" and "welfare prevents crime" statements. It may, therefore, in a very rough sense, be interpreted as a lower limit on the extent to which nonrecipient supporters of welfare spending are likely to support a simple program of cash transfers containing no work requirement provisions.

V. IMPLICATIONS OF NONRECIPIENT SUPPORT UNDER DIRECT AND INDIRECT DEMOCRACY

This section examines with the derived evidence from the California polls the degree to which nonrecipient support for welfare spending (or opposition to it) is essential to its enactment. We do this by treating the queries posed to the California sample in the May and August 1970 polls as though they were referenda or legislative motions. The relevant responses, classified by respondent income, are reported in row number 3 of Table 2 and in Table 3. Table 4 displays the levels of nonrecipient support required for enactment of each of these motions, under a variety of decision rules, given the levels of support that recipient groups have evinced.[35] These decision rules range from a minimum of one-fourth to a maximum of three-fourths. One-half is obviously the operative requirement for the overall population for a referendum decided under direct democracy with majority rule. One-fourth and three-fourths define the limiting cases for the model of indirect democracy developed in Part II. Population distribution and apportionment are, however, seldom favorable enough to permit these minimum coalitions to pass or block any motion. Thus, from a practical standpoint, limits of one-third and two-thirds seem more sensible, and even these may well be too wide.

In May 1970 poll interviewees were asked (in separate open-ended questions) which, if any, of a list of eight government programs categories involving large expenditures of money they would like to see "increased or kept at the same level of spending" or "reduced in spending." Table 3 summarizes the frequencies with which the respondents mentioned welfare spending.[36] Since some 7 percent of the interviewees mentioned welfare spending in neither case, some inconsistency is reflected in the responses. The inconsistency decreased with income, producing an upward bias in the support level required to enact a legislative motion proposing an increase in welfare spending and a downward bias in the level of nonrecipient support required to defeat it.[37]

The legislative motions implicit in the May 1970 questions for which distributional preferences are indicated (in Table 3) are set out in rows 1a, 1b, 2a, and 2b of Table 4. The right-hand side of this table reports

TABLE 3   Responses to Distributional Preference Questions on May 1970 Poll
(Sample percentage responses weighted to reflect California population)

	Income ($1,000) and Income Distribution (in parentheses)							
	Less than 3	3–5	5–7	7–10	10–15	15–20	More than 20	All
	(10%)	(10%)	(11%)	(21%)	(27%)	(14%)	(6%)	(100%)
1. Increase or maintain the same	64	75	67	59	56	52	43	59
2. Decrease	18	15	22	37	40	37	57	34
3. Inconsistent: no mention of welfare in (1) or (2)	18	9	11	4	4	10	–	7

NOTE: The explanation relates to the various rows.

1.   Frequency with which "welfare spending" was mentioned by respondents when interviewer stated: "Here is a list of some government programs which require large expenditures of money. Which would you like to see increased or kept at the same level of spending?" The query was open-ended, and the responses were neither mutually exclusive nor constrained, either by a budget limitation or by a requirement that priorities be specified.

2.   Responses to: "Here is a list of government programs which require large expenditures of money. Which would you like to see reduced in spending?" The same comments apply as in row 1.

3.   No mention of welfare in either of the above responses, reflecting implicit inconsistency. Note that this inconsistency is, on the average, lower for the income groups of $7,000 and above.

TABLE 4 Referenda Implicit in Attitudes toward Welfare Spending
(Sample percentage responses weighted to reflect California population)

Implicit Referenda on Welfare Spending	—Income[a]— Less than $7,000	More than $7,000	Required Support among Those with Incomes of $7,000 or More to Achieve Indicated Population Support Level				
	(32%)	(68%)	1/4	1/3	1/2	2/3	3/4
Questions on May 1970 Poll							
1a. Increase or maintain the same	68	55	8	19	43	66	78
1b. "Don't" decrease	81	60	3	14	38	61	73
2a. Decrease	19	40	27	39	62	86	97
2b. "Don't" increase or maintain the same	32	45	22	34	57	81	92
Questions on August 1970 Poll							
3a. Spend more	39	22	19	31	55	80	92
3b. "Don't" spend more	61	78	8	20	45	69	81

NOTE: The population is apportioned between the 32 percent with incomes "less than $7,000" and the 68 percent with incomes "$7,000 and above." This breakpoint, we assume, distinguishes between respondents who, given current economic status, are or have a significant likelihood of becoming welfare recipients. The choice of $7,000 rather than $5,000 as the breakpoint between the current and potential "poor" (recipients) and the "rich" (individuals who are unlikely to become recipients) is based on an apparent discontinuity in the responses, thus in distributional preferences, at this income level.

Figures in the right-hand half of Table 4 indicate percentage levels of support among the population with incomes of "$7,000 or more" required to achieve the indicated overall level of support (across all income groups) for the implicit referenda on welfare spending listed at the far left.

Support levels indicated in 1a and 2b are derived from reactions (and the negative complement of reactions) to: "Here is a list of government programs which require large expenditures of money. Which would you like to see reduced in spending? Which would you like to see increased or kept at the same level of spending?" and its negative complement. These questions were asked in the May 1970 poll.

Required support levels in 3a and 3b are derived from the response of "more money" to "Where should welfare, relief, and poverty programs fit in our government spending?" and its negative complement. This question was asked in the August 1970 poll.

[a]The figures in parentheses are population weights.

levels of nonrecipient support required for this enactment. For both the "increase or maintain" and the "decrease" questions, required support levels for the negative complement ("don't decrease" and "don't increase or maintain") have also been calculated to delimit the significance of the response inconsistencies discussed above. Inspection of

Table 4 indicates that the inconsistencies were not very important, since their effect, which was to produce differentials of approximately 5 percent across the board in nonrecipient support requirements, was not very important.

The necessary levels of nonrecipient support in a referendum on whether "more money" (as distinct from enough to "increase or maintain" the present level) ought to be spent on welfare programs are reported in rows 3a and 3b of Table 4. These figures are derived from the August 1970 responses summarized in row 3 of Table 2 and discussed in Part IV. Although, as mentioned earlier, the composition of the May and August samples differed, so that the responses are not strictly comparable, these outcomes are consistent with what one would expect, given an inverse relationship between the extent to which utility inter-dependence is relevant at the margin and the price of acting upon it. Still, the low level of support for higher welfare spending ("more money") among respondents with incomes of "less than $7,000" is puzzling. One possible explanation is that the August queries were not phrased in the open-ended language of the May questions but in terms of spending priorities, thus imposing an implicit but rough budget constraint into the calculus of the respondents.

In understanding Table 4, it is useful first to think of the implicit referenda as if they had been proposed in a regime of direct democracy, with enactment requiring overall support of 50 percent. In this case, enactment of an increase in welfare spending requires support (given, as the first column indicates, 39 percent support among the "poor") from 55 percent of the nonrecipient rich, while the assent of but 40 percent (a rough average of the 38 and 43 percent in rows 1a and 1b) is required to pass a motion to "increase or maintain." To effect a "decrease" in welfare spending, on the other hand, 60 percent of the "rich" (a rough average of 62 and 57 percent) must consider the present level of welfare spending too high.

These figures may now be contrasted with the actual frequencies. In fact, only 22 percent of the "rich" would like to see welfare spending increased, while 40 to 45 percent would like it decreased. However, virtually 60 percent, the same proportion enactment requires, favor its being "increased or maintained." There seems then a clear implication (to the extent the California samples are representative) that the existing level of welfare spending is stable,[38] at least under simple majority rule. The fact that nonrecipient support levels of three-fifths to four-fifths are required to pass on all two-thirds positive motions, and roughly a one-third minority among nonrecipients is in all cases sufficient to block any two-thirds motion for change in the present level of welfare spending, supports this conclusion.[39]

Under indirect democracy, the required levels of overall support may range, in theory, from 25 to 75 percent. In consequence, the variety of possible levels of required nonrecipient support multiplies. With a given decision rule, and the information Table 4 contains, one may work through the prospects of each motion, under whatever assumptions about voter participation (among recipients and nonrecipients) and the "optimality" of the spatial distribution of supporters (apportionment) he may wish to make. Since the character of this exercise is clear, specific discussion does not seem necessary at this juncture.

It is now possible to return to our crude estimate of the lower limits on "net" nonrecipient benevolence and "nonrecipient support for a cash transfer" program without work requirements and inquire, speculatively, into their implications for the likely success of proposals to institute transfer programs. Recall that the first limit, 50 percent, was derived from the "moral imperative" and "welfare prevents crime" responses and the second, 10 percent, from the deduction of the "able-bodied man" (implying a concern with the effects of income transfers on work incentives) from the "moral imperative" responses. The former can then be interpreted as a lower bound on the extent of nonrecipient support for some sort of cash redistribution program, whereas the latter indicates the minimum level of nonrecipient willingness to support such a program without imposing work requirements.

That some program of cash transfers can be enacted, whatever the decision rule, seems apparent if 50 percent is the operative limit of nonrecipient benevolence. Even the 10 percent figure, which permits some defection of recipients, is likely to be consistent with enactment if, as the case may be in representative democracy, only one-third of all voters must agree. However, the data, as available, provide no grounds on which to base estimates of the magnitude of such programs.

As indicated in the earlier discussion, the limits in themselves simply indicate prevalence and do not measure the significance or marginal relevance of benevolence at the current level of welfare spending, the base to which the implicit motions considered in Table 4 refer. To ascertain this, we require a heroic assumption about the rate at which income transfers beginning from a base of zero succeed in internalizing benevolence. To this end, assume for the sake of argument that the basis for nonrecipient support for income transfers to the poor is simple positive utility interdependence, that all welfare spending at the start is in cash, and that the initial level of cash transfers from which departures are being considered internalizes half the benevolence that would be present at a zero level of transfers. The implied operative limits of nonrecipient support for marginal changes in the initial level of cash transfers (as distinct from maintenance of the program at its current level) are then 25 and 5 percent.

The levels of required nonrecipient support spelled out in Table 4 indicate, in this case, that in direct democracy (in a referendum decided by simple majority rule) there is no "positive" motion to "increase or maintain" the level of transfer programs that could pass. But, depending upon the spatial distribution of their supporters, the same motions, set forth under representative democracy, might well stand some chance of success. If, for example, the distribution of supporters is ideal, so that overall support of but 25 percent is required, motions to "increase or maintain" and "spend more" would both do well. This also seems true for the former if one-third support is required.[40] On motions to decrease welfare spending, the benevolence limits imply that three-fourths support is simply unattainable and that other, less restrictive support levels, such as two-thirds, are unlikely to be attainable.

Admittedly, such argumentation is tenuous, as it must be, given the character of the evidence at our disposal. It does, nonetheless, suggest directions in which research must proceed if our practical understanding of the workings of democratic political process is to be meshed with theoretical models of public choice that attempt to interpret it. What is needed, first, as in discussing more conventional topics, are better structural models, with tangible counterparts in empirical evidence. To characterize democratic processes in terms of such models, one requires a consistent body of microdata, capturing the preferences of the individual actors upon which politics builds. To obtain such data, a suitable panel must be subjected to a carefully structured series of questions, capable of measuring gradations in preference and linking choice, grounded in such preference, to the price and reward systems implicit in public policies. The applicability of such data would be much less limited than that grounded in hypothetical binary choices. For the researcher interested in distributional preferences, the best of all worlds would provide matched data, relating preferences, as discerned through such surveys as the California polls that we have used, and voting through which such preferences are revealed.[41] It is obvious that this is a great deal to ask. And as if it were not already enough, or too much, the ambitious scholar may even hope for data that relate the choices of legislators and legislatures, adjusted somehow for their constituents.[42]

VI. CONCLUSION

The classical preoccupation with income distribution enjoyed a renascence in the 1960s. In motivation, this was largely pragmatic, a matter of discomfort with the apparent coexistence of social deprivation and general prosperity, rather than analytic interest in the empirical dimensions of an elusive social optimum. Disenchanted with the structure and the outcome of prevailing property rights, which define claims to human and nonhuman capital, some writers went so far as to suggest that distributive justice requires a radical restructuring of social institutions, holding that there is no way in which the social and economic system, in its present form, can accommodate the adjustments they think "necessary." Others, more cautious, and, frankly, more committed to liberal values, argued that more redistribution would occur if only the democratic political process and the social programs it produces could be made to more accurately reflect the "true" preferences of the voters from whose consent they derive.

For the practicing social scientist, which way of posing these issues is more accurate is less interesting than the question of which is more open to inquiry. To us, the apparent stability of a distributional outcome that conforms with voter preferences seems sufficient to make the investigation of redistribution as a matter of public choice, within a predefined system of rights and rules, the prior research topic. It seems more efficacious to make use of familiar concepts and methods, even when they can be adapted only with difficulty to current concerns, than to disregard them and seek, like Lancelot, a new paradigm.

Recently within the public choice frame of reference, some considerable effort has been devoted to the normative question of how much income redistribution is appropriate, and whether its form should be cash or kind. Treatment of the positive counterpart of this issue, the effort to determine the kinds of preferences reflected by income transfers carried out through private charity and public programs, has been much less satisfactory. As means of explaining redistribution, the basic deficiency of traditional neoclassical analysis resides in its formulation of the objectives, thus the preferences, which motivate voters and politicians. The requirement that rational behavior be consistent with simple self-interest, in particular, makes it far more difficult than need be to explain redistributive activities. The appropriate extension of the neoclassical paradigm, which permits more realistic interpretation of redistribution, introduces choices which reflect benevolence into the objective function.

In the present paper, we have developed this theme by building utility interdependence into models of redistribution in direct and indirect democracy. Perhaps our most significant conceptual finding is that widespread, much less universal, benevolence need not be postulated in order for its impact on the distributional outcome to be substantial. We have also attempted, using data from poll responses, to determine some of the dimensions of nonrecipient support for redistributive transfers through welfare spending. We believe the results are quite striking and offer support for assertions about the existence of benevolence and the significance of its impact on redistributive outcomes.

NOTES

1. See Aaron and von Furstenberg (1971), Becker (1969), Buchanan (1968), Goldfarb (1970), Hochman (1971), Hochman and Rodgers (1969, 1970, 1971, 1973, and 1974), Johnston (1972), Mishan (1972), Musgrave (1970), Olsen (1969, 1971a, 1971b), Pauly (1970), Peterson (1972), Rodgers (1973), von Furstenberg and Mueller (1971).
2. Robbins (1932), pp. 136–143.
3. For example, an estimate of the redistributive effects of the U.S. farm program is given in Schultze (1972).
4. See McGuire and Aaron (1970) and Gillespie (1965).
5. See Becker (1969), Dickinson (1962), Hochman and Rodgers (1973), and Schwartz (1971).
6. By a democratic system of government, we mean a set of institutional arrangements governing the procedures through which a community arrives at collective decisions in which individuals compete for the votes of a broadly based electorate. On the appropriateness of defining political democracy in this way, see Schumpeter (1942), Chapters 21 and 22.
7. Since an infinite number of transfer patterns are consistent with any total amount of redistribution, any discussion of this subject must also specify who pays and who receives. But the level of redistributive activity has some importance independent of its pattern, since it gives an indication of the proportion of resources that the community is devoting to transfer activities. For a discussion suggesting that a society, with certain institutions and rules, may be caught in a prisoner's dilemma and excessively engage in these activities, see Tullock (1971a).
8. See the references cited in note 1.
9. See Buchanan (1972).
10. For more detailed consideration of these nonmarket interactions in the two-person and N-person cases, see Hochman and Rodgers (1969), Rodgers (1973), and Rodgers (1974).
11. The essential difficulties in the view that (B, C) with equal sharing is the most likely outcome of the redistribution "game" can be seen by examining this solution more closely and comparing it with some alternatives. If the (B, C) coalition forms and votes to tax A, collecting tY_A, B and C, with equal sharing, each receive $tY_A/2$. The redistribution pattern in each period is then $(-tY_A, tY_A/2, tY_A/2)$. Whether this represents a stable solution depends on the deals that B and C, respectively, can strike with A, the expectations of each party about the behavior of the others, and the aversion of each party to the uncertainties associated with instability.

    To consider one possibility, A could bribe either B or C to forsake the coalition and to join with him. If either B or C were offered anything more than $tY_A/2$, either would be willing to defect the (B, C) coalition. At first sight, the bargaining range might appear to be between tY_A and $tY_A/2$, for C must receive at least $tY_A/2$ in a coalition with A, while A would be agreeable to a coalition with C that costs him anything less than tY_A. But this potential gain to A and C from forming a coalition as an alternative to (B, C) actually understates the potential gain, since the (A, C) coalition can also tax B, obtaining an additional tY_B. If, then, an (A, C) coalition forms, it would clearly be possible, even with no redistribution from B, for both A and C to be better off. But with redistribution from B, both A and C stand to gain even more. If C is content with $3/4$ tY_A and $1/2$ tY_B, A will suffer a net income loss of only $3/4$ $tY_A - 1/2$ $tY_B = t(3/4 Y_A - 1/2 Y_B)$. Moreover, if $tY_B \geq 1/2$ tY_A, A need pay nothing at all to C in order for C to be better off in a coalition with A than in (B, C). But before the reader gets the impression that an (A, C) coalition is more stable, he should note the possibility that B might be able to induce A to foresake C by agreeing to give A a sizable amount of his income. The possibilities are endless. Indeed, the situation is not unlike price warfare among a group of oligopolistic firms; and the outcome is indeterminate for much the same reasons.

12. The notion that income redistribution through the fiscal structure may, in part, serve the function of income insurance has a substantial intellectual history and is much discussed in the literature. See, for example, Buchanan and Tullock (1962), Chapter 13, and the summary discussion in Rodgers (1974).

13. This assumption rules out the location effects on which the Tiebout thesis focuses (1954). Implications of redistribution for location are described and discussed in recent papers by Buchanan (in Hochman and Peterson 1974) and Pauly (1972).

14. Later in the analysis, we drop this assumption and consider the significance of voter participation rates and variation in such rates across income classes.

15. In general, with K districts, each containing the same odd number of people, n, the minimum number who must favor legislation for its adoption, is given by $[(K+1)/2][(n+1)/2]$. Thus, the smallest fraction of voters who must support a proposal to insure its adoption by the legislature is given by

$$\frac{\left(\frac{K+1}{2}\right)\left(\frac{n+1}{2}\right)}{Kn} = 1/4(1 + 1/K + 1/n + 1/Kn)$$

As n and $K \to \infty$, the last three terms in the right-hand parentheses drop out and the value of this expression approaches 25 percent. See Buchanan and Tullock (1962), pp. 220–221. We have borrowed our diagrammatic representation from them.

16. With a bicameral legislature, in which constituent sets in the two houses overlap, the minimum percentage is likely to be higher. However, consistencies in voting, as between representatives of the same district in the two houses, and offsets across districts imply that it is unlikely to come at all close to doubling.

17. Note that the payment per recipient will differ in cases (a) and (b) if the tax cost of redistribution is the same for each nonrecipient. Suppose that the tax rate on the rich is a flat 10 percent, that rich persons all have incomes of $20,000 and that each poor person has an income of $4,000. Then in case (a) the nine nonrecipients each pay $2,000 and the payment to each poor person is $18,000/16 or $1,125. The single rich person who is benevolent gives up $2,000 to see the incomes of each of the sixteen poor persons raised by $1,125. Each of the other nonrecipients is made worse off since they have independent preferences. In case (b), if the benevolent rich distributed are such that only six are required to enact redistribution, the total tax collected is $20 \times \$2,000 = \$40,000$, and each poor person receives $40,000/5 = \$8,000$.

18. Table 1 also illustrates how small differences in benevolence may produce substantial differences in the degree to which societies (contrast, for example, Sweden, Great Britain, and the U.S.) pursue egalitarian social policies.

19. Related to this, for distributional adjustments at subnational levels of government, is the observation that voters, if dissatisfied with distributional connotations, can move

away. This is the phenomenon of "voting with one's feet" on which the so-called Tiebout thesis rests. One implication of utility interdependence, justifying redistributive income transfers, is that the structure of local communities is more stable than a public choice model with independent preferences might suggest. As potential transfer recipients enter a community, responding to the generosity of its welfare levels, the price of liberalism rises, leading marginal supporters of redistributive activity to emigrate and making any given level of redistributive activity more costly for those who remain. This process feeds upon itself. In these circumstances, whether redistribution will be maintained at its initial level depends on the conflicting population flows, with recipients moving in and erstwhile nonrecipient supporters moving out.

20. For the case of racial integration, this suggests that partial dispersal of the ghetto, limited to jurisdictions in which the formation of sympathetic coalitions is feasible, may be a much more effective means of increasing the political power of the minorities than the reinforcement of concentration (ghetto-gilding) or equi-proportional representation (total integration).

21. With respect to welfare spending, there are only a few obvious cases in which this assumption, with nontrivial likelihood, might be expected to fail. One is where the welfare authorities apply a "man in the house rule" or pry into private morals in screening applicants for "Aid to Dependent Children." Another is where inquiries into financial status offend potential recipients of, say, "Old Age Assistance." Even in these circumstances, however, it seems unlikely that the implied costs in terms of privacy will predominate for any more than a minority of the individuals concerned.

22. Note, however, that the examples Wilson and Banfield (1964) have cited need not be redistributive in the larger sense. Favorable votes, as for the hospital, need not imply benevolence or "public-regardingness" at all, but a desire to drain off the low-income population, permitting more effective segregation of community health facilities by income or race.

23. In general, it seems preferable to ask the reader to grant our awareness of the problems inherent in the sampling techniques of the Field Surveys, through which the data were derived, and just as important, the objective imperfections of the questions. Exhaustive presentation of qualifications, already too familiar to anyone who has worked with such data, would add little but boredom.

24. Unfortunately, to the best of our knowledge, the poll did not ask whether the respondent was or had been a welfare recipient.

25. Consider, for example, the difference between the 38 to 40 percent support for an increase in welfare spending among those with incomes of less than $7,000 and the 14 to 25 percent levels of support among those with incomes of $7,000 or more.

26. In the under $3,000 bracket, 72 percent of the respondents were sixty years of age or older, while only 49 percent of these in the $3,000 to $5,000 bracket were over sixty. A larger proportion of elderly respondents may feel that welfare is inadequate because fewer are likely to be recipients of both welfare and social security, and retirees, even if receiving social seurity, may not identify with welfare recipients. However, Radosevich (1974), in a careful study of nonsupport among the probable net recipients, found that age itself did not seem to account for such deviant responses. What seemed important, rather, was the interaction between age and level of education, inasmuch as nonsupport was more likely among those with high school or less than three years of college (as opposed to even less or more education).

27. One might also, as we mentioned in Part I, attribute a portion of nonrecipient support for welfare to government employees or others with a private interest in the magnitude of public programs. Aside from utility interdependence or insurance, however, there seems no reason for government employees, except for those who are direct suppliers of welfare spending, to be more favorably disposed to it than the average voter.

Indeed, if welfare competes with other uses of public funds, the incentives that face government employees who are not directly involved in supplying welfare services are quite the opposite.

28. This ignores support which derives from expectations of income insurance benefits and the support, based on self-interest, of government welfare workers. Both these sources of demand are likely to be small, the former because few people with 1970 incomes over $7,000 are likely to view welfare programs as providing more than the remotest possibility of potential direct benefits, and the latter for the reason already given, because the proportion of social workers in the total population is small.

29. In examining row 5, note that the rise in net benevolence with income runs counter to the decrease in the percentage of respondents who considered welfare spending a moral imperative.

30. Implicitly, we are assuming here that the housing responses are an adequate proxy for all types of particular-commodity interdependence, as we did with the crime responses and negative utility interactions. As a source of income augmentation, recipients, other things being equal, may be expected to view such in-kind transfers as inferior to cash, though they will certainly prefer them to nothing at all. If sophisticated, however, they may realize that the dollar value of transfers obtainable in kind, if interdependence is of the particular-commodity type, may well exceed that of transfers obtainable in cash.

31. Presumably, this maximum would be even larger with a more detailed income breakdown above $20,000.

32. See Hochman and Rodgers (1969), Section IV.

33. See Rodgers (1973), Peterson (1973), and Zeckhauser (1971).

34. That these responses were not unanimous may be attributed to recognition of the income deficiencies of some "working poor" and to the failure of this statement to discriminate between voluntary and involuntary unemployment.

35. Part V maintains the assumption that those with incomes of less than $7,000 are recipients and those with incomes of $7,000 or more are nonrecipients. This may well be an oversimplification. The issues the California polls posed were in terms of attitudes toward spending or public spending generally rather than in terms of income redistribution. The reasons why "recipient" groups are not unanimous in their support of motions proposing that welfare spending be increased or maintained have been discussed earlier.

36. Since these questions as posed were open-ended, the mention of welfare spending may be taken to imply that the respondent did not think it insignificant. That welfare reform was, as noted earlier, an issue in the ongoing gubernatorial primary campaign must certainly have strengthened such feelings.

37. One may speculate on the reasons for such inconsistencies, though they are of doubtful importance here. Such explanations include, for example, imperfect tax-consciousness (varying inversely with income) and general indifference. Surprising though it may seem for some respondents wishing to limit the number of their responses to open-ended questions, welfare spending may have been less salient than, say, education, the environment, and law enforcement.

38. Whether the present level of spending is stable because respondents are more comfortable with a program level to which they have been accustomed and thus favor the status quo, or viewing the political process as rational, as we have, because this level accurately reflects median voter demand, is beyond the informational capabilities of the data at hand.

39. As William Niskanen has pointed out, the two recent presidential candidates who took strong, though opposing, positions on the adequacy of present levels and systems of

welfare spending, Senators Goldwater and McGovern, were both soundly defeated. While this bit of circumstantial evidence supports our inference that the present level of welfare spending is stable, at least in terms of distributional preference, the reasons why one should not overstress it are obvious.

40. In general, Table 4 indicates that motions to "increase" or "increase and maintain" welfare spending have a somewhat better chance of success, given the parameters, than motions to decrease it.

41. It would be useful to find out if individuals, some months after voting, would repeat their choices if given the opportunity to do so. The 1973 and 1974 Gallup and Harris polls assessing the popularity of President Nixon were, to be sure, evidence of modified preference attributable to changes in perceived "prices" and "rewards."

42. Davis and Jackson (1974) provide an example of this, but make no use of underlying data on individual preferences.

REFERENCES

Aaron, Henry, and von Furstenberg, G. M. "The Inefficiency of Transfers in Kind: The Case of Housing Assistance." *Western Economic Journal* 9 (June 1971): 184–191.

Becker, G. S. "A Theory of Social Interactions." Department of Economics, University of Chicago, Sept. 1969.

Bicker, W. E. "Public Attitudes and Opinions of the Current Welfare System and Components of the Proposed Family Assistance Plan." Findings of a study undertaken for the Department of Health, Education, and Welfare. Institute of Governmental Studies, University of California at Berkeley, July 1970.

Buchanan, J. M. *Public Finance in Democratic Process.* Chapel Hill: University of North Carolina Press, 1967.

———. "What Kind of Redistribution Do We Want?" *Economica* 35 (May 1968): 185–190.

———. "Who Should Distribute What in a Federal System?" In H. M. Hochman and G. E. Peterson, eds., *Redistribution Through Public Choice.* New York: Columbia University Press, 1974, pp. 22–42.

———. "The Political Economy of the Welfare State." Research Paper # 808231-1-8. Center for Study of Public Choice, Virginia Polytechnic Institute and State University, June 1972.

Buchanan, J. M., and Tullock, Gordon. *The Calculus of Consent.* Ann Arbor: University of Michigan Press, 1962.

Downs, Anthony. *An Economic Theory of Democracy.* New York: Random House, 1957.

Dickinson, Frank G., ed. *Philanthropy and Public Policy.* New York: Columbia University Press, 1962.

Fry, B. R., and Winters, R. F. "The Politics of Redistribution." *American Political Science Review* 64 (June 1970): 508–522.

Gillespie, W. Irwin. "Effect of Public Expenditures in the Distribution of Income." In R. A. Musgrave, ed., *Essays in Fiscal Federalism.* Washington, D.C.: The Brookings Institution, 1965.

Goldfarb, R. S. "Pareto Optimal Redistribution: Comment." *American Economic Review* 60 (Dec. 1970): 994–996.

Hochman, H. M. "Individual Preferences and Distributional Adjustments." *American Economic Review* 62 (May 1972): 353–360.

Hochman, H. M., and Rodgers, J. D. "Pareto Optimal Redistribution." *American Economic Review* 59 (Sept. 1969): 542–557.

———. "Pareto Optimal Redistribution: Reply." *American Economic Review* 60 (Dec. 1970): 997–1002.

———. "Is Efficiency a Criterion for Judging Redistribution?" *Proceedings of the International Institute of Public Finance*. Leningrad Congress, 1971, pp. 1236–1248.

———. "Brennan and Walsh Reconsidered (Mutt and Jeff Ride Again)." *Public Finance Quarterly* 1 (Fall 1973): 359–371.

Johnston, John. "Utility Interdependence and the Determinants of Redistributional Public Expenditures." Ph.D. diss., Duke University, 1972.

Levy, Mickey. "A Study of Voting on the California Proposition I Referendum." Graduate School of Public Policy, University of California at Berkeley, 1974.

McGuire, M. C., and Aaron, Henry. "Public Goods and Income Distribution." *Econometrica* 38 (Nov. 1970): 907–920.

Mishan, E. J. "The Futility of Pareto-Efficient Distribution." *American Economic Review* 62 (Dec. 1972): 971–976.

Musgrave, R. A. "Pareto Optimal Redistribution: Comment." *American Economic Review* 60 (Dec. 1970): 991–993.

Olsen, E. O. "A Normative Theory of Transfers." *Public Choice* 6 (Spring 1969): 39–58.

———. "Some Theorems in the Theory of Efficient Transfers." *Journal of Political Economy* 79 (Jan./Feb. 1971): 166–176.

———. "Subsidized Housing in a Competitive Market: Reply." *American Economic Review* 61 (Mar. 1971): 220–224.

Olson, Mancur. *The Logic of Collective Action*. Cambridge: Harvard University Press, 1965.

Pauly, M.V. "Income Redistribution as a Local Public Good." *Journal of Public Economics* 2 (Feb. 1973): 35–58.

———. "Efficiency in the Provision of Consumption Subsidies." *Kyklos* 23 (Mar. 1970): 33–57.

Peterson, G. E. "Welfare, Workfare, and Pareto Optimality." *Public Finance Quarterly* 1 (July 1973): 323–338.

Radosevich, Ted. "An Estimation of Non-Support Among Probable Net Recipients of Income Transfers, State Data Program of the Institute of Governmental Studies." Institute of Governmental Studies, University of California at Berkeley, 1974.

Robbins, Lionel. *An Essay on the Nature and Significance of Economic Science*. London: Macmillan, 1932.

Rodgers, J. D. "Distributional Externalities and the Optimal Form of Income Transfers." *Public Finance Quarterly* 1 (July 1973): 266–299.

Rodgers, J. D. "Explaining Income Redistribution." In H. M. Hochman and G. E. Peterson, eds., *Redistribution Through Public Choice*. New York: Columbia University Press, 1974, pp. 165–205.

Schumpeter, J. A. *Capitalism, Socialism, and Democracy*. New York: Harper and Bros., 1942.

Schultze, C. L. *The Distribution of Farm Subsidies: Who Gets the Benefits?* Washington, D.C.: The Brookings Institution, 1971.

Schwartz, R. A. "Personal Philanthropic Contributions." *Journal of Political Economy* 78 (Dec. 1970): 1264–1291.

Tiebout, C. M. "A Pure Theory of Local Expenditures." *Journal of Political Economy* 64 (Oct. 1956): 416–424.

Tullock, G. "The Cost of Transfers." *Kyklos* 24 (1971a): 629–643.

————. "The Charity of the Uncharitable." *Western Economic Journal* 9 (Dec. 1971b): 379–392.

Wilson, J. Q., and Banfield, E. C. "Public Regardingness as a Value Premise in Voting Behavior." *American Political Science Review* 58 (Dec. 1964): 876–887.

Zeckhauser, R. "Optimal Mechanisms for Income Transfers." *American Economic Review* 61 (June 1971): 324–334.

D

Economic Justice

[9]
Contractarian Theories of Income Redistribution[1]

HAROLD M. HOCHMAN

Introduction

The redistribution of market determined incomes, fiscal or philanthropic, presumes dissatisfaction with their distribution, or with the distribution of opportunities they connote. Otherwise, redistribution would neither be appropriate nor would it occur in a democratic society. Discussion therefore must begin with the reasons for dissatisfaction, as revealed in the egoistic and the ethical choices of the individuals and communities who are party to the social contract.

The evaluation of redistributive measures is a twice-told tale. Income transfers through which redistribution is effected must be examined in normative terms to determine their consistency with the desired state of affairs. This requires positive evaluation of their effects. Without knowledge of distributional objectives and their ethical origins, which account for their legitimacy, however, such knowledge has little value. To a competent analyst there is no escape from the preferences (however inchoate) from which distributional objectives derive, or the constraints and procedures that govern the individual and collective decisions that translate this demand into policy.

The process through which a political community specifies its distributional objectives, like the objectives themselves, may be general or specific.

[1] An early draft of this paper was supported by the U.S. Department of Health, Education and Welfare. The author wishes to thank Shmuel Nitzan and Shlomo Yitzhaki for a number of insights. The usual disclaimer applies.

211

SOCIAL POLICY EVALUATION:
AN ECONOMIC PERSPECTIVE

The heart of the matter is whether the institutional context—the social contract which defines rights to nonhuman capital (property) and human capital (labor) and the income they engender—is parametric or variable. Where property rights (i.e., social rules that govern the disposition of income or its equivalent) remain open, the decision to redistribute income is a matter of constitutional choice, raising thorny ethical questions of a kind that have often been wrestled to no decision by political philosophers. In a postconstitutional context, with "defined" rights that are immune to modification in daily transactions, redistribution is political or, where its conduct is private, philanthropic. There is a distinction between the donors who finance transfers and the recipients to whom they flow. In redistribution through public choice an individual's ability to identify whether he or she will be recipient or donor is fundamental.

The distinction between constitutional and postconstitutional redistribution is central to contemporary economic thought. Without it, it is impossible to depart from the distributional nihilism that accompanied economists' rejection of classical utilitarianism. With it, some progress, definitive in a directional though not quantitative sense, can be discerned.

Even if redistributive intent is firm, it can be derailed at various crossroads, some well hidden, in the track from perception to action. Without normative guidance, constitutional and postconstitutional, the modification of market determined distribution will be random, or in accord with the preferences of decision makers rather than the preferences of those they are supposed to represent. Unless public choice reflects constituent preferences in its redistributive as well as its allocative concern, distributional choice is dependent, analytically, on a deus ex machina—the social welfare function of neoclassical welfare economics—a construct that is at best a convenient fiction.

It can be argued that classical utilitarianism is a chimera. There is no proof that individuals have identical capacity for converting income to utility. People differ in intellect and personality, as well as in economic status and access to information, and in their dissatisfaction with distribution, and thus in the basis of their support for redistributive programs. In theory and practice, utility theory is little help; at worst, it may provide a rationale for oppression.

In constraining property rights (in "constitutional" or "primary" redistribution) *and* in enacting transfer programs that modify the distribution of returns to persons and property (in postconstitutional or "secondary" redistribution), public policy must reconcile diverse preferences.[2] Incentive effects of fiscal transfers, which impinge on factor supply, are but one (though

---

[2] These terms, which help to clarify the distinction, were coined by R. A. Musgrave (1970), in his discussion of Hochman and Rodgers (1969).

the most studied) dimension of the problem of program design.[3] As impediments to attainment of the elusive distributional optimum, the factors that
blur the transmission of preferences through the political process, though
less studied, are just as important. It is difficult to design conceptual experiments or formulate positive hypotheses that link distributional objectives
and distributional outcomes; this is no secret to anyone who has tried.

To a community of but two persons, with full information, political ambiguities pose no problem. Simple self-interest leads to the voluntary definition
of distribution-constraining rules acceptable to both parties. In larger communities, problems of reference revelation and preference aggregation become apparent. Voluntarism is no longer sufficient, and enforcement costs
become significant, more so the less homogeneous the community. Redistribution as a public good becomes the business of government, and as such
the product of political compromise.[4]

To proceed from concepts to programs, isolating areas of agreement and
disagreement obligates us to understand the distributional implications of
existing social arrangements and to ascertain the effects of redistributive
actions, both direct and indirect. This is true whether our concern is with the
manner in which redistribution should occur (the normative question) or the
reasons why it does or does not occur (the positive question). But there is no
sense in which the positive evaluation of program effects is sufficient alone,
as much of the literature seems to presume, taking for granted that a demand
for more redistribution from rich to poor should be supported. To not confound distributional policy with ideological fancy, discussion must begin
with institutional premises and proceed from there, albeit imperfectly, to
operational objectives.[5]

This chapter summarizes the logical web of contemporary contractarian
theories (for a readable discussion of such theories, see Mueller 1979) of
income redistribution, as it exists in the author's mind. It strays, as it must,

---

[3] Whatever the basis of redistribution, its secondary effects on the aggregate income available for distribution will abate a preference for equality. In this regard, the limiting case, in
which incentive effects are total, is instructive, though absurd.

[4] The interpretation of redistribution as a public good is attributable to Thurow (1971) and is
developed in more detail in Breit (1974).

[5] There is little irony in the fact that extensive and heavily funded research into the likely
effects of comprehensive income maintenance proposals has yet to be translated in the United
States into the legislative reform of a cumbersome and confusing income transfer system.
Indeed, we seem farther than ever from enacting the redistributive programs—welfare reform—of the type contemplated a decade ago. It would be presumptuous as well as unfair to
blame the research community for this change in the national mood. But unless the democratic
process is hopelessly inept, it does seem that too little effort has been expended in probing the
distributional preferences of the community. Technicians, in considering means of potential
redistribution, have allowed their private normative premises and methodological commitments
to lead them down the garden path —though in democratic process, as in private affairs, the
bucket of gold can only be there if the rainbow is metaphorical.

from the traditional bounds of economics, if indeed such bounds can be meaningfully defined. Its concern is with spelling out the general guidance to the optimal amount and form and the appropriate engine of income transfers from rich to poor provided by contemporary thought. But it is not, except in an incidental way, bibliographic, and it does not provide a systematic review of the literature, or summarize findings, analytic or experimental, describing the actual or intended effects of alternative income transfer programs.[6]

Origins of Distribution and Redistribution

To obtain the income distribution, factor returns deriving from the exchange (market income) or own use (imputed income) and employment of private or common property resources (such as the imputed benefits of public services), are aggregated. The distribution, in its simplest form, can be described by a two-dimensional matrix, which classifies such flows by resource owners and resource types. Aggregation over resource type, to obtain the total incomes of resource owners (as individuals or economic units) produces the size or personal distribution of income, which is central to the discussion of equity and redistribution. Aggregation by resource type defines the functional income distribution, on which classical economics focused. The functional distribution remains a major concern in modern theories of production and economic growth.

To the extent that it enters the discussion of redistribution, concern with the functional distribution rests on a presumption that the society is divided into distinct classes. Economic units are seen as owners of capital or suppliers of labor. It is their belief in the existence of such a division that classifies "radical economists" as neo-Marxist. The class division, in which labor, as a consequence of exploitation, fares less well than capital, enables such scholars to focus the discussion of redistribution on functional shares.

In our society, however, class distinctions are less clear. Economic units at almost every level derive income from the supply of capital (through, for example, home ownership) as well as labor (now interpreted as the return to "human capital"). Thus, discussion of distributive justice focuses on total incomes of economic units and not their factor sources, except to the extent that factor returns are illegitimate or have been affected differentially by noncompetitive phenomena such as discrimination. However, it is better to treat such imperfections as exceptions which warrant correction in their own right, rather than as fundamental sources of the social demand for redistribution. Since contemporary theories of redistribution are concerned

---

[6] Two useful reviews already exist (Rodgers, 1974, and Johnston, 1975).

with the logic of income transfers from rich to poor, it seems sensible to concentrate in this chapter on attitudes toward the distribution of incomes by size.

The rationale for income redistribution, current or lifetime, must be traced to initial conditions *or* current transactions. Thus, it can be argued that property rights and the income shares they engender are improper because the process through which claims were assigned was itself illegitimate or because they give rise to a distribution of purchasing power that is unsatisfactory in terms of an independent ethical norm (such as equality). In other words, objectives can be defined in terms of process or result, or both. On the other hand, even the most classical libertarian and the most Darwinian admirer of the free-market distributional outcome may consider this distribution inappropriate because market failures prevent factors of production from receiving their true social returns. Such failures may derive from monopoly (a basis for arguing that the income shares of nonhuman capital and organized labor are excessive) or external effects, because political and bureaucratic institutions transmit preferences imperfectly.

It is often unclear which of these reasons dominates, in professional as well as lay discussion. Both supporters and opponents of redistribution seem all too willing to muster any available arguments on its behalf. Recipient self-interest aside, however, such ambiguity does seem to mask fundamental ethical dissatisfaction. On the other hand, a lack of concern with the distributional implications of market imperfections, economic or political, can be interpreted in terms of narrow self-interest *or* as a corollary of the belief that public intervention is unlikely to be worth its long-run costs. In redistribution, "the bucket" with which transfers are made, to recast Okun's (1975) metaphor, leaks freedoms as well as incentives.

This argument cannot be lightly dismissed. In a heterogeneous community consisting of people who have heterogeneous preferences it is difficult to resolve political disagreement through democratic process. Even for the actor, it is not simple to sort out the self-serving from the ethical. So it is hardly surprising that ethical arguments provide ready opening to curtailment of essential freedoms. Since freedom is multidimensional, it is resistant to simplistic interpretation. Simplistic though some may make it appear, freedom is certainly likely to require *some* redistribution. But it is unlikely to be consistent with either *negligible* or *pervasive* redistribution.

Redistribution in a Constitutional Choice Setting

In reflecting about redistribution, the major requirement is a logical artifice that distinguishes distributional preference from support for redistributive transfers that reflects simple self-interest or, to be more cynical, bargaining strategy or debating ploy. In logic, though hardly in fact, the "veil of ignorance," on which John Rawls has built *A Theory of Justice* (1971) satisfies this demand.[7] Its presupposition is that individuals deciding on social institutions in an "original position" cannot discern their prospective stations in life. This permits them to attain a consensus or constitutional contract defining the rights and rules that govern person and property. Thus constrained, constitutional choice reflects dispassionate appraisal, free of parochial interest, and produces an outcome that redounds to the benefit of all.

Though an obvious fiction, the "veil of ignorance" assumption has a number of appealing characteristics, which turn its abstract properties into a basis for discussion of redistribution, both normative and positive. Decisions behind the veil reflect not altruism, but simple self-interest. Individuals make such decisions in full knowledge of the fortunes, present and future, of the population at large, but with total ignorance of private shares. Since individuals are identical under the veil, because they are effectively ignorant of their identities, they have, perforce, identical preferences. *The concept of the veil thus denies the distinction between self and other*. This is the source of its importance to the theory of redistribution.

The veil, in contrast to prior discussion, which links distributional choice to questionable utilitarian assumptions[8] or to a "strong" social welfare function capable of incorporating interpersonal utility comparisons in preference aggregation, has a number of important implications. Since self is merged with other, interpersonal comparisons become unnecessary. Welfare comparisons are internal. Operationally, the distinction between Kantian and egoistic motives disappears. Such standard inadequacies of democratic process as the Arrow paradox, which results in cyclicity, are ruled out so that the impossibility theorem does not apply. Attention centers on the formulation of a constitution, which specifies property rights and, therefore, the endowments with which individuals enter the exchange process.

In the context defined, rights and rules turn out to hinge on the risk aversion of our "representative" (by definition) individual. To the discomfort of those who might wish for more novelty, this amounts to much the same thing as diminishing marginal utility. If individuals are universally risk averse, the marginal utility of money (obtained as factor income) diminishes throughout its range, and the "appropriate" distribution is one in which all incomes are equal, absent incentive effects or other factors that

---

[7] The "veil," as an analytic construct, differs from the "state of nature," in which property rights are unspecified, but individuals are not unaware of their status and prospects. See Buchanan (1975), Harsanyi (1955), and Vickrey (1960).

[8] Blum and Kalven (1953) provides the classic critique of the utilitarian justifications of redistributive taxation.

contradict the assumptions of the model.[9] This conclusion is remarkably robust.[10]

A rigorous line of argument verifies the emergence of the egalitarian result in a pure exchange (no production) economy under a wide variety of assumptions and decision rules (see Pazner and Schmeidler 1976; Varian 1976; other articles by Varian). Neither cardinal utility nor (external) interpersonal welfare comparisons are required. The conclusion hinges on "the fundamental symmetry of the original position [Pazner and Schmeidler 1976, p. 263]." It stands behind the veil, whether or not individuals know the content of their utility functions. Varian links this result to the more general "theory of fairness," which derives from games of fair division. Thus, if a just allocation is defined as "a Pareto-efficient allocation where the worst-off agent— the one that no one envies—is made better off, that is, envies no one," social justice, in the "opportunity fairness sense," seems to require an "equal income competitive equilibrium." An equal division of income is also "especially fair," in the sense that "no group of agents envies the average bundle of any other group" (Varian 1976, pp. 250–251).

In the fictional world of the pure exchange or all-consumption economy, then, equality satisfies the criterion of fairness and, behind the veil seems the natural positive outcome of constitutional contracting. Until knowledge of individual prospects or the need to produce goods and services for exchange are introduced, it rules the day. Once these realities are admitted, however, distributional guidance becomes far less clear.

Although one may wish for more novelty, the analogy is striking. What utilitarians obtained with "minimum aggregate sacrifice," current authors derive with the "veil of ignorance." Though the contractual nature of the contemporary theory eliminates the need for an external observer, one wonders whether the methodological improvement this implies is illusion or reality. Still, in contrast with the utilitarian version, in which there is no derivation of the authority of the state from the preferences of the governed, it does establish a direct link between social choice and individual preferences.

To build a bridge from the veil in an all-consumption setting to positive analysis requires a reconsideration of its assumptions. This uncovers many problems worthy of scrutiny, a few of which are isolated here.

---

[9] These relationships between risk aversion and the desired distribution are traced out in Hochman and Kleiman (1981). Infinite risk aversion is not required to justify perfect equality. Even if there are incentive effects, a corner outcome may be optimal if individuals are sufficiently risk averse.

[10] It should be noted that Lerner (1944) obtained this result in his utilitarian, though sophisticated, demonstration that the probable value of aggregate satisfaction is maximized if incomes are equal. He assumed that individuals know marginal utilities diminish but do not know how efficient they will be in converting income into utility.

First, if individuals differ in ability to convert money income to utility, the strict argument for equality breaks down, even if identities remain uncertain. Thus, it seems improper to lavish output on retarded persons—to the point at which their marginal utilities fall to zero—at the expense of more effective consumers.[11] Knowledge of identities strengthens this argument. As a practical matter, however, though the dilemma is clear, it is worth but limited consideration.

Second, the argument that risk aversion dominates distributional preference may rest on weak ground. Democracies, including their working-class constituencies, seem to prefer fiscal rules that retain the possibility of significant accumulation, even if it is remote. Whether this derives from narrow self-interest or a kind of economic voyeurism is not germane. Over-the-counter lotteries confirm that we cannot lightly dismiss the propensity to gamble. Thus normative models of distributional preference must, in a manner reminiscent of Friedman and Savage (1948) reconcile risk aversion with the taste for gambling. This taste, it would seem, incontrovertibly weakens the case for equality as a distributional norm.[12]

Third, the simple theory explicitly ignores production, which accounts for the major reasons why individuals demur from a constitution that mandates equality. The arguments that apply here have one characteristic in common: All imply that an equal distribution would not be Pareto-optimal. Potentially, deviations from equality can improve the welfare of at least one member of the community—or all members behind the veil.

Technological factors are at the heart of the case against perfect equality. In conjunction with differences in demand, economies of scale leading to specialization imply that market rewards will differ. Inherent differences in productivity suggest that resources, to achieve Pareto-optimal allocation, should be directed by comparative advantage. Both of these considerations, which are as relevant behind the veil as they are in the postconstitutional world, lead to real-world inequalities in the exchange process. Although a comprehensive system of transfers agreed upon in the course of constitutional choice can in theory redress such inequalities, it is likely to have incentive effects. This, in almost all circumstances, cinches the case against full equality.[13]

[11] This interpretation of Rawls's "maximin" principle requires no "external" interpersonal comparisons. Harsanyi (1975) makes this point with some force. The Karen Ann Quinlan case is a clear expression of this problem.

[12] An aside may be enlightening. If the utility-of-money function has the shape that Friedman and Savage (1948) describe, with concave segments at its extremes, the democratic preference for equality may be stronger in advanced than in low-income societies. There are many ways in which this can be played out. For example, where economic resources are scarce, it may imply a tolerance for "effective" political inequalities.

[13] Many studies have demonstrated that effects on labor supply behavior may severely limit the optimal degree of progression in the income tax. Some of the most prominent are Fair (1971), Feldstein (1973), and Mirrlees (1971).

Incentive effects, the most well researched of the factors that intrude in the case against redistribution, derive from the fact that individuals, in allocating their time, value leisure, which is not produced, as well as produced goods. (To simplify, I ignore complementaries between leisure and produced goods.) The taste for leisure implies *ex ante* that redistributive adjustments, imposed *ex post* on the outcome of exchange, may have adverse effects on labor supply, reducing the size of the pie available to be distributed. In attempting to recoup, those who must finance redistributive transfers not only shift part of the burden of redistributive taxation to the rest of the community by substituting leisure for labor, but generate a deadweight loss of economic welfare.

Once the veil is admitted to be but a scholar's artifice, the subject of redistribution as a product of social choice becomes more difficult to handle. In effect, this step moves us from normative abstraction with its utilitarian analogies toward the more complex and contradictory ceiling presented by distributional reality. It returns self-interest, as it were, to its narrow interpretation, provided (as in conventional theory) that interpersonal utility interactions are ignored. (This, however, is perhaps as unrealistic as the veil itself.) The weight of incentive effects is greater because intertemporal and intergenerational relationships are no longer impersonal.

Nonetheless, even in this more realistic and more restrictive setting, pressure for equalization, though less pronounced than equality requires, continues. James Buchanan illustrates this in *The Limits of Liberty* (1975), with a description of the metaphorical transition from Hobbesian anarchy to democratic polity.[14] Buchanan's starting point is the "state of nature" rather than the "veil of ignorance." The crucial difference is that in the "state of nature" identities and, in particular, initial endowments are known. The essence of the theory is that "economic exchange among persons is *facilitated* (emphasis added) by mutual agreement on defined rights (Buchanan 1975, p. 18)." Its logic is that of "the prisoner's dilemma."[15]

In Hobbesian anarchy participants may think that theft or expropriation is a productive means of increasing consumption share, provided each participant can act independently, without fear of reprisal. In time, however, they find this to be a two-edged sword, which may also work to their disadvantage. Energies expended in predation and defense are not without cost in real resources. Indeed, assuming that an alternative course of action is available, their cost amounts to a deadweight loss.

Thus, the adoption of self-constraining property rights, which deter predation, proves to be to the advantage of all. Redistribution is the means

---

[14] Buchanan's analysis builds on his own earlier work, with Gordon Tullock and with other colleagues, in particular the late Winston Bush (see Buchanan and Tullock 1962, and Buchanan and Bush 1972).

[15] The analogies to the theory of public goods and the free-rider problem that is central to it are, in this connection, complete.

through which the rich, with substantial endowments, induce the poor to forego predation. So long as protection is a normal good (individuals with more to protect devote more resources to protection) and the costs of enforcing agreement (through procedures built into the constitution) do not dominate the deadweight loss, redistribution is the means through which individuals induce each other to accede to the social contract and the restrictions on individual freedom it entails. Specialization and comparative advantage, which operate on the production side to bring about inequalities, simply reinforce this argument, as does the fact that individuals are not indifferent to, but value, the company of others.[16] Indeed, the closer self and other are identified, as they are behind the veil, the more redistributive the constitutional contract is likely to be. However, enforcement is unlikely to be so costly as to lead the community, by consensus, to adopt distributional rules that dictate equality, much less reversals in the exchange-determined distributional ordering.

Buchanan provides for recontracting of property rights, thus established, as objective conditions evolve and the community perceives the advantages of changing the social contract and the system of rights it encompasses. This process of rule change poses many problems for social justice. In devising rules for redistribution, prior rewards—which have cumulated over time, producing a distribution of wealth that can be traced to activities carried out with constitutional sanction—cannot be ignored.[17] Surely, no constitution could endure if the process of distributional choice were to put income and wealth up for grabs with each turn of the temporal wheel, in a perpetual effort to restore the veil, trampling existing property rights whenever they get in the way. In such a regime behavior that conforms to the law would conflict with utility maximization. If redistribution is to be consistent with respect for the law, its effects on the distribution of well-being, in both the short run and the long run, must be balanced against its effects on respect for the legal structure. The fact that the slate is never clean limits the extent to which redistribution can be carried out and the ease with which the procedures that effect it, once in force, may be modified (Feldstein 1976; Hochman 1974).

In sum, the moment the fictional identity of self and other is relaxed, the assumptions that support equality as an optimal distributional state become much stronger, and the derivation of guidelines for redistribution, set in the preferences on which democratic decision making is based, becomes more difficult. To justify equality, *individuals must be equal,* because they will no longer act as if they were equal. Problems of preference aggregation, which

[16] Note, in this context, that the distribution problem par excellence occurs within the family.

[17] This seems, in fact, to be the ultimate rationale for theories of distribution in which returns to the resources that individuals provide are considered, in essence, as "entitlements" (see Nozick 1974).

account for the distributional indeterminacy of welfare economies, reappear; no longer is there a basis for natural consensus. A practical understanding of public choice and the role of redistribution within it, as indicated by positive models of democratic process tested against real-world observations, becomes essential.

In choosing a distributional objective, the effect of the transitional equity problem is to force us away from equality per se and toward equality of opportunity, because the concept of opportunity blurs the distinction between self and other and defers the effects of change, thus discounting the costs of transition. This makes it easier to obtain agreement on rules for redistribution. But at the pragmatic level it raises the issue of how, in terms of objective characteristics, to define equality of opportunity.

In conclusion, contractarian theories of distributional preference as an element in the social contract establish the determinate optimum independent of endowments, except under assumptions as stringent and unrealistic as those of classical utilitarianism. Such theories, nonetheless, do tell us something, with weaker assumptions and little ambiguity, about the proper direction of distributional change: They imply that a voluntary social contract *should and will* provide for some redistribution from rich to poor. Risk aversion and the costs of enforcing agreed-upon claims to resources assure this.

Redistribution in a Neoclassical Setting[18]

In the postconstitutional setting there is no veil. Individuals are fully aware of their rights to resources and the returns to which these rights entitle them.[19] As a result the distributional issue is turned on its head. The income distribution determined through exchange rather than an equal distribution sets the point of normative departure. Transfers toward equality, not away from it, must be justified. The objective is attainment of a Pareto-optimal allocation of resources. If one starts from such an allocation and *the distribution it implies,* no individual's utility can be increased without harming someone else.

The allocative and distributive content of a Pareto optimum depends on preferences, as exercised by individuals, subject to property rights, and technological relationships, which control the conversion of resources into final output. Only if property rights are unambiguous and immutable is this "efficient" outcome, which differs with the specification of rights, unique.

---

[18] Much of this section is adapted from an earlier discussion (Hochman 1972, especially pp. 353–356).

[19] External effects, of course, may render such rights ambiguous, and their resolution through bargaining may have significant distributional effects (see Coase 1960). Here it is assumed that the construction has assigned all rights to resources.

There are two reasons, each of which impinges on distribution, why post-constitutional exchange, private and political, may fail to produce a Pareto-optimal allocation.

Market imperfections (deviations from competitive assumptions) inherent in the markets and motives of factors and firms, are the first. However, where market imperfections intrude, the relevant public policy issue is not redistribution per se, but fiscal or legal remedy, provided the game of correlation is worth the candle. Counterbalancing the normative danger of inaction (to which egalitarians direct their attention) are the dangers of confusing true information costs with contrived monopoly power and attempting to correct natural monopoly, through regulation, with something worse. Here, however, our concern is not to decide whether and when corrective intervention is proper, but rather to determine the incidental nature of the distributional connotations of market imperfections.

That external effects exist is the second reason why unfettered exchange may not produce a Pareto optimum. Utility interdependence, which restores, in some measure, the identity of self and other, may not only justify but require redistributive transfers. Such utility interactions may be interpersonal (utility interdependence that is positive and relevant at the margin), or intertemporal (reflecting an intrapersonal preference for income stability). Attainment of a Pareto optimum—in effect the "best" the community can do, given prevailing rights and rules—requires redistributive transfers in money or goods. This section summarizes the logic and the limits of such transfers.

REDISTRIBUTION AS A REFLECTION OF UTILITY INTERDEPENDENCE

The assumption that utility functions are independent is standard. In the mainstream of economics, utility depends on what an individual does, now and later, not on what others do, except as this is reflected (through exchange, private or public) in market prices or tax prices. This independence assumption, which forced the utilitarian justification of redistribution, obscured much of what the Pareto criterion can tell us about the proper scope and character of distributional adjustments.

Even casual observation of human behavior, both in families and in the society at large, suggests that it is appropriate to modify the model of economic choice to take utility interdependence into account.[20] This provides not only an analytic basis for discussing income transfers, but also guidance as to their proper amount and means. Indeed, it seems fair to argue (in a postconstitutional setting) that utility interdependence is essential to discussion of social justice, which is not operational unless the well-being of at

[20] Gary Becker developed this argument in a number of similar papers, including his much-cited essay, "A Theory of Social Interaction" (Becker 1974).

least one individual, in his or her own thinking, depends on what happens to others. This perception must, moreover, be Pareto-relevant; it must not only foster kind thoughts but also lead to positive redistributive actions.

The logic of this argument, as it has been spelled out in the literature, seems clear enough.[21] In the simplest of cases (two persons), A's concern for B in degree sufficient to hand over some disposable income for B's use, reflects itself in a voluntary transfer. Since both parties benefit from this transfer, it is Pareto-optimal.[22] The external effect, in other words, manifests itself in private generosity,[23] because own utility is no longer a strict function of income available for own consumption. As the number of individuals multiplies, the network of utility interactions becomes more complex. The family is perhaps the most obvious example of a social unit in which Pareto-optimal income transfers between donors with property rights in factor returns and recipients to whom they transfer such rights are a regular and significant occurrence.

Note that such transfers, which are attributable to the blurring of the distinction between self and other, are consistent with egoistic behavior. They may, in general, derive from benevolence (a concern for others) *or* a "selfish" concern with protection from the predatory behavior of others (as in Buchanan's model).[24] But they are based on intrapersonal (though not impersonal) comparison and a matter of donor volition.

Now extend the logic of Pareto-optimal transfers to the many-person case (in the limit, N persons). As the paired comparisons between donors and recipients multiply, interdependencies among individual pairs weaken and the transfers become a public good. The free-rider problem common to public goods provision emerges, and administrative costs of effecting the transfers increase. In other words, the "bucket" begins to leak.

Assume that utility interdependence, to give rise to a demand for redis-

---

[21] Early suggestion of this argument can be found in the writings of a number of economists, in particular James Buchanan and William Vickrey. However, it obtained widespread currency through Hochman and Rodgers (1969) and Olsen (1969).

[22] One can, of course, find counterexamples. For example, if B were an ascetic, whose utility is reduced by the transfer, B may find it costly to dispose of the gift. For the most part, however, the counterexamples, like this one, are aberrations, and can be fairly ignored. Their existence is evidence of a positive counterpart to the normative theory, which is refutable statistically with real-world data (if such data can be isolated). This stands in contrast to constitutional choice, for which data must be obtained through experimental procedures, because there is no real-world analogue to the veil.

[23] With predefined property rights, no transfer would result if the interdependence were negative—if, in other words, A is antipathetic to B. With more than two persons, however, negative externalities may lead to Pareto-optimal transfers (Brennan 1973). The literature on this subject suffers, in general, from loose and inconsistent use of language. In a recent paper, Shmuel Nitzan and I attempt to remedy this by developing a detailed classification, in terms of preference and price, of concepts of sympathy and antipathy (Hochman and Nitzan).

[24] In reality, then, it is usually impossible to distinguish unambiguously between constitutional and postconstitutional behavior.

tribution, requires the recipient to have a lower income than the donor. Unless A's concern is with the act of giving rather than the impact of the gift on its beneficiary, A prefers, other things equal, that C, equally well situated, make a transfer to B. This would not only improve B's welfare, as A wishes, but leave A with more income.

With many parties, the free-rider problem makes it appropriate for the public sector to engineer the Pareto-optimal transfer of income. This is accomplished by means of the fiscal process, through explicitly redistributive taxes and transfers, and through patterns of expenditure benefits that alter the distribution of real disposable income (nonzero fiscal residuals). The usual instrument is a progressive income tax—with an implicit assumption that this tax is not shifted and its incidence is independent of expenditure benefits or, alternatively, proportional to income.

Patterns of Pareto-optimal transfers, motivated by utility interdependence that is linked to income or income differentials, have been derived by a number of authors (see Hochman and Rodgers 1969; Von Furstenberg and Mueller 1971). Such transfer patterns, depending on one's precise assumptions about the relationship between interdependence and income, may be distribution-condensing, with an effect similar to risk aversion in constitutional choice, or distribution-truncating, leveling income up from the bottom of the distribution and making no transfers to anyone as long as others have lower incomes, analogous to the "maximin" decision rule.

An alternative way of stating this argument (e.g., Breit 1974, and Thurow 1971), treats the income distribution itself as a public good, in the sense of an environmental characteristic. As opposed to the utility interdependence logic, in which the public good is the set of *redistributive* transfers rather than the distribution, the Breit–Thurow perspective does not separate the object of distributional concern (the income distribution) from the logical basis of such concern (benevolence or concern with the well-being or behavior of others). It can, then, even in the abstract, encompass all redistribution, constitutional and postconstitutional. Moreover, because net recipients of fiscal transfers pay negative prices for redistribution, it is hard to think of them, in any meaningful sense, as its demanders, though it is reasonable to think of them as participants in a game (Aumann and Kurz, 1977, approach the problem in this way). Neoclassical wisdom holds transfers in cash (general purchasing power) to be preferable to in-kind transfers. Cash transfers afford recipients more options and thus, in given amounts, can have greater effects on their utility.[25] With utility interdependence, in contrast, the optimal form of income depends on the nature of the underlying external effect. Cash is appropriate, as in Friedman's argument, if donor concern is with recipient utility (if, in other words, the external effect is "general"). In-kind transfers through commodity grants (e.g., in the form of educational services

---

[25] Milton Friedman (1952) presents the classic statement of this theorem.

or housing) or price subsidies are appropriate if the interdependence is of the "particular commodity" type (Rodgers 1973). This means that the donor's primary concern is with the recipient's consumption bundle, rather than the recipient's self-perceived utility.

There are two possible reasons for this. One is the "merit want" argument, which rests on the donor's belief that the recipient lacks the knowledge required to make choices that are consistent, in a long-run frame of reference, with the recipient's own utility. The other is that the specific consumption choices of the recipient (who may, say, engage in poor health practices or antisocial activities) may offend the donor. Moreover, benevolence may be a function of the degree to which the rich think the poor are doing all they can to help themselves. Thus, if donors are averse to disincentives that lead recipients to work less and consume more leisure, wage subsidies are appropriate (Peterson 1973). Such incentive effects reduce output and constrict the set of consumption options. The case for in-kind transfers is weakened, however, by the costs, tangible and subjective, of administering in-kind transfer programs, including the implications for personal freedom of intervention in consumer choice.[26]

The one assumption needed to assure that such transfers will be equalizing is that positive interactions between the utility of the rich and the status of the poor dominate the overall interdependence pattern. Where, say, donor concern is with recipient income, diminishing marginal utility, internal to *donor* preferences, ensures this.

Despite its apparent simplicity, this interpretation of postconstitutional redistribution is not free of problems. If the objective is to explain actual distributional adjustments, difficulties in sorting out constitutional from postconstitutional explanations of real-world income transfers are a corollary of the fact that utility interdependence blurs the distinction between self and other. This is readily apparent once one asks why individuals care about each other, and recognizes the significance of defense from predation with regard to transfers that reflect certain types of particular commodity interactions. Transfers (through education, housing, and police services) motivated by concern with the crime rate are obvious examples.

Confronted with skepticism of this sort, it is important to recall that the term *constitution,* in its ordinary meaning, connotes a system of fundamental laws and principles. In effect, utility interdependence complements the constitutional basis of redistribution and serves, over time, as the engine of its revision. Recontracting, through reinterpretation of property rights, proceeds deliberately, just as compromise, which defines daily governmental

[26] In-kind transfers may, for example, be appropriate, as through education, when the donor's concern is the recipient's ability to choose (in effect, a value system). Thus, the temporal character of human development blurs the distinction between types of transfers. But it also dulls our assurance, as opposed to our presumption, that in-kind transfers can be Pareto-optimal.

procedure, gives way to consensus. It seems clear, for example, that minimal acceptable standards of living have been drastically redefined, and related aspects of equality have been restated, in the last century, or, for that matter, the last decade or two. Redistributive legislation, supported and enacted by individuals who are fully aware of their identities, has been the instrument of such change. Such legislation has been incremental, not total, and support for it has, needless to say, never been unanimous. Once adopted, however, it has come to be part of the institutional setting, immune, in the main, to reversal. The implication of this is that postconstitutional inquiry into the logic of income transfers should focus on arguments for change in the distributive and redistributive status quo, rather than aggregate patterns of redistribution.

Though the public process through which redistributive transfers are effected is anonymous, there is nothing abstract about its monetary effects. It is highly unlikely that *actual* or *potential* transfer recipients (perhaps one-fourth of the U.S. population), acting in *narrow* self-interest could have secured enactment of existing redistributive legislation without nonrecipient support, for which interdependence seems a likely explanation.[27] What scant evidence we can muster simply does not support a simple-minded interpretation of redistribution as a political manifestation of recipient self-interest (Culyer 1973, chapter 4; Hochman and Rodgers 1977).

Thus, concern for others who are thought to be receiving less than their appropriate ("fair"?) share of the social product, leading, in time, to revision of the social contract, seems to be a reasonable explanation of income redistribution from rich to poor.[28] Theories of redistribution, then, whether they begin with "the original position" or with predefined property rights, seem to converge. Because operational procedures reshape values, this convergence is iterative. In the short run the "ideal" is indeterminate. In the long run, there is reasonable assurance that the democratic political process will move us toward it, and that this distribution will reflect significant adjustment of factor incomes.

INTERTEMPORAL AND INTERGENERATION INCOME TRANSFERS

Time adds another dimension to the logic of postconstitutional redistribution. Even with deterministic income expectations, individuals, expecting income to vary over time, save and dissave to adjust to an optimal pattern of

---

[27] A complementary argument is that transfers, by making the poor more productive, will benefit all. But this seems to be a weak reason to support redistribution to many of the poor who are ill-suited (for reasons of age and social condition) to labor force participation (see Rolph 1968).

[28] Appropriateness, as this argument has developed, encompasses a concern for *narrow reasons of self-protection* with reducing the predatory activities of the poor and disadvantaged.

lifetime consumption. The result, as far as permanent income is concerned, may be no redistribution at all; in cross section measures, however, such saving and dissaving may give rise to a substantial amount of interpersonal redistribution (Polinsky 1974).

In theory, intertemporal transfers, which are *equalizing* in terms of the overall distribution *at any point in time,* can be effected without fiscal intervention; but nonzero transactions and information costs (which make borrowing and lending asymmetrical), and economies of scale in administration, justify their collectivization—at least in part. This is illustrated by the side-by-side existence of self-financed private pension programs—which relate the individual's retirement income to prior earnings—and a public social security system.

The logic of this argument is simple. Assume that the economic unit has constant preferences. Absenting time preference, then, utility maximization implies a level consumption stream, provided the process through which it can transfer disposable income from period to period is costless. In practice, the costs of making such transfers determine the extent to which the intertemporal reallocation of disposable income should be private or public.

The argument, to this point, contains no basis for linkage among economic units. Once risk and uncertainty enter, however, this is no longer the case. Risk aversion disposes individuals toward saving, as self-insurance against adverse financial prospects. It also implies that collective risk-pooling arrangements can increase private utility. In a cross section, *ex post* sense, such arrangements are inherently equalizing. As the number of individuals in the pool increases, the free-rider problem emerges and public action through redistributive programs becomes appropriate. In the extreme, individuals know no more of their own income expectations, nor have they any greater assurance of their own future claims, than they do of the prospects of others. In effect, self and other merge, returning us, from a different perspective, to the veil of ignorance and, as means of providing income insurance, the equal division it implies.

To provide further explanation of the adoption in extended self-interest of redistributive rules, the intertemporal model may be complicated by introducing utility interdependence. It is useful, to this end, to describe the individual as an evolving decision-making unit, in terms of a series of one-period utility functions linked by utility interdependence—as if the individual were a number of different individuals living in series. If this interdependence is total, there is no rivalry. This means that the consumption activities of any one period-specific individual are pure public goods, time preference aside, to the others. Redistributive transfers, which produce income equality among the period-specific individuals, are required for Pareto efficiency. Relaxation of the restrictions on time preference, risk, and interdependence weakens this conclusion, but the direction of the pressure remains the same.

There is a *tendency*—how strong it is remains open—toward equalization of the time-specific interpersonal distribution of income, manifested, for example, in the conventional Lorenz curve.

In addition, the intertemporal model enables us to understand some of the forces that underlie the redistribution of wealth and the existence of support for long-term environmental programs. Just as interdependence links the individual's well-being to his or her contemporaries, it establishes a connection with his or her descendants or heirs. Intended transfers of income and wealth, through gifts and bequests across generations (netting out intergeneration transfers that reflect the incorrect calculation of own-mortality) reflect such interdependence. (It is, of course, to be expected that such interpersonal interdependence is weaker than the linkages between the individual's period-specific utility functions.) However, a wealth owner who projects forward more than a generation or two, finds it increasingly difficult and, aside from those with whom his or her life overlaps, impossible to identify who his or her heirs will be. Once again, the self and other merge. In theory, redistributive taxation of bequests, imposed on inheritance or estates, becomes an appropriate way of taking account of intergeneration utility interdependence, and economic analysis provides us with further insight into policy actions undertaken in the ostensible interest of fairness.

Limits to Redistribution through Public Choice

Until now, a wide variety of "economic" theories, none requiring the explicit interpersonal comparisons of classical utilitarianism or a strong social welfare function, have been marshaled as support for measures that would make the distribution of income more equal. There are, however, countervailing "economic" factors, some set in motion by the reassignment of claims through redistribution and some independent of it, that temper this process, assuring that it will settle on a middle ground. These are, in the postconstitutional setting, both obvious and inevitable. As we have seen, however, many of these same considerations are apparent in constitutional choice, once production is added to the simple all-consumption model.

The most venerable, in a sense the simplest, arguments against redistribution from rich to poor are not only explicitly normative, but rest on raw ideology. Such arguments, which identify personal worth with economic contribution, reject all abridgments of rights to income and are the converse of "gut egalitarianism." [29] With but a veneer of justification, they assert that productivity, as reflected in market rewards, measures moral worth, and

[29] An extreme statement of this position would deny all basis for redistribution. A more temperate interpretation would consider that the poor are harmed by anything that others do for them, because this leads them to do less for themselves—the incentive issue, once again, in somewhat less attractive garb.

that such rewards are, as a consequence, "deserved" *and* essential to the preservation of the market institutions through which economic efficiency is achieved. (It is, of course, the first and not the second part of this statement that is objectionable.) Inherent in this one finds an interpretation of the market as divine (close, for example, to that of the economic disciples of Ayn Rand) or as a substitute for more conventional divinity, less useful for self-justification. To the few who take this stand any intervention in market-determined distribution is improper. In the extreme, even returns to monopoly power, to which others, faithful to the free market model, might object, are justified.

In bald form such arguments have little place in serious contemporary thought. It is impossible to grant them the credence that egalitarianism can derive from its concept of "the original position." In general, categorical rejection of all redistribution turns out, on inspection, to reflect an incorrect assessment of self-interest. In the face of imperfect knowledge and the need to pool risk—much less the intergeneration interdependence of utilities—it simply does not hold up.

To make a credible case, opponents of redistributive transfers must produce arguments that parallel its support, by focusing, in Paretian terms, on the effects of tinkering with the distribution that emerges under existing rights to income. These arguments are of two broad types, to which the earlier discussion has alluded. The first centers on evidence that individuals, poor as well as rich, evidence a taste for inequality, separate from the desire to retain what they have. To justify redistributive transfers, on a net basis, positive utility interdependence, increasing with income, and risk aversion must dominate this preference. The second argument, which is more conventional, asserts that efforts to redistribute income will, in themselves, have undesirable side effects. Incentive effects on the work–leisure choice are one example, narrowly economic in appearance, but deeply cultural once one probes, because of what they imply for the value systems transmitted to future generations. In the final analysis, the cost–benefit case against redistribution must rest on its implications for personal liberty, and infractions upon other rights that may undermine its appeal.

Support for inequality, in the first instance, derives from concern with security of relative position out of narrow self-interest. This need not rule out utility interdependence as a basis of transfers, but it assures that it will be dissipated well before equality is reached and reversals in the initial distributional ordering become possible. This may be as important to the skepticism about redistribution of those just above recipient status, as opposed to positive support among high-income persons (Hochman and Rodgers 1977), as monotonic variation, with income, in demands for the "goods" that redistribution supplies. (In other words, it may be as important as internalization of the interdependence that motivates income transfers.) Since well-being is multidimensional, concern with relative position seems to assure that income equalization would be accompanied by emergence, along other dimensions, of alternative inequalities, which might be far less consistent with fundamental liberties. Okun (1975, chap. 1), in his first essay, makes much of the correlation between income and political power, with allusion to the "transgressions of dollars against rights" associated with inequality. Such transgressions, however, might have been all the greater if the basis of relative position, rather than wealth, had been physical strength (which implies an ability to coerce) or demagogic skill. To recast the Okun metaphor, the "bucket" with which redistributive transfers are made may leak essential freedom, as well as output. It may also impose an uncomfortable sameness upon us. Surely, what we have observed of nonmarket economic systems, which preach an egalitarian ethic, gives us no more basis for optimism than the mixed capitalistic system with which we live.[30]

Inequality may also enter, as a good, into the preferences of the poor. Although it is unlikely to be a major factor, the poor may value the rich for their entertainment value, as evidence that money confers no incapacity to play the fool. Witness, here, public interest in the many wives of Tommy Manville, the reclusive life of Howard Hughes, and the comings and goings of the "jet set." (In New York City, for example, the *Daily News* and *Post*, which are widely read among the less than affluent, devote a great deal of space to these comings and goings. In the *New York Times*, on the other hand, they are essentially ignored.) Recognition that wealth is not a universal key to happiness provides, in this context, for relaxation of the frustrations inherent in poverty and deprivation. Popular reverence for royalty makes the same point. Unless royalty and quasi-royalty (the family of the U.S. president) were a source of utility to those without its prerogatives, their symbolism, much less their status, would not endure. Here, the major side product is not entertainment, but a sense of nationalism, which may well be as essential to the social contract as the rights and rules that give it substantive content. (Note that identification with "quasi-royalty" may even extend to those whose wealth is illegitimate, as it does when organized crime figures are treated as folk heroes.)

Ironically, the most important factor in the taste for inequality may be that it holds forth a sense of opportunity. The constitutional basis of equality rests on risk aversion. But in some measure people may be gamblers who would be worse off if denied the opportunity, however remote, of relative achievement, because they place a high value on status.[31] Whether this

---

[30] Kibbutzim, which practice an egalitarian division of output, provide a partial counterexample. But these are "small groups" (in the hundreds) of relatively homogeneous individuals, and even in this setting effective inequalities emerge.

[31] This relates to the view that alternative criteria of inequality will emerge if redistribution eliminates opportunities for economic success. An example is the emphasis on quasi-professional competitive athletics, which afford opportunities for personal recognition, in the Soviet Union and other noncapitalist countries.

preference will be reflected in public choice may hinge on the assurance that standards of living will not fall below some minimum level.

Among economists, the bulk of the attention in discussing limits to redistribution, has centered on incentive effects—specifically, its effects on work–leisure decisions. These do not appear in the all-consumption setting, but arise in two ways once the model is amended to incorporate production. First, they reduce output per capita. Since output is usually defined as a welfare index exclusive of leisure (except to the extent leisure requires the complementary purchase of marketed goods), incentive effects force the welfare frontier inward. Second, they interface with the work ethic. If recipients exhibit perverse work responses to transfers, donors will expect the full financial responsibility for the recipient population (including their dependents) to devolve on their shoulders.

Unlike the preferences discussed in preceding paragraphs, incentive effects—the "leak" in Okun's bucket—have been an important subject of empirical research, experimental and deductive. In practice, since the legislative failure of the Nixon income maintenance proposals, this research has not brought about a redefinition of welfare reform proposals that would, politically, by taking account of aversion to disincentives, prove more popular than a straightforward minimum income guarantee.

At one level, the professional preoccupation with incentive effects, relative to other factors that militate against extreme redistribution, relates to their quantitative importance. At another, it derives from the fact that their concern with labor force participation is a familiar subject of economic analysis, for which data have traditionally been collected, making it feasible to use conventional methods of conceptual and empirical research. Unfortunately, this is not true of the other factors that underlie private and public attitudes, positive or negative, toward redistribution; this hinders development of positive counterparts to the theories of redistribution discussed in this chapter.

In addition, redistributive policies are limited in the postconstitutional world by the costs of mobility among political jurisdictions, which define the boundaries of effective constitutions (Buchanan 1974). Through history, we have learned to think of migration, more often than not, as a rational response to deprivation. Within national boundaries, however, it may be as much a product of fiscal advantage, since redistributive changes in effective constitutions may conflict with the Pareto criterion (Tiebout 1956). This seems evident, as the Tiebout hypothesis suggests, in the "flight to the suburbs," and the demonstration that redistribution, unless Pareto-optimal, must be carried out at the national level. It is reflected at the national level in the incentive to "opt in or out of the society," by retreat to a tax haven or emigration to avoid the expropriation of property or the redistributive burdens—perhaps infinite—implicit in such institutions as the military draft. Indeed, there is good reason to wonder whether efforts to redistribute income and wealth, carried to the extreme, might not threaten the continuing existence of the social contract itself.

A final factual point should be emphasized in discussing the counterpressures to income equalization. This relates to the difficulty of defining, much less establishing and maintaining, precise equality, which is less a matter of its elusiveness than the fact that it is multidimensional. Only in the most shallow of senses is equality a matter of income alone. If justice is fairness and fairness requires equality, one must still inquire whether it is equality of opportunity or income that is at issue. Wherever inherent talents differ, these criteria provide different guidance. That the discussion of distribution is focused on measured income and wealth seems at best a function of our provinciality as economists, in quest of a positive counterpart to our normative model of the allocative process. As philosophers—which we become, whatever our intention, when we venture into the distributional arena—it behooves us to be more eclectic.

References

Aumann, R. J., and Kurz, M. 1977. Power and taxes. *Econometrica* 45:1137–61.

Becker, G. 1974. A theory of social interaction. *Journal of Political Economy* 82:1063–1093.

Blum, W. J., and Kalven Jr., H. 1953. *The uneasy case for progressive taxation*. Chicago: University of Chicago Press.

Breit, W. 1974. Income redistribution and efficiency norms. In *Redistribution through public choice*, eds. H. M. Hochman and G. E. Peterson. New York: Columbia University Press. Pp. 3–21.

Brennan, G. 1973. Pareto desirable redistribution: The case of malice and envy. *Journal of Public Economics* 2:173–183.

Buchanan, J. M. 1974. Who should distribute what in a public system. In *Redistribution through public choice,* eds. H. M. Hochman and G. E. Peterson, New York: Columbia University Press. Pp. 22–42.

Buchanan, J. M. 1975. *The limits of liberty: Between anarchy and leviation*. Chicago: University of Chicago Press.

Buchanan, J. M., and Bush, W. 1972. Individual welfare in anarchy. In *Explorations in the theory of anarchy*, ed. G. Tullock, Blacksburg: Center for the Study of Public Choice. Pp. 5–18.

Buchanan, J. M., and Stubblebine, W. C. 1962. Externality. *Economica* 29:371–384.

Buchanan, J. M., and Tullock, G. 1962. *The calculus of consent*. Ann Arbor: University of Michigan Press.

Coase, R. H. 1960. The problem of social cost. *Journal of Law and Economics* 3:1–44.

Culyer, A. J. 1973. *The economics of social policy*. London: Martin Robertson.

Downs, A. 1957. *An economic theory of democracy*. New York: Harper and Row.

Fair, R. C. 1971. The optimal distribution of income. *Quarterly Journal of Economics* 85:551–779.

Feldstein, M. 1973. On the optimal progressivity of the income tax. *Journal of Public Economics* 2:357–376.

Feldstein, M. 1976. Compensation in tax return. *National Tax Journal* 29:123–130.

Friedman, M. 1952. The welfare effects of an income tax and an excise tax. *Journal of Political Economy* 60:332–336.

Friedman, M., and Savage, L. J. 1948. The utility analysis of choices involving risk. *Journal of Political Economy* 56:279–304.

Harsanyi, J. 1955. Cardinal welfare, individualist ethics, and interpersonal comparisons of utility. *Journal of Political Economy* 63:309–321.

Harsanyi, J. 1975. Can the maximin principle serve as a basis for morality? A critique of John Rawls' theory. *American Political Science Review* 69:594–606.

Hochman, H. M. 1972. Individual preferences and distributional adjustments. *American Economic Review* 62:353–360.

Hochman, H. M. 1974. Rule change and transitional equity. In *Redistribution through public choice*, eds. H. M. Hochman and G. E. Peterson, New York: Columbia University Press. Pp. 320–341.

Hochman, H. M., and Kleiman, E. 1981. *Optimal inequality under the veil of ignorance.* (Working paper, Department of Economics.) Jerusalem: The Hebrew University.

Hochman, H. M., and Nitzan, S. 1981. *Concepts of extended preference.* (Working paper, Department of Economics.) Jerusalem: The Hebrew University.

Hochman, H. M., and Rodgers, J. D. 1969. Pareto optimal redistribution. *American Economic Review* 59:542–557.

Hochman, H. M., and Rodgers, J. D. 1977. The simple politics of distributional preference. In *The distribution of economic well-being*, ed. T. Juster. Cambridge, Mass.: National Bureau of Economic Research. Pp. 71–106.

Johnston, J. 1975. Utility interdependence and redistribution: Methodological implications for welfare economics and the theory of the public household. *Public Finance Quarterly* 3:195–228.

Lerner, A. P. 1944. *The economics of control.* London: Macmillan.

Mirrlees, J. A. 1971. An exploration in the theory of optimum income taxation. *Review of Economic Studies* 38:171–208.

Mueller, D. C. 1979. *Public choice.* New York: Cambridge University Press.

Musgrave, R. A. 1970. Pareto optimal redistribution: Comment. *American Economic Review* 60:991–993.

Nozick, R. 1974. *Anarchy, state, and utopia.* New York: Basic Books.

Okun, A. M. 1975. *Equality and efficiency: The big trade-off.* Washington, D.C.: Brookings.

Olsen, E. O. 1969. A normative theory of income transfers. *Public Choice.* 6:39–58.

Pazner, E. A., and Schmeidler, D. 1976. Social contract theory and ordinal distributive equity. *Journal of Public Economics* 5:261–268.

Peterson, G. E. 1973. Welfare, workfare, and pareto informality. *Public Finance Quarterly* 1:323–338.

Polinsky, A. M. 1974. Imperfect capital markets, intertemporal redistribution, and progressive taxation. In *Redistribution through public choice*, eds. H. M. Hochman and G. E. Peterson. New York: Columbia University Press. Pp. 229–260.

Rawls, J. 1971. *A theory of justice.* Cambridge: Harvard University Press.

Rodgers, J. D. 1973. Distributional externalities and the optimal form of income transfers. *Public Finance Quarterly* 1:266–299.

Rodgers, J. D. 1974. Explaining income redistribution. In *Redistribution through public choice*, ed. H. M. Hochman and G. E. Peterson. New York: Columbia University Press. Pp. 165–205.

Rolph, E. 1968. Controversy surrounding negative income taxation. In *Public finance and social security*, Travaux de l'Institut International de Finances Publique, Congress de Turin, XXIve Session. Pp. 252–261.

Tiebout, C. M. 1956. A pure theory of local expenditures. *Journal of Political Economy* 64:416–424.

Thurow, L. 1971. The income distribution as a public good. *Quarterly Journal of Economics* 85:327–336.

Varian, H. R. 1976. Two problems in the theory of fairness. *Journal of Public Economics* 5:249–260.

Vickrey, W. 1960. Utility, Strategy, and social decision rules. *Quarterly Journal of Economics* 74:507–535.

Von Furstenberg, G. M., and Mueller, D. C. 1971. The Pareto-optimal approach to income redistribution: A fiscal application. *American Economic Review* 61:628–638.

[10]

Rule Change and Transitional Equity

HAROLD M. HOCHMAN

Too often the professional analyst, in seeking a remedy for inefficiency or injustice, rests public policy discussion on simplified comparisons of the actual and the ideal. The costs of transition from the actual state to the ideal are de-emphasized. Still, the normative significance of these transitional costs which arise because pre-existing rules and institutions have legitimized claims and expectations is clear, and even a casual analysis of the legislative process verifies their importance in determining the terms on which governments enact change.

Such transitional effects raise the question of when it is appropriate to compensate those who suffer losses as a consequence of change in public policy, and on what terms. Where compensation is not desirable or feasible, transitional considerations illuminate the difficulties of obtaining an ethical consensus. In specific cases, they place constraints on the manner in which the inequities which are implicit in existing rules and institutions can be corrected.

The description and discussion of such issues of transitional equity form the objective of this paper. Because of transitional costs, we may have no unambiguous way to resolve inconsistencies between demands for rule changes which foster social justice or economic efficiency and the consensus which the Pareto criterion requires. The customary, but facile, way around this is to appeal to a social welfare function that assigns weights or social values to individual utili-

Harold M. Hochman is Senior Research Associate, The Urban Institute, and Visiting Member of the Faculty, Graduate School of Public Policy, University of California at Berkeley. He is indebted to the National Science Foundation for a supporting grant to The Urban Institute. For comments on earlier drafts, he wishes to thank Richard Bird, Martin Bronfenbrenner, Peter Brown, Cathy Gilson, George Peterson, A. Mitchell Polinsky, Edward Rastatter, Claudia Scott, and Walter Williams.

ty or wealth levels. But, given the difficulties of ascertaining a consistent social decision function of this kind, this merely begs the question.

Fortunately, to identify transitional equity issues and formulate distinctions that clarify them, so well-defined a criterion as a social welfare function is not needed. This paper addresses itself to such questions. Its focus is on the problems inherent in deciding when compensation of those who suffer interim losses can be foregone because a higher-level constitutional rule guarantees Pareto optimality in terms of a broader frame of reference. It tries to ascertain when it is legitimate in this broader sense to violate the Pareto criterion, defined in issue-by-issue terms. And it gropes toward an answer to how this might be done at least cost.

The discussion begins by inquiring into the notions of fairness and opportunity, interpreted in terms of a social contract that a community of self-governing individuals would find acceptable. The second section, focusing on a number of specific policy issues, places in context the normative problems of transition and highlights the potential for conflict between equity in the interim and the ultimate efficiency and equity objectives of social policy. The paper then turns to real-world political and economic mechanisms that mitigate the negative side effects of change and reduce transitional deviations from the Pareto criterion. The final section shows how transitional equity issues, which serve to confound public choice, have arisen in certain public education decisions of the federal judiciary.

I. SOCIAL JUSTICE AND LEGAL TRANSITION

Equity is a matter of well-being, which depends on the interpersonal distribution of entitlements to the returns from property and human capital. Usually communities hold some differences in well-being to be legitimate, while denying the fairness of others. The criteria used in evaluating legitimacy or fairness are a matter of social choice. Even so, whether equity is defined in terms of current or permanent income or some such broader but vaguer concept as opportunity (which permits stochastic variation in the relationships among prospects and outcomes) is a matter of values and intuitions. And, even if a proper measure of well-being could be agreed upon, it is essentially impossible to define a uniquely Pareto-optimal distribution when individuals have the prior benefit of endowments, whether these take the form of wealth, position, or some other measure of status.[1]

Transitional equity is a more limited concept. Its concern is with entitlements to certainty that pre-existing rights and endowments sanctioned by a social contract will continue undiminished. The basic issue is the fairness of windfall declines in the absolute wealth of some individuals that occur when the community-at-large, in its quest for a preferable long-run allocative or distributional income, alters its rules and institutions.

To gain perspective on transitional equity as a problem, one must consider the process of "constitutional choice" (that is, the process through which the high-level or general rules that govern conduct in a community are chosen) and relate it (as modern, but not elitist, theories of political economy do) to "social justice." One interpretation of this relationship, attributable to the political philosopher John Rawls, is that a "fair" (a just or equitable) distribution is one to which individuals, choosing freely, would agree in the "state of nature," in which neither rules nor endowments pre-exist. Acting behind this "veil of ignorance," no individual can identify his own distributional income, even in the probabilistic sense.[2] The social contract individuals agree upon in such ignorance of personal prospects sets up rules and institutions that govern claims to personal property and human capital and that determine, aside from random variation, the distribution of income. This distribution, moreover, carries the sanction of consensus, and being uniquely optimal (in the circumstances defined) it is socially just. Thus grounded, social justice, "indeed ethics itself is part of the general theory of rational choice."[3] There is no conflict between equity, which implies consent, and allocative efficiency. With distribution undetermined, all men prefer more wealth to less.

Under a "just" social contract, each individual, in Rawls' view, has "an equal right to the most extensive liberty compatible with like liberty for all." Included in this right, presumably, is the freedom to achieve a given standard of living: "... inequities[4] as defined by the institutional structure or fostered by it are arbitrary unless it is reasonable to expect they will work out to everyone's advantage and provided that the positions and offices to which they attach or from which they may be granted are open to all."[5] This right does not require that distribution be equal. But to be consistent with it, distributional inequalities must be justifiable in advance, as leaving the least-advantaged individual in the community at least as well off as he would be under strict equality. Since in a Pareto-efficient system, *ceteris paribus*, more output is available to be distributed than in an inefficient system, efficiency fosters justice and is desirable on its own merit. The thrust of this paradigm, given its probabilistic focus, is that distributional opportunities, not actual results, are what fairness is ultimately about. Clearly, many real-world practices that are consistent with democratic political constitutions fail this test.

Although social justice, thus conceived, may be the proper end of public policy, real-world decision making does not share its philosophic luxury. Once a "social contract" exists, as codified in rules and institutions, reality violates the assumption of probabilistic agnosticism, an assumption that is critical to the "fair game" interpretation of the choice of social rules contained in the Rawls paradigm. Most often, individual behavior presumes the permanence of pre-existing rules. Indeed, if law and the concept of rules are to be credible,[6] individuals must hold this presumption with a high degree of confidence. Not just existing rules of conduct, but changes in these rules, must be justifiable, and the process through which change is effected must itself be fair. Failing direct or indirect compensation, the fairness of a rule change is unambiguous only if the pre-existing rule was clearly inconsistent with the social contract or "constitution" that underlay it and if those whom the change has harmed have had an opportunity to anticipate and adjust to it. Public policy, in its overall concern with equity, must consider not only the beneficent effects of rule changes on individuals whom existing rules have disadvantaged but the fact that the process of change, if considered arbitrary, can itself make individuals feel it is irrational to accept the limits on behavior that rules imply.

Although Rawls provides us a backdrop against which to judge whether rules, *de novo*, are fair, he neither resolves nor claims to resolve this conflict. Rules, even if unfair or inefficient, may as custom underlie reasonable expectations. Rule changes that disappoint such expectations may themselves be considered unjust because they violate the equi-probability assumption implicit in the definition of a just practice. The problem of transitional equity is, therefore, all-pervasive. Only if the present beneficiaries of an unjust practice have attained their positions through illegitimate means is the case clear-cut. Once a social system is in motion, there is no simple logical device through which the ideal can be defined or, even if it could be defined, through which the actual can be equated with it.[7]

To illustrate the pervasiveness of transitional equity problems, consider slavery, a practice that is clearly inconsistent with fairness. Even here, where the argument is one-sided, transitional considerations, although hardly compelling, are relevant, and the factors involved are much the same as those with which policymakers must deal in considering far less dramatic rule changes than the abolition of slavery.

Consider, for example, the preferences and choices of a benevolent man, living in a regime that permits slavery, who observes a slave being beaten by his master. His preference, abstracting from benevolence, is to purchase a Rolls Royce that he himself would drive. Given his benevolent concern for the slave, however, he purchases a less expensive automobile, buys rights to the slave from his sadistic master, and installs him (still a slave) as chauffeur. In doing this, he expects that the practice of slavery, which the political constitution sanctions, is permanent and that the slave, under the old master, would have continued to suffer regular beatings. The following day, the community abolishes slavery with no compensation to slaveowners, thus subjecting this man, who had entered the practice of slavery out of benevolence alone, to a windfall loss.[8]

The point, farfetched though the example may be, is clear. Even in a less fantastic setting the same issues remain. Because of these issues proposals to change existing rules are unlikely to be acceptable, much less fair, if public policy ignores their transitional implications. Situations in which ends fully justify any and all costs of transition, however great, are uncommon. From both the practical and normative perspectives the fairness of rules for changing rules is crucial.

II. FAIRNESS AND EFFICIENCY:
CONCEPTS, CASES, AND AMBIGUITIES

With few exceptions, changes in established rules and practices create transitional equity problems. Only rarely is change Pareto-efficient in the simple sense.[9] Even if all men might prefer the long-term outcome under altered rules, some will fear decreases in wealth and the foreclosure of options in the short run and, for this reason, oppose change. Interim effects may dominate, making the present value of a change negative not just because time preference is positive but also because a man's life span is finite and intergeneration utility interdependencies are imperfect. In these cases compensation must be paid if the Pareto criterion is to be satisfied, regardless of the fact that without it the new equilibrium could leave all parties better off than they would otherwise be.

It is useful, for heuristic purposes, to distinguish (even if imperfectly) between changes in the "effective" constitution, correcting its aberrations or inconsistences, and the more restrictive modifications of rules and practices with which most public policy deals. Issues of human rights, where moral overtones predominate, are in the first category. Although such practices as slavery and *de jure* segregation, practices that use unacceptable criteria to discriminate among individuals, may emerge and endure in a world in which power is correlated with endowments, there is a strong presumption that they would not have been chosen in a world of equals. Whether there is an orderly and accepted procedure for introducing and enacting change and whether those who might be harmed have long been on notice may determine whether compensation is necessary. In the

second category the focus is on current outcomes of market and political processes rather than on fundamental human rights, and the
issues are more routine. Not elemental freedoms but the terms on
which transactions are conducted are at issue. Distributional considerations, although important, do not dominate from the start. It is in
this paper more useful to focus on this second class of issues, for
here men are more likely to agree that transitional cost considerations must temper positive action. Advocates of reform may be
more willing to honor the Pareto criterion and accept a requirement
that losers be compensated.

In determining whether compensation must be considered an
ethical requirement, the ability of individuals to anticipate change
and adjust their behavior to curtail potential losses is crucial. Consider the distinctions encountered in sorting out the negative effects
of a rule change on private wealth. One distinction is between effects on existing wealth (the expected returns of those already
engaged in the practice) and the potential losses (in an opportunity
cost sense) implicit in denying privileges to new investors. A second
distinction is between eliminating gains from continuing a practice
(which is, say, monopolistic or discriminatory) and, by imposing
change retroactively, redeeming the prior effects of this practice.
Thus suburban residents, evincing concern with the quality of local
schools, may well oppose interjurisdictional busing if they believe it
will leave their children worse off. At the same time they may well
hold that disparities between central city and suburban schools, both
in finance and in facilities, derive from rules and practices that are
unfair. The first distinction differentiates between the attitudes of
current and potential residents of the suburbs toward busing. The
second differentiates between the revealed and the abstract preferences of current suburbanites. It suggests that such individuals are
quite rational in opposing policies that they may consider to be fair
in principle because they do not wish to bear (or inflict on their
children) concentrated transitional costs.

In practice whether compensation (for past or for future losses) is
appropriate, is a far more subtle issue. Although the Pareto criterion
strictly interpreted requires compensation, it seems absurd to argue

that individuals unjustly deprived of rights under an existing rule should compensate its beneficiaries if the rule is changed.[10] Several countervailing considerations (some already mentioned) may be relevant. One is whether individuals harmed by an unfair practice participated in the "consent" process that established it. If not, the argument for compensation is less convincing. A second is whether the beneficiaries of the practice can reasonably be expected to have anticipated the change. Finally, the appropriateness of compensation may depend on whether the practice concerned involves the constitutional rights of identifiable persons or attributes of transactions that are logically distinct from the individuals who engage in them.[11]

With a rule change that is efficient in the sense that it is expected to produce net benefits it seems appropriate, even aside from ethical considerations, to compensate those who are harmed. There is little argument about compensating owners for private property "taken" through condemnation in the highway construction and urban renewal cases. But it is often unclear whether these are the only rights infringed. Destruction of familiar neighborhoods is itself costly, and many of the social difficulties of such programs derive from their effects on the intangible human capital of residents who are not property owners.[12] The ethnic or racial characteristics of these residents may, moreover, be well-defined. Can it then be said that they are not identifiable and that the rule change, in the first instance, affects the terms of transactions rather than the rights of specific individuals?

In general, the requirement that compensation be paid to neutralize distributional effects (because failure to compensate inflicts "demoralization costs") must be tempered by the proviso that the costs of violating the Pareto criterion exceed the costs of its assessment and implementation.[13] This utilitarian issue is, however, quite different from the ethical one. If public policy is concerned with compensation because interpersonal utility comparisons are impossible, the fact that transactions costs may render compensation uneconomic has no bearing on the ethical issue at stake.

Turning, for illustration, from general considerations to specific examples, consider the effort to control pollution, which deals with rights to a "common property resource." Although the objectives of such control in the long term are efficiency and equity, some individuals are sure to suffer short-run distributional harms as a consequence. Can it be argued, in this respect, that past pollution is one issue (whether retroactive compensation is appropriate) and potential pollution another? Need potential polluters be compensated for the expected effects of controls on their wealth? Might not fairness require that polluters and the community-at-large share the costs of clarifying rights to common property resources during a transition period? Can the law differentiate in logic between owners of existing firms that have capitalized known opportunities, and new or potential firms that have not? This seems at first blush a sensible course, but because it would not only spare existing firms from capital losses but provide them with a newly created source of economic rent it does not hold up.

Other rule changes, much the same in their appeal to the economist, have similar transitional equity implications. One such proposal, the elimination of quantitative restrictions on the number of taxicab franchises or "medallions" that cities authorize, is classic in its apparent simplicity. Under restricted supply the medallions sell for a high price and taxicab fares are higher than under free entry. Rationalization to the contrary, simple price theory suggests that standards of service suffer. Nonetheless, the recommendation that a community rid itself of this restrictive practice invariably raises significant political objections. These objections are justifiable because deregulation, without compensation, would inflict severe transitional losses on those who own franchises. These potential inequities would disappear, however, if the current cohort of franchise owners had instigated the medallion restrictions.[14] (Similarly, if participants in an illegal activity suffer losses when it is legalized, as private bookmakers do when public gambling ventures are created, such effects can be dismissed as fair outcomes of risky ventures.) By and large, however, current taxicab operators invested in existing franchises at the market price and did so with reason to believe that the licensing rules under which these franchises had been capitalized were both permanent and legitimate.[15] Indeed, there seems no reason (assuming that contrary legislation had not been pending and under active discussion) why they should not have considered such rules in this light, despite the fact of their inefficiency. Nor does it make any difference, in opportunity cost terms, whether the franchises have just been purchased and are yet to produce returns or whether they have already returned profits sufficient to justify the original outlay. Analytically, investment must be viewed as a continuous process and the investment decision as a choice just made.[16]

The transitional equity issue is no less important in explaining the reluctance of Congress to act on tax reform. It can be argued that many provisions catering to special interests (like percentage depletion) or to a wide class of taxpayers (like the preferential treatment of capital gains) are a travesty of distributive justice. But no tax change, however desirable it may appear in the abstract, is free of transitional effects on asset values. The fact that the community has adjusted to the established tax code is, in itself, sufficient to explain the tendency of its apparent aberrations to persist. Had active discussion of depletion reform not given wealth owners ample reason to anticipate it, it would be difficult to argue that present holders of mineral shares can justly be penalized (by failing to compensate them for the transitional effects of reform) for benefits that percentage depletion awarded to original investors in mineral properties. Nor, lacking a more definitive basis for interpreting voter preferences, have we any proof (despite ample presumption) that the political community actually prefers "statutory" to "effective" tax rates (or something in between) and that the disturbing compromises that seem endemic to the tax legislative process are unjustifiable.

It is, therefore, amply clear that the deliberation of reform proposals in isolation, without due regard for preconditions and due attention to the decision-making process from which existing institutions have emerged, risks substantial normative danger. To undo inequities without causing harm is no simple matter. Nor is it always self-evident whether the harm of transition is more or less severe than the harm of the *status quo*. For this reason, advocates of institutional change must, perforce, grant prominence on the agenda of reform to the rules that govern change. That inequity may be clothed in the garb of "justice" is small consolation.

III. PUBLIC CHOICE AND THE
PROBLEM OF TRANSITIONAL LOSS

It is neither accidental nor inappropriate that prospects of transitional loss are taken into account in the political arena. Legislators can be counted on to temper the pleas of reform-minded liberals. This is not because the *status quo* is desirable and Pareto nonoptimal change is to be avoided at all cost. It is, rather, because the prospect of transitional inequities implies that a more airtight case is required to justify rule changes than to rationalize existing rules and practices.

A variety of mechanisms, contained in the political process itself, can or do operate to reduce transitional inequities. These political mechanisms are, in a sense, imperfect substitutes for compensation and, when it is not feasible, perform a part of its function. Their effect is to make change less likely to "effectively" bankrupt specific individuals—a consequence that is irretrievable—and to reduce the concentration of transitional losses among subgroups of the population. These mechanisms, however, are not costless, for they also create political opportunities for influence and power that are more available to the strong than to the weak. Thus, whereas they help to alleviate the ethical compensation problem, they by no means eliminate it, and, depending on one's values and preferences, their overall effect may be to increase dissatisfaction with the general distributive milieu.

To focus this discussion, it is useful to refer to a simple model, constructed by Professor Buchanan, to rule out the transitional equity problem.[17] In this model the current generation defers the implementation of the rule changes it enacts until a full generation (or, to be less extreme, a decade or two) has elapsed. In consequence, individuals acting on rule changes can abstract from effects on their own status. This narrows the conflict among the alternative patterns of rights and opportunities that satisfy the Pareto criterion and brings the process of reform into closer conformity with the Rawls paradigm. Forward projection, by formalizing expectations, enables individuals to adjust to enacted change, thus softening its unintended distributional effects; and intergeneration utility interdependencies assure that time preference, through discounting, does not leave individuals indifferent to the distant future.[18]

Though a useful heuristic device, this "simple delay" model is clearly inadequate as a guide to practice. First, when the resolution of social problems is deferred, dissent is unsatisfied. The risks to a tranquil and free society that delay entails cannot help but affect the ultimate outcome. Second, for future generations, the deferral (even constitutional) of reform not only violates consent,[19] but also precludes them from changing the institutions under which they live. Third, if the effects of change can make everyone better off over time, postdating, which reduces the present value of such benefits, is inefficient—unless transitional costs alter the balance. These criticisms notwithstanding, partial delay does have its place in the real world, as in the "grandfather clause" (which permits the original rule to continue to govern on-going activities) and in explicit procedures for the gradual phase-in of rule changes.[20]

Within the more general frame of political reference, logrolling (the grouping of issues in public choice) is the primary mechanism through which the legislative process softens and mitigates transitional effects.[21] For logrolling to operate, individuals must differ in the importance they attach to issues, so that the outcome in multi-issue decisions can differ from the single-issue outcome. Although the single-issue decisions might offend some constituents, their net effect may be acceptable to all or nearly all,[22] in much the same way as the discounted effects over time of a single-issue decision may prove positive even though its short-run effects do not.[23]

The deficiencies of logrolling suggest, in themselves, certain criteria that are appropriate in weighing the likely benefits of change against its transitional costs. Rule changes with concentrated negative effects should, if possible, be avoided. If the effect on a given individual is so negative that it "bankrupts" him, issue-grouping is useless in countering transitional inequities. Consider, for argument's sake, a rule change that denies, for but a limited time, the consumption that sustenance requires. There is no way in which an individual thus affected can be compensated through issue-grouping or intertemporal logrolling and end up a net gainer. Similarly, logrolling neutralizes transitional inequities more effectively if the policies chosen have diffused rather than concentrated negative effects. Political reality, however, is quite the opposite. Despite aberrations, strength resides in numbers in a one-man—one-vote system. Legislators are more responsive to large numbers of constituents (even if these are a minority in the wider sense) who suffer well-diffused losses than to isolated individuals or local minorities. Within these groups, wealth itself is the best assurance of protection. Individuals with little capital are subject to transitional inequities as well as distributive injustice.

To carry the argument a step further, majority rule, applied in a succession of issues, is itself a means through which transitional inequities are reduced. Issues decided under this collective choice rule can, if unrelated, be considered episodes in a "convergence process," itself displaying the effective properties of logrolling.[24] Individuals, in evaluating political alternatives, trade off dissatisfaction with one rule or rule change for satisfaction with another, knowing that in some cases they will be in the majority and in some they will not. More restrictive decision rules than simple majority, such as a two-thirds rule or Wicksellian "relative unanimity," leave it less likely that a particular individual will always find himself in the minority and more likely that transitional effects, summed over issues, will be non-negative. They do this, however, at the cost of making change even more difficult to enact.[25]

Interjurisdictional mobility, within metropolitan areas (as the Tiebout model suggests) and among national communities, can also help to reconcile dissatisfaction with rules and rule changes. Individuals, over the long run, respond to (and help to bring about) majority-sanctioned changes by opting in or out of particular political communities. But in neither financial nor psychological terms are such moves costless. Moreover, their patterns are significantly affected by individual wealth. Thus, even in the potential sense, mobility is at most a partial offset to transitional costs.

Such defenses against transitional inequity, all of which hinge on the ability to delay the effects of change and to group issues, inhere in individual and legislative action, but not in judicial action. Judicial intervention, which by its nature applies on an issue-by-issue basis, thus precluding issue-grouping, is appropriate in constitutional discussions, where high-level rules for making rules are defined, and in cases where the risk is high that the pursuit of one objective will unduly compromise others. It is in these cases that the system of public choice is weakest. If negative effects are concentrated, legislative inaction (as with segregation in public education) or legislative action (legalizing the death penalty for certain convicted offenders) may "bankrupt" specific individuals or groups. Concern for their welfare may justify the dangers (in terms of side effects) inherent in the case-by-case and issue-by-issue interpretations that characterize judicial decision making.

IV. PUBLIC EDUCATION AND THE LAW:
A TRANSITIONAL DILEMMA

Perhaps the most far reaching of the transitional dilemmas in current public policy is the public education issue, and, in particular, the controversies surrounding educational finance and busing. To foster equal opportunity, both in market and in political transactions, and thereby to satisfy the Rawlsian preconditions of fairness, the courts have rendered a number of landmark decisions in the education area[26] (although as of this writing some of these are subject to reversal by the Supreme Court). A side effect of these decisions, taken to redress long-standing grievances, has been the attenuation of property rights. These have left legitimate expectations disappointed and closed or restricted channels of opportunity open to some members of the community.[27]

Consider, first, the *Hobson v. Hansen* and *Serrano v. Priest* decisions, which deal with whether differences in per pupil expenditures are consistent with equal opportunity. The *Hobson* decision, which concerns school finance within a single jurisdiction, requires the approximate equalization of per pupil spending among schools.

Intrajurisdictional differences in income and wealth are not considered a justification of expenditure differences, as they would be if
taxation were benefit based and the output of the educational process were partially a private good.[28] The *Serrano* decision extends
this logic to the state as a multijurisdictional region. It links opportunity with education and argues that interjurisdictional differences in
burdens of the local property tax are not consistent with equal opportunity. Education, *Serrano* claims, is different from other public
activities, being more like voting rights, a constitutional prerogative,
than such conventional services as fire protection and trash collection. Local differences in public education spending are, then, justifiable only if the wealth basis of educational finance has first been
normalized.

Turn now to the transitional equity issues implicit in these
decisions. *Serrano* to the contrary, it is clear that public education is
resource-using, unlike voting rights and like fire protection, and that
it must be financed, in real terms, through means that attenuate
private property. To substantiate the argument that education is different from other resource-using and tax-funded public activities,
the educational finance issue must be raised to the constitutional
level. Otherwise, if its "public-good" dimension is externality based,
as the definition of a public good implies, it seems inconsistent to
single education out for special treatment, enjoining equal services
and rejecting wealth as the basis of its finance while permitting differential expenditures and the wealth-related financing of other
public services that share its externality characteristics. Moreover,
to the extent that public action is (and is supposed to be) a reflection
of individual preferences, the case for consistent evaluation of
resource-using activities carries over to private goods. If equal opportunity is a sufficient basis for questioning the appropriateness of
the distribution of wealth as a basis of educational finance, it leaves
us uneasy about permitting private resource allocation to be
governed by endowment-related preferences.

This clearly leaves us in an uncomfortable quandary. Benefit distributions of municipal services like trash collection and the maintenance of municipal yacht harbors (much less the benefits of private
goods) surely differ, both directly and in the externalities they

produce. Moreover, there are difficulties in distinguishing equal opportunity arguments for equal provision from arguments that are little more than a particular minority's desire to extract more income
redistribution than the community, acting through its political process, is willing to provide. An avid egalitarian might argue that advantages attributable to initial position have no redeeming social value,
but so outright a rejection of property rights that are sanctioned in
the prevailing constitution is hardly constructive. It seems more reasonable to seek a middle ground, to treat education as a public trust,
managed by the community-at-large for the benefit of generations
yet unfranchised and, in particular, for minors whose interests cannot adequately be represented by their parents. On this interpretation, there is, so far as the trade-off between transitional equity and
social justice is concerned, substantial common ground between the
public education decisions discussed and the abolition of slave holding.

If the constitutional case for equal educational opportunity (and,
to the extent it is valid, other public services) could be satisfied
through guarantees of minimum levels of provision, the transitional
side effects of the Hobson and Serrano decisions (and others like
them) would be far less significant. Augmentation of these minimum
levels through endowment-related purchases of private or public education by resident taxpayers would restore the parity between
private and public choice.[29] Still, such a scheme, while assuring opportunity, would not equalize it. In a free society in which rights to
private property pre-exist—indeed, in any society that does not separate children from parents at birth—no way exists to reconcile fully
all the dimensions of equity.

Provided the discussion is restricted to the equal opportunity criterion on which the *Hobson* and *Serrano* decisions focus, neither
neighborhood schools nor "community control," nor public subsidies to private schools, are in themselves inconsistent with
fairness. To object to these delivery systems on equity grounds, an
additional consideration, "equal access" to public facilities, must be
introduced. This leads to an inquiry as to whether truly equal opportunity requires not only fiscal equalization but also a heterogeneity
in classroom composition that implies, ironically, homogeneity of

such units of production. It is with this issue of equal access that the debate over the fairness of busing within and among jurisdictions concerns itself.

Swann v. Charlotte-Mecklenburg Board of Education, written by Chief Justice Burger, deals with intrajurisdictional busing. The thrust of this decision is that equal access to physical facilities in which human capital can be formed is essential to equal opportunity and that equal expenditure is insufficient to remedy past injustices. *Swann* holds, moreover, that transitional inequity problems, so far as the matter at hand is concerned, are subordinate to the ultimate objective, the dismantling of a dual school system that is segregated by race. It concludes, more generally, although implicitly, that efforts to correct past injustice cannot accept current differences in status as a base point. Its argument is pragmatic. There is no implication that property or initial endowments are in themselves illegitimate. It simply avers that injustice cannot be corrected without infringing on endowments.

Absent a constitutional violation there would be no basis for judicially ordering assignment of students on a racial basis. All things being equal, with no history of discrimination, it might well be desirable to assign pupils to schools nearest their homes. *But all things are not equal in a system that has been deliberately constructed and maintained to enforce racial segregation. The remedy for such segregation may be administratively awkward, inconvenient and even bizarre in some situations and may impose burdens on some; but all awkwardness and inconvenience cannot be avoided in the interim period when remedial adjustments are being made to eliminate the dual school system.*[30] (emphasis mine)

In homing in on the equal access objective, Swann links the present defects of the system of public education to prior decisions on school location and construction. Its argument, however, need not be confined to such narrow terms of reference, limited to the public education case. Residential location is itself inextricably intertwined with school construction and classroom composition and has itself been shaped by exclusionary practices, including restrictive covenants, zoning and jurisdictional boundary decisions. Whatever their intent, the total effect of these practices, given the neighborhood school concept, has proved closer to *de facto* segregation than to equal opportunity in many cases.

Clearly, the total integration of educational finance and educational production, as Swann directs, would substantially attenuate the rights of self-contained communities (which could thereby be self-contained no longer) to establish and control their own school systems and finance them through wealth-related taxes. Residential sites in areas hitherto sheltered from the disadvantaged would suffer in value. Since most owners of such homesites, like the taxicab operators of our ealier example, purchased their properties with good reason to expect rules to be firm, such losses are fair reason for concern with transitional equity.[31] Moreover, the effect of busing from suburban communities to the inner city may, for many children, reduce educational opportunity, without assuring improved service to the disadvantaged, at least in terms of their preferences.

Since *Swann, Carolyn Bradley v. The Richmond School Board*, its reversal, and presidential initiatives calling for a busing moratorium have kept the busing issue in the public limelight. The *Bradley* decision ruled that satisfactory integration requires busing on a metropolitan-wide basis and ordered consolidation of the public-school systems of Richmond, Virginia, and its contiguous suburban counties. The court argued that busing cannot achieve equal access and its overriding objective of dismantling the dual school system if it continues to be constrained by jurisdictional boundaries.

Transitional equity considerations suggest, other factors aside, that the *Bradley* decision (notwithstanding its reversal) is appropriate. Areawide busing would assure that transitional effects of both property values and the quality of public education are well diffused. Since the entire metropolitan community is responsible for the *de facto* segregation implied by jurisdictional boundaries,[32] it may be appropriate for the whole metropolitan area to share in the transitional losses incurred in satisfying the constitutional guarantees of equal protection and equal access. Other than the historical accident of existing boundaries, there seems no basis in logic for requiring high-wealth residents of central cities, the political communities in which the disadvantaged are concentrated, to bear such costs, as the

Hobson decision implies. To the contrary, if "equal access" is truly a condition of justice, the unquestioning acceptance of existing local boundaries is itself arbitrary.

V. CONCLUSION

The transitional issues that the public school decisions raise are conceptually much the same as the transitional implications of other changes in social rules, institutions, and practices.[33] The illustrations of Section IV make clear the fact that on-going societies cannot often correct unfair outcomes without creating collateral harms. Indeed, one can go farther and argue that the interim effects of well-intentioned change are important not only because transitional fairness is a matter of serious normative concern but also because they may substantially alter the final outcome of the change. Concern for social justice can hardly be expected to endure unless nonmalevolent individuals believe it to be in their interest to accept legal strictures. Thus, for reason of pragmatism as well as principle the undoing of past harms must do more than shift the onus of inequity.

I hope that my inquiries, admittedly Talmudic, have surfaced a much-neglected facet of public policy. The transitional equity implications of rule changes surely deserve more scholarly attention than they have hitherto been given. For narrowly defined policy problems, at least, the clarification of transitional implications, to make clear such trade-offs, may lie within the purview of economic analysis.

NOTES

[1]See discussion of this point in Harold M. Hochman, "Individual Preferences and Distributional Adjustments," *American Economic Review* (May, 1972), pp. 353-60

[2]See John Rawls, "Justice as Fairness" in *Philosophical Review*, 1958, reprinted in Laslett and Runciman, *Philosophy, Politics and Society*, Series 2. (Oxford: Basil Blackwell, 1959), 132–57, and *A Theory of Social Justice* (Cambridge: Harvard University Press, 1971). The same construction has been developed by

John Harsanyi in "Cardinal Utility in Welfare Economics and the Theory of Risk Taking," *Journal of Political Economy* (October, 1953), pp. 434-35.

³John Rawls, "Distributive Justice," in Laslett and Runciman, *Philosophy, Politics and Society*, Series 3, (Oxford: Basil Blackwell, 1969).

⁴I interpret the word "inequities," as used here, to mean "inequalities."

⁵Rawls, "Distributive Justice."

⁶This dilemma in the theory of public policy is also discussed in Worth Bateman and Harold Hochman, "Social Problems and the Urban Crisis: Can Public Policy Make a Difference?" *American Economic Review* (May, 1971), pp. 346–53.

⁷The argument, as stated, reflects my methodological "public choice" preference for relating social practices to individual preferences. One might, in judging such practices, appeal to more "basic," nonutilitarian criteria, but these, it seems to me, are difficult to rationalize as anything more than one man's (or men's) preferences regarding the rules that govern their relationships with others. I think it preferable to remain within the social contract frame of reference as long as one can—confronting such pitfalls as the transitional equity problem as they arise rather than papering them over at the outset with strong value judgments.

⁸Another uncomfortable question—again a matter of transitional equity—arises here. When rights are established that had previously been unfairly denied to an individual or group, can this individual or group justifiably direct reprisal, retribution. and demands for reparations at individuals who might have benefited, but had not designed, the unfair practices under which the rights had been denied?

⁹Basic traffic regulations, which curtail certain rights (like driving at unlimited speeds) in exchange for the physical protection the law can provide, are such an exception.

¹⁰This is not to say that the disadvantaged, given the wherewithal, would not offer such compensation if it were essential to bring about such change. And, although it is worth little from a normative perspective, it is worth noting that such a division of the gains from the removal of injustice would be Pareto optimal.

¹¹This distinction implies, for example, that housing covenants, which exclude financially capable individuals from participating in a market, are somehow different from ghetto retail prices that exceed the community average because sellers can separate low-income from high-income markets or because costs are higher in the low-income market.

¹²Thus, in addition to compensating residents, one recent suggestion is that public-housing authorities construct new housing before razing old structures, permitting residents to respond voluntarily to new housing opportunities as they are created.

¹³This point is made clearly in Frank Michelman's justly classic paper "Property, Utility, and Fairness: Comments on the Ethical Foundations of 'Just Compensation,'" *Harvard Law Review* (April, 1971), pp. 1165-1258. But although Michelman's discussion of the ethical aspects of the compensation problem is first-rate, it leaves open the even less tractable problem of implementation. Too often, the cost of compensating is prohibitive. It is difficult to identify those to whom benefits and costs of rule changes accrue, and valuation is bound to be substantially affected by the identities of the individuals (the political entities) charged with measuring the gains and losses.

¹⁴But would the appropriate conclusion be different if the restrictions had derived

from a distributional compromise giving nonfranchise owners other privileges in return? This way out of the maze, however, is more apparent than real. Whatever the terms of such a distributional compromise, the "inefficiency" of its effect suggests that the logrolling coalition has left some parties worse off.

[15]To charge investors with responsibility for full discounting of the risk of changes in "inefficient" rules is, for my taste, too facile. It turns public confidence in property rights into a gamble, thus making mockery of the rule of law. It also implies that public choice models are tautological. There is no way around the fact that it is more difficult for communities to extricate themselves from error than to commit it.

[16]Similar arguments apply, in a more topical context, to the licensing of Cable Television franchises. Regulatory authorities cannot ignore the effects of new franchises on current licensees. (The earlier invasion of the radio market by television can be viewed in the same light.)

[17]James M. Buchanan, *Public Finance in Democratic Process* (Chapel Hill: University of North Carolina Press, 1967), ch. 4.

[18]Without such interdependence, it is difficult to reconcile simple discounting with a concern for the distant future. Even moderate interest rates would render outcomes as few as twenty years away insignificant. But this does not square with individual behavior (in investing, for example, to reforest timbered areas). See Harold M. Hochman, "Individual Preferences and Distributional Adjustments," *American Economic Review* (May, 1972).

[19]This objection, however, may be less forceful than it appears. If intergeneration utility interdependencies are sufficient, the constitutional preferences of a given social or demographic cohort may be an appropriate surrogate for the preferences of its children. See Bateman and Hochman, "Social Problems and the Urban Crisis."

[20]A variation of this, which focuses on the difficulty of assuring "reasonable expectations" when rules are subject to change, is to predetermine time limits at which all rules must be reconsidered. Thus, since individuals are on notice that changes might occur, they can discount the implied risk.

[21]The essence of logrolling is compromise based on mutual self-interest. Two individuals, with opposing preferences, each strongly in favor of one rule change and mildly opposed to another, are likely to prefer enactment of both to enactment of neither. See James M. Buchanan and Gordon Tullock, *The Calculus of Consent* (Ann Arbor: University of Michigan Press, 1962) and Roland McKean, "Public Spending and the Unseen Hand in Government," *Public Spending* (New York: McGraw-Hill, 1968), ch. 2, pp. 10–30. If queried, many social scientists, ironically, fail to see the virtue in logrolling.

[22]"Omnibus" tax legislation is a case in point. Taken singly, some provisions of such legislation seem inappropriate. Together, however, the implicit compromise that underlies them is apparent. Unfortunately, this is also true of its costs.

[23]See A. Mitchell Polinsky, "Probabilistic Compensation Criteria," *Quarterly Journal of Economics* (August, 1972), pp. 407–25.

[24]This argument is weakened if the positions that given individuals take in a series of issues are correlated. See John Jackson, "Politics and the Budgetary Process," *Social Science Research* (April, 1972), pp. 35-60.

[25]Such safeguards as the requirement that three-quarters of all state legislatures approve constitutional amendments provide little protection in more routine legisla-

tive matters. Nor do they help groups that are invariably minorities, for example, American Indians or, in the internment of World War II, the Nisei.

[26]Julius W. Hobson, individually and on behalf of Jean Marie Hobson and Julius W. Hobson, Jr., et al., v. Carl F. Hansen, Superintendent of Schools of the District of Columbia, the Board of Education of the District of Columbia et al., in the U.S. District Court for the District of Columbia, Civil Action 82-66, May 19, 1970.

John Serrano, Jr., et al., v. Ivy Baker Priest, as Treasurer of the State of California, L. A. 29820, Superior Court No. 938254, filed August 30, 1971.

Swann et al. v. Charlotte-Mecklenburg Board of Education et al., Supreme Court 402 U.S. 1.

Carolyn Bradley et al., v. The School Board of the City of Richmond, Virginia et al. In the U.S. District Court for the Eastern District of Virginia, Richmond division, filed January 5, 1972 Civil Action 3353.

[27]The transitional equity problems that these decisions imply are more acute because the rule changes they require do not operate through market transactions, permitting a smooth transition, but through discrete administrative actions.

[28]To restrict this discussion to the transitional equity implications of the education decisions, I assume that equal expenditure implies equal opportunity and ignore the question of whether equal input implies equal output in terms of educational attainment.

[29]Even if transitional equity is ignored, equal service cannot eliminate the effects of endowments as long as private education is a viable alternative. Some individuals, turning to private suppliers, will simply "waste" their tax contributions, or relocate elsewhere. Since such individuals are likely to be net contributors to the fiscal system, this behavior will exacerbate the educational finance problem.

[30]Swann et al. v. Charlotte-Mecklenburg Board of Education, pp. 23-24.

[31]There seems, after all, no reason to presume that suburban residential location is based entirely on simple prejudice, rather than a justifiable desire for access to better public services, especially education.

[32]In no way does this blame suburban residents for acting in self-interest. If the existing system of property rights is considered legitimate, the formation of communities with a preferred environment, including a fiscal base adequate to finance desired levels of public services without a great deal of intrajurisdictional redistribution, cannot be considered objectionable in its own right. However, to the extent that the formation of suburban communities masks a desire to give legal sanction to prejudice, the broader issue of whether the prevailing system of property rights is consistent with fairness is raised.

[33]The same transitional issues as the public education decisions pose arise, for example, in the preferential employment of disadvantaged minorities. In this connection, the New York *Times*, June 30, 1972, reported that Benjamin Epstein, the National Director of the Anti-Defamation League of B'nai B'rith, and Ms. Naomi Levine, acting Executive Director of the American Jewish Congress, condemned the use of the preferential quotas to equalize employment and educational opportunities for racial and ethnic minorities, calling them a distortion of antidiscrimination policies. "The fundamental wrong in preferential treatment," said Mr. Epstein, "is that individuals who have no responsibility for past discrimination are made to sacrifice their opportunities for self-fulfillment to pay the debt that society owes."

[11]

Constitutional Political Economy, 7, 3–20 (1996)
© 1996 Kluwer Academic Publishers, Boston. Manufactured in The Netherlands.

Public Choice Interpretations of Distributional Preference[1]

HAROLD M. HOCHMAN
Department of Economics, Lafayette College, Easton, Pa. 18042

Abstract. This essay examines, from the perspective of both economics and ethics, the logical foundations of income transfers in a democratic society that allocates resources, in the large, through free markets. Such transfers, enacted through the public choice process, modify the market-determined distribution of income, as a reflection of the distributional preferences of the members of a society. Both constitutional and post-constitutional explanations of redistributions are considered. A discussion of recent experimental evidence of distributional preferences leads into a critique of simple equality, built on Michael Walzer's distinction between monopoly and dominance, as a criterion of distributive justice.

JEL classification: A1, HQ, I3

1. Introduction: Economics and Ethics

For nearly three decades I have puzzled and, on occasion, written about the logical foundations of income transfers, intended to modify the market-determined distribution of income, to effect income redistribution in a democratic society that allocates resources through free markets.[2] Unlike most writings on this subject, however, my analysis is grounded in the distributional preferences of individuals and voting blocs, as these are revealed, politically, through fiscal redistribution, and not on the details of actual redistributive programs. Implicitly, then, my concern has been with the intricate and troubled relationship of political economy, in its neoclassical incarnation, to ethics.

Profoundly moral issues of this genre were central to the writings of Adam Smith and John Stuart Mill, and later for writers as diverse as Marx and Friedman or von Hayek. Substantively, this essay is a selective review of what economists have learned about distributional principles, by employing the methods of public choice, over the last generation.[3] The focus is on issues of equity or fairness, in particular, on the puzzling reality that most people do support redistributive transfers through private or political behavior, even when they seem to lose financially as a result.[4] Since such questions draw us, inevitably, on to other terrain, I shall refer liberally, though perhaps less than faithfully, to contemporary political philosophy.

The argument will have an admittedly subjective cast. Extended to distributional preference, economic discussion can be neither morally antiseptic nor ahistorical. Values are an intricate product of culture, teachers, faith, and personal history; introspection and a sense of the past, especially one's own, not only condition critical capacities, but shape analysis. Whether the argument that results can be defined as science is moot. Theory is never a failsafe guarantor of objectivity, much less common sense; this is especially true for topics like equality, property, and social justice, where the key to saying something meaningful

4   HAROLD M. HOCHMAN

is to transcend simple self-interest, while recognizing it, all the while, as the engine which drives ordinary people. What equips us for this venture is our capacity for ethical reasoning, for distinguishing what is *right*, or *moral*, from the merely instrumental. Arguably, this faculty is what differentiates people from other domestic animals and distinguishes levels of human civilization. Real life may preclude true detachment; but thought experiments, fortunately, can enable us to come close.

2.   A Qualified Defense of Market Process

In this essay, I shall explore the connection of economics, a discipline which studies mutually beneficial exchange among freely contracting parties, largely through market transactions, to distributive justice. This is construed as a synonym for equity or fairness, but not for equality, in the apportionment of market or political outcomes among economic units.

In starting, I take for granted the customary efficiency justification for market, as opposed to administrative or planned, allocation of scarce, thus economic, resources among competing and unlimited ends. For me, differences in the costs of processing information and matching buyers with sellers readily suffice to refute alternative claims. But efficiency considerations do not occupy center stage in my discussion.

Efficient allocation—i.e., a Pareto optimum—means that nothing can be done to make anyone, person or group, better off without disadvantaging another. Thus, it implies that no resources are wasted in producing output and that the division of this output among individuals cannot be improved upon, in terms of *their* evaluations, by reshuffling goods and services among them.

Market transactions, which are largely voluntary, are facilitated by property rights, private and communal, which derive from custom or law. Thanks to such property rights markets are incentive-compatible. This means that changes in the relative prices, monetary or other, at which people trade things bring about modifications of their behavior that make them as well off as they can be, given their resource constraints. It also implies that market adjustments to changes in the economic environment are automatic, minimizing the bargaining and other deadweight costs of transactions. Provided that reality satisfies a number of relatively unobjectionable assumptions, these adjustments bring about an efficient allocation of resources.

Calling an allocation efficient, however, can still leave us uneasy about some of the distributional characteristics of market outcomes. This is nothing new. Adam Smith, after all, authored *The Theory of Moral Sentiments* as well as *The Wealth of Nations*.

What, then, can the problem be? Although individual behavior, given unambiguous property rights, moves the economic system to an efficient outcome, property rights also assure that the distributional results of market allocation—the relative shares accruing to agents or participants—depend crucially on the endowments these individuals initially bring to the allocative game. Simply put, if I own all the resources, all output comes to me. There may be nothing wrong with a wealth concentration like this in efficiency terms; but it is hard to reconcile with any credible standard of fairness.

In competitive sport, most games are scoreless at the start; but in matters economic this is never the case. As in a horse race, fairness depends not only on the relative speed of the contestants, but the handicaps and the process through which they were established. Further, because resource allocation is a repeated game, wealth is cumulative. Thus, handicaps or differences that may have been acceptable in the first round are bound to cause trouble in historical context.

As I have earlier suggested, normative presumption is everywhere. Because market-determined outcomes hinge on the legitimacy of the historical processes through which endowments were established, it is palpably incorrect to treat them as if they were value-free. Few of us would rest easily if the heirs of Hermann Goering were to commission the auction house of Sotheby-Parke Bernet to sell a few long-lost Italian Renaissance paintings. In matters mundane, however, we can usually invoke the principle of consumer sovereignty and leave individuals, acting on their own volition, to work out the potential gains from trade.

Pareto optimality is an elegant criterion. Ethically, however, it does not suffice, because Pareto optima are not unique. Unless, in every sense, people are identical, each alternative configuration of property rights (resource endowments) implies, for an economy, a different Pareto-optimal outcome, distributing its social output differently among its constituents. These Pareto optima all satisfy the efficiency criterion; but most produce distributional results that seem to clash with common sense ethical norms.[5]

Even legitimate resource endowments are a remnant of history. If, individually or soci-etally, we find ourselves dissatisfied with the distributional outcome of economic activities, the remedy is to restructure property rights. When the scope of the dissatisfaction is limited, *ex post* adjustment through income transfers suffices to correct the distributional results, or errors, of the past. When it is considered endemic, however, we observe demands for radical change, ranging from land reform to outright collectivization and revolution, and an apparent willingness, on the part of the political community, to sacrifice efficiency goals to the mandates of fairness.

But as most of us have learned, or should have, this too has its shortcomings. Ethical concerns, like all metaphorical swords, cut two ways. Fairness or social justice, contingent as it is on the assurance of essential liberties, depends on far more than economic allocation, translated consequentially into a set of distributional results. In criticizing the outcomes of market allocation because endowments seem unfair, we must respond that a heterogeneous society, making collective decisions, has difficulty sustaining basic liberties unless com-modities and ideas are allocated in relatively free markets. History supplies ample evidence that the dynamics of alternative allocative systems are less consistent with the imperatives of a free society, morally, than the market realities that radical dreamers despise.

3. Government's Role in a Market Economy

A few definitions and theoretical considerations may prove helpful here. The competitive process constitutes the heart of the economic defense of markets. A market is competitive when no participant is a significant enough player, acting individually, to affect the price of anything traded. Agents are free to do as well as they can with their real or financial resources. Privately, each maximizes something, customarily called utility, which is no more than self-perceived well-being; but, except through the indirect forces of supply and demand, nobody has the power to restrict another's actions.

The virtues of this scenario are classic. Coordination is automatic, as are the behavioral adjustments that produce market-clearing prices, so we need not trouble about the motives of the agents who do the coordinating. Intermediaries, like bureaucrats and politicians, neither distort information nor interfere in price-setting. Most significant, at least for the relationship of economics to ethics, *life-arrangers*, to use James Buchanan's apt designation, have no place. Provided the essential technical assumptions are satisfied, the equilibrium to which transactions lead is Pareto-efficient; and distributional questions, if they enter the discussion at all, do so at a much higher level of generality.

Where then, aside from distribution and the endowments from which it derives, do markets fail, justifying collective action? Commonly, the answer is that markets fall short because they are not all-encompassing. Allocatively, they fail to internalize the external or spillover effects of private behavior, which arise when one individual's (or firm's) actions impinge directly, rather than through markets and prices, on another's options. When the number of people involved in these spillovers or indivisibility interactions is small, these inefficiencies can usually be handled privately, as bargaining costs are low; when it is large, however, they cannot. This accounts for a condition called *publicness*, which is the economist's conventional justification for collective action and the role of government in a market economy.

Publicness engenders inefficiency because it severs the connection between paying or being paid for one's actions or possessions and enjoying (or suffering) their use. With public goods inertia alone produces benefits—whether or not one contributes anything, in money or time, to covering their cost. Sometimes—if there is enough social pressure or bargaining costs are low—it is feasible to work out some sort of reciprocal cost-sharing scheme. When a lot of people are involved, however, or interests diverge, this is unrealistic, for most people are neither fools nor angels. In the limiting case, each individual, facing the *prisoner's dilemma*, takes up the private incentive to avoid the cost of public goods and attempts to ride free, resulting in the underprovision, relative to the efficiency norm, of goods with the characteristic of publicness. But here, unlike the market context, there is no automatic process to correct the problem, and coercion, as through taxation, becomes essential to provision. National defense is the commonplace example of such a public good. Of more immediate interest in this essay, adjustments of the income distribution, attributable to the clash of market outcomes with generally accepted ethical norms, are another.[6]

This contractarian rationale for public action is uncontroversial, neither liberal nor conservative, and acceptable to economists of every persuasion. It is tempered, however, or should be, by the recognition that real democracies, in financing the governmental provision of public goods, including distributional adjustments, confront an inherent tradeoff between the failings of markets and the inherent inefficiencies of government. Because they readily interfere with both market incentives and fundamental liberties it is dangerous to turn too quickly to collective solutions.

I have now established the background I require to elaborate on the relationship of economics to distributive ethics. In what follows I shall first explain the place of redistributive transfers in a free-market context. I shall then turn to whether income equality is an appropriate ethical norm.

4. Contractarian Theories of Redistribution

Contemporary political economy, in its public choice incarnation, encompasses both constitutional and post-constitutional representations of distributional choice. (Differences between these turn on whether the community has already established relatively unambiguous and enforceable property rights, which markets require to function effectively.) Both the constitutional and post-constitutional models respect consumer sovereignty; they assume that political acts reflect the informed consent of the electorate. The setting is contractarian and, at least in Buchanan's writings, the interpretation deontological; the focus is on process, on the rules and institutions that govern social choice and not on particularized end-states or outcomes. Ironically, both the constitutional and post-constitutional representations have largely been articulated by free-market economists—reflecting their belief that redistribution, if it is to occur, must be justified with logic, not emotion.

Economists, when trained as utilitarians, were taught that distributional judgements require interpersonal welfare comparisons. These require cardinal utility, as in the sacrifice theories of Victorian public finance, or a social welfare function that weights individual utilities. Notwithstanding their stubborn survival in some textbooks, the sacrifice theories merit no discussion, except as historical curiosities. But there is a lingering temptation to interpret the idea of a social welfare function as a promising avenue of escape from a difficult normative box.

Regrettably, appearance is deceptive. As we have learned from Kenneth Arrow, if we insist on a handful of seemingly innocent conditions, required for democracy to be meaningful, such social orderings are easier to invoke than derive. Distributional choice models that begin, however innocently, with a *strong* social welfare function[7] raise the question of moral legitimacy, swept under the rug in both classical and neoclassical economic reasoning, on which contractarian thinking centers.

4.1. Constitutional Models

James Buchanan's discussion in *The Limits of Liberty* (1975) is a suitable starting point for a discussion of this topic. Buchanan begins with the natural (i.e., market-determined) distribution that emerges in a Hobbesian state of nature, a setting in which property rights have yet to be established, in which life can be described, to credit Hobbes, "as solitary, poor, nasty, brutish and short." This Hobbesian or natural distribution is unstable because the predation and defense that anarchy engenders are too costly, in terms of deadweight loss, to all of the concerned parties. As a consequence, utilitarian incentives lead wealthier individuals, who have more to lose, to sanction redistributive transfers to those with less, as a simple matter of self-protection. This redistributive *social contract* is a voluntary response (in the small number case) to the considerable transactions costs·of unchecked anarchy. No autonomous ethical observer is required to bring it about. The net effect is a pattern of income transfers that diminishes but does not eliminate the initial or natural distributional inequalities of the state of nature.

A capacity for ethical choice is required to say anything more. The breakthrough, usually attributed to John Rawls (1958 and 1971), derives its normative power from the neutralization of egoistic preference.[8] Metaphorically, the key to understanding the Rawlsian world is the kitchen appliance that Americans commonly refer to as a cuisinart. Blended, each man is every man, or woman—equally likely to be anyone, anywhere in the frequency distribution of market outcomes.[9] Rawls achieves this methodological *tour de force* with a heuristic device he calls the *veil of ignorance*. The Rawlsian thought experiment renders social choice, in the *original position* that is its counterpart to the Hobbesian state of nature, both impartial and unanimous.

In the original position all persons in the political community know the full array of potential outcomes, which they believe themselves equally likely to receive. Individuals cannot distinguish, therefore, between outcome and opportunity, or between self and other. Their identities are probabilistic, and social choice is unanimous; there is no difference between self-interest and the golden rule. What is best for oneself is also right for others. Magically, these assumptions make the distributional indeterminacy of neoclassical welfare economics disappear. In an all-consumption economy, even minimal risk aversion is sufficient to guarantee that the optimal distributional outcome is characterized by simple income equality.

Formally, we can arrive at this conclusion by assuming that people are identical, so that they share the same endowments, preferences, and opportunities. This, too, negates the impossibility problem that plagues the search for an unambiguous social (distributional) ordering. But it also reduces social to individual choice and conceals the ethical dimension, making the whole subject of public choice appear to be superfluous. Except in a trivial sense, distributional decisions require, with identical individuals, *neither* a social welfare function *nor* a moral theory. Thus, on philosophical (as well as aesthetic) grounds, the Rawlsian representation seems much richer.

Things are different in the real world, in which people must use scarce resources to produce output. Even if the veil of ignorance is intact, market returns will turn out to be unequal, because production is characterized by specialization and comparative advantage. Political communities, pragmatically, can and do adjust the market-determined distribution, but not without impinging on basic incentives, reducing the aggregate of income and output to be distributed among their members (the deadweight loss). The preferred distribution of income will still be less unequal—it will display less dispersion—than the distribution that emerged from market activities. But every ethical criterion, even the *difference principle*, a *maximin* criterion, rejects simple income equality.[10]

Reality mirrors theory. Practical discussion typically assumes that it is possible to adequately describe economic justice in terms of an end-state principle of distribution and takes for granted the appropriateness of income as an index of individual well-being. Societies like the United States wage metaphorical wars to reduce the incidence of poverty, defined in terms of some threshold or subsistence level of income. Transfer programs, never perfect, reduce income differentials between rich and poor and nudge the income distribution in the desired direction. Typically, the result is acceptable, but insufficient; poverty, like Saddam

Hussein, invariably survives the war. One thing only is certain: the prosperity of those who administer the programs.

To the student of public choice, which requires democratic consent to legitimize collective action, something is missing in this. In America welfare reform has been, for as long as I can recall, a recurring but unrequited political theme. It seems to me that much of the chronic American discomfort with redistributive programs, including proposals for a guaranteed minimum income, derives from a failure to build policy recommendations on data that adequately describe the attitudes of ordinary people, rather than the research community, and tailor social institutions to the distributional preferences of a uniquely heterogeneous electorate.

Because, by construction, it permits agent-neutral preferences to be expressed, constitutional reasoning is the logical first step in remedying this. To fault constitutional thought experiments because, at most, they produce general guidance, like real-world constitutions, or to demean the veil of ignorance because the world is socially and temporally more complex than the Rawlsian ideal, reveals an inability to comprehend the place of abstraction in crafting an improved reality. Indeed, more often than practical people like to realize, such abstractions have operational analogues at the programmatic level; and sometimes— perhaps surprisingly—they even validate, structurally, redistributive programs that derive from consequentialist principles.

4.2. Post-Constitutional Models

Post-constitutional thinking about distributional choice, in contrast, treats the existence of property rights, which establish entitlements the legal system defends, as a given. It models people as they are, with distinct identities, aware of their particular endowments and preferences. History, therefore, matters. The public choice interpretation of post-constitutional redistribution embodies two major lines of argument.

The first, which is the central theme of my writings on income redistribution with James Rodgers, ascribes income transfers, whether in money or goods, to benevolent utility interdependence (positive interactions among individual utility functions or, more loosely, altruism). The essence of this argument is that narrow self-interest is not a realistic assumption about human behavior. Real people are not only sympathetic, caring about others as well as themselves, but display a willingness to pay for this by forgoing own consumption and transferring wealth, either in cash or goods. Here, as the theory of public goods suggests, the dispersion-reducing income transfers between donors and recipients that are required to internalize sympathetic utility interdependence and achieve a Pareto-optimal distributional outcome can readily be effected privately if numbers are small. Intra-family transfers, from child support to bequests, and charitable giving are obvious examples. With large numbers, however, as in a political community, this is not possible, and the donor-recipient relationship that underlies the redistributive transfers must be incorporated, for the usual public goods reasons, in the contractarian fiscal process.

When this interpretation of redistribution makes some simple assumptions about private preferences and the democratic process through which they are transmitted—defining, for example, systematic relationships between utility interactions and the variables that determine fiscal obligations—the social attainment of Pareto efficiency requires income transfers and, very likely, progressive taxation. These Pareto-optimal transfers, like constitutional redistribution, both reduce initial income inequalities and at the same time leave all participants in the redistributive process, donors and recipients alike, better off than they were with the market-determined distribution. Depending on the particular fiscal measures employed, they level income up from the bottom, like an income guarantee (von Furstenberg and Mueller, 1971) or reduce, but not eliminate, its dispersion across the full range of incomes (Hochman and Rodgers, 1969).[11]

I shall only mention, but not develop, the second line of argument. It interprets redistribution, within any time period, as an instrument of income insurance, which smooths the intertemporal income fluctuations (an artifice of the accounting period) to which most of us are subject and spreads risk (thus, though without the ethical connotations, paralleling the constitutional justification of distributional adjustment).[12] Under proper simplifying assumptions about the way the political process operates and the relationships among individual preferences and fiscal obligations, such transfers, which reduce within-period inequality, are similarly consistent with the Pareto criterion.

4.3. Commentary

What assures me, more than substantive argument, that these explanations of distributional choice make sense is the fact that they are anathema to extremists of both right and left. They trouble the former by justifying government's use of the fiscal process to carry out redistributive transfers and the latter by treating endowments as legitimate. With the utility interdependence argument the critics are wrong because free rider behavior becomes likelier as numbers increase, and collective provision is required to activate benevolence. Likewise, with insurance arguments for redistribution, it oversimplifies to assume that private firms are always the low-cost providers, because private decisions are complicated by moral hazard and adverse selection, and the belief that individuals will invariably act in their own best interests is no more than, except tautologically, an assumption.

The median voter model, whatever its limitations, is almost always a useful first approximation. This is true here, in asking whether, empirically, the explanations of redistribution that I have outlined hold up. Typically the poor, the major recipients of redistributive transfers, lack sufficient political, as distinct from revolutionary, capital to assure the enactment of redistributive programs, much less to make income equality a realistic objective. Nevertheless, at least in developed countries, political outcomes seem to encompass a substantial amount of redistribution from rich to poor. Moreover, if my own inferences from poll data that examined attitudes toward welfare spending and other redistributive programs are correct, such distributional preferences are quite stable (Hochman and Rodgers, 1977).[13] Theory is never as unrealistic as cynics are wont to think; this is the salvation, after all, of the scholar.

Differences between the constitutional and post-constitutional interpretations of distributional choice turn out, on reflection, to be a matter of degree. For example, extreme altruism, the limiting case of utility interdependence, can only be distinguished from Rawlsian behavior if redistributive transactions are exceedingly costly to effect. Otherwise, people who are totally other-regarding behave as if they could be anyone, as do donors who are infinitely risk-averse. Thus, it seems, in models of distributional choice, as if all roads lead to Rawls.

At this point, I have a final retrospective comment, which relates to the limitations of the self-interest assumption in explaining human behavior, be it private or political. In past writings on the place of utility interdependence in explaining redistributive transfers, I found myself attracted to this idea because utility interdependence concepts, both sympathetic (as in the explanation of redistributive transfers) and antipathetic (see Hochman and Nitzan, 1985) encompass the full range of human relations, intrapersonal as well as interpersonal, across time and generations. Utility interdependence, unlike strict self-interest, trivializes neither emotion nor our discipline. Moreover, because it frees us from the methodological need to assume, naively, that individuals are motivated differently in the private and public realms of choice, it weakens the internal barriers that separate the social sciences.[14]

In a sense, too, the discussion of utility interdependence has a great deal in common with Rawls. If, for example, people care as much for their children, or theirs in turn, as they do for themselves, the distributional outcome will be much the same as it would have been had the veil of ignorance been a reality, for it becomes ever more difficult to distinguish our descendants from other people as we project farther into the future. Clearly, such considerations would seem to account for social concern with some environmental issues, like depletion of the ozone layer, the survival of endangered species, and global warming, that rational egoists, with limited time horizon and positive time preference, find it hard to justify.

5. Experimental Evidence of Distributional Preference

Occasionally, to our delight, fact sustains theory. In its infancy the sub-discipline of public choice was almost purely speculative. In part this reflected the predilections of its founders, some of whom, if behavior does reveal preferences, displayed a marked aversion to empiricism. Perhaps this accounted for the depth of their insight; public choice was not marred by a compulsion to rush headlong into measuring and testing, casting hard questions aside and fastening on those for which data was evident and cheap.[15] While this has changed significantly, largely (but not entirely) for the better, in the intervening years, it continues to be true that the empirical surface has barely been scratched in thinking about distributional choice.

Theory's perpetual difficulty is that it is supposition. Nearly all interpretations contain a kernel of truth; but it is harder to pin this down in some cases than in others. Distributional preference is one of the hard cases. In explaining simple choices—is it easier, not to say better, to kill ourselves with guns or butter?—a minimum of assumptions is enough to infer something meaningful. But it is stickier in the realm of values, where we must grapple with commitment and meta-preference (preferences about preferences) and interpretation of indirect evidence, which is all that is available. Thus, to say anything at all invariably demands a major leap of faith.[16]

Recent literature describes a number of innovative efforts to learn something about distributional preferences through direct experiments. Indeed, the experimental literature in this area is both more extensive and more sophisticated, substantively and technically, than I had thought. Unlike most other empirical research on distributional policy, including most writings on income maintenance—which presume a social preference for the equalization of incomes, within the conventional accounting period, through redistributive transfers—the experimental inquiries focus on questions, ethical *and* behavioral, of distributional preference. Thus they do not assume away the central normative issue.

My comments will be confined to a subset of these experimental results. Specifically, they discuss three papers, by Elizabeth Hoffman and Matthew Spitzer, (1985); Norman Frohlich and Joe Oppenheimer, (1990); and John Beck, (1994).

Hoffman and Spitzer (1985) appear to have conducted the first set of major experiments dealing with distributional choice. Their experiments consisted of an extensive set of two-person games, with university students and staff as subjects, in which outcomes, decided through bargaining, indicated distributional preference. What they found is that first-movers in these games (called *controllers*) generally made more generous offers to their counterparts than noncooperative game theory would have suggested. Final settlements were less egalitarian, the stronger the second party's (the respondent's) perception that the controller's property right in the endowment had been *earned*, thus acquiring legitimacy in terms of the Lockean concept of *earned desert*. When the experimenter reinforced this legitimacy with *moral authority*—by assuring participants that the controller's property rights were indeed earned rather than arbitrary or random—the effect was even more pronounced.

While it might be excessive to claim that these experiments establish a definitive link between collective decisions and normative belief, the results obtained by Hoffman and Spitzer are unquestionably consistent with the public choice interpretations of distributional preference. When property rights are vague, as in constitutional contracting, people are much more likely to be egalitarian. Once property rights have been established, distributional outcomes move closer to the utilitarian norm, under which behavior is self-regarding. However, even in the version of the experiment that assigned maximum legitimacy to property rights, *self-interest* (measured by an *index of greed* the authors constructed) was but 70 percent of what pure egoism would have led us to expect.

To explain these findings Hoffman and her colleagues (Hoffman, McCabe, et al., 1991) subsequently conducted a series of double-blind *dictator* experiments, in which even the experimenter was uninformed of the subjects' choices. These suggested that other-regarding behavior is largely a matter of strategic considerations and expectations, as opposed to utility interdependence or a concern with equity, at least within the neutral social context of the experiments. This squares with my intuition. Benevolence is unlikely to be marginally relevant in the absence of deeper cultural ties than those that exist in the artificial communities formed explicitly for the purposes of the experiments.

The Frohlich and Oppenheimer experiments considered the choice of a distributional principle in Rawls' original position—behind a simulated veil of ignorance. My comments relate only to their experiments with production, which dealt with the redistribution of incomes the participants had earned by performing a set of defined tasks in the experimental setting.

What Frohlich and Oppenheimer (1990) found is that "concern for the poor and weak, a desire to recognize entitlements, and sensitivity to the need for incentives all enter into subjects' deliberations regarding a fair rule for implementing distributive justice" (p. 474).

Most subjects, in choosing among alternative distributional rules, preferred to maximize average income, subject to a floor or safety net (subsistence) constraint, rather than either a range (dispersion) constraint or maximin outcome. The productivity implications were more favorable when the distributional principle was chosen before the subjects could effectively estimate "their likely future productivity and economic status" (p. 464) rather than imposed by the experimenters. Similarly, commitment to group goals, the converse of free rider behavior, was greater when the distributive principle was selected unanimously rather than by majority rule.

Thus, the Frohlich-Oppenheimer subjects, through their behavior—rather than hypothetical responses—rejected both simple egoism, which would have sanctioned the market-determined distribution, and extreme redistribution. Both the restrictiveness of the decision rule imposed on the experimental group and perceptions of fairness, reflecting the impartiality of the distributive principle, proved important. And the rule chosen most often—maximization of average income, subject to a floor constraint—corresponded, more closely than its alternatives, to the type of transfer program most current in American policy debate.

Beck's experiments differ in that they examined the insurance motive for redistribution. These experiments looked at two issues, again with students as subjects. The first is whether individuals are risk-averse, the second whether they prefer a more equal distribution than individual risk aversion can explain. The setting is Rawlsian. Subjects confront the decision problem they would face behind the veil of ignorance if they know that output must be produced and that redistribution has incentive effects.

To measure their *private risk aversion*, Beck asked the participants to choose among alternative lotteries, each of which produced an income distribution with a different expected mean. While the assignment of payoffs to individuals in these lotteries is random, incentive effects make the distributions sensitive to tax rates, so that simple income *equality* violates even the *difference principle*. To ascertain their *distributional preferences*, the subjects, when choosing among the alternative lotteries, were told that everyone in their group would participate in the same lottery.

The results are revealing. While Beck's subjects did prove to be risk-averse, the tax rates associated with the distributions they chose were but half to two-thirds as high as extreme risk aversion (the maximin rule) would require. The evidence was mixed on whether individuals favored a more equal distribution than individual risk aversion implied; interestingly, however, only one of the twenty-six participants in the two experiments preferred an equal distribution.

The consistency of these results with the predictions of the theories discussed earlier is reassuring. If participants in the experiments are viewed as representative voters, democratic polities would appear to prefer some adjustment of the income distribution, albeit an incomplete adjustment, in the direction of equality. Moreover, the redistributive programs they prefer have familiar structural characteristics, similar to those considered in negative income tax experiments or the optimal tax literature.

To conclude, the studies summarized here constitute strong evidence that experimentation is a useful way to learn something about distributional preference. Adaptation of these methods to the investigation of patterns of utility interdependence, using samples designed so that benevolence is likely to be a significant factor, and to such issues as equality of opportunity would be a worthwhile extension of a highly promising avenue of research.[17]

6.   Income Equality and Justice

6.1.   Simple Equality

To here, this essay has discussed distributional outcomes, as is the custom among economists, relative to a conjectural norm of income equality, as if this were an unambiguous criterion of fairness and its attainment were desirable. But it is neither. Ethically, what is to be equalized is vague; legal income during a brief accounting period is the conventional expedient, but this obviously papers over its adequacy as a proxy for welfare. Nor does it address the broader question of whether an *economic* variable, be it income or something else, possesses enough generality to constitute a proper baseline.

The identification of equality with equity requires very special assumptions. In discussing opportunity, to wit, in reasoning deontologically, equality is sometimes a useful concept. Because identities are blurred, people tend to be more risk-averse when choosing constitutional or long-term rules. As an end-state condition, however, equality is both simplistic and unsustainable. Indeed, as Michael Walzer appears to argue in *Spheres of Justice* (1983), an emphasis on *simple equality*, defining the social norm in terms of a single dimension like income, may be inimical to constructive thinking about ethical norms.

Facts, nonetheless, help to disentangle emotion from substance. When income is recalculated in life-cycle terms, the tails of its distribution become thinner and statistical poverty is reduced substantially. The recognition that reported and actual incomes are not the same, because the quality of information differs, yields a similar result; income differentials between Third World and developed countries are always smaller than they appear in the raw statistics. This does not excuse inequities, interpreted as unacceptable deviations (not just *any* deviations) from some ethical ideal, but it does counsel caution in interpreting numbers—unless, to play the skeptic, a role that comes easily to the trained economist, one's real concern is with advocacy, or with appearance and not reality, because the agenda is centered on ideology or disguised rent-seeking.

Simple equality, of current income or any other measure, shares the imperfections of all bright-line criteria—including absolute inequality, which would give everything to me and nothing to anyone else. It is neither the right place to start a discussion of distributional equity or fairness, nor its proper conclusion.[18] Like everything else, perhaps even life and death, distributive justice is a matter of more or less, not all-or-nothing. Descriptively, the calculation of deviations from statistical equality may have pragmatic virtue; normatively, especially if selective and unbending, it demeans moral reasoning.

To students of distributional choice this is mundane stuff, related to the way our social computers are programmed, but it barely brushes the truly fundamental question of whether, ethically, economic measures can ever reveal more than a small fraction of what we need to know. Perhaps we focus on economic yardsticks because they are easier to discuss; perhaps it is conceit. But, frankly, the concept of distributive justice is too eclectic for any standard economic measure to accommodate.

If, nonetheless, we cleave to income (or some other simple indicator of wealth) in assessing the equity of social arrangements, it would seem more sensible to delineate acceptable limits of inequality than to strive for simple equality. Perhaps because I am an economist, conditioned by training to seek logical balance, I believe that an obsession with precision— here, with specific quantitative goals, independent of circumstance and custom—obscures the dialogue on distributive ethics. Unless it is realistic to work with the assumptions of the original position, it is more constructive to think in terms of tolerances, which screen out social pathology, including *unacceptable levels of inequality* and improper rules of membership.[19]

To illustrate this point, redirect your thinking to the proper or *just limits* of private markets in a political community that has made a basic commitment, for the standard efficiency reasons, to a decentralized or free-market allocation of resources. Few economists, even those who believe that pervasive intervention not only impinges on efficiency but threatens fundamental civil liberties, unqualifiedly reject all limits to market allocation. For distributional reasons, most people are troubled by insider trading in securities markets, even if it contributes, arguably, to the efficient dissemination of information about investment alternatives. They have similar qualms about the uncompromised market allocation of experimental treatments for otherwise terminal diseases, rare drugs, or vital organs; and they question the morality of rules that permit excess children to be traded like piglets. Ethics trumps efficiency in such matters, because the credibility of the same social institutions that legitimize market allocation and make it able to perform successfully is itself contingent on the existence of a widespread perception of fairness. Most of us are *not* dogmatic, at least in the end, and share in a belief that social choice, if it is to produce an ethically acceptable result, must reflect ordinary common sense.

6.2. Complex Equality and Dominance

Walzer's criticisms of uni-dimensional criteria of distributive justice, and mine, run even deeper. Simple equality, as I interpret Walzer, fails because it reflects defective peripheral vision—by treating "monopoly, and not dominance, as the central issue in distributive justice" (Walzer, 1983, p. 16). In other words, income or wealth concentration does not, by itself, indicate whether a society is just. What matters is whether political and social institutions treat income inequalities as indicators of merit or moral worth, and whether these inequalities enhance or stifle the aspirations and freedoms of those who are, in economic terms, less fortunate.

Walzer proposes, instead, a pluralistic criterion of distributive justice, *complex equality*. This criterion recognizes that many different *social goods*, each with its own distribution, are relevant to fairness. (Social goods are not the economist's public goods, but characteristics of social position that define and indicate an individual's status and influence.) What is critical for distributive justice is not the specific distribution of any of these social goods, taken by itself, but whether any of these particular distributions *dominates* social arrangements.

Thus interpreted, complex equality implies that concentrations of income or wealth are only crucial to distributive justice, in their own right, if and when individuals can transfer them to other domains, private or public, including the right to membership in the political community,[20] respect, and freedom of association, or to religion. In the economist's lexicon, complex equality mandates that the distributions of basic social goods be uncorrelated or, at worst, loosely correlated. It permits "many small inequalities," but requires that inequality "not be multiplied through the conversion process" (Walzer, 1983, p. 17). Simple though this may sound, it is a very tall order, even for a community with a highly developed network of internal values, like the Israeli kibbutz.

This argument can be carried at least one step further. Simple equality, even if it were desirable and could be attained, would not be a self-sustaining end-state characteristic because, as argued forcefully by Nozick (1974) and others, it is intrinsically unstable. Perhaps things would be different if altruism were universal, if we were each Mother Theresa; but this is not reality. Since ordinary people, both in their private and their social actions, maximize, satisfice, or otherwise strive or conspire to make the quality of their lives better rather than worse, it is in the long run an exercise in futility to push redistribution much beyond the limits of Pareto-optimal change. When democratic politics tries to force simple equality in terms of one success criterion, like income, people inevitably turn to other, usually less innocuous distributional characteristics, and a different and very likely more pernicious set of inequalities materializes.

Like Walzer, I prefer to distance myself from dominance. While my distributional preferences require some social correction of the market-determined income shares, I am not so naive as to believe that income inequalities, once attenuated, will not reassert themselves. Income, as an indicator of status, would be replaced by some other criterion with infinitely more potential for evil, including e.g., a pervasive capacity to control the lives of other people politically. Anyone who wonders why need not look beyond the postwar history of Eastern Europe, or its aftermath. There is no reason to belabor the point. The most forceful defense of free-market allocation that was published recently was not written by an affluent American, or a crusty political conservative dedicated to the preserving the old order, or an Austrian economist reminding us of eternal truth, but by Janos Kornai, the pre-eminent Hungarian mathematical economist (*The Road to a Free Economy*, 1990).

7. Epilogue

I have, in this paper, spelled out, from a number of perspectives, what I consider a compelling case for limited income redistribution through the fiscal process. I have also argued that dominance is far more to be feared than simple inequality. Even if it were within my capabilities, an analytic defense of my position would assume so much about the domain of the discussion that challenges, from every perspective, could walk unimpeded through the open door. Thus, I prefer a less formal, but richer, line of argument.

To a layman, the economist, defending market allocation, may appear to be venerating wealth, attaching a significance to the criterion of Pareto-efficiency that nothing, save decency, deserves. When the discussion of distributive ethics is recast in terms of complex equality, however, it seems to add to the case for market allocation. If markets are essentially free and external effects do not run rampant, correct incentives ensue. These incentives attach penalties to hate and, so long as dominance does not prevail, neither discriminate nor interfere with civil rights.

The so-called *man in the street*, a routine patron of the unfair gamble called the state lottery, does not crave simple equality in the distribution of income or wealth. Asked to rationalize his concern with inequality, his response is typically directed to the implications of dominance, not monopoly. Relative to alternative ways of coordinating the use of scarce resources, which is what the well-trained economist worries about, free markets loosen the bonds among social goods. Unless one is indifferent to domination, wealth inequalities have far more appeal than a system that produces a Stalin. Markets, of course, can and do co-exist with tyranny, but their general effect is to render it less stable rather than more.

There is an essential unity to the public choice interpretation of distributional preference. This holds for both method and prediction. Certainly, fundamental differences remain, which neither this essay nor a lifetime of writings can resolve, though supporters of particular redistributive measures, whether philanthropists or rent-seekers, often speak as if the debate were closed. Progress will continue so long as participants in the distributional debate confront the need for ethical legitimacy and refrain from reducing intellectual argument to a smokescreen for a partisan agenda.

Notes

1. This essay is an adaptation of two lectures, one presented to the European Public Choice Society in Turin, Italy (April 1992), and the other my inaugural lecture as the William E. Simon Professor of Political Economy at Lafayette College (February 1994). I am indebted, for comments, to Stefan Baumrin, Julian Lamont, Giorgio Brosio, and Albert Breton.

2. Hochman and Rodgers (1969) was the first of my writings in this area, and Hochman (1994) the most recent.

3. In its closing chapters, the common default location for discussions of distribution, Dennis Mueller's *Public Choice II* (1989) contains an accessible summary of public choice theories of social justice, as they relate to redistribution from rich to poor. Here, I do not recapitulate this discussion, but treat it, like some of my own early observations, as common human capital.

4. While this essay does not discuss entrepreneurial models of redistribution, in which one person's injustice is is another's desert and voters redistribute income to themselves (writings by Meltzer and Richard, 1981, and Peltzman, 1980, come to mind) this does not mean that I think them uninteresting. Their subject is simply very different. In such models support for public expenditures, including redistributive transfers, reflects self-interest, or rent-seeking, mediated by interest groups and the political process.

    While self-interest theories of this kind explain something, perhaps that much of government is a zero-sum affair, there is a great deal they cannot explain. Government spending in a typical Western society is far greater, after all, than the amount required to finance either redistributive income transfers or the survival, assured by a *nightwatchman (minimal) state*, of the democratic social contract; and net redistribution generally flows from the strong to the weak. Personally, I doubt that people are half as clever, or as dumb, as *positive* models of redistribution imply.

5. It has been demonstrated that the Pareto criterion is also problematical, logically, as a justification for (economic) liberalism. (See Sen 1970.)

6. Examples abound. My colleagues' research results produce beneficial spillovers; they add to my knowledge though I do nothing to produce them; their squabbling at faculty meetings, on the other hand, produces decidedly negative externalities.

    But these examples describe the polar case. It should be readily apparent that, in the context described, families, clubs, and ethnic communities can all be interpreted as mini-governments. While they differ in powers and enforcement methods, each functions, in its private sphere, to overcome the inefficiencies of individual choice when collective action is more promising.

7. In contrast to public choice, which has Italian and Swedish origins, this work is more in keeping with the Anglo-Saxon tradition in political economy. Typically, it derives policies, both allocative and distributional, that appear to be consistent with *reasonable* social welfare functions—additive, multiplicative, or Pareto. The Pareto interpretation, of course, effectively turns the idea of a social welfare function into little more than a security blanket.

8. Variants (formally different but substantially similar) of the Rawlsian theme had previously been developed by a number of distinguished economists, including John Harsanyi (1955), Abba Lerner (1944), and William Vickrey (1960).

9. Rawls, in *The Theory of Justice*, eschews assignments of probabilities in the *original position*. For the economist, however—at least this economist—his argument is easier to explain if we apply the principle of insufficient reason and express it, taking a step that Rawls himself rejects, as a probabilistic exercise.

10. This becomes less certain, however, when the distributional goal is defined in terms of opportunity rather than outcome.

11. Methodologically, however, this is a detail. What was important is that the argument blurs the distinction between efficiency and equity and enables the economist, contrary to neoclassical received doctrine, to use the Pareto criterion to rationalize income transfers.

12. The insurance rationale is developed in the essays by Polinsky (1974) and Zeckhauser (1974) that are included in Hochman and Peterson, *Redistribution Through Public Choice* (1974).

13. Whether this is true for countries with bipolar income distributions is not as clear. In such cases, models of revolution, in which the driving force is bribery rather than benevolence, might do a better job of characterizing the politics of redistribution.

14. In contrast, in *The Moral Dimension* (1990, p. 26) the eminent sociologist Amitai Etzioni argues that social scientists must distinguish, as economists do not, between the economic and moral domains of choice. He argues, in effect, that the individual operates with one utility function in the first sphere and a different one (describing metapreference?) in the second. This, to me, seems an arbitrary *bright line* and, because it implies that the individual is one body and two minds, methodologically inferior to the approach adopted in my writings with Rodgers. Utility interdependence captures the shading between self-interest, narrowly conceived, and ethical behavior in a way that bifurcated preferences cannot, and at least in theory its existence is empirically refutable.

15. On this I am my own authority, having been a junior member of the Department of Economics at the University in the late 1960's, and interacting with James Buchanan and Gordon Tullock.

16. It is tricky to use data collected with other ends in mind, even if it describes closely related subject matter like charitable giving or redistribution within families, to learn about distributional preference, much less ethics. In a paper witten two decades ago, Rodgers and I tried to infer something about distributional preferences and utility interdependence patterns from poll responses to questions on attitudes toward welfare spending and other redistributive programs (Hochman and Rodgers, 1977). What we seemed to learn—that a political majority, including both donors and recipients, prefers the programs to which they have become accustomed and that donors, save those at the top of the income scale, seem less concerned with the private welfare than the social behavior of transfer recipients—holds less relevance for the present discussion than our self-consciousness in interpreting such data.

17. In experimental inquiries about distributional preference the major stumbling block is not a lack of technique, but an excess of concern with technical refinement. It is very easy for experimental method to become a theology, in which the detail dominates the objectives, especially when the substantive issues seem intractable. This is an old story; professional incentives often make it easy to forget the real stakes.

    It is sometimes argued, in the United States, that the Federal Drug Administration, immobilized by risk-aversion, permits countless patients to die before approving the use of a new drug. One hopes that empirical research on distributional choice will not do the same.

18. If nothing else, this approach is not blind to the inequities inherent in frequent and unmitigated transitions in the constitutional, fiscal, and regulatory environment. Just societies have more to worry about than end-states, and like good judges we have good reason to respect precedent.

19. Walzer (1983, Chapter 2) devotes considerable attention to rights of membership in the political community, which are obviously a central factor in the distributional debate. Some of the best examples in his discussion relate to the relative treatment of citizens and guest workers, an everpresent dilemma in many European countries.

20. Returning to a point I have made earlier, one reason why complex equality is more meaningful than simple
    equality as a social goal is that it is much more likely to be accommodated by measures that limit unacceptable
    inequalities, because it demands a less comprehensive political consensus.

References

Beck, J. H. (1994) "An Experimental Test of Preferences for the Distribution of Income and Individual Risk
    Aversion." *Eastern Economic Journal* 20:2 (Spring) 131–45.
Buchanan, J. M. (1975) *The Limits of Liberty*. Chicago: University of Chicago Press.
Etzioni, A. (1988) *The Moral Dimension: Toward a New Economics*. New York: Macmillan, Free Press.
Frohlich, N., and Oppenheimer, J. A. (1990) "Choosing Justice in Experimental Democracies With Production."
    American Political Science Review 84:2 (June) 461–77.
Harsanyi, J. C. (1995) "Cardinal Welfare, Individualist Ethics, and Interpersonal Comparisons of Utility." *Journal
    of Political Economy* 63: (August) 309–21.
Hobbes, T. (1950) *Leviathan*. New York: E.P. Dutton.
Hochman, H. M. (1972) "Individual Preferences and Distributional Adjustments." *American Economic Review*
    62: (May) 353–60.
Hochman, H. M. (1983) "Contractarian Theories of Redistribution." In Helpman, E., Razin, A., and Sadka, E.
    (eds.) *Social Policy Analysis*. New York: Academic Press, 211–34.
Hochman, H. M. (1994) "Economics and Distributive Ethics." *Transaction/SOCIETY* (November/December),
    35–42.
Hochman, H. M., and Nitzan, S. (1985) "Concepts of Extended Preference." *Journal of Economic Behavior and
    Organization* 6: 161–76.
Hochman, H. M., and Rodgers, J. D. (1969) "Pareto Optimal Redistribution." *American Economic Review* 59:
    (September) 542–57.
Hochman, H. M., and Rodgers, J. D. (1977) "The Simple Politics of Distributional Preference." In: Juster, T. (ed.)
    The Distribution of Economic Well-Being. Cambridge, Mass.: The National Bureau of Economic Research,
    71–107.
Hoffman, E., and Spitzer, M. L. (1985) "Entitlements, Rights, and Fairness: An Experimental Examination of
    Subjects' Concepts of Distributive Justice." *Journal of Legal Studies* 14:2 (June) 259–98.
Hoffman, E., McCabe, K., Shachat, K., and Smith, V. (1991) "Preferences, Property Rights and Anonymity in
    Bargaining Games." (Unpublished paper, December, 1991).
Kornai, J. (1990) *The Road to a Free Economy: Shifting from a Socialist Economy: The Case of Hungary*. New
    York: WW Norton.
Lerner, A. P. (1944) *The Economics of Control*. New York: Macmillan.
Meltzer, A. H., and Richard, S. F. (1981) "A Rational Theory of the Size of Government." *Journal of Political
    Economy* 89: (October) 914–27.
Mueller, D. C. (1974) *Public Choice II*. New York: Cambridge University Press.
Nozick, R. (1974) *Anarchy, State and Utopia*. New York: Basic Books.
Peltzman, S. "The Growth of Government." *Journal of Law and Economics* 23: (October) 209–88.
Polinsky, A. M. (1974) "Imperfect Capital Markets, Intertemporal Redistribution, and Progressive Taxation." In:
    Hochman, H. M., and Peterson, G. E. (eds.) *Redistribution Through Public Choice*. New York: Columbia
    University Press, 229–58.
Rawls, J. A. (1959) "Justice as Fairness, Philosophical Review, 1958." Reprinted in Laslett and Runciman (eds.)
    Philosophy, Politics and Society, Series 2. Oxford: Basil Blackwell, 132–57.
Rawls, J. A. (1971) *A Theory of Justice*. Cambridge, Mass.: Belknap Press.
Sen, A. (1970) "The Impossibility of a Paretian Liberal." *Journal of Political Economy* 78: (January/February)
    152–57.
Vickrey, W. (1960) "Utility, Strategy, and Social Decision Rules." *Quarterly Journal of Economics* 74: (November)
    507–35.
von Furstenberg, G. M., and Mueller, D. C. (1971) "The Pareto Optimal Approach to Income Redistribution: A
    Fiscal Application." *American Economic Review* 61: (September) 628–37.

Walzer, M. *Spheres of Justice: A Defense of Pluralism and Equality.* New York: Basic Books, Inc.

Zeckhauser, R. (1974) "Risk Spreading and Distribution." In: Hochman, H. M., and Peterson, G. E. (eds.) *Redistribution Through Public Choice.* New York: Columbia University Press, 206–28.

PART II

PUBLIC POLICY

A

Tax Policy

12

THE OPTIMAL TAX TREATMENT OF CHARITABLE CONTRIBUTIONS

HAROLD M. HOCHMAN AND JAMES D. RODGERS*

ABSTRACT

Utilizing the criteria of efficient resource allocation and distributional neutrality, this paper examines the optimal method of subsidizing charity. It focuses, in particular, on the use of a tax credit as an alternative to the current method of deducting eligible contributions from adjusted gross income. Unlike many other analyses of this question, it does not employ traditional equity arguments; it proposes, rather, that subsidies, justified by the public good or externality characteristics of charity, should be structured to effect a Lindahl solution. The principal conclusion is that a tax-credit system may well conform more closely with such a solution and the criteria it satisfies than the current system.

TAKING the theory of public goods as its point of departure, this paper develops the analytical case for fiscal subsidies to charitable giving and, from this perspective, derives their appropriate structure. It deals with whether the existing means of subsidization, through the deduction of charitable contributions from adjusted gross income, satisfies the criteria of Pareto efficiency and distributional neutrality, or whether these objectives are more likely achieved with some

*The authors are Professor of Economics and Finance at the City University of New York (Bernard Baruch College and the Graduate Center) and consultant to The Urban Institute, Washington, D.C.; and Professor of Economics at The Pennsylvania State University. The theoretical sections of this paper are based on research supported by the National Science Foundation and The Urban Institute. The policy analysis was prepared at the request of the Department of the Treasury. The comments, suggestions and assistance of Robert Harris, Dick Netzer, Edward Neuschler, Oliver Oldman, John Posnett, Robert Teitel, Richard Wagner, Burton Weisbrod, and the editor of this journal are acknowledged. We retain full responsibility for anything the reader may think erroneous or outrageous.

alternative mechanism, such as a tax credit.

In 1974, charitable giving amounted to $25.15 billion. Of this, individuals gave some $19.80 billion, and $2.07 billion was transferred through bequests. The remainder was divided between corporate contributions ($1.17 billion) and foundations (2.11 billion).[1] Assuming that the marginal rate of tax, on average, to be twenty-five percent, giving by individuals alone reduced federal revenues by some $5 billion.[2] Such subsidies to individual giving are the immediate subject of this paper. Suitably modified, however, the analysis can be applied to certain other types of deductions, sometimes considered "tax-expenditures," and to corporate giving as well.

Fiscal institutions, in the public choice frame of reference, should reflect citizen-taxpayer preferences. The object of tax policy, as it relates to charitable giving, is to set up a system of subsidies, *provided such subsidies are appropriate*, that is consistent with such preferences.[3] This paper, in general terms, defines the dimensions of such a system. An important collateral purpose of the exercise is to point out that many other discussions of the tax treatment of charitable giving, in failing to approach the topic from the perspective of the theory of public goods, have failed to raise fundamental issues that are, for policy purposes, logically prior to those on which attention has focused.

Part I of the paper examines the economic justification of the fiscal subsidy to charitable giving. Part II presents a theoretical analysis of the rationale for such subsidies, utilizing the theory of public goods, and derives their optimal structure. The incentive effects of subsidization, to which conventional discussion of the tax treatment of charity has devoted most of its attention, are discussed in Part

1

III. Part IV spells out some of the policy implications of the analysis.

I. The Justification of Fiscal Subsides to Charitable Giving

There are two justifications, grounded in the Paretian concept of efficiency, for according preferential tax treatment to charitable giving. The first is the familiar notion that the activities charity finances are not private in the strict sense. Contributions to social, educational, and religious organizations not only benefit the donors, but others, both contributors and non-contributors. In other words, contributions produce positive external effects and, in varying degree, possess the characteristics of "publicness." Hence, to rely exclusively on voluntary cooperation among demanders to provide these activities, ingenious though the campaign efforts of some charitable organizations may be, seems likely to result in their under-supply. Taking benefits to others into account, the prices faced by individual contributors will be too high, leading them to under-contribute. Moreover, some persons who benefit from these activities at the margin may choose to be "free-riders" and make no contributions.

It might be argued that the undersupply of such activities will foster government provision, which replaces the voluntarism of charity with the compulsion of taxation. However, even with some "collectivization" of supply, public provision will remain suboptimal if the demanders of the activities that contributions finance are under-represented in existing political jurisdictions, and the expenditure decisions of such jurisdictions conform, approximately, to the median voter model. Such matters, needless to say, are complex. At issue are (1) just how well the political process responds to constituent demands; (2) the decision rules that political communities employ; (3) the tax instruments used to distribute the costs of government-provided goods among the members of the community; (4) the heterogeneity of citizen demands and community composition; and (5) the ease with which political boundaries can be altered and jurisdictions proliferated.[4]

To the extent that voluntary cooperation, unassisted, produces sub-optimal levels of provision, the preferential tax treatment of voluntary contributions is one way of improving matters. Such "intervention" may be viewed as a means of correcting the voluntary, cooperative outcome, or as a reflection of government failure to assess and and implement citizen desires. Through subsidies to charity, political minorities (individuals who feel strongly enough about the social value of certain activities with "public" characteristics) (a) can voluntarily allocate own-income to their provision without fiscal coercion and (b) enlist the aid of community-at-large in their financing. If individuals who are *not* primary demanders— who do not feel strongly enough about charity-financed activities to support them at the taxprices implicit in the fiscal structure—benefit from them at the margin, such cost-sharing is a requirement of efficient resource allocation. Indeed, the point of subsidies to charity is to establish sharing arrangements, among primary demanders and the community-at-large, that satisfy the normative criteria of efficiency and distributional neutrality. The community may view such sharing as a compromise between the tyranny of the majority implicit in pure collective action and the polar case of private choice, in which an individual's welfare depends entirely on his own actions.

The second justification of fiscal subsidies to charitable giving is suggested by the economic theory of bureaucracy (see e.g., Niskanen, 1971 and Weisbrod, 1976). For at least some government-provided goods, charitable organizations serve as a viable institutional alternative or supplement to public provision. Where they operate at sufficient scale, like major foundations, such organizations compete with government in providing certain services, and, as a consequence, mitigate government monopoly. This has particular import at the national level, where the softening effects of the Tiebout process, which leads individuals to move among jurisdictions when fiscal burdens dominate their expenditure benefits, are weak.

The unique role of private foundations in supporting research and social programs illustrates this argument. In a variety of areas, philanthropic enterprise finances projects that government, by reason of self-interest or law, cannot or will not undertake. Relatively speaking, philanthropy is free from bonds of political accountability, which shackle creative government, and can more readily underwrite risky projects, which hold out the hope of high, though ill-defined, social returns. For the modern scholar and research manager it takes little imagination to see the point.[5]

This line of argument also has a more subtle dimension. For some charitable activities, like those relating to religion, our political constitution precludes government provision, judging its potential costs in terms of conformity to be intolerable. Subsidization, rather than direct provision, thus seems the appropriate means through which to implement the public stake in religious activities.[6]

In the large, these arguments support the way in which charity is now defined for tax purposes. But wether it is appropriate to continue the current system of providing subsidies via deduction from adjusted gross income—so that such subsidies depend on the marginal tax rates of donors—is another matter. Employing assumptions that may approximate reality quite well, we will show that this is unlikely.

To summarize existing practice, the fiscal subsidy to individual charitable contributions in the U.S. now varies with three things. First, it depends on whether taxable income (including contributions) is positive, and whether deductions from adjusted gross income are itemized. If not, the subsidy has no direct worth to the donor, though he may gain from it, indirectly, as a beneficiary of charity, and as a member of the political community if the anti-monopoly effects of private philanthropy are important. Second, the subsidy varies with marginal tax rates, which determine the proportions in which the donor and the community share in the costs of a charitable gift. Third, the subsidy is constrained by the limits set on

deductibility by the tax code. The general limit of the charitable contributions deduction has been 50 percent of adjusted gross income since 1969; prior to this it was 30 percent. In addition, the Revenue Act of 1969 eliminated escapes from the general limit and continued the special 20 percent limit on contributions to private foundations.[7]

The discussion that follows focuses on the second aspect.[8] It provides, under specific simplifying assumptions, an analysis of the optimal tax treatment of charitable contributions, and uses this analysis as a basis for assessing how current practice compares with a practical alternative, a tax credit that rebates to all donors a pre-determined share of their contributions.[9]

II. Subsidies to Charity and the Theory of Public Goods

The optimal level of subsidies to private charity depends on how benefits are distributed between donors, the primary sharing group, and secondary demanders, comprising the community-at-large. External benefits must accrue in the demands for the specific services that charity finances or through prior constitutional choice, as with religious activities, to justify the public subsidization of charity. Otherwise, the benefits of giving are private, and no subsidy is warranted.[10]

Assume that charitable contributions finance but one activity, with pervasive "public characteristics," warranting public participation in its financing. The voluntary nature of the contributions has two immediate implications. First, each contributor attains marginal equilibrium, in which *his* incremental benefit and *his* perceived incremental cost are equal. Second, some individuals fail to contribute, not because they place no marginal value on the activity, but because they are better off as "free riders," to wit, they view the cost of its expansion, so long as they must contribute, as excessive and permit others to pay for their benefits.

The first observation implies that *any* equilibrium level of the charity-financed activity, optimal or not, will be one in which all *donors* are in marginal equilibrium. Such a solution can best be described by dividing the community into two groups, those who make voluntary contributions and those who do not. A social optimum requires:

$$\sum_{i=1}^{m} \text{MRS} + \sum_{i=m+1}^{n} \text{MRS} = \text{MRT} \qquad (1)$$

The first term on the left-hand side of (1) sums the marginal rates of substitution (MRS's) of contributors and the second sums the MRS's of non-contributors. In the solution described by (1) all voluntary contributors are in marginal equilibrium, since $\text{MRS}_i = \text{MC}_i$, the cost to the individual (as he perceives it) of a unit increment in the activity. The remaining $(n - m)$ non-contributors needs not be in marginal equilibrium. Social optimality (efficient resource allocation) requires that the second *sum*, when added to the first, equal the marginal rate of transformation (MRT) between the public good and some numeraire private good.

The objective of subsidies to charity, defined in terms of an element of the tax base that is a proxy for preferences, is to bring forth the level of contributions that satisfies (1) *and* that is also a Lindahl solution, in which, for all persons, contributors and non-contributors alike, $\text{MRS}_i = \text{MC}_i$. Such an outcome is both efficient and distributionally neutral.

To illustrate how such an outcome may be attained, assume that charity is not subsidized and that the level of contributions is such that the left side of (1) exceeds the right. Divide the community, again, into groups. Implicit in the subsidy to charity is a price reduction, which induces those in the first group, who contribute even without subsidy, to increase their nominal contributions, so long as their demands are at all elastic. The price reduction causes a second group, a subset of the initial $(n - m)$ non-contributors, to make some voluntary contributions. Despite the subsidy, individuals in the third group continue to be non-contributors. In addition, as a negative tax, the subsidy reduces federal revenues, leading all groups to contribute indirectly to support

of the activity—through some mix of higher taxes and lower expenditures on other programs, assuming full employment.

The tax literature, which dwells on the "incentive effects" of the deductibility of contributions from adjusted gross income, has focused on the net price effects of the subsidy on the first and second groups.[11] Such calculations, however, provide no information about the optimality of this (or any other) subsidy arrangement in terms of the public goods logic. It is to this question that our discussion now turns.

The allocative deficiencies of the no-subsidy situation are examined first. Then the discussion turns to the structure or system of subsidies required to bring about an optimal and distributionally neutral outcome.

A. Subsidies as a Pareto Optimal Response to Publicness

Assume that a community of three persons (or homogenous groups) is concerned with the financing of a single activity through charitable contributions and subsidy. Suppose further that both A and B choose to contribute, while the third person, C. does not, even though his valuation of an additional unit is positive at the level that A and B provide.

Consider the choice with which each person is confronted. Assuming that the publicness of the charity-financed good is pervasive, the total quantity, which is available to all, depends on their combined contributions. Moreover, with a large number of contributors (the real-world case) strategic behavior is useless, because the individual contributor presumes, rationally, that what others give is fixed and independent of his own action. Thus, each person bases his contribution on the amount of the activity it will by and his own taste for giving, taking the donations of others as beyond his control.

The circumstances just described, for three persons behaving in the mode of the "large-number" case, are illustrated in the three panels of Figure 1. The top panel shows A's choice, the middle panel

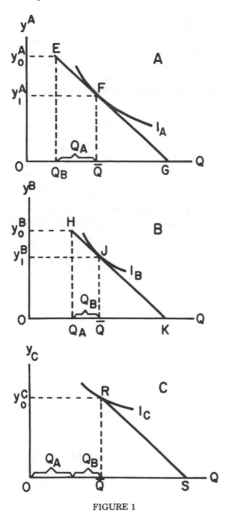

FIGURE 1

speaking, income available for other consumption) and reflects (by its linearity) a simplifying assumption that the marginal cost of Q is constant. The budget line does not extend to the vertical axis, but stops at E, because A has access to the amount of Q that others (i.e., B) finance, whether or not he contributes anything. Initially, therefore, A's position is at E, given his income Y_o^A and Q_B, the level of the activity financed by B's contribution. Given his preferences, as described by indifference curve I_A, A contributes $(Y_o^A - Y_1^A)$ and attains equilibrium at F.

B's contribution is similarly analyzed, using the next panel. Given A's contribution of Q_A, B's initial position is H on budget line HJK, which has the same slope as EFG. His contribution secures the provision of an amount Q_B.

Finally, the third individual, C, whose decision is depicted is the bottom panel, contributes nothing, given Q_A and Q_B. C prefers point R because, for him, additional units of the charity-financed good are not worth their cost.

Figure 1 describes what Buchanan, in his writings, has called an "independent adjustment equilibrium," in which each person's contribution depends on his private preferences and marginal cost, taking as given the quantities of the public good that others supply. This outcome is analogous to the Cournot equilibrium of duopoly theory and results from a similar adjustment process. [13]

This independent adjustment outcome seems a realistic description of equilibrium in the large-number case, when activities with a significant public or collective-good component are privately financed through unsubsidized voluntary contributions. It is not, however, a Pareto optimal level of provision, much less a Lindahl solution. For a Pareto optimum, it is necessary that summed incremental benefits (over A, B, and C) equal marginal cost, as in equation (1). Here, this condition is not met, because it is A's and B's *individual* (not summed) marginal rates of substitution (MRS's) that equal marginal cost. If, for example, the marginal cost of Q in terms of other goods is unity,

indicates B's, and the bottom panel, C's. Focus first on A's panel. The vertical axis measures A's income, Y^A, and the horizontal axis the quantity of public good, Q. If this good is to be provided at all, it must, by assumption, be financed by voluntary contributions. [12] A's budget constraint is the line EFG. The slope of EFG measures the rate at which A can acquire Q by sacrificing own-income (strictly and C's MRS at R is 1/2, then at $\bar{Q}$, the quantity provided,

$$\sum_{A,B} \text{MRS} (= 1 + 1) + \sum_{C} \text{MRS} (= 1/2)$$
$$> \text{MRT} = 1 \qquad (2)$$

Thus, with reference to the Pareto criterion, which defines allocative efficiency, the quantity provided in an unsubsidized, voluntary setting is too small.

Figure 2 provides an analysis of the way in which a subsidy can correct such undersupply. To abstract, for now, from the optimal structure of subsidies and focus on cost-sharing between primary demanders and the community-at-large, ignore B, leaving only A, who contributes

without subsidy, and C, who does not. The horizontal axis measures the level of the activity. The vertical axis measures: its marginal cost, assumed constant; per unit cost to A and C; and their marginal evaluations, given by the curves labeled ME_A and ME_C. A's private equilibrium is R, at which his marginal evaluation and the marginal cost of providing the good are equal. Because C's marginal evaluation is always less than marginal cost, he contributes nothing. Hence, the quantity provided is $\bar{Q}$, which is less than the optimal quantity Q^*, at which *summed* marginal evaluations, indicated by ΣME, are equal to marginal cost.

To justify public intervention, given the non-optimality of $\bar{Q}$, our two parties (or

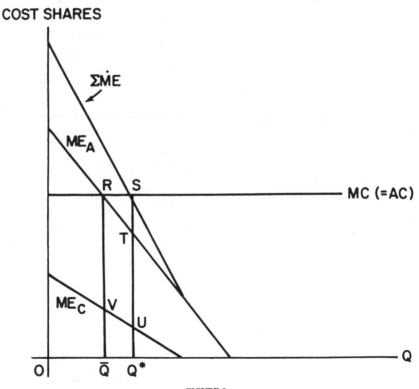

FIGURE 2

groups) must be unable to attain an optimum through voluntary bargaining. While such bargaining might occur in a genuine small-number situation, for most charity-financed activities the large number of small contributors makes it unlikely that optimality will be attained.[14] Hence, efficient allocation requires some external (governmental) modification of the budget constraints with which the participants are faced.[15]

To attain an efficient result, consider a government subsidy, effected, say, through a tax credit that reduces the contributor's income tax liability to a percentage of his gross contributions, S. A fundamental aspect of any such subsidy is that effective tax rates must be raised, public sector activities reduced, or both, to maintain the initial budgetary outcome, be it deficit or surplus. Consequently, through increased tax rates or reductions in service levels, subsidization imposes costs upon both A and C. Assume that the Treasury recaptures this revenue loss through higher effective tax rates, leaving intact the public service budget, and that A is aware that it will do this.[16]

In calculating the effect of the tax credit on the price of his contributions, A will take two factors into account. On the one hand, the tax credit reduces the price of his contributions, because it reduces his taxes, whatever his income, by S per dollar of contributions. On the other, to recoup the implicit revenue loss, A must expect higher general tax rates. The net change in price is a combination of these two effects. The second, indirect component, which operates through higher tax rates, depends on how much the individual contributes; the more he gives, the more revenue the community loses and the higher tax rates must be to maintain a given deficit or surplus.[17]

Figure 2 indicates the way in which such a tax credit would function to produce a Lindahl optimum. For optimal allocation, the subsidy must change A's contribution from its no subsidy level ($O\bar{Q} \times R\bar{Q}$) to $OQ^* \times TQ^*$. A's gross contribution must increase to $OQ^* \times SQ^*$. His net contribution, which depends on both the subsidy and the implicit tax change, may be larger

or smaller than it was before. This net contribution, plus C's implicit contribution, $OQ^* \times UQ^*$, attributable entirely to the higher effective tax rates required to replace lost revenues, finances the optimal quantity of the activity, OQ^*.

The outcome is necessarily a Lindahl solution. If A is in marginal equilibrium *and* an optimum is attained, C must, in the two-person case, be in marginal equilibrium as well, in the sense that his marginal evaluation $ME_c = UQ^*$ equals the marginal tax cost, to him, of an infinitesimal increase in A's contributions. Ironically, C reaches marginal equilibrium despite making no voluntary contribution at all.[18] For public policy, the issue this raises is that of setting the subsidy rate, S, at the level consistent with the distributionally neutral Lindahl solution.

B. The Optimal Structure of Subsidies to Charity

Discussion, thus far, has focused on (a) the failure of voluntary behavior to assure sufficient provision of a charity-financed activity and (b) the process through which the subsidies to charity, via a tax credit, can eliminate undersupply and bring about a Lindahl optimum. Attention now turns to the topic of how, if at all, the rates at which charity is subsidized should vary among contributors.

In our previous example, the subsidy took the form of a flatrate tax credit, invariant with respect to donor income or more generally, donor benefit functions. Under present U.S. law, the subsidy, as a direct function of the marginal tax rate, varies directly with taxable income. Many students of public finance have criticized this on equity grounds.[19] Here, however, the issue of subsidy structure is examined in terms of efficiency, to determine what the public goods rationale for subsidies implies for their optimal structure.[20] We do not considered the equity issue *per se*, holding, rather, that distributional choice can only be properly discussed in a much broader context than the tax treatment of contributions.

Assume, as in Figure 1, a community

of three persons: A and B, who contribute to charity, and C, who does not. Suppose, further, that all three have identical tastes, but different incomes, a standard assumption in fiscal design. Let Q*, as before, be the optimal quantity of the single charity-financed activity, with its price to each contributor being constant over quantity. Ignore, for now, the implicit effects of subsidies on tax rates and, therefore, net contributions, and proceed as if there were some authority, external to the economy in question, that stands ready to assume responsibility for the deficit.

The problem is to decide the appropriate relationship between the rates at which the community subsidizes the contributions of A and B. Given the incomes of the donors, Y_A and Y_B, we can regard their marginal evaluations, at the optimal quantity Q*, as fixed. To assure provision of the optimal quantity and a distributionally neutral outcome, the price to each person must equal his marginal evaluation; otherwise, (a) the price structure will not induce him to contribute the appropriate amount, so that Q may be under or over-supplied, and (b) the subsidy will not be distributionally neutral (income will be redistributed between A and B).

This equality of marginal evaluation and price is represented, for A and B, by equations (3) and (4):

$$\frac{C_A(1 - S_A)}{Q^*} = ME_A^* \qquad (3)$$

$$\frac{C_B(1 - S_B)}{Q^*} = ME_B^* \qquad (4)$$

C_A and C_B are the gross contributions of A and B; S_A and S_B are the subsidy rates; and ME_A^* and ME_B^* are their marginal evaluations at Q*, the optimal quantity.

To satisfy (3) and (4), subsidy rates (per dollar of contribution) must equate each individual's marginal (and average) price (his per unit cost share in the absence of monopolistic price discrimination) to his marginal evaluation at the optimal quantity. Such prices, which are obtained by dividing net contributions by Q*, define the cost shares.

Suppose now that A has the higher income. Then ME_A^* will exceed ME_B^* if Q is a normal good, an assumption the empirical evidence seems to confirm.[21] Inasmuch as quantity is fixed at the optimal level by assumption, and ME_A^* > ME_B^*, (3) and (4) imply that $C_A(1 - S_A) > C_B(1 - S_B)$. To satisfy the Lindahl condition, A's net contribution must exceed B's. However, more precise assumptions, about preferences and income elasticities of contributions (when implicit effects on tax rates are brought back into the discussion) are required to go further and establish, in general terms, the necessary relationship between S_A and S_B.

Suppose, for both A and B, an income elasticity of demand for the charity-financed activity of unity, within the relevant range (levels of output in the vicinity of Q*). With unit income elasticity, marginal evaluation (or "demand price") rises in proportion to income, so that the elasticity of marginal evaluation with respect to income is also unity.[22] Thus, if B's marginal evaluation is ME_B^* and A's income is $(1 + \lambda)$ times B's $(\lambda > 0)$, $ME_A^* = (1 + \lambda) ME_B^*$. Combining (3) and (4), this produces an exact relationship between contributions and the subsidy schedule required to satisfy the Lindahl condition:

$$C_A(1 - S_A) = (1 + \lambda) C_B(1 - S_B) \qquad (5)$$

Equation (5) indicates that A's net contribution must be $(1 + \lambda)$ times B's if each individual's marginal evaluation is to correspond to his marginal (average) per unit price. Moreover, if $S_A = S_B$, they will face the same prices per dollar of contributions and, with unit income elasticity of demand, A's gross contribution will be $C_A = (1 + \lambda) C_B$. Hence, a subsidy structure with $S_A = S_B$ will satisfy the Lindahl condition, as given by (3) and (4). Cost *per dollar* of contributions will be the same for the two donors. At the same time their shares in average (= marginal) cost will differ because they contribute different gross (and net) amounts. Other subsidy schedules, which imply different cost-sharing arrangements, violate the Lindahl condition—the public sector analogue of marginal equilibrium in a competi-

tive market—and distort the financing of the collective benefit that A and B support through charitable contributions.

Now consider an income elasticity of one-half. Marginal evaluations rise at but half the rate of income. If A's income is $(1 + \lambda)$ times B's and $\lambda > 0$, $ME_A = (1 + \lambda/2)ME_B$. Combining (3) and (4), the relationship between A's and B's net contributions to charity must be:

$$C_A(1 - S_A) = (1 + \lambda/2) C_B(1 - S_B) \quad (6)$$

Once again the Lindahl condition is satisfied by setting $S_A = S_B$. Since income elasticity is one-half, $C_A = C_B(1 + \lambda/2)$.[23]

This analysis demonstrates that the required increase, with demand, in the fiscal subsidy to a given contributor emerges naturally out of variation in the level of contributions. Attainment of the Lindahl condition does not require the variation of subsidy rates with income, as under present tax law, if the only reason for interpersonal differences in contributions is differences in income. To the contrary, the Lindahl condition requires a flat-rate subsidy, such as a tax credit, under which tax liabilities are reduced by a pre-specified proportion of eligible contributions.

Though this demonstration seems simple, it is deceptive. The assumption, contrary to previous argument, that the subsidies are externally financed engenders a conceptual problem. Properly defined, each donor's total contribution must include the compensating increase in his tax payments, inasmuch as contributors as well as non-contributors must share in its fiscal burden. By implication the cost (left-hand) side of (3) and (4) must be modified to enter the incremental tax. We do this in (7) and (8). These equations assume that the means of collection is a marginal shift in the individual income tax schedule. The incremental tax function, indicating the implicit increase in the ith individual's marginal tax rate, is denoted by $t'(Y_i)$.[24]

$$\frac{C_A(1 - S_A) + t'(Y_A)Y_A}{Q^*} = ME_A^* \quad (7)$$

$$\frac{C_B(1 - S_B) + t'(Y_B)Y_B}{Q^*} = ME_B^* \quad (8)$$

What is of interest here are the implications of different forms of this incremental tax function for the optimal subsidy structure. Specifically, we are concerned with whether this complication reverses our conclusion that a flat-rate subsidy is appropriate (that a tax credit is preferable to deductibility) in terms of the Lindahl condition.

In considering this issue, assume, as before, that the income elasticity of demand is unitary, so that marginal evaluations are proportional to income. An invariant subsidy is optimal, in these circumstances, if and only if the $t'(Y)$ terms in (7) and (8) are equal. If A's income is twice B's, the increase in A's tax payments must, in dollar terms, be twice the increase in B's. Thus the Lindahl condition requires displacement of the original marginal tax schedule by a constant, a change which makes the effective schedule slightly less progressive.

Matters become more complex when the income elasticity differs from unity, since it is marginal evaluation and not income with which charity must keep in step and, in the present argument, both Y_A and Y_B, the respective incomes of A and B, are fixed. In general, to justify $S_A = S_B$, the ratio of $t'(Y_A)$ to $t'(Y_B)$ must vary with the income elasticity. The higher the elasticity, the more progressive the "increment" in the tax must be. Conversely, with given income elasticity, the more progressive the implied increments in marginal tax rates, the more the subsidy to charity must increase with income—in the direction of its structure under deductibility—to offset its effect on tax-prices.

In policy, however, it is the magnitude and not the direction of these effects that is interesting. Cursory analysis provides ample reason to believe that such effects are inconsequential. Charitable giving is less than two percent of personal income,[25] and the implicit effects of the subsidy on marginal tax rates are even smaller because part of its cost is diverted to non-contributors. It thus seems reasonable to think of a small across-the-board differential in marginal tax rates (a marginal differential, as pointed out, that is slightly regressive) as the means through which the costs of the subsidy are offset.[26] Under this, or virtually any other assumption that is at all realistic, a flat-rate tax credit is likely to provide a good approximation to the Lindahl requirements. It is, in any case, far more likely to do this than the present structure, under which subsidies to charity are strongly progressive.

III. On the Relevance of Price Elasticities

A. Price Elasticities and Cost-Sharing Between Donors and the Community-at-Large

It is important to relate this argument, which considers subsidies to charity as a means of cost-sharing, to conventional discussion, which centers on the effect of fiscal subsidies on the incentive to contribute.

Assume, for argument's sake, that a flat-rate tax credit satisfies the Lindahl condition and there is but one charity-financed activity with pervasive public benefits. Assume, further, that the fiscal authorities have access to a suitable computational algorithm, which identifies the optimal level of charity and the terms on which donors and the community-at-large should share its costs.[27]

A legislature, deciding whether to increase or decrease its subsidy, must know more than the price elasticity of giving. A unitary price elasticity, for example, tells it only that a one percent reduction in price will increase giving by one percent; a price elasticity in excess of unity implies only that a given reduction in price (increase in the subsidy) will yield a dollar increase in contributions that exceeds its cost in terms of revenue. But it does not answer the normative question that our analysis considers basic; it does not tell us whether the price reduction is desirable.

This requires that we must know the relationship between the optimal sharing ratio, R*, defined as in Part II(A), and

the marginal sharing ratio, R_M, implicit in the incentive effect. R_M is the cost to the community (in foregoing revenue) of a one percent change in the subsidy, divided by the increase in gross contributions that accompanies it.[28] If $F_M > R^*$, the subsidy is excessive, with the community (through the fisc) bearing too large a share in the cost of financing the charity-supported activity. Alternatively if $R_M < R^*$, the subsidy is too low.

Values of R_M, for price elasticities of *net* giving (cost to the donor) and subsidy rates that span the range of reasonable estimates, are reported in Table 1. The price elasticities, which range from -0.25 to -1.50, encompass the Schwartz (1970) and Taussig (1967) estimates at the lower end of their range, and the estimates of Feldstein (1975a) and Feldstein and Taylor (1976), which range between -1.0 and -1.5, at the upper end. The initial subsidy (the complement of the price of charity to the donor) varies from 0.20, as low a marginal tax rate as can be expected to apply on returns which itemize deductions, to 0.70, the maximum marginal rate of the individual income tax.

The marginal sharing ratios in Table 1 are, from the Treasury perspective, cost-benefit ratios. Arithmetically, they are simple averages of the marginal sharing ratios implied by changes of plus and minus one percent in the net price of charity, relative to the price implicit in the subsidy rate at the head of the column (e.g., if the initial subsidy is 0.20, the price is 0.80, and becomes either 0.7920 or 0.8080 as a result of a one percent change). For practical purposes, differences between the marginal sharing ratios implied by positive and negative changes in price (in the one percent range) are insignificant (in other words, less than 0.01).

As might be expected, Table 1 tells us that the share of the incentive effect the community must pay through higher taxes declines with price elasticity and increases with the initial subsidy rate. The initial rate of the subsidy makes less difference, the lower the price elasticity; the price elasticity makes less difference, the higher the initial subsidy. In general, R_M is *much higher* than the subsidy rate itself

TABLE 1

COMMUNITY SHARE OF THE INCENTIVE EFFECTS
ON GROSS CHARITABLE GIVING

(Marginal Sharing Ratio: R_M)

Price Elasticity of Charitable Giving	Initial Subsidy Rates = Marginal Tax Rate = 1 - Price to Donor					
	.20	.30	.40	.50	.60	.70
− .25	.84	.86	.88	.90	.92	.94
− .50	.73	.77	.80	.83	.87	.90
− .75	.66	.70	.74	.78	.83	.87
−1.00	.60	.65	.70	.75	.80	.85
−1.25	.56	.61	.68	.72	.78	.83
−1.50	.52	.58	.65	.70	.76	.82

Reported figures average the cost-benefit ratio (marginal sharing ratio) for changes of ± 1 percent in the net price of charitable giving.

and is quite sensitive to the parameters, because the legislature, in granting subsidies, cannot discriminate between marginal and inframarginal contributions. In other words, changes in the subsidy are not restricted to incremental contributions, but apply to inframarginal contributions as well.

To the fiscal authorities, the point of this numerical exercise is that price elasticity, as a basis for evaluating potential changes in the tax treatment of contributions, can be quite misleading. For the general taxpayer, to whom the Treasury is responsible, liberalization of the tax treatment of contributions is only worthwhile if it has an incentive effect that is worth its marginal tax-price. Public policy involves much more than whether an additional dollar of subsidies can generate more than a dollar of charity.

Figure 3 indicates how the computations reported in Table 1 would enter an optimal contributions policy. The horizontal axis measures absolute values of price elasticities. The vertical axis measures both R^* and R_M. R^*, which is treated as exogenous, defines the "optimal share" of the Treasury (the community) in the cost of the

charity-financed activity. For each initial rate of subsidy Figure 3 plots the values of R_M, taken from the corresponding column of Table 1. If the subsidy rate is initially at $S = 0.40$, and the price elasticity is −0.50, the community is at H. At this point, $R_M > R^*$, which implies that the level of contributions is excessive. To the community, as general taxpayers, the cost of the contributions stimulated by the subsidy exceeds, at the margin, the external benefits they produce. Hence, the appropriate policy is to reduce the subsidy rate to a lower level, shifting to the curve for which $S = 0.30$, and moving from H to G to satisfy the Lindahl condition.

B. Variation in Price Elasticities and Discriminatory Subsidies

A collateral issue, which is also focused on price elasticities of giving, relates to whether income variation in price elasticity warrants the adoption of a differentiated subsidy (one which varies with income) rather than a uniform subsidy. Two distinct cases must be considered. In the first, the initial level of giving is optimal; in the second, it is sub-optimal.

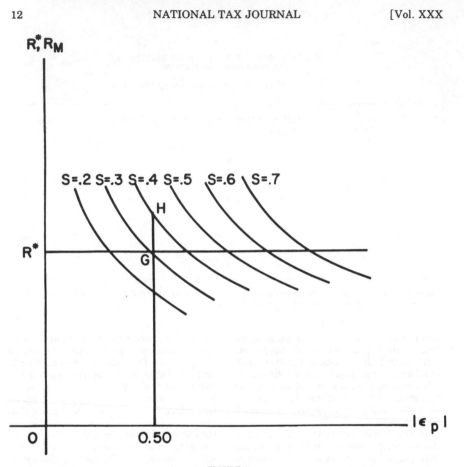

FIGURE 3

If the initial level of giving is optimal, differences in price elasticities are only relevant if distributional objectives require that the community depart from the Lindahl condition, via a non-uniform subsidy, which varies with price elasticity. The community can, no doubt, generate more charitable contributions, holding constant their cost to the public, by restructuring its system of subsidies to take advantage of differences among taxpayers, assuming they vary systematically with a practicable tax base. It may, similarly, evoke the optimal level of giving at lower cost in foregone revenue. To do

this, however, it must violate the distributional neutrality of the Lindahl condition, which "simulates" the outcome that private action ("the market") would produce if the charity-financed activities were free of their "public" characteristics. We can think of no reason, much less one that is compelling, for the structure of subsidies to charity, (in contrast, say, to the overall rate structure of the income tax) to be an appropriate vehicle through which to effect redistribution among donors.

Thus, if income variation in price elasticities of giving is to be relevant in defining the subsidy structre, the level of contributions must be sub-optimal, for conventional reasons (free-rider behavior, impediments to transactions, and the like). If giving is sub-optimal, discrimination, linked to price elasticities, may produce gains for the community-at-large, as taxpayers rather than donors. For a given total subsidy—revenue foregone— the gains from redirecting marginal subsidies to those donors with the highest price elasticities accrue at the expense of the consumer's surplus of other donors with less elastic propensities-to-contribute. If, for the community, such discrimination does make budgetary sense, equity considerations aside, the issue of whether it should effect discrimination through a device like deductibility not only depends on the precise values of the price elasticities, but their systematic and positive correlation with income. To date, the most careful studies of the relationship between income and price-elasticities are those of Feldstein (1975a) and Feldstein and Taylor (1976). They find some tendency for the price elasticity of giving to *fall* as income rises, but are skeptical of both the high price elasticity value for taxable units with adjusted gross incomes of $4,000-$10,000 and the low value for those with incomes in excess of $100,000.

Given the normative premises of our model, this suggests that the case for income variation in subsidies to charity is weak, so long as it rests on differences in price elasticities. If such a case is to be made, it must derive from systematic differences, with income, in the composition of charitable giving, in other words, in the "external" (as opposed to private or club-type) component of the benefits that charity confers.

To justify progressive subsidies, as through deductibility, from adjusted gross income, higher income groups must support activities that produce more "public" benefits (external economies) than the activities that the donations of lower income groups finance. In practice, the issue this raises is whether the tax law should treat social service activities, which have a significant redistributive component (or giving, say, to educational institutions or hospitals) differently from giving to religious causes, which are the major beneficiary of low-income charity.[29] While there are systematic differences in the composition of giving by category of beneficiary, this does not, in itself, tell us whether progressive subsidies are warranted, much less to the degree associated with marginal tax rates. Such as it is, the case for progressivity becomes weaker if we grant credence to the constitutional basis (the public good argument) for the private financing of religious activities through charity, which rests on the presumption that religion is important to the development of tastes and values that are socially desirable (e.g., it may reduce activities that impose external costs).[30]

IV. Policy Implications

Discussion turns now to specific policy implications. To this point our major conclusion is that the present system, under which contributions are deducted from adjusted gross income, producing subsidies that increase with income and marginal evaluation, may do considerable violence to the requirements of the Lindahl condition. Judged in terms of the public choice logic, this system seems decidedly inappropriate, unless there are large enough increases in the external economies associated with the ediferent activities supported as donor income rises, with no externalities associated with the contributions of persons who do not itemize deductions. This last assumption seems absurd, while there is no empirical support for the idea that the beneficiaries of the rich produce goods with more pervasive external effects. If anything, one would expect charity-financed activities having governmental substitutes (e.g., education and social welfare activities) to generate less in the way of positive external benefits than activities that are exclusively financed through charity (e.g., religion). Nor does deductibility seem an appropriate way of distributing the costs of privately provided goods which produce collective-consumption benefits between their primary demanders and the community-at-large.

Of the policy alternatives, the simplest,

in practice as in theory, is a tax credit, which reduces the income tax liability of the donor by a designated proportion of his contributions, set by the legislature to reflect the extent of their external benefits. While this recommendation is not novel, our reasons for making it are. Students of taxation have often suggested that a tax credit be substituted for the deductibility of contributions under the income tax.[31] As a rule, however, this recommendation has been associated with an aversion to the pro-rich characteristics of deductions from adjusted gross income, and it has rationalized in terms of egalitarian value judgments. To the fiscal economist, concerned with squaring policy with theory, this normative bias in the traditional case for the tax credit is a distinct methodological weakness. In our analysis, with the legitimacy of subsidies to charity (whatever their immediate distributional consequences) as a premise, we avoid this pitfall because we substitute the standard criteria of "efficiency" and "distributional neutrality" for the strong value judgment implicit in traditional use of the "equity" criterion.

It seems appropriate, therefore, to recommend, as a primary reform in the income tax treatment of charitable contributions, the adoption of a tax credit, to replace the deductibility of contributions from adjusted gross income. This seems the most practicable means of approximating the Lindahl condition.[32] To be sure, the case for a tax credit is not cut and dried. It may be vitiated by differences in the substantive composition of giving, though there is no hard evidence on this question, one way or another. Its arithmetic is complicated (as Part II has described) by the means through which the government raises the tax revenues required to finance the subsidy. But the arguments in opposition to adoption of a flat-rate credit—arguments against moving to a simple and uncomplicated cost-sharing arrangement between donors and the community-at-large—seem nowhere near so compelling, intuitively, as the arguments against the steeply progressive subsidies which deductibility implies. This in no way denies an ultimate need, from

a social perspective, for a distributional value judgment. It does imply, however, that the tax treatment of charitable contributions is not the place to implement this value judgment.

The proper level of the tax credit depends, as prior discussion has indicated, on the "external" content of the benefits that charity-financed activities confer; it depends, in other words, on the relationship between the marginal evaluations of the primary sharing group, namely, voluntary donors, and the community-at-large.[33] In academic discussion, though not actual policy, the specification of this proportion can be thought of as a matter for democratic decision-making, which faces the same problems here as in setting tax-prices for conventional public goods.

In practice, however, there is nothing simple about the business of obtaining such an algorithm. As an initial approximation, the legislature might set the tax credit to maintain the budgetary cost of the subsidy at its current level, under deductibility—with an upward adjustment to reflect those contributions that are now subsumed under the standard deduction and thus denied the subsidy. According to Feldstein and Taylor (1976, p. 1219), a 25 percent tax credit would hold both the total volume of contributions and its cost to the Treasury approximately constant. While this approach would ignore the non-optimality of the outcome under deductibility, our principal reason for advocating reform, it is a starting point that avoids first-order effects on public revenues.[34]

Second, it is not only appropriate, but important, to remove charitable contributions from the umbrella of the standard deduction. So long as charity produces external benefits, there is no logical basis for denying the subsidy to the broad class of donors who do not, for whatever reason, elect to itemize.

Nor do we see compelling reason to set a quantitative limit, relative to income on any other index of ability-to-pay, on the amount of a taxpayer's contributions (direct or through a bonafide foundation, properly monitored) that the community is willing to subsidize, provided it sets the tax credit at its proper level. The present limit is a vestige of an improper interpretation of the rationale for fiscal subsidies to charitable giving, which considers the subsidy to be a tax dodge or loophole, adopted as a matter of political expedience rather than allocative efficiency. No doubt repeal of the limit might enable more of the very rich to pay no tax at all. But to do so, provided the tax credit is less than 100 percent, the rich must assign a larger share of their own income and wealth to social purposes, reducing their expenditures on private goods and, in so doing, producing benefits (through mixed private and public financing) that are valued at cost by the community-at-large.

On these grounds, the twenty percent limit on giving to private foundations seems questionable, assuming, of course, that "the public" has not erred in its definition of eligible foundations. In addition, the efficient use of donations to charity is hampered by the inability of donors to regulate their disposition. As Tullock (1966) has pointed out, individuals have little incentive to acquire such information, since its cost is greater than their private gain. Thus foundations, functioning as intermediaries, acquiring information for donors and monitoring the use of charity by those to whom they dispense funds, play a very significant role in the philanthropic process. The twenty percent limit, by discouraging donor use of the foundation vehicle, not only inhibits efficiency in the disposition of contributions, but, by so doing, reduces the level of giving, even through external benefits might justify additional subsidies.

The final question is whether a "floor" should be placed on eligible contributions, limiting the deduction to persons whose gifts exceed a certain percentage, such as three percent, of adjusted gross income. This limitation has been recommended, among others, by Goode (1964) and Taussig (1967). To rationalize a floor in terms of efficiency, one must argue that activities financed by individuals having deductions lower than the floor generate no positive external effects, or that at least the benefit the floor generates by precluding subsidies to truly private goods offsets the harm it inflicts by stifling contributions to activities with positive external effects. If the former argument is used to rationalize a floor, simply removing these private activities from the list of those that will be subsidized is a better solution. However, either argument requires knowledge about the external effects associated with various charitable activities, and in the absence of such knowledge, no clear position is possible.

In conclusion, it should be pointed out that the logic of this paper is not limited to the tax treatment of charitable contributions. It can be extended to other deductions allowed by the tax law, referred to (in some cases with inappropriate value connotations) as "tax-expenditures." Such deductions, in contrast to those that reflect costs of earning income, include, among others, medical expenditures, and certain casualty losses, which warrant special tax treatment because they reflect a kind of constitutional decision to share risk. With the medical deduction the case against subsidy rates that vary directly with income seems even clearer than it does for contributions. Though full evaluation of such considerations lies beyond the scope of this paper, we strongly recommend that the preferential tax treatment of other non-business expenditures of the household be re-evaluated in light of analysis of the kind this paper has developed.

FOOTNOTES

[1] American Association of Fund-Raising Counsel, *Giving USA: 1975 Annual Report*, p. 6. Foundation giving, of course, derives from prior gifts of corporations and individuals.

[2] The figure of twenty-five percent is taken from Feldstein (1975a). It was calculated by applying the marginal tax rate for joint returns to contributions in each taxable income class.

[3] Thus, within the framework of this paper, it is inappropriate to think of subsidies to charity as a "tax loophole." Such a characterization, pejorative in tone, implies that the community really prefers nominal and effective rates of tax to be one and the same (though there is little evidence that it does) or that the state's claims on the individual's income are logically prior to his own.

[4] For a model that discusses these issues in more detail, see Weisbrod (1975). Also see Buchanan and Tullock (1962).

[5] We are, of course, ignoring abuses, as occur when the foundation vehicle is used, without social purpose,

as a simple tax-dodge, reducing the taxation of private income. But this is a separate issue.

[6] If governance and the political process were costless and the federal system ideal, both of these justifications for the subsidization of charitable giving would vanish. There would be no need for "private jurisdictions" of demanders, acting without the coercive powers of government, to provide collective wants. Moreover, individuals would not need charitable organizations as counterpoise to the abuses and inefficiencies inherent in government monopoly.

[7] For more detailed discussion of these limits, and the special 30 percent limitation on certain gifts of capital gain property, see Internal Revenue Service Publication 526, "Income Tax Deduction for Contributions," 1974 edition.

[8] In the policy discussion of Part IV we return briefly to the other two factors.

[9] What qualifies as a legitimate contribution (a topic which preoccupies much legal discussion) is ignored, as are abuses of the preferential treatment of contributions, such as gifts of overvalued assets. As a policy issue, questions of legitimacy stand on their own, separate from the concerns of this paper. Vickrey (1975) examines some aspects of abuse, particularly those involving gifts of non-cash assets.

We should note that our analysis does provide a rationale for liberalizing the tax treatment of political contributions and rethinking the present practice of disallowing contributions to organizations engaged in non-partisan political activity (e.g., the League of Women Voters), this depite the ambiguities inherent in the adjective "partisan." Such participation in the political process is itself a public good.

[10] If the benefits of a charity-financed activity have a restricted domain in, say, political or spatial terms, those who do not benefit should not be required to help finance it. The members of the "club," as a self-contained community, should be fully responsible for costs. See Buchanan (1965) and Polinsky (1973) for discussion of cost-sharing in a community club context. This implies, strictly speaking, that the subsidization of much charity should be, say, local rather than federal. It has its institutional counterpart in restrictions on deductibility, in some states, to philanthropic organizations that concentrate their activities in-state. Our analysis assumes all this away, implying, if effect, that such differences wash out in the aggregate. To do otherwise would make an already unwieldy analytic framework even more unmanageable.

[11] See Feldstein (1975a, 1975b), Feldstein and Taylor (1976), Kahn (1960), Schwartz (1970), Taussig (1967), and Vickrey (1962).

[12] The simplest rationalization of this is that public provision requires the acquiescence of a political majority, but that the set of jurisdictional boundaries and opportunity costs of relocation preclude the formation of such a majority.

[13] See Breit (1968), Buchanan (1967, 1968), and Fellner (1960).

[14] Of course, bargaining may occur if a few large contributors account for a charity's support. For discussion of the possibility of such group bargaining, where the distribution of the relevant characteristic among participants is very skewed, see Stigler (1974).

[15] Whether the government has the information to improve matters, rather than make them worse, is not dealt with here. We assume that *some* form of subsidization can improve resource allocation to *some* degree.

[16] Introduction of the subsidy will increase the quantity of the charity-financed activity, and alter the optimal amounts of public sector activities that are complementary with it or substitutes for it. Throughout this paper such interdependence is assumed to be absent.

[17] Strictly speaking, this means that A cannot be viewed as a pricetaker, since price varies with quantity. However, in a large-number setting (analogous to a firm in competition) this can be ignored, since an increment in A's contribution will have negligible influence on effective tax rates.

[18] Of course, introduction of the subsidy might well induce C to make *some* voluntary contribution, unlike the situation depicted in Figure 2, if it reduced his net price, at some levels of contributions, below the corresponding marginal evaluation.

[19] See, for example, Schaefer (1968) and Vickrey (1974).

[20] We are still assuming that charity finances but a single activity and that the publicness of its benefits is pervasive. Whether subsidy rates should differ among activities because they differ in degree of publicness is essentially an empirical question, which is considered, though in a manner more cursory than its importance warrants, in Part III.

[21] This is confirmed in Feldstein (1975a) and Feldstein and Taylor (1976), and by both Taussig (1967), using cross-section data, and Schwartz (1970), in time series analysis. Although there are wide differences in the estimates of income elasticities of giving reported in these studies, the values are uniformly positive.

[22] Proof: The elasticity of ME_i, the marginal evaluation of the ith person in the community, with respect to income is defined as:

$$\eta_M = \frac{dME_i}{dY_i} \cdot \frac{Y_i}{ME_i}$$

If person i's net contribution in Lindahl equilibrium is

$$C_i = ME_i Q^*$$

and the change in contribution as income changes (i.e., as we move from one person to another) is given by

$$dC_i = d(ME_i)Q^*$$

The elasticity of contributions with respect to income is, therefore,

$$\frac{dC_i}{dY_i} \cdot \frac{Y_i}{C_i} = \frac{d(ME_i)Q^*}{dY_i} \cdot \frac{Y_i}{ME_i Q^*} = \eta_M$$

Thus, with unit income elasticity, $\eta_M = 1$.

[23] This exercise can be repeated, with identical effect, for other values of the income-elasticity, such as one and one-half.

[24] Note that what we are talking about here are increments in marginal tax rates. It seems reasonable to assume that the individual income tax is the vehicle through which marginal revenue adjustments are made.

[25] American Association of Fund-Raising Counsel, *Giving U.S.A.: 1975 Annual Report*, p. 10. Note that personal and not disposable income is the appropriate base. Public choice theory, which governs this analysis, looks at taxes, which account for the difference between personal and disposable income, as costs, to individuals, of government-provided services, including charity-financed activities and certain income transfers. Such government-provided services figure in taxpayer utility functions in the same way as private goods.

[26] For non-contributors, like C, the Lindahl condition requires that

$$\frac{t'(Y_c)Y_c}{Q^*} = ME_c$$

If a non-contributor places no value on the charity-financed activity at the margin when the optimal quantity is provided (i.e., $ME_c = 0$), the incremental tax rate for this person, $t'(Y_c)$, should, strictly speaking, be zero. Hence, unless those with a zero marginal evaluation continue to pay no tax after the across-the-board evaluation continue to pay no tax after the across-the-board incremental increase in marginal tax rates, the Lindahl condition will be violated. However, with the assumption that marginal evaluations vary positively with income, the non-contributing individual with the lowest marginal evaluation will pay, correspondingly, the lowest share of the cost.

[27] There are, in theory, systematic methods, independent of current giving, through which such information can be obtained. Three suggestive papers are Bohm (1972), Kurz (1974) and Tideman and Tullock (1976).

[28] Assume, for example, that there are two individuals, A and C, with A a contributor (subject to 50 percent subsidy) and C a noncontributor. If A has a price elasticity of giving of -2 and initially gives $100 gross, a one percent decrease in price (from 50 to 49.5 percent) would increase net contributions by 2 percent, to $51, and gross contributions to $103 ($= \$51 \div .495$). Initially, the community's share was $50. This share now increases to $52 ($= 0.505 \times \$103$). R_M is the ratio of the increase in the community's cost to the increase in gross contributions, i.e., $2.00/3.00 \cong 0.67$. Notice that the increase in the community's cost comes about by applying the higher subsidy rate to the new level of gross contributions ($103) rather than the increment of $3.

[29] See Tables 1 and 2 in Feldstein (1975b).

[30] To pursue this in more depth would raise a whole new set of technical issues, taking us well beyond the range of this paper. An inquiry into the extent to which activities of local government are "public," which might help in examining whether subsidies to charity should vary with its composition, is provided by Borcherding and Deacon (1972).

[31] See, among others, Vickrey (1947).

[32] Recall the logic of our argument—that charity finances the provision of "goods" and is not an expense of earning income. As to why deductibility was given its present role in the tax treatment of charity, convenience seems the best answer. But one can also point to the failure of decision-makers to understand the public choice logic of the subsidy to charity, inasmuch as the contributions deduction predated

full-scale development of the theory of public goods.

[33] This also tells us something about the proper relationship between the rates at which the community subsidizes individual and corporate giving. If corporate contributions are passed through to shareowners, imputation problems are confronted, as in any assessment of the distributional implications of corporate income taxation. Such problems are no more (and no less) severe in this context than they are generally. However, to the extent that the corporate tax is shifted forward to the community-at-large through higher product prices, so that the social price of a given sharing ratio is higher for corporate than individual giving, nominal rates of subsidies to corporate giving should be lower.

[34] While replacing the current system of deductibility with a 25 percent tax credit would leave the level of giving approximately the same, a substantial change could be expected, again using the Feldstein and Taylor estimates, in its composition. Religious organizations would receive almost 10 percent more and educational institutions 24 percent less in contributions than under the present system. Whether this compositional change represents an improvement or a worsening of resource allocation depends on the optimality (or the size and direction of deviation from optimality) of the present position under deductibility.

REFERENCES

American Association of Fund-Raising Counsel, Inc., *Giving USA*. New York: American Association of Fund-Raising Counsel, 1975.

Atkinson, A.B. "The Income Tax Treatment of Charitable Contributions," in Ronald E. Grieson, ed., *Public and Urban Economics, Essays in Honor of William S. Vickrey*, New York: D.C. Heath & Co., 1976, pp. 13–29.

Baumol, William J., and David F. Bradford, "Optimal Departures from Marginal Cost Pricing," *American Economic Review*, 60:3 (June, 1970), pp. 265–83.

Bohm, P., "Estimating the Demand for Public Goods: An Experiment," *European Economic Review*, 3:3 (Oct. 1972), pp. 111–30.

Borcherding, Thomas E., and Robert T. Deacon, "The Demand for the Services of Non-Federal Governments," *American Economic Review* 62:5 (Dec. 1972), pp. 891–901.

Breit, William, "Public-Goods Interaction in Stackelberg Geometry," *Western Economic Journal*, 6:2 (March 1968), pp. 161–64.

Buchanan, James M., "Cooperation and Conflict in Public Goods Interaction," *Western Economic Journal*, 5:1 (March 1967), pp. 109–21.

———, "An Economic Theory of Clubs," *Economica*, 32:1 (Feb. 1965), pp. 1–14.

———, *The Demand and Supply of Public Goods*. Chicago: Rand McNally & Co., 1968.

———, and Gordon Tullock, *The Calculus of Consent*. Ann Arbor: University of Michigan Press, 1962.

Feldstein, Martin, "The Income Tax and Charitable Contributions: Part I—Aggregate and Distributional Effects, *National Tax Journal*, 28:1 (March 1975a), pp. 81–100.

———, "The Income Tax and Charitable Contributions: Part II—The Impact on Religious, Educational, and Other Organizations," *National Tax Journal*, 28:2 (July 1975b), pp. 209–26.

———, and Amy Taylor, "The Income Tax and Charitable Contributions," *Econometrica*, 44:6 (Nov. 1976), pp. 1201–22.

Fellner, William, *Competition Among the Few*. New York: Augustus M. Kelley, 1965.

Goode, Richard, *The Individual Income Tax*. Washington, D.C.: The Brookings Institution, 1964.

Hochman, Harold M., and James D. Rodgers, "Pareto Optimal Redistribution," *American Economic Review*, 59:4 (Sept. 1969), pp. 542–57.

——— and ———, "The Simple Politics of Distributional Preference," forthcoming in *The Distribution of Economic Well-Being*. New York: National Bureau of Economic Research, 1977.

Internal Revenue Service, *Statistics of Income 1962: Individual Income Tax Returns*. Washington, D.C.: U.S. Government Printing Office, 1965.

———, *Income Tax Deduction for Contributions*, Internal Revenue Service Publication No. 526, Washington, D.C.: U.S. Government Printing Office, 1974.

Kahn, C. Harry, *Personal Deductions in the Federal Income Tax*. Princeton: Princeton University Press, 1960.

Kurz, Mordecai, "Experimental Approach to the Determination of Demand for Public Goods," *Journal of Public Economics*, 3:4 (Nov. 1974), pp. 329–48.

Niskanen, William A., Jr., *Bureaucracy and Representative Government*. Chicago: Aldine-Atherton, 1971.

Polinsky, A. Mitchell, "Collective Consumption Goods and Local Public Finance: A Suggested Theoretical Framework," Proceedings of the XXVIII Congress of the Institut International de Finances Publiques, Saarbrücken, 1973, pp. 166–81.

Schaefer, Jeffrey M., "Philanthropic Contributions: Their Equity and Efficiency," *Quarterly Review of Economics and Business*, 8:2 (Summer 1968), pp. 25–34.

Schwartz, Robert A., "Personal Philanthropic Contributions," *Journal of Political Economy*, 78:6 (Nov./Dec. 1970), pp. 1264–91.

Stigler, George J., "Free Riders and Collective Action: An Appendix to Theories of Economic Regulation," *The Bell Journal of Economics and Management Science*, 5:2 (Autumn 1974), pp. 359–65.

Taussig, Michael K., "Economic Aspects of the Income Tax Treatment of Charitable Contributions," *National Tax Journal*, 20:1 (Mar. 1967), pp. 1–19.

Tideman, T. Nicholas, and Gordon Tullock, "A New and Superior Process for Making Social Choices," *Journal of Political Economy*, 84:6 (Dec. 1976), pp. 1145–60.

Tullock, Gordon, "Information Without Profit," *Public Choice*, 1 (Fall 1966), pp. 141–59.

Vickrey, William S., *Agenda For Progressive Taxation*. New York: Ronald Press, 1947.

———, "Private Philanthropy and Public Finance," in Edmund S. Phelps, ed., *Altruism, Morality, and Economic Theory*. New York: Russell Sage Foundation, 1975, pp. 149–70.

———, "One Economist's View of Philanthropy," in Frank G. Dickinson ed., *Philanthropy and Public Policy*. New York: National Bureau of Economic Research, 1962, pp. 31–56.

Weisbrod, Burton A., "Toward a Theory of the Voluntary Non-Profit Sector in a Three-Sector Economy," in Edmund S. Phelps, ed., *Altruism, Morality, and Economic Theory*. New York: Russell Sage Foundation, 1975, pp. 171–96.

———, "Some Collective-Good-Aspects of Non-Government Activities: Not-For-Profit Organizations," paper prepared for the 32nd Congress of the Institut International de Finances Publiques, Edinburgh, Scotland, September 1976.

B

Urban Economics and Urban Policy

13

Social Problems and the Urban Crisis: Can Public Policy Make a Difference?*

By Worth Bateman and Harold M. Hochman

The Urban Institute

Originally, we had planned to call this paper "Social Problems and the Urban Crisis: Reflections on the Unheavenly Prospect," as a bow in the direction of Professor Banfield and *The Unheavenly City*. [2] For some reason, John Kain objected to that. Nevertheless, because 1970 has been the Year of Banfield and Benign Neglect, it seems appropriate to begin with a few observations on the relationship of Banfield's analysis to ours.[1]

Both for Banfield and ourselves, the term urban crisis connotes a set of unwanted social and economic conditions. As Banfield is the first to acknowledge, it is disagreeable to be confronted with undernourished and poorly educated children, dilapidated housing and abandoned neighborhoods, or rising unemployment and high rates of crime. However, while Banfield's analysis reflects concern with these conditions, it implies that the more affluent members of society can do little about them, for it sees the lower classes as enmeshed in a culture of poverty which virtually guarantees the failure of positive action programs. In a sense, Banfield's interpretation suggests that the middle and upper classes are also victims of the urban crisis; perceiving the conditions in which

the lower classes live, they wish to help, but every attempt is frustrated because the patient fails to respond to treatment. In these circumstances, Banfield's counsel of resignation is a comfort to the frustrated do-gooder who can thus continue to live comfortably, though social problems remain unchanged.

Basic to our analysis, as to Banfield's, is the presumption that the urban crisis derives from the dissatisfaction of the lower classes. This dissatisfaction is based on their perception that the conditions in which they live are unacceptable in relation to what *they* would like them to be. The problem thus posed is primarily an urban one for two reasons: (1) the poor have tended more and more to concentrate in urban areas, and (2) the disparities between income and wealth are much more obvious in urban areas where the very rich and the very poor live in physical proximity. If either of these conditions did not hold, there would be no urban crisis *per se*.

Primarily, our analysis differs from Banfield's in its explanation of *why* our society has not made more progress in dealing with the crisis in urban communities. For Banfield, the "present-orientedness" of the lower classes is responsible for the failure of public policy; for us, it is the political majority that has failed, by not adopting the essential reforms in social and economic institutions. If this majority could remedy its own shortsightedness, it would recognize that such reforms are in its own self-interest. In other words,

* We wish to thank Stuart Altman, Richard Bird, Peter Brown, Richard Burton, Grace Dawson, Frank de Leuw, Harvey A. Garn, William Hamburger, William Gorham, Joel Rosenblatt, Alice Rivlin, and Kathleen Sproul for substantive and editorial criticisms of earlier drafts, though we alone retain responsibility for our interpretation of the urban crisis.

[1] For a more detailed evaluation of Banfield's thesis, see [1].

346

our belief is that responsibility for the urban crisis stems neither from the lower classes nor from market failure, but from the deficiencies of the process of governance itself and the systems of rights it sanctions.

I. *Dimensions of the Urban Crisis*

In our view, two characteristics of our society are the heart of the urban crisis. The first is a judgment, held by significant political minorities, that the present degree of inequality in the distribution of income, wealth, and social opportunity is unjust; the second is the spillover effects of such distributional inequality: crime, family disintegration, poor education and health services, and the deterioration of the physical environment. While in themselves these problems are not peculiar to cities, the spatial concentration of people and industry which characterizes urban areas makes their effects both more acute and more apparent and, at the same time, facilitates the political organization of those who are most dissatisfied. Taken alone, however, the existence of these problems in urban areas is not sufficient to justify a diagnosis of "urban crisis."[2]

What has given the current situation its crisis proportions is that governments at all levels—local, state, and federal—have been unable to achieve a rate of progress, in dealing with distributional inequalities and their negative spillovers, acceptable to the individuals and groups pressing for

[2] Thus, as we use it, the term "urban crisis" connotes something more than the fact that urban society is not a utopia, that cities are not perfect and some wants of city dwellers go unsatisfied, as they always must, because public means are constrained. Not all externalities with which cities must deal originate in distributive injustice. Simpler externalities in consumption give rise to many urban allocation problems and are, in large measure, the basis for the public provision and financing of many local public services. But such problems, in our definition, are something different from the urban crisis itself and relate to it only to the extent that they interact with and exacerbate the primary causes identified in the text.

social change. [6, 9, 11, 15, 16, 18, 19, 20] Discrimination in employment and housing persists; public education is in a shambles in many urban school systems; wide disparities are evident in the quality and availability of such basic public services as fire protection, police, and sanitation; the incidence of poverty is high; and for generations the distribution of income has remained much the same. Most of all, the critical divisions between rich and poor in our society have increasingly been drawn along racial lines, even though racial differences in some socioeconomic measures have narrowed. Thus, despite some well-intentioned efforts and some progress in absolute terms, the Kerner Commission's portrayal of our society as "separate but unequal" seems as accurate now as it did in 1966.

Three interacting reasons can be cited for the failure to deal decisively with these problems. First, population mobility has produced patterns of settlement in metropolitan areas (within and among jurisdictions) that are sharply stratified geographically and therefore, politically, along economic, social, and racial lines. Second, the existing distribution of public authority within the federal structure and, in particular, the division (among levels and units of government) of the fiscal power to tax and spend has obstructed political action. Finally, the political process itself has tended to cater to pluralistic and powerful special interests. [2]

Metropolitan areas continue to collect a growing proportion of the nation's population, income, and wealth. Rising incomes in these areas are associated with suburbanization, a lateral movement which has had a distinctive racial bias. Low-income households and racial and ethnic minorities are increasingly concentrated in the central cities, with the relatively more affluent tending to the suburbs. On the one hand, this location process has increased

the extent to which central city residents must bear the fiscal and administrative burdens of providing basic public services; on the other, it has severely undercut the financial capabilities of central city governments. Central cities, without significant change in the structure of metropolitan government and its financing, can do little to deal with the distributional problems that pervade urban society and give rise to the urban crisis. Moreover, by accelerating the migration of industry and middle and upper-income residents to the suburbs, attempts to implement a strongly redistributive central city budget or to use public expenditure patterns in such areas as education and recreation as *de facto* means of redistribution are likely to be counterproductive. [3][3]

While cities lack the resources and authority to deal effectively with the problems which confront them, other levels of government—state and federal—are limited in what they do by the political forces they represent.[4] These forces reflect the interests of political majorities (or majority coalitions of minorities) who reside (and vote) primarily *outside* the jurisdiction of the city. The interests of these majorities and the legislators who represent them are frequently in conflict with the fundamental structural reforms needed to deal with distributive injustice and its external effects. This is seen, for example, in the actions of state legislatures in which rural-suburban coalitions block reforms intended to ease distributional inequities in school finance, law enforcement, and health services. [5] At the federal level, also, the Congress has been overwhelmingly effective in frustrating attempts to

[3] What we refer to here—"the prisoner's dilemma" in which cities and suburbs find themselves—is well known. For a somewhat different diagnosis of the urban crisis and what to do about it, see [10].

[4] Of course, these same political forces operate among districts and neighborhoods within central cities, but within cities the critical factor of rigid political boundaries is absent.

reconcile the distributional problems of urban areas and overwhelmingly ineffective in adapting its procedures to the demands which an increasingly diverse and troubled society place upon it. [7] In part, as Banfield's perceptive critique of current public policy points out, this is because reasonable-sounding programs have been misguided. But much of the responsibility rests in the hands of vested interests—sectional, economic, and political—operating through the Congress or the President, opposed to distributional change or bent on diverting public resources to parochial goals, through such measures as oil depletion allowances, agriculture and maritime subsidies, educational aid to federally impacted areas, the interstate highway program, and, certainly not least, many military programs.

This situation is not new. Cities have always spawned more problems than their financial resources or political authority would permit them to resolve, and state and federal governments have always been heavily influenced by interests that appeared indifferent or even hostile to the people and problems of the city. If anything, the situation in an absolute sense may now be better than before, because cities, the disadvantaged, and racial minorities have benefited from such measures as voting rights legislation and reapportionment. Nevertheless, the situation in which the cities now find themselves is distinguished from the past by a number of factors, all of which justify a current diagnosis of "urban crisis." Our generally affluent society has heightened aspirations of all social and ethnic groups in relation to realizations, and the twin processes of urbanization and suburbanization have themselves widened the gap between actual and minimally acceptable social conditions. A series of constitutional and legislative victories have legitimized the grievances and claims for justice of racial and economic minorities. Thus encour-

aged, these groups have stepped up their pressure for reforms to make such legal and moral rights a reality. However, the slow adjustment of social institutions and practices, plus the inevitable effects of a heritage of discrimination and prejudice on human attributes and capabilities, have kept measurable progress well below the pace of expectations.[5]

Thus, perceived distributive injustice, coupled with the urban concentration of those who are most dissatisfied, is what the urban crisis is all about. What triggers the crisis is a judgment that the structure of rights to property, income, and political power, and the institutions and rules determining the way in which these rights are established and enforced are inequitable and unlikely to change. [6, 8, 9] Repeated frustration of attempts to change prevailing practices increases the likelihood of recourse to violence or other extra-legal protest and separation (effective secession of the disaffected minorities) from the rest of society.[6] In the extreme, neither of these alternatives is likely to be successful. The threat or fact of violence to protest perceived injustice makes more likely the formation of majorities which will enforce restraints on individual freedom, particularly the freedom of those most dissatisfied with the *status quo*. This multiplies the resentment, discontent, disagreement, disorder, and repression which is already characteristic of the urban scene. Extreme separation is also not a tenable solution, though it may be advantageous for a small number of the disaffected. Unless the separatist minorities are willing to accept a permanent position of inequality (and inferiority) conflict will result. Thus, separation, as a long-term arrangement, seems unstable and unsustainable. [13] Moreover, like other social institutions which impede resource mobility, separation is inefficient. On balance, it will reduce not only the welfare of the political majority, but also that of minorities which practice it.

II. *Can Public Policy Make a Difference?*

Our diagnosis, if correct, suggests that the urban crisis is a crisis of legitimacy, deriving: (1) from a failure of existing institutions to produce outcomes consistently which all members of society can believe to be in their long-run interest, and (2) from a conviction that the process by which these outcomes are achieved is itself unfair. In our view, resolution of the crisis requires fundamental structural reforms in economic, social, and political institutions. [11] The accomplishment of this objective requires that the *de facto* system of legal, political, and economic claims be acceptable to all members of society. Such consensus must develop from a conviction that the obligations and rewards of a just and stable society are a matter of universal self-interest.[7]

If self-interest is narrow in scope, then the best to be hoped for is action to reduce the unwanted spillover effects of distributional inequalities that are felt by both majorities and minorities (either because of utility interdependence or because they affect individual welfare narrowly conceived). Stricter law enforcement, urban

---

[5] For an excellent analysis of this point, see [14].

[6] One side-effect of this situation is a loss of faith in the idea, basic to a free society, that rational and unfettered inquiry, given enough time, will yield a just and acceptable solution. One might argue that disadvantaged minorities themselves have never harbored any such presumption; however, it has surely been a basic premise of idealists, including students and intellectuals. To the extent that the urban crisis is manifested in violence and disdain for law, not just on the part of the disadvantaged but among some idealists at all levels of economic well-being, this belief appears to have broken down.

[7] Little can be gained by arguing over a definition of consensus. Surely, it seems reasonable to assume that malevolent people are not a politically relevant force. If they were, a free society could not endure. In any case, true malevolence is an uncommon condition. Other things equal, few men prefer the Pareto nonoptimal to the good of one and all.

renewal, and a number of environmental programs fit this description. However, such measures are insufficient to set in motion the corrective forces needed to relieve the urban crisis because they do not come to grips with fundamental deficiencies in the "rules of the game" or "effective constitution" which govern social interaction and determine the distribution of income, wealth, and social opportunity. Use of the fiscal structure to redistribute income and wealth directly (e.g., universal income supplementation) is one way of effecting such change. In addition, other changes which govern market or nonmarket rules of the game (e.g., voting rights reform and open housing) can in due time significantly alter the distribution of private and social claims. The latter changes, in contrast to direct action programs, need neither strain the public budget nor require periodic authorizations, or annual appropriations, and do not rely on the bureaucratic structure for success.

At a practical level, all of this suggests that civil rights legislation and enforcement, income maintenance, open housing, and programs which assure equal access to education and equal protection of the law hold much more promise for the future of a "free" and harmonious (though still heterogenous) urban society than an admixture of functional and categorical programs of limited scope. Urban renewal, the hodgepodge of *ad hoc* welfare programs now in force, and large-scale efforts to induce technological change and innovation in such areas as home construction and urban transportation are unlikely, or less likely, to make much of a dent in the urban crisis.[8]

[8] Indeed, it is not always clear that disadvantaged families are the primary beneficiaries of programs ostensibly designed to help them or that the programs benefit the disadvantaged at all. One result of urban renewal, after all, has been neighborhood dissolution; another has been the opportunity for gain it presented

Changes in "rules of the game" which are basic to the urban crisis directly modify the effective structure of property rights and the structure of claims associated with them. In conjunction with market forces, such rights and claims largely determine the long-run distributional characteristics of our society and whether they are perceived as fair or unfair.

Thus, the system of private rights to property is very much bound up with the "urban crisis," not just because the distribution of such rights is unequal and the use of resources for private gain generates some diseconomies, but because these rights are not absolute. One man's rights are often another's deprivation. The issue of fairness or distributive justice arises, thus, in any discussion of property rights because the distribution of claims, which in a market-oriented society imply political as well as economic power, derives from such rights.

For a social practice like rights to private property to be acceptable to all members of a community, Rawls has argued it must be fair, and to be fair, it must satisfy two conditions: (1) all parties whom the practice will affect must be given an opportunity to make claims on its design,[9] and (2) the practice must apply equally to all affected by it unless a deviation from equal application will benefit all concerned (e.g., unless a deviation is Pareto optimal, as might be the case if equal application, through effects on productivity, implies lower though more equal incomes for all.) [11] This definition provides a

to home builders and land developers [8]. Similarly, claims on the agricultural surplus are surely preferable to hunger. But are the subsidies which generate this surplus preferable to the direct income transfers which they might otherwise finance?
[9] Note that this criterion provides a philosophical basis for black Americans, whose ancestors did not voluntarily opt into our society, to object to its existing system of property rights and prevailing distributive characteristics.

rationale for attenuating or modifying some existing property rights through a consent mechanism (e.g., through redistributive taxation, which alters rights to earned income). It also gives the reason why society characteristically proceeds with caution in doing so. The interests of those adversely affected are crucial in determining the degree and speed with which unjust practices are changed. It is one thing to begin *de novo* to build a system of law which restricts the rights attaching to private property; it is quite another to modify existing rights, thereby changing rules of the game in midstream.

The distinction we are making here is between "payoff problems," [12, 17] which are evaluated within a given system of rules, and "choice of game" problems, in which the rules themselves are decided. There are two ways of viewing the proper procedures for changing an unfair practice. They differ fundamentally on the issue of compensation. One approach holds to the view that the process of change requires compensation of the injured party; i.e., even the party now benefiting from an unfair practice whose interests will be adversely affected by a change in the practice. The second approach distinguishes between those claims which are legitimate and those which are not and holds to the view that the claims of those who benefit from an unfair practice can be overridden. These are primarily differences in moral views. As a practical matter, compensation or long lead times, or both, are generally associated with fundamental changes in the rules of the game.[10]

The problem of fairness in transition is, of course, less significant when the effect

of rule changes on individuals is indirect, as with congressional reform and measures designed to make federalism more effective (such as revenue sharing or changes in metropolitan or regional political structures). [5] It is more significant (and difficult) when rule changes affect individuals directly (as when property rights are modified or attenuated, since property and income attach to particular individuals). When rule changes *do* affect property rights directly, the assurance of orderly transition is greater if changes are such that they can work themselves out through market transactions. To be specific, open housing, which is a change in market practices, is clearly preferable to a system of residential quotas or enforced and uncompensated scattered-site housing.

An instructive approach to the dilemma of constitutional change—both in terms of the goals of change and the process for getting there—has been suggested by Buchanan. [4][11] In his view consensus on basic changes in social institutions is more likely to be achieved if individuals have a dispassionate and detached view of their expected effects (because projection forward in time narrows the set of Pareto-optimal outcomes). This is true if constitutional-type changes, once adopted, do not take effect until a later point in time (say, 25 years), thus exempting the present generation from their effects. It may well be that we can do little to resolve the urban crisis equitably in the short run, but that in the long run, appropriate constitutional-type changes, capable of consensus, can bring about social justice and, thereby, dissipate the crisis itself. But, whatever its conceptual appeal, a delayed

[10] Thus, for example, a community of risk-averse individuals, totally ignorant of their future income prospects, might choose a fiscal constitution which calls for equalizing redistribution. But immediate income prospects are not at all uncertain in the real world and consensus on such a rule is hardly realistic. [4]

[11] Buchanan has argued, as we have, "in fiscal theory, as in politics generally, scholars need to pay more attention to the working out of rules or institutions through which final outcomes emerge and less attention to the shape of these outcomes themselves." [4, p. 300]

solution (and much less one that puts change off for a full generation) does not come to grips with the interim problem of preserving a free society in the face of what appears to be a degenerative (perhaps rapid) movement away from consensus.[12]

III. *Conclusion*

Reduced to its common denominator, our discussion suggests that a "solution" of the urban crisis, in the short or long run, requires that the various constituencies in our nation be able to see the kinds of constitutional-type changes described (including changes in the fiscal constitution) as a matter of their own long-run self-interest. To attain justice with fairness, what is needed is a broad moral consensus, founded in a heightened perception of human interdependence and an understanding that a just and free society are the stakes of a game which must be played out within a viable time frame.

While we interpret the urban crisis quite differently from Banfield, some of our policy recommendations are similar to his. But while Banfield, in large part, sees the crisis as deriving from the present-orientedness of the lower classes, our analysis suggests that it is precisely the lower classes' ability to project an intolerable situation forward, together with the present-orientedness of the political majority and the political incentives of their representatives, which leads to action or inac-

[12] The idea of postdating change is not fully consistent with the premise that all parties whom a social practice will affect must be given claims on its design. Pragmatically, however, this counterargument is less troublesome than our prior reservation, for it is not necessarily inappropriate to interpret the constitutional preferences of any given social or demographic cohort as a surrogate for the preferences of its children. The implication of Buchanan's argument, moreover, is that the realistic alternative to fairness in the future is not fairness at present, which may be unattainable in any case, but the perpetuation of legally-sanctioned inequities.

tion that exacerbates or perpetuates the crisis.

Thus, while Banfield's counsel is one of pessimism and resignation, ours is not. We believe that resolution of the crisis is possible if political majorities are future-oriented enough to adopt constitutional reforms which not only benefit the lower classes but serve the majority's long-run self-interest. If these political majorities have the foresight to adopt fundamental, constitutional-type change, fulfillment can be harnessed to hope, and an urban society that is just, humane, and truly free can be a reality.

REFERENCES

1. Harvey A. Averch and Robert A. Levine, "Two Models of the Urban Crisis: An Analytical Essay on Banfield and Forester" (RAND, RM-6366-RC, September 1970).
2. Edward C. Banfield, *The Unheavenly City* (Little, Brown, 1970).
3. David F. Bradford and Harry H. Kelejian, "An Econometric Model of the Flight to the Suburbs," Econometric Research Program, Research Memorandum No. 116 (Princeton University, October 1970).
4. James M. Buchanan, *Public Finance in Democratic Process* (University of North Carolina Press, 1967).
5. Richard Burton, "The Metropolitan State: A Prescription for the Urban Crisis and the Preservation of Polycentrism in Metropolitan Society," presented before the Subcommittee on Urban Affairs, JEC, Oct. 15, 1970.
6. Eldridge Cleaver, *Soul on Ice* (Delta Publishing Co., 1968).
7. *Making Congress More Effective*, a Statement by the CED Research and Policy Committee (Committee for Economic Development, Sept. 1970).
8. Otto A. Davis and Andrew B. Whinston, "Economics of Urban Renewal," *Law and Contemporary Problems*, Vol. 26 (Winter 1961), pp. 105–117.

9. William O. Douglas, *Points of Rebellion* (Random House, 1970).

10. Jay Forester, *Urban Dynamics* (MIT Press, 1969).

11. John Gardner, "The Common Cause," mimeo, July 20, 1970.

12. Harvey Leibenstein, "Long Run Welfare Criteria," Julius Margolis, ed., in *The Public Economy of Urban Communities* (Resources for the Future, 1965).

13. Edward H. Levi, "The Crisis in the Nature of Law," *The Record* (March 1970), pp. 3–23.

14. Elliott Liebow, *Tally's Corner* (Little, Brown, 1967).

15. Richard P. Nathan, "Reforms of the New Federalism," *New York Times*, Oct. 10, 1970.

16. Richard M. Nixon, "A Call for Cooperation," Presidential Message to Congress (Sept. 1970).

17. John Rawls, "Justice as Fairness," *Philosophical Review*, Vol. 67 (April 1958), p. 83.

18. Charles A. Reich, *The Greening of America* (Random House, 1970).

19. Elliott L. Richardson, "Towards a Workable Federalism," Address Before the National Association of Counties, Atlanta, Georgia, July 27, 1970.

20. Sir Geoffrey Vickers, *Science and the Regulation of Society* (Columbia University, The Institute for the Study of Science in Human Affairs, 1970).

21. Robert Wood, *The Radner Lectures*, delivered at Columbia University, April 7, 8, 14, 1970.

[14]

CLEARING THE REGULATORY CLUTTER

Harold M. Hochman

Persistently and pervasively, through licensing requirements, development regulations, and price controls, government in New York City has displayed an uncommon gift for interfering with private behavior and turning good intentions into harmful results.

While few of its specific practices are distinctive, New York's regulations are unmatched in breadth and, in some instances, stringency. The city requires licenses and permits to protect consumers from risk (putatively), and producers from competition (inadvertently), for 600–700 different activities. The administrative code and municipal ordinances restrict development through building codes and bulk requirements (which specify conditions of construction and occupancy) and zoning rules (which limit what can be done at particular locations). Moreover, New York City controls prices in 16 areas. Some of these such as apartment rents or taxi fares, are much discussed, but others are obscure. In addition, the state imposes controls, such as the minimum markups in retail liquor sales that were recently invalidated by the courts, in many more. Indeed, for a business to locate in New York as matters now stand, the advantages must be overwhelming.

Basic economic changes and unsound fiscal practices, not regulation, precipitated the extensive deterioration in New York's economic fortunes during the 1960s and 1970s. But the panoply of regulatory practices in which New York indulged, ostensibly to "protect" its residents, its labor force, and its visitors from predatory activities, had systemically weakened New York's economy, both by raising the private costs of everyday activities and by making the city a more troublesome and expensive place in which to conduct

93

HAROLD M. HOCHMAN

business. Indeed, in their existing form, some regulations seemed to serve no practical public purpose, but rather to promote the private goals of the regulated interests themselves by protecting them from competition.

Admittedly, only a small minority of the regulations seemed totally unnecessary. Usually, the problem lay in their administration, in their intensity, and in the interaction among ostensibly sensible rules that made the cure worse than the disease. Whereas regulation, properly administered, should function like laser surgery, New York often appeared to be wielding a butcher knife, carving more deeply into the substance of market transactions than public objectives warranted, and ignoring the implicit epidemiology of its actions. There seemed to be little or no understanding that tinkering with the self-correcting properties of the market process to enhance the good of each ultimately operates to the detriment of all.

Beginning in the 1970s, there have been some changes in New York's regulatory practices, initiated primarily by officials charged with making the city more attractive to business. These include some changes in licensing, in occasional opportunities for "one-stop-service" to reduce the difficulties of coping with multiple licensing requirements, and in inspections. Such cosmetics notwithstanding, New York remains an overregulated city.

LOOKING FOR A RATIONALE

It is a bit disconcerting that public policy in New York seems more readily explained by social philosophy, well-intentioned though naive, than by dispassionate analysis. In its *Consumer Affairs Information Guide* the Department for Consumer Affairs asserts, with manifest pride, that "the New York City Consumer Protection Law Regulations constitute the most effective, comprehensive set of remedies against abuses in the market place available to any jurisdiction in the country." Though this objective, enunciated by the agency most prominent in administering licenses and permits, sounds admirable, it reflects without subtlety a fundamental and unqualified distrust of markets that is symptomatic of the syndrome of overregulation. It presumes that consumers cannot or will not protect themselves from abuse by refraining from repeated transactions with sellers who fail to offer fair value, *and* that it is worth incurring the *full* costs of statutory protection—including its intrusiveness, active and latent—even if abuses are isolated and few

CLEARING THE REGULATORY CLUTTER

in number. Each time an abuse is uncovered, the city's instinct seems to demand a new regulation, regardless of whether the contingency is one against which it is really worth insuring. If the benefits of regulation were free, this position might withstand scrutiny. Unfortunately to those who enact and administer regulations, the benefits do seem unambiguous, for they provide gainful employment and agency revenue, while the cost is borne by the community-at-large.

The fact that regulation interferes with market allocation is not, in itself, damning. After all, its purpose is to provide for the correction of market failure. Indeed, in this sense regulation is singularly attractive, because it absorbs minimal fiscal resources. If, however, a specific regulation is to be justified, the market failures it is correcting must entail social costs that exceed the negative side effects of intervention. Political determination of whether a particular statute meets these criteria is complicated, however, by the fact that the allocative or deadweight costs of regulation attributable to distortion of choice are diffused and ill-understood, whereas the effects of the market abuses at which regulation is directed are concentrated and readily discernible.

One way to try to evaluate regulations would be to distinguish between those that improve markets by reducing risks against which self-insurance is impractical or collective insurance is less expensive, and those that hinder markets. But contingencies or risks vary, ranging from the risk of purchasing shoddy merchandise to the risk of a rent increase attributable to broad shifts in the housing market. In addition, the fact that the availability of private insurance varies with the degree of risk and the income of the insurer raises the question of fairness.

Instead, regulations might be evaluated in terms of whether the stakes are large or small, whether the victims are average citizens or people who lack adequate means of self-protection, or whether the alleged market failure is actually a rationalization, enshrined in the fabric of law, of vested interest. Though such distinctions are invariably ambiguous, common sense usually suffices.

Based on considerations such as these, when intervention through regulation still seems justified, it is important to determine whether it is too stringent and whether its administration is expeditious or cumbersome. This is what most observers, including many city officials, believe true in New York.

HAROLD M. HOCHMAN

A THEORETICAL JUSTIFICATION

The economic analysis of much local regulation involves a shifting of risk from the individual to the general public, or from buyers to seller. For example, consumer regulations reduce uncertainty for buyers about the quality of the goods and services offered. As a result of such uncertainty, bid-prices are lower than sellers are willing to accept, causing a progressive decline in the quality of the goods available in the market, a phenomenon economists call adverse selection. An example can be found in the used-car market. Because consumers cannot distinguish between good cars and "lemons," used-car prices, to a large extent, appear to be independent of quality. Good cars are held off the market, and the quality of the used cars that are for sale is understandably suspect.

In theory, governments impose consumer regulations, through licensing and other standards, to circumvent the unfortunate result of quality uncertainty. The solution, however, can produce new and even more severe problems. To compensate for the direct costs in money and time and the indirect costs in inconvenience and intrusiveness that regulation entails, sellers raise their effective prices. This transfers wealth to three groups: to the most risk-averse of prospective buyers, to those with a bureaucratic or political stake in intervention, and to sellers who obtain monopolistic protection as a consequence of measures such as occupational licensing. Such groups gain at the expense of the average buyer, who would prefer lower prices and more risk. Moreover, because regulation inherently alters prices, especially if it engenders monopoly, it distorts consumer choices and the composition of economic activity, and thus reduces the average consumer's welfare. Accordingly, regulations that are unwarranted, too stringent, or improperly structured, given the underlying justification, can easily result, even in the short run, in a net social loss.

In general, the losses individuals can suffer in isolated transactions are small. Competition and the flow of information, given the breadth of the markets in question, usually provide consumers with adequate protection. Ironically, regulatory intervention often reduces the scope of competition. It is unclear whether regulations reduce the costs of search, and compliance costs can be quite high. For many activities, then, simple registration combined with more-vigorous enforcement of the statutes against fraud might turn out

CLEARING THE REGULATORY CLUTTER

to be just as effective as regulation in protecting buyers from consumer abuse.

The fact that, within a large perspective, the direct effects of regulation on city revenues may seem inconsequential does nothing to vitiate these conceptual arguments. While administrative agencies are not permitted to make a profit and the direct costs of inspection do not dominate agency budgets, revenue considerations do motivate agencies, because both their prestige and their budgets are correlated with the range of their activities. Thus, agencies pay less attention than they should to real compliance costs in money, time, and inconvenience, even when the type of regulation in question is warranted, because the agencies do not bear them. In New York, these compliance costs are graphically illustrated by the existence of a corps of specialists known as expediters, who have the connections and skills required to "walk" multiple applications for licenses through the bureaucratic maze.

WHY NEW YORK LOVES REGULATION

While it seems obvious that a distrust of the market process is particularly pervasive in New York, other factors that underlie the impulse to overregulate are more elusive. In the large, this bias does not seem to be a response to the political demands of minorities or the poor, but the unintended product of a dialogue among elites, reflecting (absent understanding of economic principles) their vision of a well-ordered world. Even those New Yorkers who should understand the pitfalls of endemic regulation seem to place more trust in conscious actions of government than in the self-corrective properties of markets. Millionaires participating in New York politics seem to behave philosophically like socialists, calling for enactment of protection from risks of all sorts without due regard for cost. Though never admitted, and rarely understood, there seems to be a prevalent belief, reinforced by the media, that public and vested interests coincide, that perceived problems can be cured without undue side effects simply by promulgating or perpetuating rules.

There is no entirely satisfactory explanation for why the entrepreneurial spirit for which New Yorkers are acclaimed has thus been tempered in public affairs by paternalism. Sociologically, it may be derived from an intellectual identification with the socialist tradition, which treats as given a divergence of interest between active investors and a large, changing, immigrant-and-minority population that is

97

HAROLD M. HOCHMAN

limited in its ability to protect itself from predatory business practices. Or perhaps it is simply that political interests, inherently short-sighted, find it useful to define *predatory* broadly, thus capitalizing on the empathy of those who feel obliged to do something active about conditions they perceive as unfair.

The argument might also be made more generally in terms of a "public choice" interpretation of political behavior. Drawing on Mancur Olson's book *The Rise and Decline of Nations* (New Haven: York University Press, 1982), this argument attributes the antimarket ethos to the city's political age. Through overregulation, mature and entrenched bureaucracies act out their own political interests, particularly if civil service protection and public service unions insulate them from competitive forces. Rigidities inherent in the political activities of special interests cumulate. Such reinforcement is greatest in older and larger urban areas with well-developed and self-sustaining systems of patronage, such as New York. It is intensified if regulation infringes on the liberties of people who, being less active politically, seem anonymous, such as the recent immigrants who operate many small retail businesses.

At the political level—in the Board of Estimate, the City Council, and the Borough Halls—regulations, cloaked in the pious garb of community well-being, often reflect trades among interest groups or between consumers and the media, at the expense of those with less political clout, especially small businesses.

Another reason for the pervasiveness of regulation in New York may be the unremitting coverage of crime by the city's assiduous reporters and media. While no isolated instance of crime elicits a political response, even from activist politicians, repeated abuses assuredly will, even if their frequency is no greater, relative to the total number of transactions, than in smaller cities. The larger a city, and the larger its legislative body, the more media coverage there will be and the more frequently remedial legislation will be written.

If, however, the general perception is that a statute is too stringent or too inconvenient, it will be weakly enforced—a pattern that breeds disrespect for justified and unjustified regulations alike. As an alleged abuse is absorbed in the fabric of the local economy, like the omnipresent street peddlers, it draws decreasing attention. While legislation may ensue, it is ignored if it flies in the face of accepted characteristics of city life. If everyone in a society violates a law, it is unlikely to be enforced at all.

CLEARING THE REGULATORY CLUTTER

LICENSES AND PERMITS

Licensing illustrates most of the problems created by overregulation. Inherently, licensing places the right to participate in a market activity in the hands of the government and, in so doing, shifts the burden of proof to the individual consumer or producer. It is this factor (not the license fees, which invariably are small potatoes) that accounts for licensing's intrusiveness and, where it is unwarranted, its distortive effects. Even at its worst, licensing is not a powerful destructive force like rent control, but a nuisance, resembling insect bites rather than cancer. Yet we all know that a vacation resort in which the mosquitoes are ubiquitous is less likely to prosper.

Government construes a license as a revocable privilege, valid for a specified time period, usually a year, so long as the license-holder satisfies certain restrictions or side conditions—such as cleanliness, safety standards, or "good moral character"—that it deems in the public interest. Permits are similar, but apply to one-time events. Fees are a minimum cost of entry. Unless a licensee is willing to proceed illegally, licensing power can determine his economic life. In practice, violation is not uncommon, especially when multiple licenses, each requiring a different inspection, must be obtained from different agencies and the costs of delays in forgone revenues, inconvenience, and time exceed the expected penalties for noncompliance.

Table 1 categorizes the various licensing requirements in New York City in terms of appropriateness and justification. Only where public health and safety are at issue—the best example is bulk storage of flammable materials—do the stakes seem high enough to make the case for regulation incontrovertible. Obviously, fires spread more readily in densely populated areas, and risks are higher for people less likely to take self-protective measures, such as residents of low-income areas. Although death or injury can never be prevented entirely, random third-party effects, as well as abhorrence of preventable tragedy when even a single life is at stake, dictate intervention when density and clearly perceived hazards are involved.

Similarly, the licensing of places of public assembly, such as theaters, is necessary because given the large number a mishap might affect, no single individual can make a reasonable assessment of risk. Thus, individual protection is costly relative to public action, and the classic "public good" argument for intervention

HAROLD M. HOCHMAN

Table 1 Categories of Licensing in New York City: Validity of Rationale

Category	Rank
Use and storage of flammable materials Places of public assembly Protection of children Cleanliness Use of public streets and sidewalks	Significant rationale
Temporary business Health services Tourist-oriented business Transfer of possession of personal property Bingo and Las Vegas nights Employment agencies Crime-oriented businesses Fences for stolen merchandise The protection of public morals Final disposition of the deceased	Debatable rationale

Source: Hochman, *op. cit.*, p. 205.

applies—provided, that is, that the good is equally available to all at no increase in cost.

But the same is hardly true of some other licensing categories, particularly in the consumer affairs area. With the licensing of auctioneers, for example, the risk is monetary rather than mortal, the amounts involved are relatively small, transactions are independent, and proper incentives are in place. Although information is imperfect, dishonesty will drive away trade, albeit with delay. Statutes against fraud would seem sufficient to protect the public. Similarly, regulating church bingo nights because gambling is infiltrated by criminal elements (or, in these days of public lotteries, because bingo competes with government) seems to stretch logic. Even organized crime, one might expect, would shrink at skimming the profits of a local parish fund-raiser.

Licensing to protect public health poses similar issues. Restaurant inspection, if efficient, honest, and tolerant of trivial oversight, seems a reasonable way around limited consumer information. However,

CLEARING THE REGULATORY CLUTTER

as recently revealed scandals prove, restaurant inspection seems to invite corruption. Other licenses are especially perverse. Reason is not well served by the fact that barbers and beauticians, who earn incomes that vary with individual competence and do only trivial damage if they are incompetent, require occupational licenses, whereas "mohels," who perform ritual circumcisions, do not, because their market is "self-regulating." Behind the rhetoric, ostensible objectives often prove spurious, with licensing actually serving to control entry and protect vested interests. Why else would the plumber's examination include essay questions? Do writing or a command of English bear any relationship to a plumber's competence?

On the other hand, there is a valid rationale for licensing use of the public streets and sidewalks. Fees, if set properly, are appropriate charges for use of a common property resource, just as property taxes are, in effect, user charges for other government services, such as police protection and trash collection. Sidewalk cafes pay significant fees, which may reflect both site rent and public service charges. Sidewalk vendors also use both sidewalks and public services, but they pay no property tax and collect little or no sales tax—the one sense in which they represent unfair competition. Moreover, since license fees do not vary with location, peddlers and pushcarts tend to congregate in well-trafficked commercial areas where site values are high. Basic economics suggests that rules and fees for mid-Manhattan ought to be more stringent than are those for other areas.

In most cases, the rationale for licensing requirements is debatable. Frequently, common law, private interest, and simple registration to supply information would suffice without inspection. Examples include businesses such as the few remaining pawnbroker shops in the city, which, it is feared, might be used to "fence" stolen merchandise; bowling alleys, which are thought to be criminal hangouts; and, stretching reason, coin laundries, which house "slot machines." The first two examples ignore the fact that the target activities can readily shift venue. The third, though patently ridiculous, was used, in a classic example of the regulatory mentality, as a rationale for a proposal to extend consumer affairs licensing to coin dry-cleaning establishments.

The economic effects of licensing are in large part a function of the administrative procedures applied to implement them, particularly when there are multiple restrictions. To open a new luncheonette or restaurant for example, requires fully 11 procedures that take some two to three months to complete and must often be helped

HAROLD M. HOCHMAN

along by an "expediter." But for every potential establishment, whether it is to be operated by experienced restaurateurs or by novices, by native Americans or by those who speak mainly Chinese or Greek, having to send a representative to a Health Department training course for a two-week series of one-hour sessions seems of dubious value. The question is not whether such a program has benefits, but whether the benefits exceed the costs. Furthermore, since compliance costs seem more-or-less independent of scale, there appears to be a bias against smaller firms.

Perhaps the most troubling aspect of licensing is its ambiguity. Agencies possess a variety of discretionary powers and tend to be enforcement-minded and prosaic. They control entry by requiring examinations and by screening for "good moral character"; they investigate and inspect to enforce rules; and they adjudicate disputes, imposing sanctions such as fines, suspensions, and revocations. A licensee must satisfy them from start to finish, for allegations of violation, even if untrue, are costly to contest or disprove, and the loss is not compensated.

DEVELOPMENT REGULATIONS

Development regulations differ from licensing in subtle but important ways. Like occupational licensing, some standard development regulations, such as zoning, confer monopoly power, because locations are distinctive and not interchangeable. Deviation from permitted uses and building sizes is only possible if the applicant, on whom the burden of proof resides, obtains a variance. Implicitly, the operative property right is the city's, not the agent's.

In an important way, however, building regulations and land-use controls are more critical to the well-being of the urban economy than is licensing. While the implications of licensing may loom large for the business environment in the aggregate, their first-order effects usually impinge on activities for which reasonable alternatives exist. Licensing makes the urban economy run like a five-year-old automobile with its original spark plugs, like Leningrad or Mexico City rather than Hong Kong. Though embarrassing, this can hardly be fatal.

Excessive or inappropriate intervention in development and land use, on the other hand, can prove crippling, because it impinges directly on location, the engine of the urban economy. If development regulation is improper, what results is more like a systemic infection

CLEARING THE REGULATORY CLUTTER

than a bruise. Since a long-lasting stock is at issue, current effects may be impossible to reverse. Once land rents and the cost of space are driven up and businesses shift from Manhattan to Stamford or Englewood Cliffs, it may be near-impossible to entice them to return, even with costly tax abatements or other distortive subsidies. This is true also for the residential choices of upper- and middle-income families who move to the suburbs because they find taxes too high and city services inadequate.

Particularly troubling is the city's tendency to change the rules of the game in midstream, especially to the extent that it adds to investor uncertainty. A good example of midstream rule changes is the moratorium on conversion or replacement of single-room occupancy (SRO) rooming houses and hotels, which inhibits the filtering of such properties to higher-valued uses. To the extent it reflects a concern with gentrification, the regulation demonstrates a blindness to fiscal realities, which are ill-served by redistributive measures that create perverse demographic and developmental incentives.

Another example of midstream rule changes is the "loft law." When, a decade or so ago, New York suffered a major decline in manufacturing, many lofts were converted to residential use through leases with specified expiration dates and conditions of occupancy. Subsequently, as the economy recovered and residential leases expired, owners found it preferable to restore such properties to commercial use. However, they found that in the interim, residential tenants had gained the protection of housing regulations that, in effect, converted their leases to grants of tenure. Again, the implications are clear.

Building regulations are substantively more rigorous in New York than in other cities. Whether such rigorousness is warranted by differential third-party effects of uncontrolled private actions depends on such variables as the age and height of structures, population density, and demographic, economic, and racial factors. It is harder to argue against, for example, a requirement that fail-safe electrical wiring be used in New York's high rises, stacked one against another and occupied by thousands, than it would be to argue against similar regulations in Arizona. But it is also inappropriate to apply the same standards to a duplex in Staten Island as to an apartment block in Brooklyn or an office building in Manhattan. Although little more can be said on this subject without careful study, general caution is in order. Regulations are designed and enforced by specialists with a bureaucratic and professional incentive to overvalue the benefits

103

HAROLD M. HOCHMAN

and understate the costs of stringent standards. It is difficult for a layman to argue with the Fire Department over methods of fire prevention. But some external audit of standards, with the participation of private firms affected by the rules, would assure balance.

The city not only has adopted many special zoning districts to preserve or encourage significant residential or commercial neighborhood characteristics, but also carries on an active landmarking program to protect buildings and neighborhoods with architectural or historical significance. Landmarks cannot be altered without a complicated authorization process. While such land-use restrictions involve some of the same issues as the more mundane licensing regulations, they also share some of the more important characteristics of takings under the power of eminent domain. The difference is that in landmarking cases, the owner has no right to monetary compensation, even though the restrictions imposed can significantly damage the market value of his property. Thus, balancing preservation of the urban heritage against efficient land use inevitably raises broad problems of fairness. Given the ease with which "causes" are politicized in New York, ostensibly sensible landmarking and rezoning programs add to investor uncertainty about property values and inhibit development.

Interestingly, building developers and owners do not see the stringency of the development codes as their most onerous problem. Typically, systemic effects tend to be ill-understood, while particular features or aspects of the regulations are magnified. Among professionals, the major source of dissatisfaction is over the way the codes are administered—over the transactions costs rather than the allocative distortion. Zoning is administered by the City Planning Department, by local community boards, and by the Board of Standards and Appeals. Decentralization, even within agencies, delays in inspection and enforcement, the monetary and time costs of complying with multiple licensing, the Uniform Land Use Review Procedures (ULURP), and the need to "expedite" arouse virtually universal criticism. The main issue is whether "one-stop service" could be implemented on an interagency basis, reinforced by incentives forceful enough to stem resistance, by a strong mandate from the Mayor's office or through reorganization. But it is the essence of tautology that the byways of an established bureaucracy are easier to criticize than to change.

All in all, the best policy for New York might be a "nonpolicy" of not trying to fix what isn't broken—doing as little as possible to

104

inhibit the flow of locational resources to their highest-valued uses. It would be eminently more sensible to build in checks and balances and refrain from measures that only make the city locationally unattractive, than to impose well-intentioned constraints, mostly in response to distributional politics, and after the fact, attempting to remedy their damaging effects through expensive economic development programs and selective dispensations.

PRICE CONTROLS

Price controls, like other regulatory instruments, are uncommonly prevalent in New York. Of the services subject to price regulation in New York City, only five were controlled by 50 percent or more of the cities that responded, approximately a decade ago, to a questionnaire on this subject. The explanation lies in the impulse in New York, discussed above, to regulate not just serious abuses, but typical market risks, without acknowledging that compliance can create new and even worse problems.

No price regulation has had an impact as pervasive as rent control, which produces nonprice rationing, discourages investment, and invites corruption. Because it was thought that free-market rents would be unfair to some tenants, those tenants fortunate enough to occupy rent-controlled or rent-stabilized apartments, by virtue of tenure, family ties, or "key money," enjoy large subsidies from landlords. Others, as a consequence of implicit redistribution and the welfare loss associated with distortion, pay more than they would if the market were free.

Consumer protection against potential monopoly is the standard rationale for administrative price ceilings. But the local monopolies to which price controls apply result, as often as not, from licensing itself. Regulation of private-bus fares reduces the quality of service in the outer boroughs so that public transit will not suffer "unfair" competition. Public park concessionaires, along with taxis, also enjoy publicly protected monopolies. Though the number of taxi medallions has lagged demand by decades, taxi operators recently sought to protect their valuable monopoly by organizing protests against the Taxi and Limousine Commission's proposal to issue new medallions, even at a rate modest enough to cushion windfall losses; and jitneys, a potential source of competition for medallion taxis, are altogether prohibited.

This is not to say that price oversight is invariably improper from

HAROLD M. HOCHMAN

a public-interest perspective. Market outcomes may seem patently unfair to consumers confronted by "temporal" monopolies, as in roadside automobile emergencies. Such monopolies are often present, as well, when specific services are minor complements of something else, such as with wardrobe checking in public buildings.

To some—particularly short-term visitors with neither the time nor the background to learn the byways of navigating by bus or subway—taxi fares reflect such a monopoly. Uniform posted prices negotiated by the government as agent for consumers may be justified because the latter cannot identify suppliers in advance of purchasing their services. But however valid this argument, pervasive controls are a *non sequitur*. In general, the elimination of most entry restrictions would lead to improved service and more competitive fares. The case for liberalizing taxi regulations is supported by evidence from cities such as Washington, D.C., where entry is essentially free, subject to driver certification, and shared rides are permitted, despite the fact that crime is no less prevalent. Ironically, however, New York has moved in the opposite direction by extending regulation to gypsy cabs, even though they may make service less available in low-income areas. If nothing else, this fact surely raises doubts that the political drive for regulation has weakened.

Another instance of the ambiguous welfare effects of price ceilings is found in the regulation of interest rates. People who borrow from pawnbrokers typically do so because they lack an alternative. But interest ceilings that ignore the inherent riskiness of such loans have led to a severe contraction of this trade, making loans less available to high-risk borrowers.

There is no good reason to regulate cable television tariffs. Cable is not a natural monopoly, and the service is neither a public good nor a necessity. To be sure, over-the-air competition is regulated; but cable regulation simply compounds the wrong. Access to public utility rights-of-way could readily be negotiated competitively. New York created a monopoly where none need have emerged when it divided Manhattan into service territories, rejecting a proposal by the FCC that would have franchised a third firm and then taxed the "monopoly surplus" through franchise fees and a requirement that cable companies provide free or low-cost channels for public use. As a consequence, cable companies suffered consistent losses, and thanks to the scandal-tainted system of public franchising, most residents of the outer four boroughs are, to this day, without cable service.

106

CLEARING THE REGULATORY CLUTTER

CONCLUSION

In the parable of "the prisoner's dilemma," two prisoners fail to achieve gains that are possible if both accept the risks of trust and cooperation; seeking safety through distrust, both suffer losses. Regulation provides the comfort of good intentions; its full consequences are ill-understood. The gains to individuals for whom the issue is salient dominate, even though they fall short of the loss to the full community, which is well diffused.

In New York, regulation has created a cluttered landscape, which design by deletion could surely improve. New York, in a sense, seems characterized by an impulse to regulate. It is difficult to put one's finger on the total costs of its regulation, but they are clearly higher than most people realize. Like the public welfare effects of an extortionate tax, the relationship between regulatory excess and its side effects is exponential, nor proportional. The compulsion to act, out of fear of the impersonal forces that drive markets, betrays a failure to understand that trying to achieve an urban utopia through social engineering winds up serving vested interests while harming the economy as a whole.

Overregulation in New York will not be corrected by changing the puzzle piecemeal, because the obstacle is its overall design. Naively, one might wish for a restructuring of urban political incentive, producing a change of heart and a new faith in markets. But it is fantasy to expect overregulation to disappear overnight, or in the next year or the next decade. Political ideas are not concepts but habits, which are self-perpetuating—all the more so when one political party remains dominant, without significant competition, for generations. Progress can at best be incremental, reflecting changes in the cast of characters and the prevailing ethos.

Nonetheless, it remains useful to think through ways of altering the intellectual and political ambience so that regulation can facilitate, not stifle. A first step would be to place the burden of proof on the regulator, not the individual or firm at which regulations are directed. This would mean that government, rather than automatically stepping in to set things right at each perceived injustice or quasi-catastrophe, would bear the burden of proof, especially when proposed regulations are broader and more stringent than the national norm. At a minimum, each measure would be backed by benefit-cost calculations that take side effects into account, and such studies—the more cynical the better—would see the full light of day.

HAROLD M. HOCHMAN

Something close to unanimous public approval, rather than the minority support of those with intense interests, should be required to put new regulations in place. Existing statutes should be subject to periodic reexamination and to sunset provisions. Where feasible, registration should replace licensing, and each specific requirement should be tailored to its essential dimensions. Just as the city managed to strip away problems of compliance to encourage the movie industry, it should remove impediments to other industries that can contribute to its economic base.

If New York does nothing about its propensity to regulate, it will not slip away into the Hudson, but it will slowly be crippled by what was called, a decade ago, the British disease—an economic lethargy that derives from the dulling of incentives. In the long run even the vested interests who benefit from overregulation will be worse off for their indulgence, and other cities will set the urban standard for the country.

Urban Studies, Vol. 29, No. 2, 1992 237–250

New York and Pittsburgh: *Contrasts* in Community

Harold M. Hochman

[Paper received in final form, October 1991]

Summary. This essay develops the theme of Chinitz's 1961 paper. To understand cities, Chinitz argued, urban economists must pay attention to the supply side, especially to economies and diseconomies of agglomeration, which result from the interaction of density, scale and heterogeneity. This paper, in contrast to Chinitz, emphasises the diseconomies, which become predominant as urban scale increases and account for many of the deep-seated social problems with which urban economics is concerned. The failure of urban models to incorporate agglomeration seriously limits their usefulness and is partially accountable for the decline of interest in urban economics. Throughout, recent histories of New York and Pittsburgh are used, as in Chinitz's paper, to illustrate the argument.

Reprise: 'Contrasts in Agglomeration'

Ben Chinitz presented 'Contrasts in agglomeration: New York and Pittsburgh', his classic essay on urban structure, at the December 1960 meeting of the American Economic Association (Chinitz, 1961). He was, by then, a seasoned veteran of the New York Metropolitan Region Study; the Pittsburgh Economic Study was at its midpoint. As we have all come to expect of Ben Chinitz, 'Contrasts' was free of differential equations, without cant or conceit, and composed from start to finish in plain English, a mode of discourse that has now become, among economists, almost obsolete.[1]

While rich in intuition and generous with examples, 'Contrasts' did not offer a comprehensive explanation of urban or regional structure; nor did it suggest solutions for urban problems, real or imagined. Its focus was methodological, to show that regional models in which export demand singularly determines the scope and composition of economic activities are seriously incomplete. Inherently, such models ignore secondary industries; thus, they cannot account for effects of spatial concentration that reflect the interdependence of basic and non-basic activities.

'Contrasts' argued that we must, to understand what makes cities different or unique, examine "the assets and liabilities" of agglomeration. This is brought about by the interactions of supply-side externalities (across firms and industries) with increases in scale and population density. These interactions become more important in shaping economic and social arrangements in an urban region, at both the industry and aggregative levels, as density and scale increase. Consequently, patterns of agglomeration, as characteristics of a city, reflect its complexity as a network of interdependent relationships

Harold M. Hochman is Professor of Economics at Baruch College and the Graduate Center, The City University of New York, USA. The help of Kappie Hochman, Jose Pacheco and James Walker was invaluable in its preparation. The author is also grateful to Christopher Shea, Principal Economic Planner in the Department of City Planning of the City of Pittsburgh, for providing background information.

among the persons and sub-groups that comprise its population. Thus, following Marshall, agglomeration is traceable to economies that are external to firms and even industries but internal to the local economy. Over time these relationships shape what we might call location-specific economic and social history. To emphasise agglomerative forces is to manifest a deep belief that community life is heavily affected by the social feedback of economic relationships, past and present.

The present essay will extend this theme in a number of ways, including a few even Chinitz might question. It will be confined to the urban dimension of regional enterprise, because it is this with which I am familiar, and the effects rather than the causes of agglomeration.[2] In the spirit of 'Contrasts', I shall contend that agglomerative and not basic factors (namely, export demand, which is determined outside the region) hold the key to whether an urban environment will be able to retain its attractiveness, through economic fluctuations and trends, as a place in which to live, work and visit.

Moreover, as Chinitz recognised but did not emphasise, I shall argue that agglomeration engenders social liabilities as well as assets. To illustrate my argument—because the occasion is proper for sentimentality—I shall focus on the recent histories of New York and Pittsburgh.

Usually, when it is discussed at all, agglomeration is construed as a source of external economies. But they are but half the story. Agglomeration has a dark side, and it is the source of much of our dismay about US cities. Moreover, the effects of agglomeration on the urban social fabric seem to be factorially, or exponentially, rather than linearly related to scale. Whichever, the cumulative effects and the epidemiology seem to be more rapid and pronounced for the diseconomies than the economies.

The asymmetry in thinking about the positive and negative side-effects of agglomeration is both enlightening and chastening. Chinitz enunciated these concerns in his summary of 'Contrasts':

> It should be apparent by now that what I am reaching for is the specification of a function which relates external economies and diseconomies to industry structure, size being held constant. My feeling is that we have been too prone to associate external economies and diseconomies with size. We have been disturbed at not being able to derive a satisfactory correlation between the two. What I have tried to do is explore some of the residual variation around the size function. *I recognize the difficulties of adequately formulating and testing these notions. But I do not think we can afford to ignore them because they are difficult* [emphasis mine] if, as I maintain, they are relevant to an understanding of the dynamics of area development. (Chinitz, 1961, p. 289)

My suspicion is that the relative neglect of the general subject of agglomeration in urban economics derives from the fact that agglomerative forces and their effects are difficult to model or measure. After all it is such skills that typically elevate assistant professors to higher rank. While we are young and creative, professional incentives persuade us to sweep ambiguous concepts like agglomeration under the rug. The same incentives also nurture a false presumption that reality is infinitely malleable, that timely correction of social and economic outcomes would be feasible if only politicians were less venal. Urban economists stress the positive and not the negative side-effects of agglomeration, when they mention them at all, for two reasons. First, self-selection has made them what they are, and they would prefer to like the cities they study. Cities, at least in the sectors they frequent, seem vibrant and sophisticated, even if degradation can usually be found, as in Manhattan, a stone's throw from the fancy shops and cultural attractions. Second, because it is often difficult, given the demographic

facts, to separate urban from racial issues, *urban* is sometimes a code word for minority in the US. Urban economists are sensitive, perhaps unduly, to the dangers of saying anything which might be interpreted as having negative racial connotations—even if the sense in which the issue is racial is a statistical artifact.

This said, I have set two tasks for this paper. The first will be a pleasure. It is to build on the intuition, method and examples of 'Contrasts', simple but faithful to urban reality, to further our understanding of agglomeration. In doing this I shall try to understand why, contrary to my expectations and those of most trained observers, things have turned out as they have for New York and Pittsburgh over the intervening years. The second, I fear, will be work, possibly without useful product. It is to think through why the field of urban economics now seems suspended in time, and how we might help it to become unstuck.

New York and Pittsburgh: Description and Perception

In what follows I have tried to be selective and present a minimum of numbers so as to highlight the differences between the New York and Pittsburgh regions (Toker, 1986; US Bureau of the Census, 1986, 1988; Gill, 1989).

Pittsburgh was the first of the older US manufacturing cities to decline as the US comparative advantage in producing steel and other primary metals diminished. Metals, though once synonymous with its region, now account for only 5 per cent of earnings (compared to a high of 40 per cent) and manufacturing, altogether, contributes little more than one-fourth (double its share in New York). In finance the shares are reversed (6 per cent in Pittsburgh compared to 18 per cent in New York).

Overall, both metropolitan areas (PSMAs) lost population (Pittsburgh 5 per cent and New York 8 per cent) between 1960 and 1984, largely during the 1970s. Such totals, however, mask Tiebout shifts from the central city (in New York's case from the Bronx, Brooklyn and Manhattan, the boroughs with the heaviest concentrations of minority and poor residents) to other jurisdictions in the region, leaving the former worse off, fiscally and socially, than aggregates can imply. Changes in employed paralleled population. Recently, however, job losses have been reversed in both areas, with white-collar service jobs replacing blue-collar employment. Pittsburgh, for example, thanks to its universities, has become something of a centre in R&D in such areas as health care, computers, artificial intelligence and robotics. Continued growth is projected for the immediate future.

New York's transformation to a service base was accompanied during the mid-1970s by fiscal problems so severe that they brought it to the brink of bankruptcy in 1976. This fiscal crisis, which recurs in economic downturns, had many causes. These included: a type of political management, effectively single-party, that treated budget constraints as non-binding; New York State's imposition of uniquely heavy responsibilities for social service expenditures (50 per cent of welfare spending) on the city itself; and a pervasive distrust of market process as a remedy for urban problems, both allocative and distributive. In the New York PSMA local government expenditures per capita are twice Pittsburgh's and carve away roughly 20 per cent of per capita income. Nevertheless, because taxes are so high and satisfaction with its urban services so low, the perception is that New York's government is permissive, not generous. Rightfully, government in New York is seen as intrusive, because its regulatory intervention in market activities far outstrips that of any other US city in breadth and intensity. New York's apparent failure to understand the connection between the benefits and costs of intervention, for example, has enabled each of the diverse and heterogeneous political interest groups in New York to act as if it could

ride free on the others. The result, the opposite of the standard inference from public expenditure theory, in which tax avoidance is the assumed objective, has been an excess of local governance, with overprovision of services and neglect of infrastructure. Of course, there is also no dearth of tax avoidance in New York; but the nominal burden is so much higher than in other US cities that it hardly makes a dent. I have discussed New York's penchant for regulation in Hochman (1981, 1988).

Among my lesser heresies is a belief that as economists we typically make entirely too much of the economic characteristics of our environment. So far as satisfaction with where we live is concerned, they are at most secondary. Nonetheless, every urban resident evinces some concern with employment opportunities and the cost-of-living. On the first count, New York has fairly consistently outperformed Pittsburgh and much of the rest of the country—on average; where it has been deficient, however, the problems are much deeper and the spillovers to the community-at-large more debilitating. On the second, Pittsburgh is among the best of our large metropolitan areas, while New York is close to the worst. Major differences in housing costs and the burdens of taxation dominate the comparison. Though it is to be commended for its compassion, it is doubtful that New York's responses to its social problems, which have turned its budget into an engine of redistribution, have left its economy more viable.

Demographic comparisons between the two metropolitan areas are revealing. In 1988 the population of New York's PSMA was roughly four times Pittsburgh's (8.4m vs 2.2m). In Pittsburgh, however, Allegheny County dominates; the central city populations differ by a factor of 20. This implies a much higher concentration of people and problems in New York than Pittsburgh. New York's density (over 24 000 per square mile) was the highest in the US, roughly four times Pittsburgh's (which is similar in this respect to Los

Angeles, St Louis and Buffalo). Within New York's boroughs (excluding Staten Island), roughly one-third of the population is Black, one-fourth Hispanic (PSMA fractions are smaller), and a fifth foreign-born (with obvious overlap); in Pittsburgh, Blacks account for about 8 per cent of the PSMA population (20–25 per cent in the central city) and the Hispanic and foreign-born fractions are minimal. Just as important, because it reveals something about the stability of the two communities, more than 40 per cent of New York's population (55 per cent in Manhattan) were born out of state; in Pittsburgh this measure of in-migration was only 15 per cent. In addition, while Pittsburgh's per capita income is 6 or 7 per cent below New York's, poverty (as defined officially) is twice as common in New York as in Pittsburgh. In other words, there is much greater dispersion in New York's income distribution (though whether it is fair to call it bipolar, making it quasi-Third-World, can be debated).

These histories notwithstanding, the *Places Rated Almanac* (Boyer and Savageau, 1985, 1989) has awarded both metropolitan areas high marks, with Pittsburgh ranking first in 1985 (out of the 33 metropolitan areas in which 75 per cent of Americans live) and third in 1989 (Seattle was first). New York, though near the bottom in cost-of-living and crime, on which only Miami outperformed it, registered a composite ranking of 25th in 1985 and, less credibly, seventh in 1989.[3] However, quite aside from the inherent limitations of urban scorekeeping it is quickly apparent that this rating is misleading; five of the nine (equally weighted) indicators—the arts, education, health care, recreation and transportation—are quantity-based (reflecting a count of facilities, like hospitals or museums) and markedly biased towards large metropolitan areas.

Residents see today's Pittsburgh as a vibrant and comfortable city, diverse and multi-ethnic, rich in culture, low in crime, and free of the pervasive blight, social and

visual, that makes so many US cities, and once made it, so unpalatable. To quote Gill (1989), writing in *The New Yorker*,

> The note struck in Pittsburgh is not one of hysteria but one of equilibrium. According to the FBI the city has one of the lowest crime rates of any major city—its crime rate is actually lower than that of little Peoria—and it is certainly [in the words of Toker (1986)], *"psychically an open city, one that people can walk about in without dread"* [emphasis mine].

Its style is somewhat European, with the added variety of a US immigrant community, even in its third or fourth generation. New York, on the other hand, seems the epitome of everything there is to dislike about large cities. Diehard New Yorkers will counter that this is a matter of taste, of differences between perception and reality, an illusion of urban scale. After all, if a city is large enough, one can find examples of everything, majestic and degenerate, within its borders; New York has plenty of both, inviting both envy and contempt. Other US cities, with fewer amenities and stingier public services, have trouble filling out the nightly news.

I strongly suspect, however, there is something more to the current chorus of condemnation. Central Manhattan is not all of New York. To paint with a broad brush, much of the rest (save Staten Island, where one now finds sentiment to secede) is an even less attractive place to live than in 1976. This is not just because New York is more dense or heterogeneous than a city like Pittsburgh, but because its density, diversity and scale (in short, its patterns of agglomeration) interact with its demographic make-up, income distribution and, not least, its dominant political ethos, as reflected in the style and substance of local governance, in ways that nurture an ever more unpleasant epidemiology.[4] Consequently, though the average New Yorker is not poor and New York spends more on public services than other cities do, most people, extrapolating from the subways or

the emergency rooms of public hospitals, perceive the quality of these services as low.[5]

Whether this is a true picture may be less pertinent than the fact that people believe it. To the dismay of economists, especially positivists, perception does as much to foster alienation or nurture a sense of deprivation, absolute or relative, as fact. For example, perceptions (unmeasurable?) of danger, derivative from the tone (again unmeasurable) of local street life, or perceptions of discrimination, whether accurate or strategic, determine how comfortable urban residents are with their environment. And the interactions of these perceptions with density, heterogeneity, scale (with agglomeration), and with the rhetoric of urban politics are major reasons—if not *the* major reasons—why urban problems appear to be much stronger in New York than in other cities.[6]

Nobody expects cities to be idyllic; that is not what urban life is about. Most of us judge locations, once a few major economic indicators are factored out, by whether they are liveable, by whether our children and our parents can freely navigate their streets—by foot, car or public transportation—without fear or disgust. We ask, too, whether daily routine consumes so much energy that nothing is left for diversion. It is in these terms that New York suffers most when compared with Pittsburgh or other medium-sized US cities.

Agglomeration and the Realities of Urban Living

Everything, even in economics, has its special history, which teaches us how we came from there to here. In its beginnings, urban economics evolved from regional analysis and centred on the Marshallian interdependence, essentially in demand, of basic and non-basic activities. To this was added, as interest in urban structure increased, the location models of Alonso, Mills and Muth. Neatly enough, the overall result effectively restated, with little disaggregation, the classic characterisation of an open economy, for the special case in which the community cannot print money.

Central place theory, the conceptual core of urban models, starts with the premise that economic agents, in deciding where to locate in an urban area, minimise transportation costs. Gravity models generate spatial attributes, including rent and density gradients, with a minimum of assumptions. Because transport costs increase, rents and densities diminish as households and firms, trading convenience for space, distance themselves radially from the hub of a circular city (Mills and Hamilton, 1989). The comparative statics of factor price changes or innovations are straightforward. As in all theory, the (evolving) equilibrium also depends on parameters (natural advantages), initial conditions (location-specific urban history) and exogenous changes in the economic or political environment (immigration).[7] Moreover, depending on how the puzzle fits together, this equilibrium can be stable or unstable. This is important if our concern is with whether a city, having been harmed by short-term changes in its environment, can anticipate a reversal of fortune.

But spatial models suffice only so long as objectives are tidy. They run into trouble when our concerns are less antiseptic, like why real cities are distinctive, or life is a pleasure in some and a nightmare in others. Elementary modelling can tell us much, but not all. For this we require common sense, and powers of observation as well. Both more specificity and more ambiguity than spatial theory can tolerate are required to describe urban reality. Agglomeration is a concept with these attributes, and thus with effects that are easier to recognise than derive. It takes us a giant step closer to understanding the implications of scale for the quality, as well as structure, of urban communities, and their meaning for perceptions of urban life.

'Contrasts', as has been pointed out, contains a convincing argument that a city's economic prospects are profoundly influenced, through inter-industry supply relationships, by its existing economic structure, and thus by what has happened there before. Industrial tradition, which has been co-determined with local custom, shapes the aptitudes and attitudes that people bring to participation in the community. This reminds us that location-specific history really does matter—because, at each point in time, it is parametric and defines initial conditions that constrain the future. In particular, agglomerative economies and diseconomies, which are side-effects of industrial structure and urban scale, interact with and colour local communities, establishing their distinctiveness, both good and bad. They act, in essence, as bonding agents, glues that hold together the diverse strands of urban life, for better or worse.

The implications of this argument are instructive. This essay will argue, subsequently, that well-intentioned thinking about cities often errs in its optimistic assessment of the healing powers of collective action. For example, even if, perhaps through some metaphorical war, racial discrimination were obliterated, its effects would linger in the minds and acts of its victims for generations. In the meantime unattainable expectations may deepen both perceptions and realities. Because social mobility is greater in a more competitive environment, caste is less important. Akerlof (1970) has written a classic paper on this general subject. Please keep in mind also that the arguments that follow simply point out some hidden secondary effects of agglomeration. They do not indicate my prejudices and no attempt has been made here to measure or otherwise verify any of these effects.

It is useful, in developing this theme, to start with a few examples from 'Contrasts' and trace, with reference to the present argument, some of their contrasting implications. As hypotheses, each is ample fare for additional investigation, with some being worth an empirical literature of their own. It is soon evident that the effects of agglomeration need not be simple, or benign.

Entrepreneurship

'Contrasts' pointed out that New York is largely a city of small and medium-sized firms, while Pittsburgh was historically dominated by capital-intensive basic industry. Small, highly competitive businesses (as in New York's garment industries) do more to breed risk-takers among managers (Chinitz's definition of entrepreneurs) than large oligopolistic corporations (heavy industry). Moreover, people who must cultivate their competitive skills to compete successfully can adapt to change more readily than managers whose hierarchical status is traceable to pedigree or table manners. In short caste matters less in a competitive and mobile social environment (Akerlof, 1970).

These stylised facts imply, quite generally, that social status should be less important to determining the distribution of returns to effort in New York than Pittsburgh. They also suggest that New York, over and above its gateway advantage, will be more attractive to have-nots, like most immigrants, with limited command of English and dreams of economic success (because the division between workers and capitalists does not project the same sense of permanence).

With all blessings, however, comes an unintended curse. Inherent in risk-taking is a possibility of failure, both absolute and relative; and it is nothing if not normal for people to become dissatisfied if they observe others enjoying what they can only desire. If more risk is taken in New York than in Pittsburgh, failure will be more common, even after deflating for scale, and cohesion within ethnic and racial groups will inflate perceptions of relative deprivation. The failures, too, will be more likely to remain in the central city, over generations, than the successes, who are more apt to migrate to the suburbs, for the usual reasons. By implication the central city will become a locus of more despair, more alienation and, of course, more social diseconomies of agglomeration.

Labour Force Participation of Women

Heavy industry (Pittsburgh) is less conducive to the labour-force participation of married women than apparel or services (New York) because it is less concentrated in space (more land-intensive) and time (typically requires three-shift operation). Consequently (controlling for market wage rates and urban demography) female labour-force participation and family incomes will be lower in a city like Pittsburgh, by virtue of custom and history, than New York.

While this would appear to favour New York over Pittsburgh, the balance is less apparent. For example, when mothers are employed outside the home, some childcare responsibilities devolve on others. Logistically, the arrangements are easier to work out if the nuclear family is intact, or the primary caregiver can afford to hire competent replacements, or there is an extended family to step into the breach. But, for both economic and social reasons, we would expect better access to such resources for industrial workers in Pittsburgh's tightly-knit ethnic neighbourhoods than for disadvantaged families in Bedford–Stuyvesant or East New York— all the more if these are female-headed —because both funds *and* human capital are required to obtain quality day-care.

Perhaps all this is moot when parent(s) are lawyers or investment bankers, but its salience increases as we move down the economic ladder. Public schools are a vastly inferior substitute for home care, and teachers cannot teach *and* break the cycle of poverty unless, thanks to their home environment, pupils are receptive to education. Problems of supervision and discipline are even worse, at least in terms of their spillovers, with adolescents and teenagers than with small children. Short-run effects are intensified, among all age groups, by secondary effects on behaviour and opportunity, and by their historical interplay with social pathology (for example, teenage pregnancy and other correlates of adolescence) and institutions (examples include some union-membership restrictions and certain juvenile justice and civil-rights enforcement practices). Urban density, by facilitating the transference of negative values outside the family setting, reinforces all of these problems and makes it more difficult to interdict the asocial behaviour they engender.

Industrial Diversification

The breadth and scope of an area's service industries are determined by the structure of its dominant industry. Large interregional firms in heavy manufacturing, like those that used to dominate Pittsburgh, provide more of their own infrastructure, from accounting to trucking, than small firms. Thus, if an urban area dominated by large industrial corporations (like steel-producers) suffers an export-based decline, cyclical or secular, it is less well-positioned for a recovery driven by industries like office services. Because, in conjunction with scale, diversification is a built-in stabiliser, this suggests that New York's economy should have been more resilient than Pittsburgh's. Aggregates, however, conceal structural differences and ignore dispersion.

In New York, for example, the labour market has had trouble absorbing low-skill individuals, particularly minority youths with limited education, because they are numerous *and* because more educational accomplishment is needed to function effectively in the growing sectors than in the declining sectors (at least in legitimate jobs). This perception of chronic mismatch has persisted in bad times and good during New York's secular transformation from light manufacturing to office employment. On the other hand, civic pride and a strong

work ethic pervade Pittsburgh's tightly-knit blue-collar enclaves of second- and third-generation Eastern Europeans. The occupational transition has been smoother because attitudes in these communities, after generations of manufacturing employment, seem conducive to adaptation and self-improvement, even though the acquisition of new skills holds out little hope of instant wealth.

Contact Externalities

These three examples of agglomerative economies and diseconomies originate in familiar ground for economists. However, a different, potentially more analytical slant, in which the practical significance of agglomeration derives from the ease and frequency of interpersonal contact and the compounding of contact externalities, may shed even more light on the connection between agglomeration and urban social problems (Jacobs, 1969; Mills and Hamilton, 1989).

In discussing the benefits (in terms of productivity and innovation) of spatial concentration, some writers, notably Jane Jacobs (1969), focus on the high level of personal interaction that characterises city life. Thus, the fact that the number of potential contacts multiplies factorially, not proportionally, as a city's population and work force increase gives rise to both economies and diseconomies of agglomeration. This, over and above savings in costs of transportation, underlies the centralisation of markets and the geographical clustering of competing, yet complementary, dealers in financial instruments or such commodities as diamonds, flowers, electronic equipment and Chinese food to be found in all major urban centres, and especially in New York. Arguably, modern communications technology reduces the need for personal interaction, making it efficient to decentralise many business functions, including much office work, to economise on location costs. Many corporations, previously headquartered in central Manhattan, have relocated managerial functions to the suburbs or other PSMAs, leaving skeleton staffs to interact with, say, the media or advertising in the city centre. But this is a matter of degree. The argument still explains one of the major advantages of large cities.

As every New Yorker is all too aware, however, the proliferation of personal interactions also produces an explosion of unpleasant contact externalities, often with baleful repercussions for the quality of urban life. Not just beneficial, but antisocial interactions (copycat criminals and graffiti artists are stereotypes) display scale economies. The synergy that results is all too familiar. For example, the formation of a gang that is effective in terms of its expressionistic objectives requires some threshold number of delinquents; and a threshold number of gangs (within, say, a police precinct) can paralyse a neighbourhood. Similar reasoning applies to the drug culture and organised crime. Drugs are more dangerous when addicts share needles, and protection more lucrative when potential victims interact and transmit the fear. It is also a fair description of the petty delights that seem to dominate our perceptions of big-city living: panhandling, littering, honking horns and bicycle messengers who are apparently unable to distinguish red from green or read one-way arrows. In short, negative contact externalities, deriving from agglomeration, account for much of the real cost of congestion, as it is borne collectively by urban communities.

I hypothesise, in this connection, a persistent tension, with economies of agglomeration dominating in most small to medium cities and diseconomies becoming more and more controlling as agglomeration (interpreted, again, as an amalgam of density and scale) increases. Unchecked, moreover, the diseconomies can and sometimes do assume epidemic proportions.[8] Obviously, local customs, demographic characteristics, location-specific history and other factors can be grafted on

to this argument to discern why, in specific cases, the facts might deviate from central tendencies. Hartford is surely no paradise, while many would argue that Seattle, which is a much larger city, comes close.

It remains to explain why the empirical rule is that diseconomies overtake economies as cities become denser and larger and not the reverse (in which very large cities are pleasant and smaller ones hellholes). One answer is that the proportion of problem residents is much smaller (to pick arbitrary numbers, one in 100 or, even in the worst neighbourhoods, one in 20) than the share of those whose contribution to community life is non-negative. A second is that the social cost of negative contact externalities escalates rapidly because of demonstration effects; on the other hand, because inputs are not infinitely variable, the benefits of scale taper off as bottlenecks develop.

However powerful the compounded effects of diseconomies of agglomeration may be, they do not dominate until the population, adjusted for density, becomes large enough. Up to a point, city-dwellers may see some negative contact externalities as a fair price for urban amenities. Then the balance changes swiftly. In other words, cities have limited ability to absorb disaffected people. Nor need the reasons for their disaffection—whether it is justifiable or not—have much to do with its effects. This is the situation as I see it in the largest US cities. But I caution the reader that this interpretation is assertion, not fact. While this thesis is certainly loose, my conjecture is that it could be tightened up and tested, using rough measures of disamenities—so long as we recall that relevance is more important than precision. Just as 'Contrasts' gave us a better handle on the economic structure of urban areas, my hunch is that such an analysis, centring on the facts of agglomeration, would teach us a great deal about what makes cities livable.

Urban Pathology and Urban Paradox

While medical analogies may be imperfect, they are almost always illuminating, and ordinary people can relate to them. In essence I have argued that formal urban models are more useful for understanding urban anatomy than urban physiology, or pathology, or epidemiology. If urban economists cared only about cities as still-life, it would be enough to learn about industrial and spatial structure, or the internal workings of markets for housing, labour and transportation, and then stop; but we appear intent upon using what we know to inform policy. To accommodate reality the analysis must be dynamic; it must accommodate non-economic variables; and it must recognise that it is outliers, not the median resident, who cause the most intractable urban problems.

In the 1960s, the decade that followed 'Contrasts', professional interest in urban economics, which was then in its adolescence, mushroomed; since then, except among those with an ideological or ethnic axe to grind, it has clearly waned. Even in New York, where one would expect urban economics to be popular, courses in the field have difficulty attracting students. One wonders why! Surely it is not because all the work has been done. Nor is it that the remaining work holds little promise of a free trip to Stockholm. Somewhere on the track from then to now, urban scholars, collectively, seem to have missed the train.

Since its heyday urban economics has travelled two distinct though crossing paths. The first was formal and technical; the other sought counsel on contemporary policy issues. Along the first path the reasoning was orderly and the insights clear. Once the seminal ideas were in place, however, academic inquiry retreated to the testing and retesting of subsidiary hypotheses, and sometimes to inconsequential refinement. (A more cynical view is that it degenerated into a series of extended footnotes to the works of the masters.) The second path found economists attempting to harness their skills to challenges posed by a familiar list of social problems, from poverty to ugliness, which are aggravated by urban density. Here ideological and methodological bias could intrude more readily, both in the framing of the questions and in the quest for answers; perhaps innocently, both questions and answers hinge in hidden ways on value premises, because doctrine colours perception and rent-seeking is universal. In general, urban votes are more likely to turn on self-interest, as interpreted through distributional expectations, than on whether public actions are efficient. If, for example, it were possible to discern who would lose from the advent of racial harmony, we would know who benefits from the perpetuation of disharmony; great insight is not required to recognise that gainers and losers do not sort by race.

Now, after decades of well-funded research, vast public expenditures, a decade of prosperity and a short period of stagnation, the US's largest cities are no closer to being problem-free than they were a generation ago. Indeed, most of the old problems—fiscal inadequacy, debilitated infrastructure and immigration/emigration—remain, some worse, some better: for example, fiscal inadequacies, some self-inflicted; an infrastructure debilitated by deferred maintenance; and patterns of immigration and emigration, amplified by fiscal incentives, that beggar the central city. Other problems that are even more grotesque, like drugs and homelessness, or more impenetrable, like ethnic and racial animosities that seem to foreclose dialogue, have escalated. Though constrained by the public budget, especially in times of fiscal stress, the quest for solutions, at least for improvements, endures. But without far more emphasis on agglomeration, especially the diseconomies, than it has been accorded before, we should not expect much new insight to come from urban economics.

Urban pathology does not derive from standard allocative problems that are apt to yield to conventional policy (like fighting fires in neighbourhoods where law and order is the norm) but from those that do not (like juvenile crime or disruptive behaviour in the schools). To right the troubles in our cities, particularly the inner cities, we must refocus our professional attentions on the intangibles of urban life, on location-specific customs and culture and the moral codes that underlie and reinforce them. Since we live and work in an age in which technique seems to dominate substance, this is not easy stuff for economists, even urban economists, to accept. Ingenuity, however, should never be underestimated. With sufficient time, or gin, I suspect that agglomeration can be incorporated in formal, even if imprecise, models of urban life. This would be a useful step; when structure exists, better measurements, and insight, follow.

Because agglomeration is a residue of history, the correction of urban pathology is at best slow. Diseconomies may deepen even as material conditions improve. Though ominous, especially to anyone familiar with the recent ethnic confrontations in New York and other cities, it does not imply that *any* deliberate course of action is preferable to none. Market process is usually self-correcting, and self-correction may not only be the optimal, but the *only*, real remedy for many urban problems.

Once a city has adjusted to decline, as New York and Pittsburgh did, initially through reductions in land rents and then through relocation, it is likely to regenerate. Lower land prices will make it, as it had been, an attractive location to a different set of economic activities—unless the social damage, which is not accounted for in static models, has been so extensive and, by virtue of its transmission from one generation to another, ingrained that the degeneration is irreversible. In this sense short-run damage, no matter how severe, will be less crippling to a city's economy than chronic maladjustment, even if softened by ameliorative policies,

because elapsed time is a major factor in the erosion of established customs, culture and moral codes. Indeed, if political actions block essential change, to protect pre-existing interests, regeneration may be thwarted.[9] In reacting to changes in a general equilibrium process, it is definitely possible to try too hard.

During the era of the New York and Pittsburgh studies anyone with the audacity to suggest that Pittsburgh might be considered more attractive than New York 30 years into the future would have been written off as deluded. Yet this is more or less as it has turned out. No doubt New York has had the harder row to hoe. It is vastly larger and more diverse in every respect, like Los Angeles; more divided racially and socially, like Washington; more open, through immigration, to problems imported from the outside world, like Miami; and, most troubling of all, more vulnerable to the politics of special interests with narrow constituencies, like Beirut. But this is as it has always been. Such considerations cannot in themselves explain why many people perceive New York, as an urban place, to be worse than ever and Pittsburgh as something of an urban miracle.

The answer is not simple. Despite everything, I have argued, something about Pittsburgh's agglomerative life-support system has remained in essential balance, enabling it to emerge whole, though not unscarred, from its industrial decline. Thus Gill (1989) virtually glows in comparing Pittsburgh's success in urban planning with the experiences of Atlanta and Dallas, and its ambience with New York's, referring to it as "a model of survival against high odds". Central to his argument is the idea, which I share, that older industrial cities like Pittsburgh and Buffalo have attributes that make them better places to live. Many factors are relevant, including the presence of established cultural and philanthropic organisations, but I suspect that migration patterns of unskilled labour are the most important consideration. Unskilled labour is unlikely to move to an area that has undergone a major decline in its manufacturing base unless, like New York, it is a haven for immigrants. Sociologically, this stabilises the city, converting an ostensible deficit to an asset. On the other hand, New York, despite the reversal of its economic fortunes in the 1970s, continues to be immersed, socially, in perpetual struggle. Part of the difference may be ascribed to scale and demography, but it is largely attributable to two factors. One is the seemingly limitless multiplication of negative contact externalities that has taken place in New York. The other is the difference in the substance and style of urban leadership, both within and outside the city government.

In civic affairs, Pittsburgh comes across as a city of doers; witness the rejuvenation of its downtown and the success of its Golden Triangle. New York, on the other hand, has established itself as a city of meddlers. Though entrepreneurial skills may be more widely distributed in New York, vision is not. Horizons are parochial, limited by the boundaries of the block, or by ethnic, racial and neighbourhood lines of division.

Repeatedly, New York politics has shown itself to be unable to withstand distributional imperatives, or to comprehend the costs of succumbing to them. Policy error, sometimes understood but rarely corrected, has been a major factor in the perpetuation of New York's problems, thanks to an apparent conviction that others will foot the bill. Examples abound: rent control, over-regulation, a commercial-occupancy tax, welfare policies that encourage a dependent population to immigrate and remain dependent, development restrictions that treat decrepit hotels as essential housing, and sentimental landmarking of buildings or districts with supposed historical significance. Such practices magnify transaction costs by establishing powerful incentives to litigate. Moreover, they are not self-correcting, but

cumulative, given the vesting of interests; even if mistakes are uncovered, backtracking is generally a practical impossibility. One result has been a broadening of the omnipresent diseconomies of agglomeration.

Urban problems are resolved and perceptions altered for the better, as in Pittsburgh, by fundamental institutional change, not rhetoric. Prime examples are fiscal practices that actively encourage commercial development (without worrying, in each petty instance, whether something is in it for every interest group with a finger in City Hall) and heavier taxation of land than office space in the city centre. New York, in contrast, has a tax system that is biased against commercial use.

Conclusion

Urban economics seems to have arrived at a resting place in the cycle of discovery. Even the simplest of moral standards rouses our concern with the lives and prospects of people who feel trapped by the blight of the urban landscape. The temptation to do something, indeed anything, is strong; but it is often perverse as well. Wisdom cautions us that anything we do, however well-meaning, may have effects that run counter to intention. Even worse, such effects may be irreversible, at least within a meaningful time-frame, for reasons that can be political, social or economic—as they have been in the well-documented case of rent regulation. Salins (1990) reminds us that New York's "untraditional priorities [have not] purchased much relief from social pathology. [As he argues, New York] may not be much worse off than other major US cities when it comes to the underclass, but it is not visibly better off. Nor can we say that without its extraordinary expenditures New York's social malaise would be even deeper, because many city programs, conspicuously its housing programs, clearly have made things worse". Outcomes depend, too intimately, on the relationship between the distribution of wealth and the distribution of urban votes. Thus, it is just as wrong to care too much, to indulge a hyperactive conscience in its ultimate fantasy, the belief that there are quick solutions to chronic problems. This is the urban paradox in a nutshell.

In the social sciences all swords, like the effects of agglomeration, have at least two edges, and sometimes more. This guarantees our continuing employment.

Notes

1. It was Ben Chinitz, to his credit, who first stirred my interest in urban economics, by (what else?) recruiting me for the Pittsburgh Economic Study (a position which, retrospectively in error, I did not accept). What a judge of (erstwhile) talent! For a quarter-century Ben has been, for young economists, both agent and rabbi. Friends make no moves without first consulting him. The fact that he has no charge for these services reflects only his utility function and not their value. It also bears mention that my children, through third grade, believed 'Uncle' Ben to be among the most celebrated of Americans, having invented rice.
2. Frankly, in the 20 years of my acquaintance with urban economics, I have yet to come across a satisfactory definition of agglomeration; nor do I expect to be fully satisfied with my own effort. Yet, as with most concepts that resist definition, we know when we see it, and we can recognise its effects more clearly than its cause.
3. The *Places Rated Almanac* (Boyer and Savageau, 1985, 1989) has been published since 1981 at four-year intervals, first by Rand McNally and now by Prentice-Hall, essentially as a guide for people who are thinking of relocating. Like all such compendiums it is replete with facts, some more and some less meaningful, but all fascinating.
4. The news reports chronicle a seemingly endless succession of ugly incidents—racial attacks by both Blacks and Whites, sexual assaults, drive-by shootings of innocent bystanders, including children, and the full laundry list of crimes associated with the distribution and use of illicit drugs. It is not as if New York has ever been free of crime, but it has now become more random. Setting aside higher sensibilities, some New Yorkers even talk as if organised crime, thanks to its discipline, were their protector.
5. Peter Salins, an astute observer of New York (though, like me, a long-time resident of its suburbs) makes the point that "New York's particular tragedy is that 30 years ago the city's services were so well managed that they served as models for other cities, not object lessons in failure" (Salins, 1990, p. 17).
6. Progress seems to have been far more rapid among other ethnic groups, like Asians or West Indian Blacks, whose perceptions of history are less crippling and who act, individually and politically, as if education and participation in the market economy are the most promising paths to self-betterment. For a discussion of this, see Sowell (1981).
7. Each of these factors is part of the answer to why Chinese immigrants initially settle in Chinatowns. Locational advantages place such communities where they are, and immigrants settle in them because their predecessors, the only people who speak their language, have clustered in them.
8. This point is well illustrated by the successful salesman's belief that a satisfied customer will tell two other persons, but a dissatisfied customer will tell 10.
9. Thus we would eventually expect the South Bronx to prosper, as did Park Slope and SoHo, so long as politics does not thwart change.

References

AKERLOF, G. (1970) The economics of caste and of the rat-race and other woeful tales, *Quarterly Journal of Economics*, 84, pp. 488–500.

BOYER, R. and SAVAGEAU, D. (1985, 1989) *Places Rated Almanac*. New York: Prentice-Hall.

CHINITZ, B. (1961) Contrasts in agglomeration: New York and Pittsburgh, *American Economic Review: Papers and Proceedings*, May, pp. 279–289.

GARWOOD, A. (Ed.) (1984) *199 American Cities Compared*. Burlington, VT: Information Publications.

GILL, B. (1989) The sky line: the malady of gigantism, *The New Yorker*, 9 January.

HOCHMAN, H.M. (1981) The over-regulated city: a perspective on regulatory procedures in the City of New York, *Public Finance Quarterly*, 9, pp. 197–220.

HOCHMAN, H.M. (1988) Clearing the regulatory clutter, in: P. SALINS (Ed.) *New York Unbound*, pp. 93–108. New York: Basic Books.

JACOBS, J. (1969) *The Economy of Cities*. New York: Random House.

MILLS, E.S. and HAMILTON, B.W. (1989) *Urban Economics*, 4th edn. Glenview, IL: Scott, Foresman.

SALINS, P. (1990) Is New York going down the tubes?, *NY: The City Journal*, 1, pp. 13–18.

SOWELL, T. (1981) *Markets and Minorities*. New York: Basic Books.

TOKER, F. (1986) *Pittsburgh: An Urban Portrait*. University Park, PA: The Pennsylvania State University Press.

US BUREAU OF THE CENSUS, US DEPARTMENT OF COMMERCE (1986) *The State and Metropolitan Area Data Book*.

US BUREAU OF THE CENSUS, US DEPARTMENT OF COMMERCE (1988) *The County and City Data Book*.

C

Addictive Behavior

[16]

ADDICTION AS EXTREME-SEEKING

THOMAS A. BARTHOLD and HAROLD M. HOCHMAN*

This paper examines addictive and compulsive behavior within a new framework, in an effort to establish a stronger link to the psychological and sociological literature on the subject. Individuals who suffer an addiction are not the classic homo economicus of textbooks, but are instead extreme-seekers. Concavities in indifference curves provide a simple characterization of extreme-seeking. The consequences of consumption which is physiologically or psychologically addicting and which threatens the individual's health are modeled in terms of capital and threshold effects. The model is then used, tentatively, to assess policies aimed at controlling substance abuse.

I. INTRODUCTION

To skeptics, the economist's model is an intellectual puzzle, pandering to esoteric tastes but producing little in the way of useful findings. Our objective is the conversion of a few nonbelievers, by providing insight into addictive behavior, a persistent aspect of human perversity to which economists (with but a few provocative exceptions) have given scant attention.

In 1980 there were half a million heroin addicts, more than thirteen million problem drinkers (including over three million teenagers), and fifty-three million habitual smokers in the U.S. Perhaps ten million Americans had tried cocaine. Twenty percent of young adults had reported non-medical use of amphetamines, and 13 percent, tranquilizers. Nor were older adults immune; 3 percent had used tranquilizers and 6 percent, barbiturates.[1] While it would be ridiculous to consider all of these people addicts, such figures do place the issue in empirical perspective. Completion of the picture would require the addition of compulsive gamblers and victims of overeating, sexual obsession and, for that matter, shopping at Bloomingdale's.

Compulsion, which drives addiction, assumes many forms, some innocuous but many harmful. While headlines lead us to think of addiction in terms of heroin and cocaine, alcoholics and chronic smokers consume legal goods. Indeed, some addicts, like workaholics, evoke puritanical pride and often produce beneficial third-party effects. We are all aware of people who are driven, working round the clock (at what productivity?), to the detriment of their

* Staff Economist, Joint Committee on Taxation, and Professor of Economics at Baruch College (Center for the Study of Business and Government) and the Graduate Center of the City University of New York. This paper has benefited (we think) from the kibbitzing of our wives and of armies of our friends. A few like Colin Campbell, William Campbell (a psychiatrist), Sidney Carroll, Herbert Glejser, Donald F. Gordon, and Jacob Paroush warrant special mention. We are indebted to the Earhart Foundation for support of this project.

1. Figures from the Alcohol, Drug Abuse, and Mental Health Administration [1980].

89

health; and of "saints," consumed by altruism, who sacrifice themselves for the sake of others. However, legal or illegal, genetic or environmental, all addictive behavior seems to share some common characteristics. These commonalities enable us to model it.

Our premise is that sustained addictive behavior is neither normal or typical. Addicts tend to behavioral extremes, an aberration in tastes which may through time make it more difficult for them to derive utility from nonaddictive goods.[2] Nature does not take kindly to imbalance, and addictive behavior is a pathological imbalance in consumer choice which sustains itself and is reinforced in some cases by illicit markets.[3]

Whether addiction is rational behavior (consistent with self-interest or negatively sloped demand curves) or reflects something more (myopia?) seems beside the point. For addicts, as we model them, indifference curves may lack the convenient property of universal convexity and are, for at least part of their range, concave. We know that this can mean that some relative prices generate corner (all or none) outcomes, at which the consumer dedicates his full endowment to the addictive activity. It can also imply that his response to small price changes may be discontinuous.

On the other hand, many (perhaps most) participants in (potentially) addictive activities do respond to changing relative prices. Robins et al. [1975; 1977] report that 35 percent of American enlisted men in Vietnam, where drugs were inexpensive and sanctions weak, used heroin. Of these, 54 percent became addicts. Since the U.S. had experienced a 97 percent rate of recidivism for treated heroin addicts, law enforcement and public health officials believed that thousands of new addicts would flood the U.S. at the war's end. Surprisingly, however, the record refutes this. It reveals no significant increase in the addict population, in the demand on treatment centers, or in the street price of heroin. Although Zinberg [1972] found U.S. Army anti-drug programs an abysmal failure (correlated, in fact, with increased heroin use), at most 10 percent of the Vietnam addicts continued using it upon returning home, according to Robins et al. While behavioral psychologists, sociologists and physicians attribute this drastic reversal to differences in mores, this explains neither the high level of drug abuse in Vietnam, because the mores of American servicemen had been formed before they went to war, nor the fact that so many (10 percent is not a trivial proportion) persisted in their addiction.

A meaningful model of addictive behavior should describe not only abuse, but also its reversal. It should provide insight into the differences between addiction, both physiological (entailing withdrawal problems) and psycholog-

2. This squares with the view that individuals with "dependent" or "borderline" personalities are more likely to become addicts. Terms like dependent and borderline, however, are diagnostic and not inductive. They refer to discernible behavior or the enunciation of beliefs conducive to such behavior.

3. One common characteristic is that addiction is almost always self-destructive, whether positive (like the compulsive work habits of the artist or some contributors to this journal) or negative in its social effects.

ical (entailing, in the limit, obsession) and compulsion or habit (simple repetition). The crux is the degree to which addictive behavior, during a brief span of time, reinforces itself and, as it continues through time, forecloses options. Thus, the model ought to tell us why Vietnam addicts differed from the stereotype; why some individuals appear to lose control, while others, seemingly identical, suffer but minor detrimental effects. This will in turn provide insight into policies that might, if appropriately structured and targeted, limit or reverse compulsion.

II. ALTERNATIVE VIEWS OF ADDICTIVE BEHAVIOR

Psychologists and sociologists claim little success in describing an "addictive personality," finding at most that "alcoholics (and drug addicts) appear ... different from others," according to Lang [1983, 207]; but not in a discernible, systematic way (at least from the variables they examine). Still, the concept of personality, if nothing more, must imply that preferences are not identical and that personal history matters. Thus, our model of addictive behavior takes as its point of departure the hypothesis that compulsive and addictive individuals are different.[4]

Our premise is that individuals can be divided into at least two types. Innate characteristics, reinforced by market forces, drive the first type, "extreme-seekers," to addictive behavior. Perhaps because this darker side of human personality is unimportant for most people, conventional theory ignores it. The second type, "continuous adjusters," displays little or no extreme-seeking, even in an unfavorable environment. The two groups are distinguished by the way the behavior in question (quantity and intensity of a compulsive activity) can be triggered by price changes (opportunity cost) and how past participation modifies its current transformation into utility. Thus, "capital" and "threshold" effects, which can prove irretrievable, are central, because extreme-seeking would be of little concern if it had no lasting effects on opportunities.[5]

---

4. O'Leary and Wilson [1975, 355] state the following: "Despite decades of research and therapy, distressingly little progress has accrued from traditional psychodynamic and pychometric approaches to understanding or treating alcoholics. The search for the prealcoholic personality has consistently failed to identify any specific physical factors, psychological traits or underlying personality dynamics which reliably differentiate alcoholics from either the normal population or other groups judged to be abnormal." Because alcoholics act differently, they are thought to be different, but only after the fact. (For further comment see Lettieri, Sayers, and Pearson [1980].) It is not clear whether noneconomists' failure to define a distinctive addictive personality derives from substantive factors or empirical methods. As economists we need not, nor can we, probe whether personality differences are innate, deriving from genetic traits, or developmental. In essence, we postulate differences, sketch behavioral implications, and ask what can be done. Note, however, that our attribution of addiction to a common personality trait finds support in evidence that the drug naltrexone (see the *New York Times*, November 29, 1984, p. A1) reduces the craving associated with withdrawal from both nicotine and narcotics.

5. This paper contains the beginnings of a theory of behavior with links to other fields such as psychology and psychoanalysis. Because we seek different insights, it would be self-defeating to dwell on whether our usage is consistent with theirs. Nonetheless, communication mandates some effort to be consistent. Both addiction and compulsion, Webster's *New World Dictionary* tells us, imply habituation. Compulsion entails an "irresistible, repeated, irrational impulse to perform

Whether psychological or physiological, addiction neither develops overnight nor can be shed instantaneously. As Stigler and Becker argue in "De
Gustibus . . ." [1977], a legacy of cumulative consumption, a kind of "capital
effect," characterizes all addictive behavior. Past participation creates a stock
or "history," which adds, positively or negatively, to the utility of current or
future consumption. If this capital effect is strong enough, the behavior is
labeled addictive. Thus, over time it takes more and more martinis to unwind,
and tolerance can escalate to alcoholism.

Unfortunately, Stigler and Becker confine their discussion to "happy addicts"
(Winston's term [1980, 302]). Whether individuals develop a taste for classical
music or succumb to alcohol, they are treated as if they were functionally
similar. Innate characteristics establish no priors, leaving to whimsy the question of why one man develops a craving for Beethoven and another becomes
a devotee of Jim Beam. Protagonists lack distinct personalities, or have personalities they have crafted entirely through past consumption. Addicts feel
no remorse and seek no help. While it is possible to observe compulsion one
period and not the next, the sequence of choice depends upon the constraints.
Stigler and Becker see the potential for policy in those constraints. In so doing
they appear to assume smooth adjustment to changing relative prices. If,
however, people who become addicted tend to be extreme-seekers, this may
be unrealistic. In sum, for Stigler and Becker addiction is simple habit, reflecting a rational (consistent with self-interest) response to preferences and
opportunities. If an addict believes that an exotic mix of uppers and downers
will make him happier, there is no more to it, even if death reveals that his
reasoning was flawed.

Habit, which economizes on the processing of information, implies a smooth
dynamic path to addiction. However, for Winston [1980] addiction is characterized by loss of control and attempts to reverse behavior. To capture this
he posits stable but nonconstant preferences, "between the extremes of petri-
fication and randomness" (p. 296). The individual has two preference modes,
one myopic, the other farseeing. Meta-preferences ("preferences about one's
preferences," p. 298) control his behavior, which alternates randomly, subject
to capital effects, between myopia and enlightenment. Whether in any specific
period he acts like Jekyll or Hyde depends on expected utility, calculated
under the utility function, myopic or "normal," operative at the moment. If
Hyde surfaces in several consecutive periods, the individual is labeled an
addict. This parable of random dual preference, however, does not fit the
experience of the Vietnam veterans. If Hyde's emergence were truly random,
we could explain neither its prevalence in Vietnam nor its subsequent reduction
in frequency. Thus, while Winston's model does demonstrate that many aspects
of addiction yield to neoclassical interpretation, the *deus ex machina* of dual

---

some act," while addiction connotes passivity. This translates, for the economist, into the notion
that addictive and compulsive acts are atypically unresponsive to incentives. When behavior is
unresponsive to all feasible incentives it can be thought of as obsessive.

preference and the nebulous character of the switching mechanism limit its usefulness.

Loss of control is also central to Elster [1979] and Schelling [1978; 1980]. Habit, with its smooth dynamics, lends itself to "self-command" and to reversal through precommitment. Weight Watchers and Alcoholics Anonymous rely in part on this rationale. But this does not come to grips with why an individual will precommit to something different if he is doing what he wants.[6] Precommitment implies that the addictive good is *not preferred* and, by implication, that self-control is unstable.[7]

Our discomfort with such interpretations leads us to a somewhat more eclectic model of addictive behavior. It combines extreme-seeking (as an outcome of personality aberration), capital effects (which represent personal history), and thresholds (which reflect its noneconomic limits, beyond which it causes irreversible harm). Indeed, some libertarians might argue that the only types of addictive behavior worth addressing in policy discussion are those that violate such thresholds. While extreme-seekers and continuous adjusters may be indistinguishable at low levels of consumption, a failure to distinguish between them can lead to moral hazard and adverse selection.[8] Thus, preventive measures which cannot differentiate between low and high risk populations have limited use in controlling addictive behavior and are cost-effective only if inexpensive.

III. RUDIMENTS OF A MODEL

Concavity

While revealed preference may reflect poor judgment, it is our sole source of data. An individual cannot describe his present preferences, much less meta-preferences. Even if behavior is time-inconsistent, there is no way to tell whether this derives from miscalculation, endogenous taste change, or randomness in the relationships among acts and outcomes. Interpretation of addictive behavior as extreme-seeking steers us away from this black box.

To start, consider a one-period model in which utility derives from two goods, x and y:

6. Precommitment also assumes that self-control (self-insurance against unwanted outcomes) is feasible and that willpower, grounded in private principles or social norms, can stem temptation. But while it may help to convince someone that addictive consequence will follow choice as night follows day, it may also turn him to an even more deleterious alternative.

7. It may also be unstable if neurological or pharmacological evidence can trace addictive behavior to personality traits that reflect objective biological attributes.

8. One often expects to find moral hazard and adverse selection in tandem. Pauly [1974] and Akerlof [1970] provide excellent discussions of these issues. Moral hazard occurs when the consumer, by his own actions, can affect the probability or magnitude of loss; legalization of offtrack betting to fight organized crime, by lowering opportunity cost, may help compulsive gamblers discover themselves. Adverse selection occurs when a policy designed to spread risk over a large group attracts only the most unfavorable risks. If addiction implies perfectly inelastic demand, a policy that raises the price of cocaine may reduce its consumption among continuous adjusters, but have minimal effects on current addicts.

$$U = f(x, y). \tag{1}$$

Think of x as the relatively compulsive (addictive) good and y as a composite of all else.[9] Figure 1 maintains the assumption that more is better, assuming positive marginal utilities, f_x and f_y;[10] and that, for some domain, marginal utility does not diminish: $f_{xx} > 0$ or $f_{yy} > 0$ or both. But it also permits $f_{xy} <$ 0, meaning that the marginal utility of y need not increase with x. Prices, income, and time, including costs of violating social convention, all constrain choices.

For activities that reflect an absence of self-control, such assumptions are not at all outrageous.[11] Preferences in commodity (x, y) space are characterized by marginal rates of substitution and the extent to which indifference curves, as the assumptions imply, display concavity. While slopes are invariably negative, the assumptions permit marginal rates of substitution to increase within each decision period. Higher levels of x reinforce a craving for more. While downward-sloping, indifference curves have at least one inflection point and possibly two. U_1 and U_2 are concave to the right of the inflection point; U_3 and U_4 are concave between the two inflection points. Because it measures degree of compulsion, the distance between inflection points can be critical.

All this can be seen in Figure 1. If the opportunity locus is aa', the optimum is a^* on U_1, to the left of the concave range. But when the opportunity locus is either bb' or cc', the optimum is $b^* = c^*$. So long as relative prices favor x, the optimum is either a corner (b^* on U_2) or to the right of the inflection point (d^* on U_4).

As they are usually interpreted, indifference curves indicate rates of consumption at a point in time, not sequential choice. But this hardly characterizes the way individuals, say, eat peanuts at cocktail time, and it has limited descriptive value for commodities or activities that are subject to short-run saturation, like all the common addictive goods. In the case of peanuts it seems more realistic to think ex ante of one handful leading to the next until indigestion grinds the process to a halt. This is essentially how we interpret com-

---

9. This does not mean that all y goods are nonaddictive, but that x dominates a lexicographic ordering. If an individual is addicted to both heroin and nicotine, heroin dominates and cigarette consumption is subsumed in y. Later we discuss some implications of defining x as a vector of addictive goods.

10. The notation f_x denotes the first derivative of the function f with respect to changes in the commodity x. Similarly, f_{xx} and f_{xy} denote second derivatives.

11. If, for example, x were alcohol, its consumption to the point of stupor would diminish enjoyment of food, family, books, etc. (see Winston's remark, p. 307); and if y were a composite of food, family and books, $f_{xy} < 0$. Alternatively, if x were cocaine, one "line" might lead to giddiness, while two or three would invite rapture; mathematically, $f_{xx} > 0$.

12. Thus concavity may be shorthand for a dynamic process consisting of instantaneous taste changes, which we treat for convenience as if it were static. It seems best to sidestep this theoretical nicety and leave the distinction between statics and dynamics to effects on current consumption that extend beyond the current decision period through the development of tolerance (see next subsection). Different moments in time never present the same opportunities, independent of prior choices, without limits imposed by personal experience. To some extent the limits are physiological.

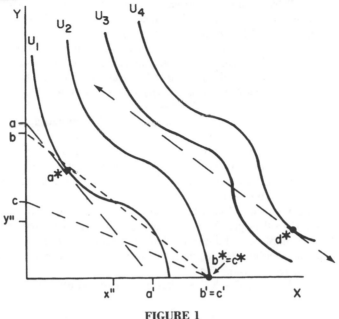

FIGURE 1
Indifference Curves of Extreme-Seekers

pulsion.[12] In the concave range the compensated demand curve is completely inelastic or discontinuous. Within a decision period successive units of x increase marginal utility until the consumer exhausts his resources or his preferences again become convex.[13] This description suggests that continuous adjusters, whose preferences do not display concavity, are less likely to become addicts than extreme-seekers.

With concavity, the price expansion path (whether we think of opportunity cost in terms of market price, time, or ostracism) is not continuous. Relative prices favorable to x drive the consumer to a corner or to an allocation at the right of the lower inflection point. Such shifts, moreover, need not be smoothly reversible.

But compulsion is also limited in the short run by the fact that work force participation precludes some kinds of consumption, like the use of alcohol, during the workday; by the need to sleep; or by the legal closing time of neighborhood taverns. In the long run it is limited by the threshold effects we discuss later.

13. The reader may ask why we have chosen to focus on the indifference map rather than examining the demand functions, suitably restricted, that might engender addictive behavior. To this our answer is pragmatic. Indifference curves with concave segments make it easy to visualize extreme-seeking. This should make the model more intelligible, especially to clinicians who are concerned with devising ways of treating it. Note, too, that if we concentrated on the correlation of addiction with conventional variables like income and price, we would be focusing on market (not individual) behavior, masking the link between behavior and personality, which controls preferences.

Stigler and Becker, on the other hand, do not distinguish between compulsion, which drives the susceptible individual to a corner, and addiction,
which must be established over time. Purchase of x initiates a drive that
produces permanent or irreversible addition. This capital effect is specific to
consumption of x and independent of everything else, including the consumer's
characteristics and the attributes of y.[14] But consumers of x who are not
extreme-seekers—probably the vast majority—never build up enough of such
a capital stock to become addicts.[15]

Personal History. Compulsion occurs in spurts—at the country club, the race
track, or the gaming table—when an extreme-seeker finds himself in an environment that supports it. It becomes addiction as he learns, after a compulsive
episode, that repetition satisfies the craving created by past consumption. But
such deferred capital effects of prior consumption, while central to addiction,
are not the driving force behind the compulsion itself.

A basic premise of our discussion is that people have distinctive, evolving
personalities, shaped in part by prior choices, including those that manifest
compulsion. A simple model illustrates the interaction in determining current
behavior among extreme-seeking, personal history, and the capacity to extract
utility from current consumption.[16]

We assume that the individual maximizes an n-period utility function.

$$V = \sum_{j=1}^{n} U_j, \tag{2}$$

where

$$U_j = (y_j - b)^{\frac{1}{2}} + e_j^{\frac{1}{2}} \tag{3}$$

14. To a point, then, our model mirrors Stigler and Becker. Their consumer maximizes lifetime
utility subject to a wealth constraint, choosing between euphoria (produced through the present
and past consumption of x_j) and y. They make the usual assumptions about the utility function
and define addiction as occurring when consumption of x has a positive effect on the production
of current euphoria and a negative effect on future euphoria. Note, however, that such a definition
is not inconsistent with nonconvex preferences.

15. Thus, ours is a more general model than Stigler and Becker's. Concavity, which describes
compulsion, reflects personality differences among individuals who are more susceptible to addiction and those who are relatively immune to it—between cases in which discontinuous responses
to relative price changes in favor of the addictive good are potentially significant and those in
which they are not (because responses are continuous, or the discontinuities reflect inconsequential
blips in the indifference map).

16. This interaction is captured quite graphically in the "Opponent-Process Theory of Motivation" developed by Solomon and Corbit [1978]: "Aversive states, manifesting themselves after
the sudden termination of pleasurable inputs, become more intense with repeated experiences.
Mild loneliness later becomes grief. Mild craving later becomes abstinence agony and intense
craving. In addition, after many repetitions the steady level of pleasure produced by the continued
presence of the pleasurable stimulus input has decreased. The confirmed opiate user experiences
a 'loss of euphoria,' and the rush is gone. The pleasure-affective systems seem eventually to yield
to opponent processes which keep departures from hedonic equilibrium relatively small. The
aversive opponent process, when it is manifest, is more intense and longer lasting than it once
was. So frequently repeated pleasure has its costs, psychologically, in an increased potentiality for
displeasure."

and, for simplicity,

$$e_j = x_j - \delta x_{j-1}. \tag{4}$$

Utility in the jth period is derived, in (3), by combining the composite commodity y with e, "euphoria," a good that cannot be purchased directly but must be created by consuming x. Current consumption of x, (4) tells us, contributes to e; but previous consumption, by establishing an unfavorable personal history, diminishes it.[17]

In addition, we assume that a no-borrowing, cash-flow budget constraint must be met period by period:[18]

$$W_i = P_i y_i + P_i x_i \qquad \text{for } i = 1, 2, \ldots, n. \tag{5}$$

For the preferences of (2) to (4) and Figure 1, the budget constraint (5) controls choice. Depending on prices an interior or a corner solution results. It is easy to specify parameters (b and δ) and prices that produce interior solutions in the first and last periods, but corners in intervening periods. This occurs, for example, if x is relatively expensive in the first and last periods, but freely available between, a scenario corresponding to the market for heroin in Vietnam.[19]

The parameter δ represents the capital effect of past x. This capital effect operates through both tolerance and craving. In (4) ever-higher levels of x are required to sustain a specified level of utility, so long as $\delta > 0$, as the individual builds tolerance to the addictive good. If x creates e of euphoria in period j, $(1 + \delta)x$ is required to create e in period $j + 1$. Alternatively, only δ percent of prior x continues to have a negative effect on the present production of e.[20] In terms of Figure 1, prior x, by creating (negative) capital, repositions the indifference map in (x_j, y_j) space, shifting it to the left. A given consumption bundle (x, y) yields less (ordinal) utility.[21]

The effect of cumulative consumption of x on craving itself is hidden by the linear form of (4). Generalizing to make e_k a function of present and past x, $f_k(x_k, x_{k-1}, \ldots x_1)$, the decay to time k of a unit of x consumed at j is $1 + f_{x_j}$. Prior consumption can alter the marginal utility of future x, changing the

17. The specific form of (3) is illustrative. We choose this particular algebraic example because it generates indifference curves like U_1 and U_2 in Figure 1. Obviously, other mathematical specifications can also produce concavities.

18. Such a no-borrowing constraint biases the model against extreme-seeking. In lore and practice, borrowing can perpetuate compulsion. Stories abound of borrowing at exorbitant interest rates to finance a drug or gambling habit.

19. Superficially, this validates Winston's claim that a consumer can act like an addict—increase x dramatically—in one period, while reducing it the next. Winston, however, makes random switching responsible for the change. Our model is more neoclassical, with relative prices driving behavior.

20. Thus, $(1 - \delta)$ percent of the original x has decayed or depreciated between j and $j + 1$. A good with no capital effects has a 100 percent rate of decay.

21. In the reverse case δ's effect is positive. It becomes easier to enjoy good music, the more one hears.

shape, not just the positioning, of the static indifference curves. In Figure 1 the convex regions become less convex, while the concave regions become more concave. In theory the capital effect can even create concavity, turning a continuous adjuster into an extreme-seeker.[22] But this begs the question of whether a continuous adjuster will ever consume enough x, at realistic relative prices, to transform his personality. The fact that some 90 percent of Vietnam returnees did stop their use of heroin supports the conjecture that such transformations are the exception and not the rule. Obviously, the capital effect is more important for an extreme-seeker, because the discontinuous jump inherent in the choice of a corner implies that a compulsive consumer can rapidly accumulate a substantial stock of addictive capital.

Violation of Thresholds. Since household production is nonadditive, a functional human being must consume more than x. Some minimum or threshold y is required to sustain utility or, to add a bit of drama, life itself. If in Figure 1 the consumer's choice implies a level of y lower than y'', the shortfall is damaging.[23] Like the capital effect, imbalance in consumption (e.g., failure of the alcoholic to eat nourishing meals) reduces his ability to benefit from consumption. The longer this imbalance persists, physiologically or socially, the greater the harm.

Though it may be difficult to disentangle their effects, two separate thresholds pertain to y'' and x''. A down-in-the-gutter alcoholic not only fails to eat but probably drinks enough to damage his liver permanently. He reduces his survival prospects by consuming less than the threshold amount of the y good ability $\Pi_j(y)$ that an individual alive in the first period will remain alive in

The thresholds may be current or cumulative, and they may be interdependent. As we are reminded all too often, an overdose of cocaine can be fatal within moments, regardless of whether the consumer had previousy used cocaine that day, or ever. Or cocaine (exceeding the x threshold) can exact its toll over time by constraining choice, leading to inadequate nutrition or crippling supportive social relationships (violating the y threshold), quite aside from the buildup of craving and tolerance incorporated in the capital effect.

Indeed, the likelihood that the consumer will violate thresholds is a good indicator of the severity of an addiction as a social problem. Few chain smokers find their ability to earn income, enjoy their families, or eat nourishing meals

---

22. The second derivative of lifetime utility V with respect to any x_j is

$$V_{x_j x_j} = \Sigma \, (U_{e_k} f_{x_k x_k} + U_{e_k e_k} f_{x_k}).$$

If U is always convex, a convex f could make V concave. That is, the capital effect could create compulsion. But this is not a necessary consequence. Indeed, if f is linear, the capital effect would never produce compulsion.

23. Unless there are two inflection points, a corner allocation implies that y is zero. With two inflection points, what is relevant is whether y is above or below some minimum, y''. A reasonable presumption is that it will vary with income, so that the damage done by a given level of x may vary inversely with wealth.

significantly diminished, though their habit is destructive. They pass the x threshold, but not the y. Compulsive handwashers may find it difficult to sustain employment or shop for necessities, but medically there is no way this addiction can cause death. They violate the y threshold, but not the x. So long as a compulsive gumchewer sticks to sugarless gum, his habit is unlikely to induce choking or periodontitis, and is otherwise benign. Neither threshold is violated.

As these examples suggest, distinctions between x and y thresholds are fuzzy. Exceeding either diminishes survival probability or, less dramatically, makes utility more difficult to produce.[24] Because it affects health, heavy smoking, like excessive handwashing, can eventually reduce the capacity to enjoy life. The critical question is whether a large enough endowment could, despite addictive behavior, sustain someone. After all, fastidiousness did not kill Howard Hughes, but a similar craving for nicotine would probably have hastened his demise.

To formalize this discussion, we focus on the y threshold, y'', interpreting it in terms of survival probabilities. Think of y as current consumption or as a vector of all past consumption of the composite good, and define the probability $\Pi_j(y)$ that an individual alive in the first period will remain alive in j as

$$\Pi_j = h(y'' - y), \qquad \text{with } h' \leq 0 \text{ for } y < y'' \text{ and } h' = 0 \text{ for } y \geq y''. \quad (6)$$

Deviations below y'', whether current or cumulative, not only matter but can take many different forms. Deficient nutrition during childhood can have permanent effects on health, but the detrimental effects of insufficient exercise in one's twenties can subsequently be reversed by an appropriate regimen in one's thirties.

Assuming full knowledge of survival probabilities from (6), the consumer maximizes expected lifetime utility—the system of equations (2)–(5). So long as it is below the threshold y'', survival probability is nondecreasing in y. The marginal impact of an increase in y on lifetime utility will be greater than it would be in the absence of threshold effects. Consequently, the marginal rate of substitution at $y < y''$ is the same or smaller when we account for thresholds than when we did not. For $y > y''$ there is no threshold effect. In terms of Figure 1 indifference curves retain their initial shapes above the y threshold, but flatten out below it. If individuals correctly perceive the full consequences of consuming too little y, x would have to sell at a lower price to effect a corner allocation.

Thus, both personal history and consumption imbalance suggest that addictive behavior is unstable. If harmful enough, the capital and threshold effects

---

24. The capital effect repositions the indifference map indirectly by making it more difficult to convert x into utility. Violating thresholds adjusts its position by making it more difficult to convert anything (x or y) into utility.

can bring about the functional demise—eventual elimination—of an addict.[25] Morbidity and mortality are altered, for example, by addiction to chocolates, cigarettes, or alcohol—because they foster obesity, respiratory diseases, and cirrhosis.[26] It thus seems obvious that research findings measuring such effects can enrich our formal analysis.

Summary of the Model. Declines in the relative price of an addictive good lead to corner allocations, which imply that respon~~—~~ses to price changes are d~~~~scontinuous. Successive declines slide the consumer across the horizontal axis to higher indifference curves. At corners, however, given the quality of x, substitution effects are absent and income effects are entirely dedicated to x. With subsequent rises in the price of x, behavior is sticky and difficult to reverse through relative price changes. This stickiness becomes more pronounced as addiction transforms preferences through its capital effect. Moreover, failure to maintain a minimum level of consumption of y or excessive consumption of x may reduce prospects of survival.

IV. TENTATIVE BEHAVIORAL HYPOTHESES

Reversal of Addictive Behavior

With all else constant, only a price change can trigger extreme-seeking or, symmetrically, initiate its reversal (in section III's model). The linear capital effect of (6) cannot, in itself, drive consumption to a corner. Concavities, however, mean that the price-consumption path is not continuous. Reversal may require a quantum increase in the price of the addictive good. The addict, while resisting withdrawal, may endure it if there is a strong enough movement against x in relative prices.

With the capital effect, which enhances the taste for the addictive good, the subsequent period's indifference curves become more concave and price changes are less likely to reverse addiction. Price incentives are less effective where x has more of a direct effect on tastes or past consumption has more staying power (where δ is higher).[27] With such reinforcement an extreme may

25. Dynamically, addiction is a process of elimination by self-selection, analogous to the failure of firms to maximize profits discussed by Alchian [1950]. Just as Becker [1962] argues that survivors in competitive markets are profit maximizers, we maintain that normal (not self-destructive) individuals have convex preferences.

26. Statistics add some insight. More than 1 percent of heroin-dependent Americans die each year. Physicians link heavy alcohol use to at least 65 percent of cases of cirrhosis of the liver, the fourth leading cause of death among Americans aged twenty-five to sixty-four. Mortality rates of male smokers average 70 percent above rates for nonsmokers. Together, alcohol and tobacco are blamed for 25 percent of premature mortality in the U.S. Morbidity is also higher among extreme-seekers. Smokers miss more days of work than nonsmokers (50 percent more among males, 25 percent among females) and are more likely to be hospitalized (26 percent among males, 7 percent among females). Heavy users of alcohol exhibit higher incidence of heart disease, ulcers, and nutritional deficiencies. Sources: Report of the Surgeon General [1979]; Institute of Medicine [1980]; Alcohol, Drug Abuse, and Mental Health Administration [1980]; and Commission of Inquiry into the Non-Medical Use of Drugs [1973].

27. It is likely that price changes would be less effective in reversing chronic smoking, because the physical craving for nicotine is strong and long-lasting, compared to marijuana, which is not physically addictive.

be sustained even if price returns to a level at which an otherwise identical consumer, unburdened by personal history, would engage in balanced consumption.

Income changes lead consumers to new corners on different indifference curves but do nothing, in themselves, to promote reversal. By reducing x, diminishing the capital effect, income reductions can make price changes more efficacious, but they also make violation of the y threshold more likely.[28]

In sum, once a consumer moves to a corner, imbalance is best reversed through changes in tastes or nonprice constraints. While other avenues exist—ability to learn from the past or to respond to new information—they require the modification of behavior through self-control. The 1964 Surgeon General's Report, which prompted many chronic smokers to quit, indicates how new information, easily interpreted in terms of the x threshold, can initiate reversal by altering perceived survival probabilities.[29]

If a substitute for x could eradicate its capital effects, have we any reason for confidence that an addict would use it? Replacement of heroin with methadone is a case in point. If through experience an addict learns his compulsion is destructive, substitution is likely. Since he benefits from eliminating the negative effects of past consumption, he would even pay for methadone, in an amount that depends on the strength of the capital effect. But such an alternative, to accomplish reversal, must be combined with price increases that make x unattractive after it has dried up the cumulative effects of prior consumption.

Substitution Among Addictive Alternatives. While the argument has so far treated compulsion as a fixation on some unique behavior, reality requires that we consider substitution among addictive alternatives. Central to the household production concept is the instrumentality of addictive, like other, goods. The consumer values peer status, immediate gratification or—because it facilitates a flight from reality—euphoria, not alcohol or cocaine. He can produce such ends in various ways, switching among addictive inputs as the environment alters.

Thus, interpret the x of our model as a vector of nonexclusive alternatives, some of which are potentially addictive and some not. Whether an individual consumes addictive goods and, if so, addiction ensues is controlled by production possibilities and costs, on the one hand, and by personality, on the other. Within the vector x economic criteria control choice. An addict may be indifferent, other things equal, among alternative means of gratification. If heroin is unavailable or (just the same) its price is too high, a drug addict

28. Implications of thresholds for reversibility appear minimal. If the consumer is already at a corner, thresholds provide no impetus to reversal, even though diminished survival probabilities flatten the indifference curves in the neighborhood of the corners. Above the y threshold the indifference curves remain the same, so there is no difference in the response to price.

29. While backsliding may be all too easy, drying out, as Winston argues, does produce short-run benefits. Alcoholics Anonymous tries to make the alcoholic believe that the costs of his drinking are high, for himself and his family. AA proselytizes that even one drink can have an infinite price, despite evidence (Thank God!) that moderate drinking can improve cardiovascular function.

will switch to something cheaper; and as cirrhosis threatens, a problem drinker may turn to compulsive shopping, fingernail biting, beachcombing, or religion. Thus, should concavities make complete reversal of addiction difficult, a proper objective is to divert behavior to a nonaddictive alternative, or to an addiction that is thought innocuous, like methadone or gumchewing, even if the gum must be laced with nicotine to make it appealing.

This interpretation of x as a vector within which the extreme-seeker substitutes can go far to explain age/use profiles among susceptible individuals. Opportunity cost increases (use decreases) with age for substances conducive to euphoria. When a minor indulges in illicit drugs, it results in a lighter penalty and does not establish a permanent criminal record; and because alcohol and cigarettes are more acceptable than drugs, their use and potential abuse begins earlier and lasts longer. Thus, correlation of shadow price with age predicts abuse profiles that start and rise in the teens and decline in the twenties and thirties. Since such findings refer to "typical" individuals, however, they have limited clinical value. A theory of addictive behavior is still needed to understand why some people build and maintain their consumption of alcohol, tobacco or drugs to harmful levels while others do not, despite repeated warnings about effects on life expectancy.

Income is another age-dependent factor. While adults derive most of their income from labor, minors receive much of theirs as endowment. If, through absenteeism or reduced productivity—both linked to alcohol and drug abuse— consumption of euphoria is anti-complementary with labor supply and earnings, its shadow price is higher for adults. It is also higher if euphoria is anti-complementary with such goods as "home life" or "playing with the children." We can then expect more abuse among single or divorced persons and among the unemployed. If anything, higher income will lead a committed addict to improve quality. The well-to-do drink Wild Turkey, not Thunderbird, sometimes rationalizing this by posing as connoisseurs.

V. PRELIMINARY POLICY DISCUSSION

Assuming for the sake of argument the correctness of our characterization, what can be done programmatically to control compulsion and addiction? Here we look briefly at a few alternatives. Their common thread is a recognition that it is best to keep the cost, particularly future cost, of addictive activities high.

One alternative is to make such activities illegal. However, since extreme-seekers display inelastic demand, this creates profit opportunities for illicit suppliers, as underscored by Prohibition and by the lively markets for illicit drugs. In illicit markets consumers are susceptible to pricing strategies that create demand. Initially consumption is inexpensive, to bait and hook the user; as demand develops, price is raised and the market broadens.[30]

---

30. Our model squares well with evidence of so-called heroin epidemics in U.S. cities. DuPont and Greene [1973] document one such epidemic in Washington, D.C., where heroin use grew rapidly in the late 1960s, peaking in 1969–70. This peak coincided with a police crackdown on

A possible remedy is the creation of legal alternatives, limited in access, to nurture a reasoned approach. State liquor stores and offtrack betting (OTB) shops are examples. (In New York the advertising slogan of OTB is "Bet with your head, not over it.") But it is moot whether they can limit consumption to levels that lie to the left of the corner. Politicians, like much of the electorate, see such markets as a less vexing source of revenue than taxation and so set prices that are suboptimal, at least in terms of controlling addictive behavior. Compulsive gamblers, seeking high returns, deal with illegal bookmakers because they offer better odds (transactions costs are lower). Revenue seeking, therefore, may adversely select continuously adjusting users, diverting extreme-seekers to the illegal market.

Sanctions with third-party monitoring, often in combination with social regulation, represent a second way of deterring extreme-seeking by sustaining cost. If objectionable enough, the public shuns alcoholics as a nuisance, even in private clubs—though revenue potential again suggests an indelicate balance—and as a threat to license and reputation.

Some consider self-enforcement, reinforced by group norms, the only truly effective strategy. The examples of Alcoholics Anonymous and Weight Watchers, in which commitments to reveal behavior are essential to treatment, merit careful investigation. We have already pointed out how self-command, as in Schelling, might *counteract* addictive forces. But another credible explanation of its effectiveness is that it *redirects* extreme-seeking to its obverse. Alcoholics Anonymous attempts to transform preferences by converting the inebriate into an ardent nonalcoholic, so that abstinence dominates alcohol in the array of addictive alternatives. Weight Watchers tries to replace an addiction to food with a compulsion to diet. In either case extreme-seeking may remain a salient characteristic of personality; but group norms, making behavioral lapses more expensive, reinforce the intended transformation of preferences.

Some countries, (e.g., Great Britain and Israel) have used certification of identified addicts, a third method of dealing with extreme-seeking, which divides the population at risk between addicts and nonaddicts, to contain the market for drugs. Subsidization of methadone clinics is a variant of this. Methadone programs implicitly accept the premise that "addicts are different" and assume, in effect, that addictive behavior, once established, cannot easily be reversed through price changes or self-command. To be eligible for methadone maintenance, which offers the certified addict a chemical replacement

the narcotics traffic and the establishment of new treatment facilities. Although use declined precipitously between 1970 and 1972, it still exceeded 1965 levels at the time of their study. If the cash price remained constant or fell in the late 1960s and group norms encouraged people to try heroin (DuPont and Greene report that the pusher was viewed as a "glamorous individual"), it was to be expected that the total number of users would grow. The capital effect, moreover, implies that each user would have consumed a greater amount. Washington's law enforcement efforts raised the price of heroin. In February 1972 it sold for $1.53 per milligram and by March 1973, $5.80 per milligram. In addition, the community developed an anti-heroin attitude. Given this change in constraints, the model suggests that continuous adjusters would have cut back on consumption, but that extreme-seekers would, for the most part, have remained at the corners to which they had moved during the period of low heroin prices.

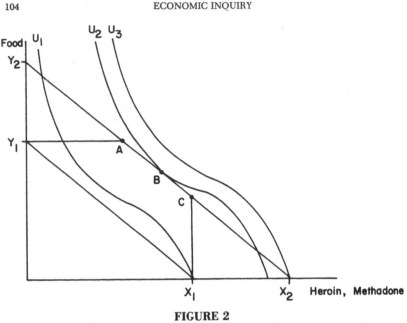

FIGURE 2
Free Methadone vs. Free Food

for heroin, addiction must be acknowledged. Participation can thus entail substantial nonmonetary cost, much of it sustained because admission of addiction may have continuing effects on employment opportunities. Since methadone maintenance without controls reduces to a voucher for euphoria, price effects suggest that side conditions are fundamental. Unless monitored, the addict will respond by consuming more euphoria through free methadone *and* street-priced heroin.[31]

Addict welfare could also be increased by subsidizing food or distributing vouchers restricted to food purchases. In Figure 2 a methadone program shifts the budget constraint from Y_1X_1 to Y_1ACX_2, with aggregate consumption of heroin *and* methadone increasing from X_1 to X_2. If, instead, the addict were given X_1C in free food, requiring the same public expenditure as free methadone of Y_1A, he would face the constraint Y_2CX_1 and choose bundle B. Though he would prefer the methadone, the food subsidy would increase y and reduce his use of heroin, making him less likely to violate the operative thresholds. While vouchers can sustain y above its threshold, measures that lower heroin or methadone prices without controlling total expenditures on x cannot be expected to cure addiction, because x is partially dependent on the decay of capital created by past consumption. Overall, then, our model predicts that a

---

31. Zinberg reports that *more* heroin was consumed by participants in U.S. Army treatment programs.

free outpatient methadone clinic would be less successful than an inpatient program, because it would do less to restrict consumption possibilities.[32]

VI. CONCLUDING REMARKS

Extreme seeking is not typical. We think of addicts as caricatures because that is what they are. All but the most intransigent of libertarians are bound to have their faith in consumer sovereignty shaken by a tour of the Bowery.

Public policy must consider not only the dimensions of such self-destructive behavior, but also its social cost, which varies by type of addiction and by the personal characteristics of the addict. Such costs are measurable in higher premia for homeowners', renters', auto, and life insurance, and in the resources devoted to nonfinancial insurance, through locks, guns and burglar alarms, to say nothing of inconvenience and fear. Drunk drivers clearly impose external costs, and drunken fathers and mothers batter their children. Even overeating, which seems at first an entirely private affair, may be epidemic within families.

Implicitly, our defense of the theory this paper has developed is that it is flexible enough to explain prevalent types of addictive behavior. But we have done almost nothing to attach numbers to concepts. Expansion and verification of the model is the logical next step. This will require data that can validate both its static (within-period) and dynamic (intertemporal) components. In the first instance, we need to gauge the importance of extreme-seeking as opposed to continuous adjustment; and, perhaps from psychiatric findings, to identify the levels at which individuals lose control, leading them to select extremes, as well as their receptivity to substitution among addictive alternatives. To flesh out the dynamics it is necessary to get a handle on values of δ, the rate of decay of addictive capital, and identify specific descriptors or quality of life characteristics in terms of which thresholds can be delineated. Comparisons of such descriptors (e.g., measures of morbidity and mortality) across individuals, in light of interpersonal differences in incidence, can serve as a point of departure for initial tests of the model.

REFERENCES

Akerlof, George. "The Market for Lemons: Qualitative Uncertainty and the Market Mechanism." *Quarterly Journal of Economics*, August 1970, 488–500.

Alchian, Armen, A. "Uncertainty, Evolution, and Economic Theory." *Journal of Political Economy*, June 1950, 211–21.

Alcohol, Drug Abuse, and Mental Health Administration. *The Alcohol Drug Abuse, and Mental Health National Data Book*. Rockville, MD: U.S. Department of Health, Education, and Welfare, 1980.

Becker, Gary S. "Irrational Behavior and Economic Theory." *The Journal of Political Economy*, February 1962, 1–13.

---

32. A free methadone program also nurtures moral hazard. Unless clinics can screen successfully, continuous adjusters can pose as addicts (moral hazard) to take advantage of cheap highs, making treatment programs (prohibitively?) expensive.

Commission of Inquiry into the Non-Medical Use of Drugs, *Final Report of the Commission of Inquiry into the Non-Medical Use of Drugs.* Ottawa, Canada: Information Canada, 1973.

DuPont, Robert L. and Mark H. Greene. "The Dynamics of a Heroin Addiction Epidemic." *Science,* 24 August 1973, 716–22.

Elster, Jon. *Ulysses and the Sirens: Studies in Rationality and Irrationality.* Cambridge, U.K.: Cambridge University Press, 1979.

Institute of Medicine. *Alcoholism, Alcohol Abuse, and Related Problems: Opportunities for Research.* Washington, D.C.: National Academy Press, 1980.

Lang, Alan R. "Addictive Personality: A Viable Construct?" in *Commonalities in Substance Abuse and Habitual Behavior,* edited by Peter K. Levison, Dean R. Gerstein, and Deborah R. Maloff. Lexington, MA: Lexington Books, 1983, pp. 157–235.

Lettieri, Dan J., Mollie Sayers, and Helen Wallenstein Pearson, eds. *Theories on Drug Abuse: Selected Contemporary Perspectives.* National Institute on Drug Abuse Monograph 30, Washington, D.C.: U.S. Government Printing Office, March 1980.

O'Leary, K. Daniel and G. Terrence Wilson. *Behavior Theory: Application and Outcome.* Englewood Cliffs, N.J.: Prentice-Hall, 1975.

Pauly, Mark V. "Overinsurance and Public Provision of Insurance: The Roles of Moral Hazard and Adverse Selection." *Quarterly Journal of Economics,* February 1974, 44–62.

Robins, L. N., J. E. Helzer, and D. H. Davis. "Narcotic Use in Southeast Asia and Afterwards." *Archives of General Psychiatry,* August 1975, 955–61.

Robins, L. N., J. E. Helzer, M. Hesselbrock, and E. Wish. "Vietnam Veterans Three Years After Vietnam: How Our Study Changed Our View of Heroin," in Problems of *Drug Dependence. Proceedings of the Committee on Problems of Drug Dependence,* edited by L. Harris. Washington, D.C.: National Academy of Sciences, 1977.

Schelling, Thomas C. "Egonomics, or the Art of Self-Management." *American Economic Review,* May 1978, 290–94.

————. "The Intimate Contest for Self-Command." *The Public Interest,* Summer 1980, 94–113.

Solomon, Richard L. and John D. Corbit. "An Opponent-Process Theory of Motivation." *American Economic Review,* December 1978, 12–24.

Stigler, George J. and Gary S. Becker. "De Gustibus Non Est Disputandum." *American Economic Review,* March 1977, 76–90.

United States Department of Health and Human Services. *Smoking and Health, A Report of The Surgeon General: The Health Consequences of Smoking, The Behavioral Aspects of Smoking, Education and Prevention.* Washington, D.C.: U.S. Government Printing Office, 1979.

Winston, Gordon C. "Addiction and Backsliding: A Theory of Compulsive Consumption." *Journal of Economic Behavior and Organization,* 1980, 295–324.

Zinberg, N. E. "Heroin Use in Vietnam and the United States: A Contrast and Critique." *Archives of General Psychiatry,* March 1972, 486–88.

Name index